Fuzzy Preference Queries
to Relational Databases

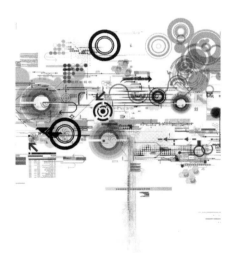

Fuzzy Preference Queries to Relational Databases

Olivier Pivert & Patrick Bosc

IRISA/ENSSAT, University of Rennes 1, France

Imperial College Press

Published by

Imperial College Press
57 Shelton Street
Covent Garden
London WC2H 9HE

Distributed by

World Scientific Publishing Co. Pte. Ltd.
5 Toh Tuck Link, Singapore 596224
USA office: 27 Warren Street, Suite 401-402, Hackensack, NJ 07601
UK office: 57 Shelton Street, Covent Garden, London WC2H 9HE

British Library Cataloguing-in-Publication Data
A catalogue record for this book is available from the British Library.

FUZZY PREFERENCE QUERIES TO RELATIONAL DATABASES

ISBN-13 978-1-84816-869-5
ISBN-10 1-84816-869-1

Typeset by Stallion Press
Email: enquiries@stallionpress.com

Printed in Singapore by World Scientific Printers.

3 3001 00966 3443

To Ewa (O.P.)

Foreword

Databases are pervasive in our information-focused world. While in many cases, such as corporate databases, they are apparent to the user, in many other cases they are the hidden backbone of applications. This is particularly the case in web applications. Many of the widely used popular web applications make considerable use of databases. This is true for websites such as Amazon.com, Facebook and even Google. As we move into a future world in which there will be even more demand for smart user-friendly computing, the requirement for intelligent manipulation of databases has become extremely important. Successful websites will be required to allow users to interface in what can be called "computing with words". The concept of a fuzzy set, introduced by L.A. Zadeh of the University of California at Berkeley, provides an ideal framework for the digital representation of words and their associated semantics. It allows for the capturing of the nuances and grayness of human language. A further feature, as the name "fuzzy sets" implies, is that, like database theory, it is a set-based theory. Thus the joining of fuzzy set theory with databases, and particularly relational databases, is very natural. Together they become a very rich framework on which to build the type of intelligent information technologies that will underlie future user-friendly smart applications. The authors of this book, Patrick Bosc and Olivier Pivert, are internationally recognized leaders in the field of fuzzy relational database theory. They have worked for many years in this field and have made many important contributions to its development. They have a deep understanding of the subject matter. Their team at Enssat in Lannion, France, is perhaps the best in the world in fuzzy relational database theory. Over the years I have always been impressed by, and enjoyed, the lucidity and clarity of the authors' writing style. This book manifests this notable feature. Their presentations have always been, for the most part, self-contained: they will tell you everything you need from beginning to end. This book displays the same characteristic. In addition to providing the formal theoretical underpinnings, the authors provide clear examples illustrating the ideas.

I enjoyed the book and I thank the authors for the effort put into providing such a pleasant and useful book.

Ronald R. Yager
New York, December 2011

Acknowledgments

The authors wish to thank their colleagues Ludovic Liétard on the one hand, and Allel Hadjali and Grégory Smits on the other hand, for their contributions to Chapters 6 and 10 respectively.

Contents

in many other computer science areas, thus contributing to the definition of "intelligent systems". As to relational database management systems, the challenge resides in their ability to translate "what" into "how" efficiently, in other words to produce querying programs running sufficiently fast compared to *ad hoc* programs. This issue was controversial for a while, but finally, technological evolutions (both of processors and disks) made the performances reached by relational systems credible; relational DBMSs became the standard and have been widely deployed since the mid-eighties.

Initially motivated by business applications, databases have spread to new domains such as CAD, office automation, and geographic systems, which has led to extensions to the model in order to capture richer structures than "simple" relational tables. Object orientation has been an important step, and database systems have incorporated facilities to deal with objects, rather than relations, since the end of the nineties. Many other evolutions have occurred, for instance data warehouses and data marts to support decision applications based on "online analytical processing" (OLAP). Here the underlying model is a multi-dimensional one and related operations apply to a hypercube of data, in particular aggregations over dimensions. But once again, relational systems are at the heart of this technology since they serve to feed and to interface data warehouses. One of most recent trends is the accounting for web data with XML models and the development of associated query languages.

1.2 Preferences and Fuzzy Sets

It is worth noting that, in most research works and commercial database management systems, it is assumed that the aim of a query is the delivery of a (multi-)set of answers where all elements are implicitly "equally" satisfactory. Behind such a view is the use of Boolean predicates and operators supporting the notions of acceptance and rejection. Except for some pioneering works, the idea of preference queries has received attention only recently in the database community. Various approaches have been proposed, but most often the objective of efficient implementation constrains the functionalities the user is provided with. For instance, specifying preferences is considered a complementary step after some Boolean selection, and/or is restricted to the selection operation. In contrast, the suggestion advocated in this book is to envisage preferences as a central concern in

Chapter 1

Introduction

1.1 Databases and their Evolution

Databases cover the domain of computer science dedicated to the management of huge quantities of permanent data. A database represents the computerized image of a given universe (e.g., sales, deployed products, employees of a company, etc.). Its main use is the retrieval of information from the data stored inside it, but this implies updates to be performed as changes happen in the real world to make the database as faithful to reality as possible. The birth of databases can be situated in the sixties as a response to the growing need for the automation of various data management tasks in the industry, for overcoming the limitations of both manual procedures and/or the use of file structures associated with dedicated programs. The first commercial systems were simple, fairly empirical (i.e., without any formal basis) and their efficiency was highly dependent on programming skills. However, they had the merit of providing developers with more advanced tools than those previously available.

In 1970, E. F. Codd, a researcher from IBM Research Labs, proposed the foundations of a formal approach to database management systems (DBMSs) relying on the mathematical concept of relation. In his view, it was possible to express queries in a high-level language, namely relational algebra, leading to formulations much more compact than traditional programs. This characteristic remained in the SQL language designed in the middle of the seventies, such that the user has to focus on what he or she is interested in, not on how to get it, thus hiding the programming aspects to a large extent. This tendency, aimed at offering high-level concepts rather than interacting with computers through basic programming languages, is not specific to databases, and has widely developed

Contents

database queries and to call on fuzzy sets, a concept initially introduced by L.A. Zadeh in 1965, instead of regular sets. By its very nature, a fuzzy set is strongly related to preferences, inasmuch as a membership function is nothing but the description of the values that are more or less acceptable regarding a given concept, i.e., more or less preferred values. By doing so, a sound foundation of queries is obtained and preferences may appear wherever it makes sense, thus designing a fully fledged preference query language. The key idea is that of graduality, i.e., the fact that a given statement is more or less true, which naturally extends the usual Boolean framework of truth/falsehood. This point of view somewhat differs from that of the binary relations used in Pareto-based approaches (e.g., Skyline queries) where only a partial order is provided which leads to incomparable pairs of elements/answers. In addition, fuzzy predicates are generally expressed as natural language expressions and, as such, they convey a "human touch" to a query language. Last, the fuzzy-set-based framework makes it possible to deal with two levels of preferences, since one can assign different importances to fuzzy predicates intervening in a given expression. In this respect, such languages have a greater expression power as they go far beyond what Boolean languages offer.

1.3   Overview of the Book

Numerous aspects of preferences are tackled in this book, after some reminders on databases (Chapter 2) and a presentation of some basic notions about fuzzy sets (Chapter 3) that are necessary for the forthcoming chapters. We should emphasize that, although presented in the context of relational databases, the topics tackled could apply to other data models (especially object-oriented ones).

The two main families of approaches to preferences in database queries are reviewed in Chapter 4: those based on scores, called quantitative, and those relying on preference relations, called qualitative.

Chapters 5 and 6 are devoted to a presentation of an extended relational algebra on the one hand, and SQLf — an SQL-like language offering a wide range of querying capabilities including preference features — on the other hand. It is shown how the various concepts of SQL (the base block as well as nesting and partitioning) can be enhanced to incorporate preferences at the limited expense of defining fuzzy terms (mainly predicates, binary operators, and quantifiers used in a query).

Chapter 7 is entirely dedicated to the division operation which has the distinction of being an operator with very rich semantics. Its original version allows for the retrieval, inside a relation called dividend, of the values associated with all the elements of a given set (the divisor). Several basic cases of extension can be imagined, among which are those defining the division: i) when the dividend and/or divisor relations involve preferences over the tuples, ii) in a tolerant way if we look for the values associated with "almost all" of the values of the divisor, iii) when the domain common to the dividend and the divisor is provided with a similarity relation, iv) in the presence of a divisor made up of a hierarchy of subsets.

Next, the concept of bipolarity comes into play. Chapter 8 deals with fuzzy bipolar queries in the sense that a query involves two (possibly fuzzy) components, one describing a constraint and another where the condition plays the role of a wish, as in the query "I am interested in a low-consuming car around $9,000, if possible grayish with good comfort". The basic interpretation principle relies on the fact that the two poles are treated separately and never aggregated; it is shown that the relational algebra can be extended to handle such queries.

Chapter 9 is about an extension of the "group by" clause present in SQL in order to define a fuzzy partition of the tuples instead of a crisp one. Beyond the interest of this feature for end-user queries, it turns out that it makes it possible to write queries intended for mining association rules "on demand".

The issue of empty and over-abundant answers to fuzzy preference queries is at the heart of Chapter 10. It may seem reasonable to consider empty answers on the one hand, and over-abundant ones on the other hand, as dual problems. With this point of departure, dual transformations of the queries (in terms of modification of the involved fuzzy predicates) lead to dual solutions. Nevertheless, it is also shown that some specific solution to each of these problems can be devised which breaks their apparent duality.

The conclusion part (Chapter 11) summarizes and highlights the principal contributions of the book and discusses some directions for future work, for instance preference queries in the presence of imperfect data.

Chapter 2

Reminders on Relational Databases

This chapter is mainly devoted to recalling the notions of the relational model of data which are essential for understanding most of the aspects dealt with later in this book. It may be omitted by readers who are familiar with the domain, but the reader who would like to go deeper is encouraged to refer to Date (1995), Korth and Silberschatz (1998), and Ullman (1989).

The data model grounded in the notion of relation is first described, then the algebraic operators which constitute the basis for manipulating relations are presented. The next subsection is devoted to querying relational databases using the SQL language, which is available in commercial DBMSs and used by a large number of application developers.

2.1 Basic Notions and Vocabulary

The relational model, proposed by E.F. Codd in 1970 (Codd, 1970), has its foundations in the mathematical theory of relations. The principle is to consider a database as a set of relations, each of which describes a part of the underlying universe (personnel of an enterprise, real-estate transactions, scientific observations, management of a stock of components, etc.). In this framework, a relation r corresponds to a subset of a Cartesian product of possibly non-distinct domains $D_i, i \in [1, n]$, therefore:

$$r \subseteq D_1 \times \cdots \times D_n.$$

This subset is called the *extension* of relation r. From a concrete point of view, a relation gathers the associations of values (*tuples*) describing the elements of the considered universe. For instance, a relation about services (or departments) of a company with an identifying number, a name, and

5

a budget, includes only triples corresponding to the actual services of the company, like $\langle 149,\ sales,\ 20.5 \rangle$.

The *schema* (also called *intention*) R of a relation r is defined over a set of distinct attributes A_j associated with each of the domains. Every attribute A_k represents the role played by its corresponding domain and $R(A_1, \ldots, A_n)$ denotes a relation schema. For example, one may have the attributes *l-city* and *place* built over the domain of cities, the former (resp. latter) standing for the city where an employee lives (resp. the city where a company is located). Two different attributes are not *a priori* comparable, except if they share the same domain, in which case these attributes are said to be *compatible*. Such attributes may then appear in comparison operations (equality/inequality, or even superiority if their underlying domain is provided with an order relation; see the selection and join operations in Section 2.2).

The number of attributes of a relation is called its *degree* and its number of tuples (elements) is its *cardinality* (as for sets). Any relation involves at least one identifier called a *key*, i.e., a minimal set of attributes allowing for distinguishing among any two tuples. Such a set does exist, since the whole set of attributes is a potential (perhaps not minimal) identifier due to the fact that a relation does not contain duplicates. One of the principal interests of the notion of key is from the query-processing point of view, since a key may serve to build an index, thus providing efficient access to tuples (provided that the key value is known as an input).

Example 2.1. Consider the schema $S(sid,\ ss\text{-}number,\ name,\ birth\text{-}date)$ about students of a university with a number given by the university (*sid*), a national social security number (*ss-number*), a family name (*name*), and a date of birth (*birth-date*). It may be reasonably assumed that a relation built over S has two keys provided that student IDs and social security numbers are uniquely assigned to students. A more sophisticated case is the following, where the schema $ZC(zcode,\ city,\ street)$ is considered for the description of zip codes in a given country. No isolated attribute constitutes a key, but there are possibly two keys: {*city, street*} on the one hand, if it is assumed that a given street in a given city is not "split" over several codes, and {*zcode, street*} on the other hand.◇

Usually, a relation is represented as a bi-dimensional array (or table) whose columns are the attributes and whose lines are the tuples of the considered extension. The order of both lines and columns does not matter, since the notion of set (of attributes and tuples here) does not convey any order over the elements.

As can be seen, there are only a few concepts in the relational model, which emphasizes its simplicity and ease to learn. However, this also reflects some semantic poorness, mainly because in this model, everything is either an attribute or a relation. In particular, no distinction is made between the representation of an entity (or object) of the real world with an intrinsic existence (e.g., employee, service, customer, vehicle) and that of an association between several entities (e.g., an order connecting a customer and a product) whose existence depends on that of the referenced entities. Thus, the assignment of an employee to a given service supposes the prior existence of that employee and that service. This is also the case for the purchase of a car by a customer. Indeed, complementary concepts do exist, among them the important notion of integrity constraints, which represent properties of the data that must be enforced both at their creation and when updates are performed. From a practical point of view, in most of the DBMSs, these can be checked through "triggers", i.e., programs which are activated when needed. In practice, the analysis aiming at building up a database relies on a richer semantic model (typically the *entity–relationship* model) that offers the tools appropriate for modeling the concepts and properties of interest. In this approach, the relational data model is the target of a translation of the schema thus designed.

Example 2.2. Consider a company willing to have an employee database. Each employee is described by an identifier (*e-id*), his/her name (*e-name*), surname, birth and living cities, as well as the department of the company he/she works for. Then, the schema of the considered relation is *EMPLOYEE*(*e-id, e-name, surname, birth-city, living-city, work-serv*) whose key is *e-id*, where the attributes *birth-city* and *living-city* share the same domain, namely names of cities. An extension of this relation is given in Table 2.1; each line (tuple) describes the data related to a given employee of the company. Adding a relation with schema *SERVICE*(*s-id, s-name,*

Table 2.1   An example of an extension of the relation *emp*(*EMPLOYEE*)

e-id	*e-name*	*surname*	*birth-city*	*living-city*	*work-serv*
14	Dupont	Jacques	Paris	Nantes	9
3	Mesnard	Yves	Lyon	St Nazaire	1
5	Lucat	Pierre	Marseille	Aix	9
21	Robin	Louis	Rennes	Rennes	5
7	Perrin	Marc	Lannion	Angers	2
12	Marival	Jean	Lens	Paris	2

budget), whose key is *s-id*, will enable the name and budget of each service of the company to be taken into account. We remark that although similarly named, *e-name* and *s-name* are not compatible attributes, in contrast to *s-id* (in relation *ser*) and *work-serv* (in relation *emp*).◇

2.2   Algebraic Operations

As was seen before, the relational model has a double characteristic, since a relation is a set (of tuples) on the one hand, and the elements of this set are structured on the other hand. As a consequence, operators allowing for the manipulation of relations take advantage of both aspects. The *relational algebra* constitutes the formal basis for manipulating relations, although it is not the language in use from a practical point of view (see Section 2.3 devoted to the SQL language). This algebra is made of setoriented and relational operators which have relations as inputs and which also deliver relations as results. So it is a closed calculus system allowing for the composition of operators using expressions such as:

$$op2(op1(r),\ s) \quad \text{or} \quad op1(op2(op3(r,\ s),\ t)),$$

where r, s and t are relations, $op1$ is a unary operator, and $op2$ and $op3$ are binary operators. These operators are presented below, and X, Y and Z stand for sets of attributes appearing in schemas of relations.

2.2.1   *Set operations*

The *union, intersection,* and *difference* of two relations r and s, whose attributes must be pairwise compatible, return a relation with the same schema. They are defined as follows:

- $union(r,s) = \{t|t \in r \textbf{ or } t \in s\}$,
- $inter(r,s) \ = \{t|t \in r \textbf{ and } t \in s\}$,
- $differ(r,s) \ = \{t|t \in r \textbf{ and } t \notin s\}$.

The cardinality of the results is such that:

- $max(card(r), card(s)) \leq card(union(r,s)) \leq card(r) + card(s)$,
- $0 \leq card(inter(r,s)) \ \leq min(card(r), card(s))$,
- $0 \leq card(differ(r,s)) \ \leq card(r)$.

These operations are illustrated in Figures 2.1, 2.2, and 2.3. The *Cartesian product* of two relations r and s (unconstrained as to their schemas $R(X)$

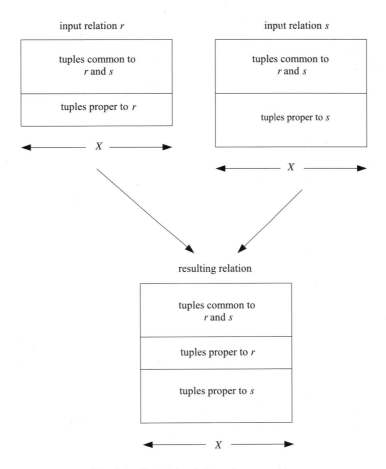

Fig. 2.1   Principle of the union operation

and $S(Y)$), delivers a relation defined as:

$$cartprod(r,\ s) = \{t = \langle u,\ v \rangle \mid u \in r \textbf{ and } v \in s\}.$$

Formally, the schema of the resulting relation is $T(X \cup Y)$ assuming that $X \cap Y = \emptyset$, which can always be achieved using the renaming of attributes if needed. The cardinality of the Cartesian product is known exactly:

$$card(cartprod(r,\ s)) = card(r) * card(s),$$

which expresses the combinatorial nature of this operator and the computational complexity which may then occur. Figure 2.4 illustrates the principle

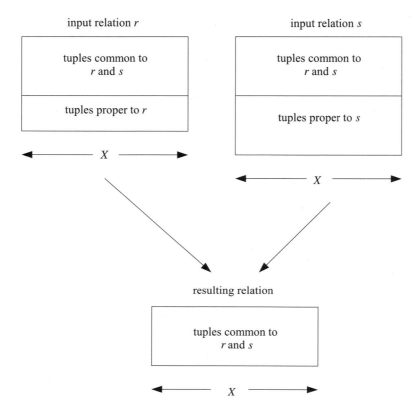

Fig. 2.2   Principle of the intersection operation

of this operator. Except for the difference operation, these operations are associative and commutative. Finally, it must be remarked that the difference is useful for answering certain queries involving negations, such as "retrieve the services where no engineer works". The answer to this type of query calls on the general scheme:

{searched items} = *differ*({referential of elements}, {unsatisfactory elements}),

knowing that these two sets are generally fairly easy to specify. In the previous example, this procedure produces:

differ({all the known services}, {those services where at least one engineer works}).

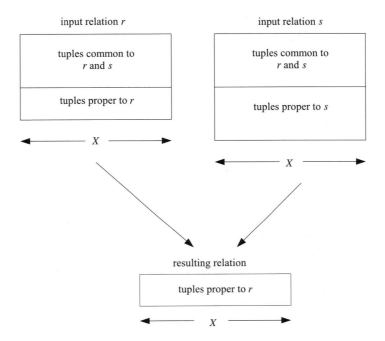

Fig. 2.3   Principle of the difference operation

2.2.2   *Relational operations*

The relational operators exploit the fact that relations possess a structure in terms of attributes. The four most common operators, namely *selection*, *projection*, *theta-join*, and *division*, are presented in turn.

Selection is a unary operator aimed at extracting a subrelation from an input relation by means of a condition (predicate or constraint) applying to every tuple. Such a condition is a logical expression where elementary conditions are built with constants, comparators and the sole attributes of the concerned relation (which may be either a base relation, i.e., part of the schema of the database, or an intermediate relation resulting from preceding operations). The atomic conditions may be connected by conjunctions and disjunctions, and parentheses are used to force priority if needed. Formally, if r is a relation with schema $R(X)$ and p is a predicate referring to attributes of X, one has:

$$select(r,\, p) = \{t \mid t \in r \textbf{ and } p(t)\}.$$

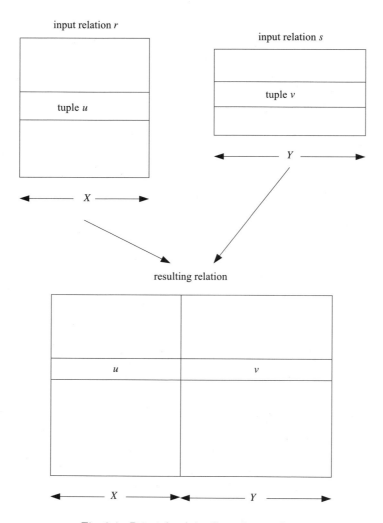

Fig. 2.4   Principle of the Cartesian product

The operating principle of this operation, aimed at keeping only those tuples that comply with the condition, is graphically represented in Figure 2.5.

The second unary operator is projection, whose goal is to retain a subset of desired attributes from those initially present in the input relation. It removes some columns and may be seen as the counterpart of the selection, which discards lines. If r is a relation with schema $R(X)$ and Z is a proper subset of X $(Z \subset X)$, the projection of r onto Z is defined as:

$$project(r, Z) = \{z \mid \exists t,\ t \in r \ \textbf{and} \ t.Z = z\},$$

input relation *r*

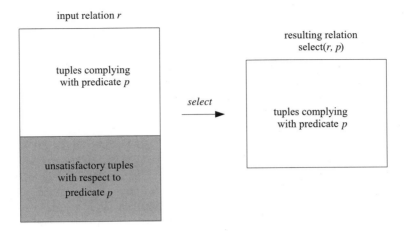

Fig. 2.5   Principle of the selection operation

input relation *r*

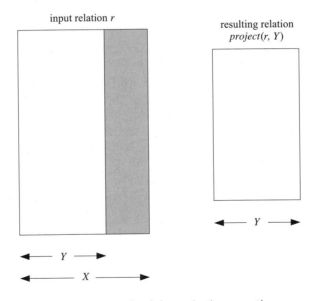

Fig. 2.6   Principle of the projection operation

where $t.Z$ denotes the value of the constituent Z in tuple t. Figure 2.6 illustrates the functioning principle of the projection. Note that, a relation being a set, the result of a projection does not contain any "duplicate". So, in the case where two initially distinct tuples share the same value on Z, they collapse and a single tuple is generated in the result.

Example 2.3. Consider the database composed of the relations *emp* and *ser* with respective schemas *EMPLOYEE*(*e-id, e-name, age, birth-city, living-city, work-serv*) with key *p-id*, and *SERVICE*(*s-id, s-name, budget*) with key *s-id*, where *work-serv* and *s-id* are compatible attributes. The query aimed at the retrieval of any service (number) whose budget is over $20M or where there is at least one employee less than 35 years old living in his birth city may be written as:

$$union(project(select(ser, budget > 20), s\text{-}id),$$
$$project(select(emp, living\text{-}city = birth\text{-}city \textbf{ and } age < 35),$$
$$\{work\text{-}serv\})).$$

With the extensions of Tables 2.2 and 2.3, the result is made up of the two values 5 and 9.◇

The two remaining operators are binary, and correspond to particular (useful) combinations of previously defined operators. Theta-join stems from the Cartesian product, but differs from it by keeping only the pairs of tuples matching a given (joining) property according to the formula:

$$join(r, s, \theta, A, B) = \{\langle u, v \rangle \mid u \in r \textbf{ and } v \in s \textbf{ and } \theta(u.A, v.B)\}$$
$$= select(cartprod(r, s), \theta(A, B))$$

Table 2.2   Relation *emp* of Example 2.3

e-id	e-name	age	birth-city	living-city	work-serv
14	Dupond	32	Paris	Nantes	1
3	Mesnard	47	Lyon	St Nazaire	1
21	Robin	29	Rennes	Rennes	5
7	Perrin	52	Angers	Angers	10
12	Marival	34	Lens	Paris	9

Table 2.3   Relation *ser* of Example 2.3

s-id	s-name	budget
5	sales	17
1	manufacturing	14
9	secretariat	30
10	marketing	12

where R (resp. S), the schema of r (resp. s), is defined over X (resp. Y), A and B are two compatible respective subsets of X and Y, θ is a comparator, and $\langle u, v \rangle$ denotes the tuple gathering the elements u and v. This operation, very often used in practice, allows for combining relations with a semantic link conveyed by the presence (in their schema) of one of several attributes sharing the same domains. The principle of the join is illustrated by Figure 2.7. In practice, the comparison operator is often equality, and it

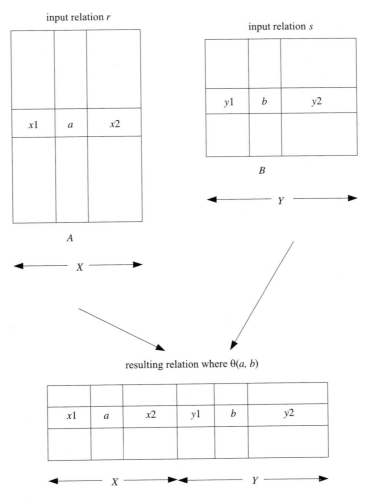

Fig. 2.7 Principle of the join operation

is possible to define a variant called equijoin in the following way:

$$equijoin(r,\ s,\ A,\ B) = \{\langle u,\ v' \rangle \mid u \in r \textbf{ and } v \in s \textbf{ and } (u.A = v.B)$$
$$\textbf{and } v' = v.(Y - B)\},$$

or:

$$equijoin(r,\ s,\ A,\ B) = project((join(r, s, A, B, =), X \cup Y - B),$$

where $X \cap Y = \emptyset$. A side-effect is to avoid generating useless (duplicate) information, since in every tuple of the output relation the B-value would be equal to the A-value (with the previous definition). The interest of the equijoin is shown in the next example.

Example 2.4. The two relations of Example 2.3 have a semantic link due to the presence of the compatible attributes *work-serv* (in *emp*) and *s-id* (in *ser*). The query to look for any pair (*e-name, s-name*) such that *e-name* works in *s-name* and *s-name* corresponds to a service which has a budget less than \$15M can be written thanks to an equijoin, as follows:

$$project(equijoin(emp, select(ser, budget < 15), \{work\text{-}serv\}, \{s\text{-}id\}),$$
$$\{e\text{-}name,\ s\text{-}name\}).$$

With the extensions given in Tables 2.2 and 2.3, services numbered 1 and 10 fulfill the budget requirement, and the final result is the binary relation of Table 2.4.◇

Table 2.4   Result of Example 2.4

e-name	s-name
Dupond	manufacturing
Mesnard	manufacturing
Perrin	marketing

Several other specific forms of join exist, among which are:

- self-join, where the same relation is used twice, which enforces the renaming of the attributes in the resulting relation,
- natural join, which corresponds to the equijoin of two relations over the set of attributes having the *same name* in both. With the schemas

$R(X, Y)$ and $S(X, Z)$ with $Y \cap Z = \emptyset$, the natural join of $r(R)$ and $s(S)$ is defined as:

$natjoin(r,\ s) =$
$$\{\langle x, y, z \rangle \mid \exists t \in r,\ \exists u \in s \text{ such that } t.XY = xy \textbf{ and } u.XZ = xz\},$$

- antijoin, which delivers those tuples of the first relation which match none of those of the second relation, i.e.:

$antijoin(r, s,\ \theta,\ A,\ B)) =$
$$\{u \mid u \in r \textbf{ and } \not\exists v \in s \text{ such that } \theta(u.A,\ v.B)\},$$

- semijoin, which may be seen as a join followed by a projection over the sole attributes of the first relation, i.e.:

$semijoin(r, s,\ \theta,\ A,\ B))$
$$= project(join(r,\ s,\ \theta,\ A,\ B)),\ X)$$
$$= \{u \mid u \in r \textbf{ and } \exists v \in s \text{ such that } \theta(u.A,\ v.B)\}.$$

The last operator is called division. If r and s are two relations with respective schemas $R(A, X)$ and $S(B, Y)$ where A and B are compatible (sets of) attributes, the division is defined as follows:

$$div(r, s, A, B) = \{x \mid \forall\, a, (a \in project(s, B)) \Rightarrow (\langle a,\ x \rangle \in r)\}, \qquad (2.1)$$

or equivalently:

$$div(r, s, A, B) = \{x \mid project(s, B) \subseteq \Gamma_r^{-1}(x)\}, \qquad (2.2)$$

with $\Gamma_r^{-1}(x) = \{a \mid \langle a,\ x \rangle \in r\}$. In other words, a value x belongs to the result of the division if and only if it is associated with at least all the values of the (set of) attribute(s) B of relation s, as illustrated in Figure 2.8. It is worth noting that the set of attributes Y in relation s does not play any role and can be empty. The justification of the term "division" assigned to this operation relies on the fact that a property similar to that of the quotient of integers holds. Indeed, the resulting relation *res* obtained with Expression (2.1) or (2.2) is called a "quotient" and has the double characteristic:

$$\forall t \in res,\ cartprod(s,\ \{t\}) \subseteq r,$$

$$\forall t \notin res,\ cartprod(s,\ \{t\}) \not\subseteq r.$$

Example 2.5. Consider the relation *emp* given in Table 2.2 and the relation *stay* with schema $ST(s\text{-}num,\ emp\text{-}num,\ duration)$ describing how long

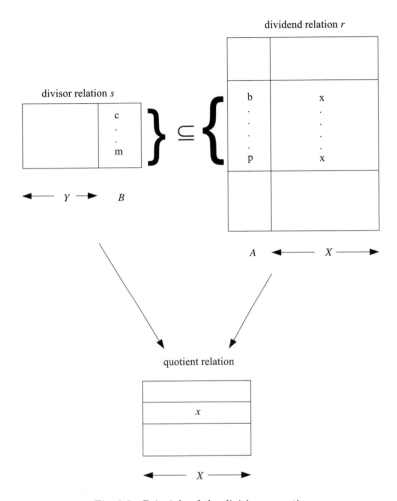

Fig. 2.8   Principle of the division operation

employees have stayed in various services. The query looking for any service where all the employees older than 40 have stayed for more than three
months, is expressed as:

$$div(project(select(stay, duration \geq 3), \{s\text{-}num, emp\text{-}num\}),$$
$$select(emp, age > 40),$$
$$\{emp\text{-}num\}, \{e\text{-}id\}).$$

With the extensions of *emp* and *stay* given in Tables 2.2 and 2.5, the
result of the previous query contains only the service number 5 where both

Table 2.5   Relation *stay* of Example 2.5

s-num	emp-num	duration
2	3	5
2	7	2
2	14	10
10	7	12
5	7	24
5	3	6
5	21	8

employees 3 and 7 (who are older than 40) have stayed more than three months. We remark that it is necessary to discard attribute *duration* (by means of a projection) so as to get the correct result. Otherwise, the result would be a binary relation composed of pairs (service number, duration) such that all the employees older than 40 have stayed for this same duration (over three months).◇

It can be easily shown that the division may be written as:

$$
\begin{aligned}
div&(r,\ s,\ A, B) \\
&= differ(project(r,\ X), \\
&\qquad\quad project(differ(r, \\
&\qquad\qquad\quad cartprod(project(r,\ X),\ project(s,\ B))),\ X)).
\end{aligned}
$$

(2.3)

This expression can be justified as follows:

- the sub-expression $r_1 = cartprod(project(r, X), project(s, B))$ computes the pairs (a, x) which should be in relation r for all x's to be qualified,
- the sub-expression $x_1 = project(differ(r, r_1), X)$ delivers the values (x) for which at least one association with the B-values of s is missing in r,
- the final difference $differ(project(r, X), x_1)$ keeps the values x of r for which no association is missing.

Closely related to division is antidivision. This operator aims at selecting the X-values present in relation r which are associated with *none* of the B-values present in s. It is defined as follows:

$$
\begin{aligned}
antidiv(r,\ s,\ A,\ B) = \{x \in\ &project(r, X)\ | \\
&\forall\, a, (a \in project(s,\ B)) \Rightarrow (\langle a,\ x \rangle \notin r)\},
\end{aligned}
$$

(2.4)

or equivalently:

$$antidiv(r, s, A, B) =$$
$$\{x \in project(r, X) \,|\, project(s, B) \subseteq cp(\Gamma_r^{-1}(x))\}, \tag{2.5}$$

$cp(rel)$ denoting the complement of rel. Here also, relation r (resp. s) is called the dividend (resp. divisor) and the result obtained by Expression (2.4) or (2.5), called an "anti-quotient", has the property:

$$\forall t \in \ res, \ cartprod(s, \{t\}) \subseteq \ cp(r),$$
$$\forall t \notin \ res, \ cartprod(s, \{t\}) \not\subseteq \ cp(r).$$

2.2.3 *Properties*

The operators of the relational algebra possess a number of properties. It is, in particular, possible to design a minimal set of operators from which any other one can be built. This is the case with {union, difference, selection, projection, Cartesian product}. Then, the intersection can be written as:

$$inter(r, \ s) = differ(union(r, \ s), \ union(differ(r, \ s), \ differ(s, \ r))).$$

Some properties express equivalences between algebraic formulas, for instance due to the distributivity of one operator with respect to another. So, if r and s are two relations with respective schemas $R(X)$ and $S(X)$, one has:

- $union(select(r, p), select(s, p)) = select(union(r, s), p),$
- $inter(select(r, p), select(s, p)) \ = select(inter(r, s), p),$
- $differ(select(r, p), select(s, p)) = select(differ(r, s), p).$

Moreover, if Y denotes a subset of X, the following properties hold:

- $union(project(r, Y), project(s, Y)) = project(union(r, s), Y),$
- $inter(project(r, Y), project(s, Y)) \ \supseteq project(inter(r, s), Y),$
- $differ(project(r, Y), project(s, Y)) \subseteq project(differ(r, s), Y).$

The following example shows their validity using a simple case.

Example 2.6. Consider the relations r and s with schema (A, B) and their extensions given by:

$$r = \{\langle a, \ b_1\rangle)\}, \ s = \{\langle a, \ b_2\rangle\}.$$

Let $X = \{A, \ B\}$ and $Y = \{A\}$. The projections $project(r, \ Y)$ and $project(s, Y)$ yield:

$$project(r, \ Y) = \{a\}; \ project(s, \ Y) = \{a\}.$$

Moreover:

$$union(r,\ s) = \{\langle a,\ b_1 \rangle,\ \langle a,\ b_2 \rangle\};\ inter(r,\ s) = \emptyset;\ differ(r,s) = \{\langle a,\ b_1 \rangle\}.$$

The results, corresponding to the left- and right-hand sides of the previous formulas, are synthesized as follows:

$$union(project(r,\ Y), project(s,\ Y)) = \{a\};$$
$$project(union(r,\ s), Y) = \{a\};$$
$$inter(project(r,\ Y), project(s,\ Y)) = \{a\};$$
$$project(inter(r,\ s), Y) = \emptyset;$$
$$differ(project(r,\ Y), project(s,\ Y)) = \emptyset;$$
$$project(differ(r,\ s), Y) = \{a\}.\diamond$$

Finally, we point out the following property concerning selection and join:

$$join(select(r,\ p),\ s,\ \theta,\ A,\ B) = select(join(r,\ s,\ \theta,\ A,\ B), p),$$

where p is a predicate bearing only on the attributes of relation r.

The interest of these properties resides in the possibility for: i) the user to translate his or her natural language need into different correct expressions, and ii) the DBMS to carry out some transformations for optimization purposes.

2.3 An Overview of SQL

The SQL language is the most commonly used tool to manipulate relational databases. It can be used either directly to submit queries, or through programming languages (e.g., C and Java) which provide appropriate interfaces. The foundations of the language were laid in the mid-seventies with SEQUEL, developed in the context of a prototype called System-R (Chamberlin *et al.*, 1976). The set of operations offered by SQL includes the design and modification of the schema of a database, the management of access rights, querying and data updates. It involves extensions with respect to the relational algebra, in particular in order to ease the formulation of complex queries. It is a *de facto* standard which is found in most (not to say all) commercial DBMSs. The principal components of SQL related to querying capabilities are reviewed in the rest of this section.

2.3.1   *The base block*

The SQL base block "**select** ... **from** ... **where** ..." is a key element which allows for the expression of several relational operators. One of its commonly used forms is written as:

> **select** [**distinct**] *attributes* **from** *relations* **where** *condition*

which is interpreted the following way (regardless of the effective processing strategy of any DBMS):

(1) compute the Cartesian product of the relations in the "from" clause, which are either base or temporary relations,
(2) select the tuples agreeing with the condition of the "where" clause,
(3) retain the sole attributes appearing in the "select" clause and remove duplicates if "distinct" is mentioned; when * is used instead of a list of attribute names (star convention), all attributes are kept.

This interpretation scheme "covers" several operators of the relational algebra. Table 2.6 gives the correspondences between algebraic operators and forms of the base block.

Example 2.7. Consider the relations *emp*(*e-id, e-name, age, birth-city, living-city, work-serv, resp, salary*) and *ser*(*s-num, s-name, budget*), whose respective keys are *e-num* and *s-num*. Attribute *resp* represents the employee's senior; 0 means that this employee has no senior. The query aimed at the retrieval of any pair (employee's name, service name) such that the employee works in the service, this employee does not live in his/her birth-city, and this service has a budget less than $15M, may be written as:

> **select** *e-name, s-name* **from** *emp, ser*
>
> **where** *budget* < 15 **and** *birth-city* ≠ *living-city* **and** *work-serv* = *s-num*.

Here, the join condition is integrated inside the "where" clause and the distinction between selection and join conditions made in relational algebra

Table 2.6   Correspondences between relational algebra and SQL

operator	algebraic expression	SQL expression
selection	$select(r, p)$	**select** * **from** r **where** p
projection	$project(r, \{A_1, \ldots, A_n\})$	**select distinct** $A_1, \ldots, A_n$ **from** r
Cartesian product	$cartprod(r, s)$	**select** * **from** r, s
theta-join	$join(r, s, \theta, A, B)$	**select** * **from** r, s **where** $A \, \theta \, B$

vanishes. With the extensions of *emp* and *ser* shown in Tables 2.7 and 2.8, this query delivers the result reported in Table 2.9.◇

When a relation is used several times (for instance twice as is the case in a self-join), it is necessary to know which occurrence an attribute refers to. To this end, a variable is associated with every occurrence of the relation; this variable serves as a prefix for attribute names. We will see later other situations where variables are of interest.

Example 2.8. With the relation *emp* of Example 2.7, the query to look for the pairs (employee's name, senior's name) such that the employee earns more than his senior, requires two occurrences of relation *emp*, and it written as:

select *E.name, S.name* **from** *emp E, emp S*

where *E.senior = S.e-id* **and** *E.salary > S.salary,*

where E and S refer to two copies of relation *emp* (more specifically, S plays the role of the seniors of the elements of E).◇

The two preceding examples illustrate some of the predicates that usually appear in a "where" clause, i.e., founded on a conjunctive or disjunctive

Table 2.7   Relation *emp* of Example 2.7

e-id	e-name	age	birth-city	living-city	work-serv	resp	salary
14	Durand	37	Paris	Nantes	5	3	9000
5	Milon	49	Lyon	St Nazaire	1	34	21500
34	Rocca	28	Le Croisic	Rennes	1	3	12000
3	Perrol	34	Lannion	Redon	5	0	7600
7	Robin	30	Nantes	Nantes	5	3	11000

Table 2.8   Relation *ser* of Example 2.7

s-num	s-name	budget
1	sales	19
5	marketing	13

Table 2.9   Result of the query of Example 2.7

e-name	s-name
Durand	marketing
Perrol	marketing

combination of terms (predicates) of the form "*attribute θ constant*" or "*attribute-1 θ attribute-2*" where θ is a comparator. There are also many dedicated predicates (e.g., "*attribute* **is null**") which are not dealt with here.

A variant of the base block allows the delivery of a result made of a single tuple using one or more aggregate functions according to the syntax:

select *ag-1*(*att-1*), ..., *ag-p*(*att-p*) **from** *relations* **where** *condition*,

where *ag-i*(*att-i*) denotes an aggregate (i.e., a set-oriented) function, *ag-i* applying to attribute *att-i*. This is interpreted as follows:

(1) perform the Cartesian product of the relations of the "from" clause,
(2) select the tuples complying with the condition of the "where" clause,
(3) compute the value of each aggregate function of the "select" clause over the tuples resulting from the previous step.

The most common aggregate functions, generally predefined in available DBMSs, are: maximum (*max*), minimum (*min*), average (*avg*), sum (*sum*), variance (*var*), standard deviation (*std*), median (*med*), and cardinality (*count*). With the except of the last function, it is assumed that the argument used is numeric.

Example 2.9. With the previous relations *emp* and *ser*, the query to look for the number of employees working in a service having a budget less than $15M, along with their average salary, may be written as:

select count(∗), **avg**(*salary*) **from** *emp*, *ser*

where *work-serv* = *s-num* **and** *budget* < 15.

Here, "**count**(*)" returns the cardinality of the tuples resulting from steps (1) and (2), while "**avg**(*salary*)" computes the average of the attribute *salary* over those tuples. With the data of the extensions given previously in Tables 2.7 and 2.8, the result obtained is the tuple: ⟨3, 9200⟩. If one wants to know how many employees of service 5 play the role of a senior, it is necessary to use "count" applied to the attribute *senior*, together with the keyword "distinct" so that any senior is taken into account only once. Such a query would be formulated as:

select count(**distinct** *senior*) **from** *emp*

where *senior* ≠ 0 **and** *work-serv* = 5.

With the extension of *emp* in Table 2.7, this query returns 1 as a result, while 2 would have been delivered in the absence of the keyword "distinct". ⋄

2.3.2 *Combining base blocks*

Several blocks may appear inside an SQL query by means of two major constructs: predicates based on *subqueries* and *set-oriented combinations*.

Besides those mentioned previously, SQL allows for more sophisticated predicates with a nested block, also called a "subquery"; this can even be used recursively if needed. The principal forms of nested predicates are the following:

(1) *att-1* [**not**] **in** (**select** *att-2* **from** ...) where *att-1* and *att-2* are compatible attributes; this predicate is true if the value of *att-1* in the current tuple of the outer block belongs (resp. does not belong when "not" is used) to the set of values returned by the inner block (the subquery),

(2) [**not**] **exists** (**select** * **from**...); this predicate is true if the result returned by the inner block is not empty (resp. empty if "not" is used),

(3) *att-1* θ {**any** | **all**} (**select** *att-2* **from**...) where *att-1* and *att-2* are compatible attributes; with "any" (resp. "all"), this predicate is true if the value of *att-1* in the current tuple of the outer block is in relation θ with at least one (resp. all) the values of *att-2* returned by the inner block,

(4) *att-1* θ (**select** *ag(att-2)* **from**...) where *att-1* and *att-2* are compatible attributes; this predicate is true if the value of *att-1* in the current tuple of the outer block is in relation θ with the single value (aggregate) returned by the inner block.

It is worth noting that some equivalences hold between these expressions, as illustrated in Example 2.10.

Example 2.10. Consider relations *emp* and *ser* as defined previously. The query to look for the name of any service whose budget is over \$17M where there is no employee born in Nantes may be written as:

select *s-name* **from** *ser* **where** *budget* > 17 **and** *s-num* **not in**
(**select** *work-serv* **from** *emp* **where** *living-city* = "Nantes")

or:

select *s-name* **from** *ser* **where** *budget* > 17 **and** *s-num* $\neq$ **all**
(**select** *work-serv* **from** *emp* **where** *living-city* = "Nantes")

or:

> **select** *s-name* **from** *ser* **where** *budget* > 17 **and not exists**
> (**select** * **from** *emp*
> **where** *living-city* = "Nantes" **and** *work-serv* = *ser.s-num*).

In the last expression, the subquery refers to the outer block thanks to the predicate "*work-serv* = *ser.s-num*" where the dot notation "relation.attribute" is used. This method enhances the readability of the formulation, even if it is not mandatory here since one could also write "*work-serv* = *s-num*".◇

It is also possible to combine base blocks by means of compositions corresponding to the set operators presented in Section 2.2.1. The general syntax is:

> (**select** *att1-1*, ..., *att1-n* **from** *relations1* **where** *condition1*)
> {**union|intersect|except**}
> (**select** *att2-1*, ..., *att2-n* **from** *relations2* **where** *condition2*)

where the attributes from *att1* and *att2* are pairwise compatible. Except in the case of the union, which is mandatory since it builds a superset of each incoming relation, this kind of expression may be replaced by a construct with a subquery. So the intersection:

> (**select** *A*, *B* **from** *r*) **intersect** (**select** *A*, *B* **from** *s*)

may be formulated as:

> **select** *A*, *B* **from** *r* **where exists**
> (**select** * **from** *s* **where** *A* = *r.A* **and** *B* = *r.B*)

and the difference:

> (**select** *A*, *B* **from** *r*) **except** (**select** *A*, *B* **from** *s*)

may be replaced by:

> **select** *A*, *B* **from** *r* **where not exists**
> (**select** * **from** *s* **where** *A* = *r.A* **and** *B* = *r.B*).

Example 2.11. Consider the preceding relations *emp* and *ser*, and the query to look for any service (number) with a budget over $6M where there is at least one employee living in Nantes. Such a query may be expressed either as:

> (**select** *s-num* **from** *ser* **where** *budget* > 6)
>
> **intersect**
>
> (**select** *work-serv* **from** *emp* **where** *living-city* $=$ "Nantes")

or as:

> **select** *s-num* **from** *ser* **where** *budget* > 6 **and exists**
>
> (**select** * **from** *emp*
>
> **where** *living-city* $=$ "Nantes" **and** *work-serv* $=$ *ser.s-num*).◊

2.3.3 *Partitioning*

Consider a user who would like to know the average salary in each service. Using the constructs presented so far, it would be necessary to submit first a query to get the number of any service where at least one employee works, then to process as many queries delivering the average salary of the corresponding service as there are services. Such a process would be tedious, and can be avoided using the partitioning facility of SQL.

The principle consists of partitioning a relation on the basis of one or more attributes sharing the same value, according to the schema of Figure 2.9. From now on, the result of the query concerns the subsets generated by the partitioning, and not tuples individually. The syntax of a query is:

> **select** *att-set-1*, *ag-set* **from** *relations* **where** *ind-cond*
>
> **group by** *att-set-2* **having** *set-cond*

where:

- *ind-cond* is a condition for the selection of tuples of the relation to be partitioned,
- *att-set-2* is the set of attributes onto which the partitioning is done,
- *set-cond* is a condition for the selection of subsets coming from the partitioning,
- *att-set-1* is a subset of the attributes pertaining to *att-set-2* since only attributes of *att-set-2*, which have a same value in a subset, make sense at the subset level,
- *ag-set* stands for a list of aggregate functions applying to attributes of the partitioned relation.

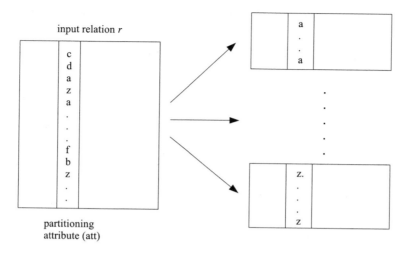

Fig. 2.9   Partitioning using a single attribute

The interpretation of a partitioning query is the following (regardless of any actual processing in a DBMS):

(1) perform the Cartesian product of the relations of the "from" clause,
(2) select the tuples complying with the condition (*ind-cond*) of the "where" clause,
(3) from the relation resulting from the previous step, build subsets of tuples with the same value over the attribute(s) mentioned in the "group by" clause (see the schema of Figure 2.9),
(4) remove the subsets which do not comply with the condition (*set-cond*) of the clause "having" (which makes use of aggregate functions),
(5) for each subset, retain the value of the attributes appearing in the "select" clause (*att-set-1*) and compute the value of the aggregates of this same clause.

Example 2.12. The query to look for any service where the average salary of its employees born in Nantes is over \$12K may be written as:

> **select** *s-num* **from** *emp* **where** *birth-city* = "Nantes"
> **group by** *s-num* **having** *avg(salary)* > 12.

The query returning the number of employees, the average salary, the lowest and highest salary of any service where more than 15 employees work is expressed as:

> **select** *s-num*, **count**(*), **avg**(*salary*), **min**(*salary*), **max**(*salary*)
>
> **from** *emp*
>
> **group by** *s-num* **having count**(*) > 15.◇

2.3.4 *Expressing division and antidivision*

No specific feature is available in SQL to express division queries. Such a need is covered, thanks to partitioning. Recall that the division of relation r with schema $R(A, X)$ by relation s with schema $S(B, Y)$ retains a value x appearing in attribute X of r if it is associated with at least all the values of attribute B in s. It turns out that partitioning enables the computation of the set of values associated with every x (using X as the partitioning attribute). However, it is still necessary to overcome the lack of set containment (or any other set comparison operation) in SQL. Fortunately, it is possible to replace this operation by a comparison over cardinalities of sets, although not the original ones of course, once one remarks that:

$$A \subseteq B \Leftrightarrow A = A \cap B \Leftrightarrow card(A) = card(A \cap B).$$

From this observation, the dividend relation is seen to be restricted to tuples whose value of the division attribute (A) pertains to the divisor relation. Now, a value x is acceptable if it is associated with a set whose cardinality is exactly that of the divisor. This results in the following generic expression:

> **select** X **from** r **where** A **in** (**select** B **from** s)
>
> **group by** X
>
> **having count**(**distinct** A) = (**select count**(**distinct** B) **from** s).

An alternative expression of division is possible using subqueries (nested predicates) based on a convenient rewriting of Expression (2.1), since one has:

$$\{x \mid \forall a, (a \in project(s, B)) \Rightarrow (\langle a, x \rangle \in r)\} =$$
$$\{x \mid \nexists a, (a \in project(s, B)) \text{ and } (\langle a, x \rangle \notin r)\}.$$

This second expression leads to the following possible expression for the division of r by s:

select distinct X **from** r $r1$ **where not exists**

(**select** * **from** s **where** B **not in**

(**select** A **from** r **where** $X = r1.X$)).

Example 2.13. Consider the query to look for the number of any service where all the employees over 40 have stayed for at least three months (Example 2.5). Using partitioning, its expression is:

select s-num **from** $stay$ **where** $duration \geq 3$ **and** emp-num **in**

(**select** e-id **from** emp **where** $age > 40$)

group by s-num **having count**(**distinct** emp-num) =

(**select count**(*) **from** emp **where** $age > 40$).

The introduction of the condition "emp-num **in** (**select** e-id **from** emp **where** $age > 40$)" guarantees the correctness of the statement.

The other possible formulation (using subqueries) is:

select s-num **from** $stay$ $s1$ **where** $duration \geq 3$ **and not exists**

(**select** * **from** emp **where** $age > 40$ **where** e-id **not in**

(**select** emp-num **from** $stay$

where $duration \geq 3$ **and** s-$num = s1.s$-num)).

The use of a variable ($s1$) in the outermost block is mandatory for the reference to attribute s-num made in the innermost block (s-$num = s1.s$-num).◇

The expression of an antidivision of relation $r(A, X)$ by relation $s(B, Y)$ (see Section 2.2.2) is much easier, and calls on a difference. Indeed, an element x is satisfactory if it does not belong to the set of values from X for which at least one association with a value B of s exists. This gives the formulation:

select X **from** r **where** X **not in** (**select** X **from** r, s **where** $A = B$).

Chapter 3

Basic Notions on Fuzzy Sets

3.1 Introduction

Set theory is used in various domains of computer science (for instance principles of programming) and is one of the foundations of relational databases, as seen in the previous chapter. It is of interest to note that this theory has both a set-oriented side and a logical side, each set operation having its counterpart in logic. Several extensions of set theory have been studied in recent years, among which rough sets (Pawlak, 1982) and fuzzy sets (Zadeh, 1965) are of particular interest in the database area. Rough sets are used for data mining (see, e.g., Quafafou and Boussouf, 1997) and are not dealt with later on. Fuzzy sets were initially created for the design of automated systems, and they constitute a central topic in this book.

The key idea behind fuzzy sets is their ability to represent categories or classes of elements where the boundary between membership and rejection is not clear-cut (or abrupt), but on the contrary *gradual*. This approach is especially suitable for dealing with numerous concepts in everyday life (and terms of natural languages) for which there is a progressive transition between full- and non-membership, in the sense that the concept of interest associated with the fuzzy set (*high* temperature, *inexpensive* price, *fair* color, etc.) is observed to a greater or lesser extent. If the interpretation of such terms is clearly contextual, it is generally hard to represent them using regular sets, as illustrated by Figure 3.1. In this case, one can observe an abrupt transition between the values which pertain to the concept "high temperature" and those which do not. Thus, a temperature of 25°C is definitely not a "high temperature", while 25.1°C definitely is a "high temperature", which is not in accordance with common

31

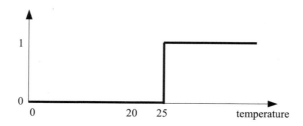

Fig. 3.1   The regular set of temperatures over 25°C

sense. The history of fuzzy sets has been rich; its main events are listed below:

- 1965: Zadeh's seminal paper is published (Zadeh, 1965),
- beginning of the seventies: birth of the "expert system" approach in control with fuzzy rules,
- 1973: first book about fuzzy sets written by A. Kaufmann,
- 1975: first results of the use of fuzzy rules by Mamdani and Assilian,
- 1978: paper introducing possibility theory which is closely related to fuzzy sets; this theory is introduced by Zadeh (1978) as a new theoretical framework for dealing with uncertainty,
- 1978: first issue of the international journal *Fuzzy Sets and Systems*,
- second half of the seventies: intensive activity in fuzzy control in Europe (United Kingdom, Denmark, Netherlands especially) with numerous applications to industrial processes,
- 1985: first congress of IFSA (International Fuzzy Systems Association) with a biennial occurrence ever since,
- end of the eighties: fuzzy boom in Japan with a wide range of applications such as the Sendai subway, washing machines, photocopiers, rice cookers, hi-fi sets, camcorders, and cameras,
- beginning of the nineties: growing interest in fuzzy sets in Germany (with the strong support of the authorities), France, Spain and North America; many national and international scientific conferences are launched,
- 1992: first international conference of the IEEE (FUZZ-IEEE) in San Diego, which has since become a yearly event,
- 1993: first issue of the international journal *IEEE Transactions on Fuzzy Systems*,
- 1999: creation of the European society EUSFLAT (EUropean Society for Fuzzy Logic And Technology).

The initial application of fuzzy sets was in the area of control, since L.A. Zadeh was an automatician. However, fuzzy sets received huge interest in many other communities, even if the applications have not been as spectacular as in fuzzy control. The use of fuzzy sets has been, and is still, a topic of research and development in mathematics, image processing, classification, data analysis, artificial intelligence, operations research and optimization, decision making, information retrieval, and database systems, this last topic being the main concern of this book.

This chapter is limited to introducing those notions strictly necessary for understanding the following chapters. The reader interested in complementary aspects of fuzzy sets is invited to refer to Dubois and Prade (1980, 2000); Klir and Yuan (1995); Leondes (1999); Ruspini *et al.* (1998). After presenting some definitions and notations, the principal operations over fuzzy sets (composition and inclusion) are detailed. Then, the notions of fuzzy measures and integrals are given, as well as the extension principle and some key aspects of fuzzy quantified propositions.

3.2 Definitions and Notations

In the following, regular sets are denoted by A, B and fuzzy sets by E, F. In the usual case, a set A is associated with a *characteristic function* f_A taking its value from the pair $\{0, 1\}$. For any value x of the domain X (also called the universe or referential), $f_A(x)$ indicates whether x belongs to A or not. This view extends to a fuzzy set which is associated with a characteristic function denoted by μ valued in the interval $[0, 1]$ of the real line $\mathbb{R}$, also called the *unit interval*. The value $\mu_E(x)$ expresses the extent to which the element x of X is a member of the fuzzy set E:

$$\mu_E : X \longrightarrow [0, 1]$$

$$x \longrightarrow \mu_E(x).$$

If $\mu_E(x)$ equals 0, x does not belong to E at all; if it is 1, x is a full member of E. The closer $\mu_E(x)$ is to 1 (resp. 0), the more x belongs (resp. does not belong) to E. A regular set is a special case of a fuzzy one, where the characteristic function takes only the two values 0 and 1.

In practice, a fuzzy set is often used to model a linguistic term, in particular an adjective, as illustrated in Figures 3.2 and 3.3. A fuzzy set provides a *symbolic/numeric* (and vice versa) interface, between the symbolic aspect

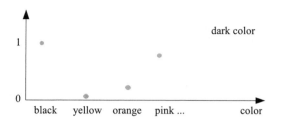

Fig. 3.2   The fuzzy set of dark colors

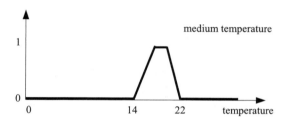

Fig. 3.3   The fuzzy set of medium temperatures

of the term and the numeric aspect of the characteristic function valued in the unit interval.

Most often, the modeled fuzzy concepts correspond to functions that are either monotonic, or increasing–decreasing represented by a trapezium (possibly left or right open), or a triangle. The part of the function corresponding to transitions is then linear, which is generally sufficient for coping with most requirements. For convenience, it may happen that a discrete function (for instance over the variable *age*) is represented in a continuous fashion. In such a case, the function makes sense only for the effective values of the variable (for instance, integers between 18 and 70 for the variable *age*).

In the case of a finite discrete fuzzy set E (which will be considered in what follows since it is sufficient in the database context), we use:

$$E = \{\mu_1/x_1, \ldots, \mu_n/x_n\},$$

which means that E has the associated characteristic function:

$$E : \{x_1, \ldots, x_n\} \longrightarrow [0, 1]$$

where $\mu_E(x_i) = \mu_i$ is the degree of membership of x_i to E. By convention, the associations for which the degree equals 0 are omitted.

The *support* of a fuzzy set E, denoted by $supp(E)$, is the regular set made of the elements with a strictly positive degree, i.e., which belong *somewhat* to E:

$$supp(E) = \{x \mid x \in X \text{ and } \mu_E(x) > 0\}.$$

The *core* of a fuzzy set E, denoted by $core(E)$, is defined as the regular set of the elements whose degree is 1, i.e., which are full members of E:

$$core(E) = \{x \mid x \in X \text{ and } \mu_E(x) = 1\}.$$

These two notions collapse in the case of a regular set, since if x is somewhat in A it belongs (totally) to A.

A fuzzy set E may be described as a collection of nested regular sets using the concept of α-*level cut* or α-*cut* defined as the regular set E_α of elements whose degree is greater than or equal to α:

$$E_\alpha = \{x \mid x \in X \text{ and } \mu_E(x) \geq \alpha\}.$$

The strict α-*cut* of E denoted by $E_{\overline{\alpha}}$ is obtained by replacing the symbol $\geq$ by $>$ in the above formula.

The following properties hold:

- $\alpha_1 > \alpha_2 \Rightarrow E_{\alpha_1} \subseteq E_{\alpha_2}$,
- $E_1 = core(E)$,
- $E_{\overline{0}} = supp(E)$.

The notion of α-cut establishes a natural link between fuzzy and regular sets, in the sense that a fuzzy set is expressed by more or less demanding interpretations in terms of α-cuts. Moreover, a fuzzy set may be recovered from its α-cuts by considering the proper elements $P_E(\alpha)$ of each α-cut, i.e., the elements of E that belong to none of the α-cuts with a degree strictly higher than α. The initial fuzzy set E is then made of the elements of each $P_E(\alpha)$ which are assigned their associated degree α.

The *cardinality* of a regular set extends to fuzzy sets as follows:

$$card(E) = \sum_{x \in X} \mu_E(x).$$

The *height* of a fuzzy set E is given by the degree of the element of maximal membership. E is said to be *normalized* if its height is 1.

In the following, the *complement* of fuzzy set E is defined as:

$$\forall x \in X,\ \mu_{\overline{E}}(x) = 1 - \mu_E(x).$$

This operation is involutive, i.e., $\overline{\overline{E}} = E$ $(\mu_{\overline{\overline{E}}}(x) = \mu_E(x))$.

Example 3.1. Let $X = \{a, b, \ldots, j, k\}$ and $E = \{1/a, 0.7/c, 0.2/e, 0.3/f, 0.6/h, 0.7/j, 0.9/k\}$. The height of E equals 1 (E is normalized) and:

- $\overline{E} = \{1/b, 0.3/c, 1/d, 0.8/e, 0.7/f, 1/g, 0.4/h, 1/i, 0.3/j, 0.1/k\}$,
- $E_{0.3} = \{a, c, f, h, j, k\}$; $E_{0.5} = \{a, c, h, j, k\}$,
- $E_{\overline{0.6}} = \{a, c, j, k\}$; $E_{0.8} = \{a, k\}$,
- $supp(E) = \{a, c, e, f, h, j, k\}$,
- $core(E) = E_1 = \{a\}$,
- $card(E) = 4.4.\diamond$

3.3   Composition of Fuzzy Sets

The operations combining fuzzy sets extend the usual set operations; they are presented along with their logical counterpart.

3.3.1   *Intersection and union of fuzzy sets*

Norm and *co-norm* operators constitute the foundation of the extension of intersection and union for fuzzy sets whose logical counterpart is the pair conjunction/disjunction (and/or). In the unit interval, the norm $\top(x, y)$ is a binary operator with the following properties:

- associativity : $\top(x, \top(y, z)) = \top(\top(x, y), z)$,
- monotonicity (non-decreasing with respect to each argument):

$$\text{if } x_1 < x_2 \text{ then } \top(x_1, y) \le \top(x_2, y),$$

$$\text{if } y_1 < y_2 \text{ then } \top(x, y_1) \le \top(x, y_2),$$

- existence of the neutral element 1: $\top(1, x) = \top(x, 1) = x$.

Similarly, a co-norm $\bot(x, y)$ is associative, commutative, monotonic, and admits 0 as a neutral element. The following inequalities hold for norms and co-norms:

$$\forall y, \top(x, y) \le x \le \bot(x, y) \quad \text{and} \quad \forall x, \top(x, y) \le y \le \bot(x, y),$$

which look like the triangular inequality and lead to the terms *triangular norm* and *triangular co-norm* . Any pair norm/co-norm $(\top/\bot)$ is tied by duality relationships:

$$\top(x,y) = 1 - \bot(1-x, 1-y) \quad \text{and} \quad \bot(x,y) = 1 - \top(1-x, 1-y),$$

which correspond to the De Morgan laws in the usual set-theoretic framework, i.e.:

$$(a \text{ and } b) = (\overline{\overline{a} \text{ or } \overline{b}}) \quad \text{and} \quad (a \text{ or } b) = (\overline{\overline{a} \text{ and } \overline{b}}).$$

The intersection and union of fuzzy sets are defined as:

- $\forall x \in X, \mu_{E \cap F}(x) = \top(\mu_E(x), \mu_F(x)),$
- $\forall x \in X, \mu_{E \cup F}(x) = \bot(\mu_E(x), \mu_F(x))$

where $\top(x,y)$ (resp. $\bot(x,y)$) stands for a norm (resp. the dual co-norm).

Norms have a *minimal element* called *Weber's norm* defined as:

$$\top_W(1,y) = y, \top_W(x,1) = x; \top_W(x,y) = 0 \text{ otherwise.}$$

Indeed, any norm $\top$ is such that:

$$\top(x,1) = x, \top(1,y) = y; \text{ in any other case } \top(x,y) \geq 0.$$

They also admit the *minimum* $(min(x,y))$ as a *maximal element*.

Proof. Assume that $min(x,y) = x$. Due to the properties of norms, one has:

$$\top(x,y) \leq \top(x,1) \quad \text{and} \quad \top(x,1) = x.$$

Then, $\top(x,y) \leq min(x,y)$. ∎

Due to the relationship between co-norms and norms, the minimal co-norm is the maximum $(max(x,y))$ and the maximal co-norm is *Weber's co-norm* defined as:

$$\bot_W(0,y) = y, \bot_W(x,0) = x; \bot_W(x,y) = 1 \text{ otherwise.}$$

In addition, 0 (resp. 1) turns out to be an *absorbing element* for any norm (resp. co-norm).

Proof. From the fact that $min(x,y)$ is the largest norm, any norm $\top$ complies with:

$$\forall x \in [0,1], \top(x,0) \leq min(x,0).$$

But $min(x, 0) = 0$ and then: $\forall x \in [0, 1], \top(x, 0) = 0$. In an analogous way, for any co-norm $\bot$: $\forall x \in [0, 1], \bot(x, 1) \geq max(x, 1)$ and $max(x, 1) = 1$ leads to the conclusion that $\forall x \in [0, 1], \bot(x, 1) = 1$. ∎

Norms and co-norms generalize the usual conjunction and disjunction operators:

- $\top(0, 1) = \top(1, 0) = \top(0, 0) = 0$ since 0 is absorbing for any norm $\top$,
- $\top(1, 1) = 1$ since 1 is the neutral element of any norm $\top$,
- $\bot(0, 1) = \bot(1, 0) = \bot(1, 1) = 1$ since 1 is absorbing for any co-norm $\bot$,
- $\bot(0, 0) = 0$ since 0 is the neutral element of any co-norm $\bot$.

Example 3.2. Let E and F be the fuzzy sets:

$$E = \{1/a, 0.3/b, 0.7/c, 0.2/e\}$$

$$F = \{0.3/a, 1/c, 1/d, 0.6/e\}.$$

With min/max, the intersection and union of E and F are:

$$E \cap F = \{0.3/a, 0.7/c, 0.2/e\}$$

$$E \cup F = \{1/a, 0.3/b, 1/c, 1/d, 0.6/e\},$$

whereas with the probabilistic norm and co-norm (see Table 3.1) one has:

$$E \cap F = \{0.3/a, 0.7/c, 0.12/e\}$$

$$E \cup F = \{1/a, 0.3/b, 1/c, 1/d, 0.68/e\},$$

and with Łukasiewicz's norm and co-norm (see Table 3.1):

$$E \cap F = \{0.3/a, 0.7/c\}$$

$$E \cup F = \{1/a, 0.3/b, 1/c, 1/d, 0.8/e\}.\diamond$$

The number of norms (and co-norms) is infinite; the most common ones are given in Table 3.1. Example 3.2 shows that the result of the intersection and union of two fuzzy sets may vary widely according to the choice made for the norm and co-norm. Moreover, it is impossible to find a couple $(\top, \bot)$ for which all the properties of Boolean algebra hold. In particular, idempotency and non-contradiction/excluded-middle laws are incompatible.

Proof. Consider an idempotent norm $\top$ such that $\forall x \in X, \top(x, x) = x$. Moreover, assume that $E \cap \overline{E} = \emptyset$, i.e.: $\forall x \in X, \top(x, 1 - x) = 0$. We should have, simultaneously: $\top(0.5, 0.5) = 0.5$ and $\top(0.5, 0.5) = 0$, which is impossible.

Table 3.1   Principal norms and co-norms

norm: $\top(x,\ y)$	associated co-norm: $\perp(x,\ y)$	name
$min(x,y)$	$max(x,y)$	Zadeh
xy	$x+y-xy$	probabilistic
$max(x+y-1,0)$	$min(x+y,1)$	Łukasiewicz
$\dfrac{xy}{\gamma+(1-\gamma)(x+y-xy)}, \gamma \in [0,1]$	$\dfrac{x+y-xy-(1-\gamma)xy}{1-(1-\gamma)xy}, \gamma \in [0,1]$	Hamacher
$\begin{cases} x \text{ if } y=1 \\ y \text{ if } x=1 \\ 0 \text{ otherwise} \end{cases}$	$\begin{cases} x \text{ if } y=0 \\ y \text{ if } x=0 \\ 1 \text{ otherwise} \end{cases}$	Weber

Similarly, an idempotent co-norm $\perp$ is such that $\forall x \in X, \perp(x,x) = x$. Moreover, if the excluded-middle law holds: $E \cup \overline{E} = X$, i.e.: $\forall x \in X, \perp(x, 1-x) = 1$. Here, we must have both: $\perp(0.5, 0.5) = 0.5$ and $\perp(0.5, 0.5) = 1$, which is impossible. ∎

Double distributivity is not guaranteed for a given pair $(\top, \perp)$. It turns out that the couple (min, max) is of particular interest, because it preserves most of the properties usually valid:

- computational simplicity,
- applicability to a purely ordinal scale, coarser than the unit interval, where symbolic values are provided for the grades. For instance, with the ordered symbols *bad* $\prec$ *weak* $\prec$ *small* $\prec$ *medium* $\prec$ *large* $\prec$ *huge*, it is possible to compare any pair of symbols (a,b) and then to evaluate $min(a,b)$ and $max(a,b)$,
- preservation of both idempotency and double distributivity,
- distributivity of the α-cut operation with respect to intersection and union:

$$(E \cap F)_\alpha = E_\alpha \cap F_\alpha \quad \text{and} \quad (E \cup F)_\alpha = E_\alpha \cup F_\alpha.$$

A drawback of the minimum (resp. maximum) lies in its inability to discriminate between two situations where vectors of degrees are compared and share the same minimal (resp. maximal) value. So, $min(0.8, 0.3, 0.5) = min(1, 0.3, 0.9) = 0.3$. Of course, other norm/co-norm couples have better discrimination power, but generally they do not offer the ordinal feature of minimum and maximum. Several refinements of min/max have been proposed (Dubois *et al.*, 1997) in order to stay within an ordinal framework and to reach a better discrimination power. These refinements no longer correspond to norm/co-norm pairs. We now illustrate two representatives:

the *discrimin* and the *leximin* operators (the case of *discrimax* and *leximax* being quite similar).

We consider two vectors x and y over $[0,1]^p$. We use the notations: x_i (resp. y_i) for the ith component of x (resp. y), $D(x,y) = \{i \mid x_i \neq y_i\}$. The *minimum, discrimin* and *leximin* operations over x and y are defined as:

$$x >_{min} y \Leftrightarrow min_{i\in[1,p]}x_i > min_{i\in[1,p]}y_i,$$

$$x >_{disc} y \Leftrightarrow min_{i\in D(x,y)}x_i > min_{i\in D(x,y)}y_i,$$

$$x >_{lex} y \Leftrightarrow \exists k \in [1,p] \text{ such that } \forall i < k, x_i^* = y_i^* \text{ and } x_k^* > y_k^*,$$

where x_i^* stands for the ith component of the vector x^* obtained from x by ranking its components in increasing order. *Leximin* refines *discrimin*, which in turn refines the minimum, i.e.:

$$x >_{min} y \Rightarrow x >_{disc} y \Rightarrow x >_{lex} y.$$

For instance, if $x = (0.1, 0.2, 0.7, 0.3)$ and $y = (0.2, 0.2, 1, 0.1)$, we have:

$$x^* = (0.1, 0.2, 0.3, 0.7),$$
$$y^* = (0.1, 0.2, 0.2, 1),$$
$$D(x,y) = \{1, 3, 4\},$$
$$min_{i\in D(x,y)} x_i = 0.1,$$
$$min_{i\in D(x,y)} y_i = 0.1,$$

then x and y are incomparable using *discrimin*, just as they are for the minimum, but $x >_{lex} y$ ($k = 3$). Now if we take: $x = (0.1, 0.2, 0.7, 0.3)$ and $y = (0.2, 0.2, 1, 0.8)$, we obtain:

$$x^* = (0.1, 0.2, 0.3, 0.7),$$
$$y^* = (0.2, 0.2, 0.8, 1),$$
$$D(x,y) = \{1, 3, 4\},$$
$$min_{i\in D(x,y)} x_i = 0.1,$$
$$min_{i\in D(x,y)} y_i = 0.2,$$

then $y >_{disc} x$, $y >_{min} x$ and $y >_{lex} x$ ($k = 1$).

It is worth noting that the only case where two vectors x and y cannot be ranked according to *leximin* is when they have exactly the same values (regardless of their order in the vectors).

Another pair of operators stemming from the min/max couple is their weighted versions (denoted by *wmin* and *wmax*), intended for preserving the ordinal feature and most of its properties (in particular associativity, commutativity, neutral element). So if the importances $w_1, \ldots, w_n$ (with $max(w_i) = 1$; i.e., at least one set E_j is *completely* important) are associated with the fuzzy sets $E_1, \ldots, E_n$, one has:

- $\mu_{wmin(E_1,\ldots,E_n,w_1,\ldots,w_n)}(x)$
  $= min(max(1 - w_1, \mu_{E_1}(x)), \ldots, max(1 - w_n, \mu_{E_n}(x)))$,
- $\mu_{wmax(E_1,\ldots,E_n,w_1,\ldots,w_n)}(x)$
  $= max(min(w_1, \mu_{E_1}(x)), \ldots, min(w_n, \mu_{E_n}(x)))$.

The normalization condition over the weights is imposed by the fact that, in its absence, the maximal (resp. minimal) degree of satisfaction 1 (resp. 0) cannot be reached for *wmax* (resp. *wmin*) even though all the input degrees $(\mu_{E_i}(x)'s)$ equal 1 (resp. 0). The usual minimum and maximum are recovered from the previous expressions by assigning the maximal level of importance 1 to every set, i.e., $w_1 = \ldots, w_n = 1$. Finally, the properties:

- $wmin(E_1, \ldots, E_n, w_1, \ldots, w_n) = \overline{wmax}(\overline{E_1}, \ldots, \overline{E_n}, w_1, \ldots, w_n)$,
- $wmax(E_1, \ldots, E_n, w_1, \ldots, w_n) = \overline{wmin}(\overline{E_1}, \ldots, \overline{E_n}, w_1, \ldots, w_n)$

hold.

3.3.2 *Difference between fuzzy sets*

An initial approach to the difference, whose logical counterpart is the operator *"except"* (or *"and not"*), consists of extending the usual definition over two regular sets A and B:

$$A - B = \{x \mid x \in A \text{ and } x \notin B\}. \tag{3.1}$$

More generally, from the definition of an operator given as:

$op(< parameters >) = \{t \mid \text{formula } \Phi \text{ defining the acceptable elements t}\}$,

the characteristic function $\mu_{op}(t)$ is obtained by making the following replacements in formula Φ:

- a conjunction (resp. disjunction) by a norm $\top$ (resp. co-norm $\bot$),

- the universal (resp. existential) quantifier by a generalized conjunction (resp. disjunction); the n-ary version of min/max is taken later on (except otherwise stated),
- the negation by the complement to 1,
- membership $(x \in E)$ by a degree of membership $(\mu_E(x))$.

In the specific case of the difference, letting E and F be two fuzzy sets, one obtains:

$$\forall x \in X, \mu_{E-F}(x) = \top(\mu_E(x), \mu_{\overline{F}}(x)) = \top(\mu_E(x), 1 - \mu_F(x)),$$

which, with particular choices for the norm $\top$, leads to:

$\mu_{E-F}(x) = min(\mu_E(x), 1 - \mu_F(x))$ with $\top(x, y) = min(x, y)$,
$\mu_{E-F}(x) = max(\mu_E(x) - \mu_F(x), 0)$ if $\top(x, y) = max(x + y - 1, 0)$ is chosen.

Example 3.3. Consider the fuzzy sets:

$$E = \{1/a, 0.3/b, 0.7/c, 0.2/e\} \text{ and } F = \{0.3/a, 1/c, 1/d, 0.6/e\}.$$

Using the minimum for the conjunction, one obtains $\{0.7/a, 0.3/b, 0.2/e\}$ for the difference $E - F$, while $E - F = \{0.7/a, 0.3/b\}$ with the other choice.◇

Other approaches may be envisaged based on different points of view about the formulation of the usual difference between regular sets, which, of course, are equivalent to Expression (3.1). For instance, one may take:

$$E - F = \text{ the smallest set to add to } E \cap F \text{ to obtain } E,$$

as a starting point. Then, it follows that:

$$E - F = \cap \{G \mid G \cup (E \cap F) \supseteq E\},$$

and the characteristic function of the difference between the fuzzy sets E and F is defined as:

$$\mu_{E-F}(x) = inf \{u \mid \bot(u, \top(\mu_E(x), \mu_F(x)) \geq \mu_E(x)\},$$

where $\top$ (resp. $\bot$) is a triangular norm (resp. co-norm).

Example 3.4. With the fuzzy sets E and F of Example 3.3, the norm "*minimum*" and the co-norm "*maximum*", one obtains the difference $E - F = \{1/a, 0.3/b\}$. This result is quite different from those obtained previously (see Example 3.3), which highlights the variety of behaviors observed according to the choice of difference operator.◇

This kind of approach is particularly appropriate when it is impossible to call on the notion of complement, for instance if one wants to deal with fuzzy bags (see Rocacher and Bosc, 2002; Rocacher, 2002). A somewhat similar view is based on:

$$E - F = \text{ the smallest set to add to } F \text{ to obtain } E \cup F,$$

which leads to:

$$\mu_{E-F}(x) = inf \{u \mid \bot(u, \mu_F(x)) \geq \bot(\mu_E(x), \mu_F(x))\},$$

where $\bot$ is a triangular co-norm.

3.3.3 *Cartesian product of fuzzy sets*

The Cartesian product of the two regular sets A and B, defined as:

$$A \times B = \{xy \mid x \in A \text{ and } y \in B\},$$

where xy denotes the concatenation of x and y, extends to fuzzy sets as soon as a triangular norm $\top$ is taken for the conjunction, which yields:

$$\mu_{E \times F}(xy) = \top(\mu_E(x), \mu_F(y)).$$

Example 3.5. Let E and F be the fuzzy sets:

$$E = \{1/a, 0.3/b, 0.7/c, 0.2/e\},$$
$$F = \{1/y, 0.6/z\}.$$

Their Cartesian product $E \times F$ is:

$$\{1/(a, y), 0.6/(a, z), 0.3/(b, y), 0.3/(b, z),$$
$$0.7/(c, y), 0.6/(c, z), 0.2/(e, y), 0.2/(e, z)\}$$

if the minimum is taken for $\top$, while one would obtain:

$$\{1/(a, y), 0.6/(a, z), 0.3/(b, y), 0.18/(b, z),$$
$$0.7/(c, y), 0.42/(c, z), 0.2/(e, y), 0.12/(e, z)\}$$

with the product.$\diamond$

3.3.4 *Trade-off operators*

The preceding operators correspond to an adaptation of the operators working on regular sets. However, there are operators which make sense with fuzzy sets but which do not in the usual context, for instance because their result would not be in the pair $\{0, 1\}$. This is the case in particular for mean operators which perform a trade-off over their arguments. This view is obviously quite orthogonal to the use of the minimum (resp. maximum) which keeps only the worst (resp. best) value among the arguments. It is possible to combine several fuzzy sets by means of diverse simple mean operators (e.g., arithmetic, geometric, or harmonic). If a weighted mean is used, a specific importance is given to each of the input sets. So, if W denotes a normalized set of weights (whose elements add up to 1), the weighted mean of the fuzzy sets $E_1, \ldots, E_n$ returns the fuzzy set characterized by:

$$\mu_{wm(E_1,\ldots,E_n,W)}(x) = \sum_{i=1}^{n} (\mu_{E_i}(x) * W[i]).$$

Using this operator, weight assignment is static. Yager (1988) has introduced a variant, called ordered weighted averaging (OWA), where the assignment is dynamic. Instead of combining the values by assigning $W[1]$ to E_1, $W[2]$ to E_2, and so on, the principle relies on a weight assignment once the values of the vector $E_1(x), \ldots, E_n(x)$, are ranked decreasingly. By doing this, the weight $W[1]$ applies to the largest value of the vector, $W[2]$ to the second largest, $\ldots$, and $W[n]$ to the smallest. The resulting definition is:

$$\mu_{OWA(E_1,\ldots,E_n,W)}(x) = \sum_{i=1}^{n} (\mu_{E_i'}(x) * W[i])$$

where $\mu_{E_i'}(x)$ is the ith largest value among $\{\mu_{E_1}(x), \ldots, \mu_{E_n}(x)\}$. It has been shown that:

- this operator is monotonically non-decreasing with respect to each entry $(\mu_{E_i}(x))$,
- its result lies between the minimum and the maximum of the input values,
- the minimum, maximum, and average of the entries are recovered when appropriate weights are chosen, namely

$$W_{min} = (0, \ldots 0, 1),$$
$$W_{max} = (1, 0, \ldots, 0), \text{ and}$$
$$W_{avg} = \left(\frac{1}{n}, \ldots, \frac{1}{n}\right).$$

Fig. 3.4 Respective position of norms, co-norms, and mean operators

Example 3.6. Consider the fuzzy sets $E_1 = \{0.4/a, 0.8/b\}, E_2 = \{1/a, 0.2/b\}, E_3 = \{1/b\}$, and the weight vector $W = (0.2, 0.5, 0.3)$. The regular weighted mean over E_1, E_2, and E_3 delivers the set $F_1 = \{0.58/a, 0.56/b\}$, while $F_2 = \{0.4/a, 0.66/b\}$ is obtained with the OWA aggregation.$\diamond$

The relative position of mean operators with respect to norms and co-norms is given in Figure 3.4. There are many other trade-off operators: see in particular Dubois and Prade (1985b, 2000); Fodor and Yager (2000) Yager (1993).

3.3.5 *Nonsymmetric operators*

Here, we focus on three operators that have a counterpart in natural language, and can be seen as a way to define a sophisticated interaction between predicates in order to build three new types of condition:

- P_1 *and if possible* P_2, which is related to conjunction,
- P_1 *or else* P_2, which is connected with disjunction,
- P_1 *all the more as* P_2, which expresses a reinforcement of P_1 when P_2 is more and more satisfied.

These constructs can be nested to consider, for instance, statements like P_1 *and if possible* (P_2 *and if possible* P_3), or combined with each other, as in the statement P_1 *or else* (P_2 *all the more as* P_3), but the scope of this section is restricted to binary statements. A more complete presentation of these operators can be found in Bosc and Pivert (2011).

3.3.5.1 *"And if possible"*

The expression "P_1 *and if possible* P_2", where P_1 and P_2 are two (possibly complex) predicates, expresses both a weak and asymmetric conjunction, in the sense that P_2 is less important than P_1 and does not have a full compensation power. An example of its use is the query "find houses with four rooms, a price around \$300k and if possible a small garden and a garage". In such a context, the presence of a small garden and a garage intervenes only for houses having four rooms and a price somewhat around \$300k. The basis for defining this operator, denoted by *aip*, is the following set of axioms (where μ_i stands for the degree of satisfaction of predicate P_i for a given element onto which "P_1 *and if possible* P_2" applies):

- AIP1: "P_1 *and if possible* P_2" is less drastic than "P_1 *and* P_2", i.e.: $aip(\mu_1, \mu_2) \geq min(\mu_1, \mu_2)$,
- AIP2: "P_1 *and if possible* P_2" is more demanding than P_1, i.e.: $aip(\mu_1, \mu_2) \leq \mu_1$,
- AIP3: *aip* must have asymmetric behavior, i.e., it is noncommutative and: $\exists x, y : aip(x, y) \neq aip(y, x)$,
- AIP4: *aip* is increasing in its first argument, i.e.: $x \geq y \Rightarrow aip(x, z) \geq aip(y, z)$,
- AIP5: *aip* is increasing in its second argument, i.e.: $y \geq z \Rightarrow aip(x, y) \geq aip(x, z)$,
- AIP6: "P_1 *and if possible* P_2" is equivalent to "P_1 *and if possible* (P_1 *and* P_2)", i.e.: $aip(\mu_1, \mu_2) = aip(\mu_1, min(\mu_1, \mu_2))$.

It follows that when P_1 is not at all satisfied, neither is "P_1 *and* P_2", which makes it impossible to call on a mean operator to model *aip*. Moreover, the effect of "if possible" intervenes when μ_2 is less than μ_1 and one wants the value returned to be greater than μ_2, which is the result in the presence of a regular conjunction. In other words, the result must be upgraded with respect to μ_2 without going beyond μ_1. Several ways to perform this upgrade can be envisaged; we suggest the following modeling whose behavior is illustrated in Table 3.2, and which complies with axioms AIP1 to AIP6:

$$\alpha_1(\mu_1, \mu_2) = min(\mu_1, k \cdot \mu_1 + (1 - k) \cdot \mu_2)$$

with $k \in [0, 1]$. For instance, if $k = 0.5$ is chosen, one gets:

$$aip_1(\mu_1, \mu_2) = min\left(\mu_1, \frac{\mu_1 + \mu_2}{2}\right).$$

3.3.5.2   *"Or else"*

The expression "P_1 *or else* P_2", where P_1 and P_2 are two predicates, expresses both a strong and asymmetric disjunction, in the sense that P_2

Table 3.2   Behavior of "P_1 and if possible P_2"

μ_1	μ_2	$k = 0.3$	$k = 0.5$	$k = 0.8$
0.3	0	0.09	0.15	0.24
0.3	0.4	0.3	0.3	0.3
0.3	0.7	0.3	0.3	0.3
0.3	1	0.3	0.3	0.3
0.6	0	0.18	0.3	0.48
0.6	0.4	0.46	0.5	0.56
0.6	0.7	0.6	0.6	0.6
0.6	1	0.6	0.6	0.6
1	0	0.3	0.5	0.8
1	0.4	0.58	0.7	0.88
1	0.7	0.79	0.85	0.94
1	1	1	1	1

is not considered at the same level as P_1 and then is not a "true alternative" for P_1. As with "and if possible", this operator, denoted by *oe*, can be defined on the basis of the following axioms:

- OE1: "P_1 *or else* P_2" is more drastic than "P_1 *or* P_2" since, as said above, P_2 is not as good as P_1: $oe(\mu_1, \mu_2) \leq max(\mu_1, \mu_2)$,
- OE2: "P_1 *or else* P_2" is softer than P_1 since P_2 constitutes a "choice", i.e.: $oe(\mu_1, \mu_2) \geq \mu_1$,
- OE3: *oe* must have asymmetric behavior like *aip*, i.e., it is noncommutative (cf. axiom AIP3),
- OE4: *oe* is increasing in its first argument, i.e.: $x \geq y \Rightarrow oe(x, z) \geq oe(y, z)$,
- OE5: *oe* is increasing in its second argument, i.e.: $y \geq z \Rightarrow oe(x, y) \geq oe(x, z)$,
- OE6: "P_1 *or else* P_2" is equivalent to "P_1 *or else* $(P_1$ *or* $P_2)$", i.e.: $oe(\mu_1, \mu_2) = oe(\mu_1, max(\mu_1, \mu_2))$.

From axiom OE2, it follows that when P_1 is fully satisfied, so is "P_1 *or else* P_2". In addition, the effect of "or else" intervenes when μ_2 is greater than μ_1 and one wants the value returned to be less than μ_2, which is the result in the presence of a regular disjunction. In other words, the result must be discounted with respect to μ_2 without going below μ_1. In the spirit of the definition of *aip*, that proposed for *oe* is:

$$oe(\mu_1, \mu_2) = max(\mu_1, k \cdot \mu_1 + (1 - k) \cdot \mu_2)$$

with $k \in [0, 1]$. For instance, if $k = 0.5$ is taken:

$$oe_1(\mu_1, \mu_2) = max(\mu_1, \frac{\mu_1 + \mu_2}{2}).$$

It can easily be proven that this definition conforms to axioms OE1 to OE6 (see Bosc and Pivert, 2011). Moreover, interestingly enough, De Morgan's laws hold $\forall k \in [0, 1]$ between operators aip and oe, which makes them dual as conjunctions and disjunctions based on norms and co-norms:

$$1 - aip(1 - \mu_1, 1 - \mu_2) = oe(\mu_1, \mu_2),$$

$$1 - oe(1 - \mu_1, 1 - \mu_2) = aip(\mu_1, \mu_2).$$

Table 3.3 illustrates the behavior of operator oe.

3.3.5.3 *"All the more as"*

We now deal with the modeling of conditions of the type "P_1 *all the more as* P_2". An example of such a condition is: "find a Honda Accord with a low price, and the price must be all the lower as the mileage is higher", which can be written as:

$$low(price) \ all \ the \ more \ as \ high(mileage).$$

Once again, different interpretations of such a condition can be devised. The idea advocated here is to strengthen predicate P_1 in a way proportional to the satisfaction of P_2. In other words, for an element t, $\mu_{P_1 \ all \ the \ more \ as \ P_2}(t)$ ranges from $\mu_{P_1}(t)$ when $\mu_{P_2}(t) = 0$ to $\mu_{(very \ P_1)}(t)$

Table 3.3   Behavior of "P_1 or else P_2"

μ_1	μ_2	$k = 0.3$	$k = 0.5$	$k = 0.8$
0.3	0	0.3	0.3	0.3
0.3	0.4	0.37	0.35	0.32
0.3	0.7	0.58	0.5	0.38
0.3	1	0.79	0.65	0.54
0.6	0	0.6	0.6	0.6
0.6	0.4	0.6	0.6	0.6
0.6	0.7	0.67	0.65	0.62
0.6	1	0.88	0.8	0.68
1	0	1	1	1
1	0.4	1	1	1
1	0.7	1	1	1
1	1	1	1	1

when $\mu_{P_2}(t) = 1$. According to this, the following axioms are used to construct the operator *atma*:

- ATMA1: *atma* is decreasing in its second argument, i.e.: $y \leq z \Rightarrow atma(x, y) \geq atma(x, z)$,
- ATMA2: *atma* is increasing in its first argument, i.e.: $x \leq y \Rightarrow atma(x, z) \leq atma(y, z)$,
- ATMA3: when P_1 is not at all satisfied, so is "P_1 all the more as P_2", i.e.: $\forall y, atma(0, y) = 0$,
- ATMA4: when P_2 is not at all satisfied, "P_1 all the more as P_2" is equivalent to P_1, i.e.: $\forall x, atma(x, 0) = x$
- ATMA5: when P_1 is partly satisfied and P_2 is somewhat satisfied, "P_1 all the more as P_2" is a "true" strengthening of P_1, i.e.: $\forall x \in]0, 1[, \forall y > 0, atma(x, y) < x$.

From these properties and the choice of:

$$\mu_{very\ P_1}(x) = (\mu_{P_1}(x))^2$$

as the powering strengthening modifier supporting "very", several definitions of *atma* can be derived, among which are:

$$atma_1(\mu_1, \mu_2) = \mu_1^{(\mu_2+1)},$$
$$atma_2(\mu_1, \mu_2) = (\mu_1^2 - \mu_1) \cdot \mu_2 + \mu_1,$$

whose behavior is illustrated in Table 3.4. By analogy with the operator "P_1 *all the more as* P_2", one may think of a predicate "P_1 *all the less as* P_2" for which predicate P_1 is weakened. Thus, $\mu_{P_1\ all\ the\ less\ as\ P_2}(t)$ varies from $\mu_{P_1}(t)$ when $\mu_{P_2}(t)$ equals 0 to $\mu_{more\ or\ less\ P_1}(t)$ when μ_{P_2} is completely true.

Table 3.4   Behavior of "P_1 all the more as P_2"

μ_1	μ_2	$\mu_1^{\mu_2+1}$	$(\mu_1^2 - \mu_2) \cdot \mu_2 + \mu_1$
0.6	0	0.6	0.6
1	1	1	1
0	0.25	0	0
0.8	0.5	0.715	0.72
0.6	1	0.36	0.36
0.2	0.75	0.06	0.08

3.4   Inclusions and Implications

The usual definition of the inclusion of A in B relies on the expression:

$$(A \subseteq B) \Leftrightarrow (\forall x \in X, (x \in A) \Rightarrow (x \in B)) \qquad (3.2)$$

which shows the close relationship between inclusion and implication. For this reason, we first present how the usual (material) implication extends to a fuzzy framework, before moving to several types of extension of the inclusion.

3.4.1   *Fuzzy implications*

3.4.1.1   *Introduction*

Usually, the implication $(P \Rightarrow Q)$ expresses a link between the values p and q of the propositions P and Q. It returns "*true*" when proposition Q is true or when proposition P is false, according to the truth table reported in Table 3.5. This table is also associated with the expression ((*not P*) *or Q*). Several approaches to extending the implication can be envisaged when propositions P and/or Q are no longer Boolean, but instead take their values in the unit interval. Any fuzzy implication is a function defined as:

$$\Rightarrow_f : [0,1] \times [0,1] \longrightarrow [0,1]$$

$$(p,q) \longrightarrow (p \Rightarrow_f q),$$

and it is increasingly true (resp. false) as its result approaches 1 (resp. 0). Fuzzy implications can be presented according to various classifications; in what follows they are divided into three families covering the most frequent and useful ones. Their principal characteristics are discussed along with their semantics, in order to highlight their *rational* usage.

Table 3.5   Truth table of the proposition $P \Rightarrow Q$

	Q	
P	**true**	**false**
true	*true*	*false*
false	*true*	*true*

3.4.1.2 *S-implications*

This name stands for *strong* implications. Their starting point is the expression of the material implication as:

$$((not\ P)\ or\ Q),$$

and the class of S-implications (denoted by $\Rightarrow_S$) is defined as follows:

$$P \Rightarrow_S Q = \bot(1 - p, q). \tag{3.3}$$

where the disjunction ("or") is generalized by a co-norm ($\bot$). There is an infinity of S-implications: the three most common are given in Table 3.6. These implications are their own contraposition, since from Expression (3.3):

$$not\ Q \Rightarrow_S not\ P = \bot(1-(1-q), 1-p) = \bot(q, 1-p) = \bot(1-p, q) = P \Rightarrow_S Q.$$

As for the material implication, one has:

$$(P \Rightarrow_S false) = \bot(1 - p, 0) = 1 - p.$$

Furthermore, the S-implications of Table 3.6 can be ranked as follows:

$$(P \Rightarrow_{KD} Q) \le (P \Rightarrow_{Rb} Q) \le (P \Rightarrow_{Lu} Q).$$

and the Kleene–Dienes implication is the smallest among S-implications, because it is built using the smallest co-norm. The largest S-implication, denoted by $\Rightarrow_{SM}$, is found when Weber's co-norm is taken in Expression (3.3), which yields:

$$P \Rightarrow_{SM} Q = \begin{cases} (1 - p) \text{ if } q = 0, \\ q \text{ if } p = 1, \\ 1 \text{ otherwise.} \end{cases}$$

All the S-implications $P \Rightarrow_S Q$ are lower bounded by $(1 - p)$.

Table 3.6 The three main S-implications

name	definition	underlying co-norm $\bot$
Kleene–Dienes	$P \Rightarrow_{KD} Q = max(1 - p, q)$	$\bot(u, v) = max(u, v)$
Reichenbach	$P \Rightarrow_{Rb} Q = 1 - p + pq$	$\bot(u, v) = u + v - uv$
Łukasiewicz	$P \Rightarrow_{Lu} Q = min(1 - p + q, 1)$	$\bot(u, v) = min(u + v, 1)$

3.4.1.3   *R-implications*

The second class of fuzzy implications contains the R-implications, whose name derives from the *residuation principle*. Usually:

$$(P \ and \ (P \Rightarrow Q)) \Leftrightarrow (P \ and \ (not \ P \ or \ Q)) \Leftrightarrow$$

$$((P \ and \ not \ P) \ or \ (P \ and \ Q)) \Leftrightarrow (P \ and \ Q),$$

and then the truth value of the proposition $(P \ and \ (P \Rightarrow Q))$ is upper-bounded by that of proposition Q, i.e., $(p \ and \ (p \Rightarrow q)) \leq q$). In the fuzzy case, this inequality serves as the basis for searching for the maximal element for which it holds:

$$(P \Rightarrow_R Q) = sup \{u \in [0,1] \mid \top(p, u) \leq q\}, \tag{3.4}$$

$\top$ denoting a triangular norm. Of course, there is an infinite number of R-implications: they can be rewritten as:

$$P \Rightarrow_R Q = \begin{cases} 1 \text{ if } p \leq q, \\ f(p, q) \text{ otherwise,} \end{cases}$$

where $f(p, q)$ is specific to the considered R-implication. The commonest R-implications are given in Table 3.7, along with their associated generative norms. The Rescher–Gaines implication may be considered as a specific R-implication which takes fuzzy propositions as inputs and delivers a Boolean result. It derives from a formula close to Expression (3.4), namely:

$$(P \Rightarrow_{RG} Q) = sup \{u \in \{0,1\} \mid \top(p, u) \leq q\} = 1 \text{ if } p \leq q, 0 \text{ otherwise}$$

whatever the norm $\top$. These implications can be ranked as follows:

$$(P \Rightarrow_{RG} Q) \leq (P \Rightarrow_{Gd} Q) \leq (P \Rightarrow_{Gg} Q) \leq (P \Rightarrow_{Lu} Q).$$

Gödel's implication is the smallest proper R-implication (i.e., excluding that of Rescher–Gaines), because it is built using the largest norm (the "minimum"). It is worth noting that Łukasiewicz's implication is both an

Table 3.7   The three main R-implications

name	definition	underlying norm $\top$
Gödel	$P \Rightarrow_{Gd} Q = 1$ if $p \leq q, q$ otherwise	$\top(u, v) = min(u, v)$
Goguen	$P \Rightarrow_{Gg} Q = 1$ if $p \leq q, q$ otherwise	$\top(u, v) = u * v$
Łukasiewicz	$P \Rightarrow_{Lu} Q = 1$ if $p \leq q, 1 - p + q$ otherwise	$\top(u, v) = max(u + v - 1, 0)$

R-implication and an S-implications, since its expression given in Table 3.7 is such that:

$$P \Rightarrow_{\text{Lu}} Q = \begin{cases} 1 \text{ if } p \leq q, \\ 1 - p + q \text{ otherwise} \end{cases}$$

$$= min(1 - p + q, 1),$$

this latter expression being the one given in Table 3.6. Any R-implication may be reformulated in a format close to that of an S-implication by replacing the co-norm appearing in Expression (3.3) by an appropriate operator. This format is used in Chapter 6. As an illustration, we now deal with Gödel's and Goguen's implications. Gödel's implication ($P \Rightarrow_{\text{Gd}} Q = 1$ if $p \leq q, q$ otherwise) must be rewritten:

$$P \Rightarrow_{\text{Gd}} Q = op(1 - p, q).$$

Then:

$$op(1 - p, q) = \begin{cases} 1 \text{ if } p \leq q, \\ q \text{ otherwise,} \end{cases}$$

which leads to:

$$op(u, v) = \begin{cases} 1 \text{ if } u + v \geq 1, \\ v \text{ otherwise.} \end{cases}$$

This operator returns 0 if and only if u and v both equal 0 and 1 when u, or v, or both equal 1, which is identical to the behavior of the regular disjunction. Of course, it is noncommutative; this is the reason it is called a *noncommutative disjunction* (ncd_{Gd}). A dual (in the sense of the De Morgan laws) *noncommutative conjunction* (ncc_{Gd}) can be associated with this noncommutative disjunction, allowing the following to be stated:

$$P \Rightarrow_{\text{Gd}} Q = ncd_{\text{Gd}}(1 - p, q) = 1 - ncc_{\text{Gd}}(p, 1 - q),$$

where:

$$ncc(u, v) = 0 \text{ if } u + v \leq 1, v \text{ otherwise.}$$

The same holds for any other R-implication (Dubois and Prade, 1984), for instance with Goguen's implication:

$$P \Rightarrow_{\text{Gg}} Q = ncd_{\text{Gg}}(1 - p, q) = 1 - ncc_{\text{Gg}}(p, 1 - q),$$

where:

$$ncd_{Gg}(u, v) = \begin{cases} 1 \text{ if } u + v \geq 1, \\ \dfrac{v}{u} \text{ otherwise,} \end{cases}$$

$$ncc_{Gg}(u, v) = \begin{cases} 0 \text{ if } u + v \leq 1, \\ \dfrac{u + v - 1}{u} \text{ otherwise.} \end{cases}$$

Similarly, any S-implication can be rewritten in the format of an R-implication, by replacing the norm with the appropriate noncommutative conjunction in Expression (3.4). In fact, the close connections established in Dubois and Prade (1984) are summarized in Figure 3.5.

3.4.1.4 *Contraposition of R-implications*

The third family of implications correspond to the contraposition of R-implications which turn out not to be their own contrapositions (except Łukasiewicz's implication, which is also an S-implication). Their general definition is:

$$(P \Rightarrow_{\text{contrapR}} Q) = ((not\ Q) \Rightarrow_{\text{R}} (not\ P)).$$

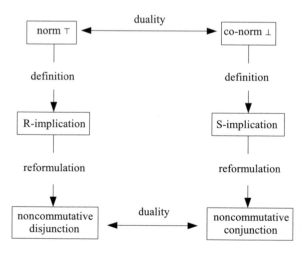

Fig. 3.5   Connections between norms, co-norms, implications, noncommutative conjunctions, and disjunctions

In particular:

$$P \Rightarrow_{\text{contrapGd}} Q = \begin{cases} 1 \text{ if } p \leq q, \\ (1-p) \text{ otherwise,} \end{cases}$$

$$P \Rightarrow_{\text{contrapGg}} Q = \begin{cases} 1 \text{ if } p \leq q, \\ \dfrac{1-q}{1-p} \text{ otherwise.} \end{cases}$$

Notice that the Rescher–Gaines implication is its own contraposition, since:

$$(not\ Q) \Rightarrow_{\text{RG}} (not\ P) = \begin{cases} 1 \text{ if } p \leq q, \\ 0 \text{ otherwise} \end{cases}$$

$$= (P \Rightarrow_{\text{RG}} Q).$$

3.4.1.5 *Some characteristics of fuzzy implications*

All of the fuzzy implications presented above generalize the usual material implication; i.e., when the input values are 0 or 1, their result coincides with that of the regular implication. Indeed, since 1 is an absorbing element and 0 a neutral element, for any S-implication one has:

- $(0 \Rightarrow_{\text{S}} 0) = \perp(1,0) = 1$,
- $(1 \Rightarrow_{\text{S}} 1) = \perp(0,1) = 1$,
- $(1 \Rightarrow_{\text{S}} 0) = \perp(0,0) = 0$,
- $(0 \Rightarrow_{\text{S}} 1) = \perp(1,1) = 1$.

In a similar way, for R-implications and their contrapositions:

- $(0 \Rightarrow_{\text{R}} 0) = (0 \Rightarrow_{\text{R}} 1) = (1 \Rightarrow_{\text{R}} 1) = 1$ since the first argument is less than (or equal to) the second one,
- $(1 \Rightarrow_{\text{R}} 0) = sup\,\{u \in [0,1]\,|\,\top(1,u) \leq 0\} = sup\,\{u \in [0,1]\,|\,u \leq 0\} = 0$.

These last two properties also hold for the Rescher–Gaines implication.

The three classes of fuzzy implications considered so far possess the following properties according to the requirements described in Yager (1980):

- $\forall p \in [0,1] : p \Rightarrow_{\text{f}} 1 = 1$,
- $\forall q \in [0,1] : 0 \Rightarrow_{\text{f}} q = 1$,
- $\forall q \in [0,1] : 1 \Rightarrow_{\text{f}} q = q$,
- $\forall p, q_1, q_2 \in [0,1] : \text{ if } q_1 > q_2, (p \Rightarrow_{\text{f}} q_1) \geq (p \Rightarrow_{\text{f}} q_2)$,
- $\forall p_1, p_2, q \in [0,1] : \text{ if } p_1 < p_2, (p_1 \Rightarrow_{\text{f}} q) \geq (p_2 \Rightarrow_{\text{f}} q)$.

Some fuzzy implications can operate in a purely ordinal setting, i.e., it is not mandatory to be provided with numeric truth values in the unit interval and an ordered scale suffices. This is the case for Kleene–Dienes', Gödel's and Rescher–Gaines' implications (see Example 3.7), but not for those of Goguen, Reichenbach and Łukasiewicz. Indeed, the first three implications depend only on comparison operations and scale reversing (associated with the negation), while the other three need arithmetic operations.

Example 3.7. Consider the following ordered symbols $A < B < C < D < E$, where A (resp. E) is the minimal (resp. maximal) element corresponding to 0 (resp. 1) in the unit interval. For the sake of simplicity, we use $A \Rightarrow_f B$ to represent the implication $P \Rightarrow_f Q$ when A is the value of P and B is that of Q. Table 3.8 gives the result obtained for a sample of situations.◇

3.4.1.6 *Semantic aspects of fuzzy implications*

It is important to pay attention to the meaning which can be associated with the various fuzzy implications. This allows in particular for an appropriate choice in the context of a given domain of application (such as the division operation tackled later in Chapter 6). S-implications (in particular, those of Kleene–Dienes, Reichenbach and Łukasiewicz) have the characteristic of guaranteeing a minimal level of satisfaction ($P \Rightarrow_S Q$ returns a value at least equal to $(1 - p)$) as illustrated in Figures 3.6 and 3.7. Moreover, in the case of the Kleene–Dienes implication, the antecedent P acts as an important level assigned to the conclusion Q. Indeed, when p, the value of P, is low, only the high values of Q are "seen" (i.e., have an impact on the result of the implication), in contrast to the case of a high value of p for which Q is "seen" over a wide range of values (the interval $[1 - p, 1]$ which is large if p is small). As to R-implications, the value of the antecedent P has the role of a threshold, and full satisfaction is reached when the value

Table 3.8   Ordinal framework for some implications

	$A \Rightarrow_f D$	$B \Rightarrow_f E$	$C \Rightarrow_f D$	$B \Rightarrow_f A$	$D \Rightarrow_f B$	$E \Rightarrow_f B$
Kleene–Dienes	E	E	D	D	B	B
Gödel	E	E	E	A	B	B
Rescher–Gaines	E	E	E	A	A	A

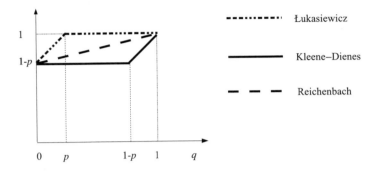

Fig. 3.6 Behavior of S-implications when p is small

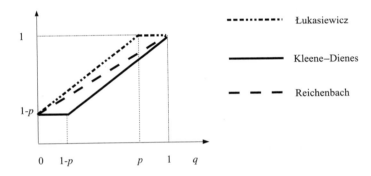

Fig. 3.7 Behavior of S-implications when p is large

of the conclusion Q is greater than (or equal to) p. Otherwise, the level of satisfaction is less than 1, and:

- depends on the sole conclusion with Gödel's implication,
- varies with the ratio between the value of the conclusion Q and that of the antecedent P ($\frac{q}{p}$) using Goguen's implication,
- is all the lower as the difference between the values of the antecedent and the conclusion increases with Lukasiewicz's implication.

Example 3.8. Table 3.9 summarizes the results obtained with the Rescher–Gaines, Gödel, Goguen, and Lukasiewicz implications for a sample of situations. It may be seen that these results may be close (or even equal), or on the contrary quite different values. Moreover, it can be observed that they comply with the properties described previously, in particular the order over these four implications given in Section 3.4.1.3.◊

Table 3.9   Illustration of the behavior of R-implications

implication	$0 \Rightarrow_R 0.3$	$0.3 \Rightarrow_R 0.8$	$0.6 \Rightarrow_R 0.2$	$0.8 \Rightarrow_R 0.1$	$1 \Rightarrow_R 0.8$
Rescher–Gaines	1	1	0	0	0
Gödel	1	1	0.2	0.1	0.8
Goguen	1	1	0.33	0.125	0.8
Łukasiewicz	1	1	0.6	0.3	0.8

3.4.2   *Inclusions*

3.4.2.1   *Introduction*

It may happen that sets are compared in terms of their inclusion or equality. Usually, this type of comparison leads to a Boolean answer, and the fuzzy set framework suggests a triple approach:

- to define these operations when the operands are fuzzy sets,
- to deliver a graded result instead of a binary one, whatever the type (fuzzy or not) of the operands,
- to allow for some tolerance in the inclusion (or equality) mechanism, in the sense that exceptions may be more or less acceptable.

3.4.2.2   *Regular inclusion between fuzzy sets*

The usual definition of the inclusion of A in B given by Expression (3.2) can also be written in terms of a constraint on the characteristic functions of A and B as:

$$(A \subseteq B) \Leftrightarrow (\forall x \in X, f_A(x) \leq f_B(x)). \tag{3.5}$$

This expression extends in a canonical way to two fuzzy sets E and F by:

$$(E \subseteq F) \Leftrightarrow (\forall x \in X, \mu_E(x) \leq \mu_F(x)), \tag{3.6}$$

which is often called "inclusion in the sense of Zadeh". Figures 3.8 and 3.9 illustrate the cases of inclusion and non-inclusion according to Expression (3.6). It is notable that Expression (3.6) may serve as a basis for defining the *crisp* equality of two fuzzy sets E and F:

$$(E = F) \Leftrightarrow (\forall x \in X, \mu_E(x) = \mu_F(x)). \tag{3.7}$$

Starting from Expression (3.2), which calls on an implication, one may define a more demanding inclusion, namely:

$$(E \subseteq F) \Leftrightarrow (\forall x \in X, (x \in supp(E)) \Rightarrow (x \in core(F))). \tag{3.8}$$

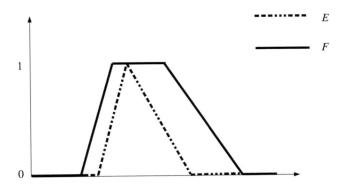

Fig. 3.8 E included in F according to Zadeh

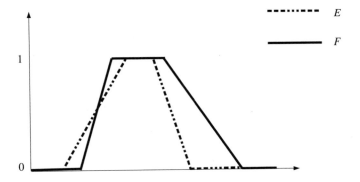

Fig. 3.9 E not included in F according to Zadeh

Figure 3.10 illustrates the inclusion of E in F according to Expression (3.8). The major drawback of such definitions stems from the fact that a negative answer is obtained when the inclusion of E in F (for regular or fuzzy set) is "obviously" violated, but also when it *almost* holds. More generally, this phenomenon may be interpreted as the inability to distinguish between quite different situations. This is obviated by using a *graded* inclusion.

Example 3.9. The fuzzy sets $E_1 = \{1/a, 1/b\}$ and $E_2 = \{0.5/a, 0.7/b\}$ are not included in the fuzzy set $F = \{0.4/a, 0.7/b\}$ using Expression (3.6). However, intuition may suggest that it is definitely more obvious for E_1, which certainly contains F, than for E_2, which is "almost included" in F.◇

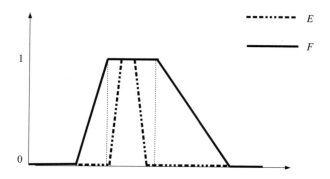

Fig. 3.10　Strong inclusion of E in F

3.4.2.3　*Graded inclusion*

Devising an inclusion whose result is a matter of degree allows for finer accounting than with an "all or nothing" view. By using a degree, a graded inclusion extends the notion of inclusion of one set (fuzzy or not) in another. Here again, several approaches may be taken.

Cardinality-based view of graded inclusion.　Taking the following definition of the regular inclusion of A in B:

$$(A \subseteq B) \Leftrightarrow ((A \cap B) = A),$$

it follows that:

$$(A \subseteq B) \Leftrightarrow (card(A \cap B) = card(A)).$$

It is then possible to define a graded inclusion through the degree of inclusion, defined as:

$$deg(A \subseteq B) = \frac{card(A \cap B)}{card(A)}.$$

In this way, the inclusion becomes gradual by evaluating the proportion of elements in the intersection of A and B with respect to those present in A. More generally, if E and F are two fuzzy sets, the degree of inclusion of E in F is given by:

$$deg(E \subseteq F) = \frac{card(E \cap F)}{card(E)} = \frac{\sum_{x \in X} \top(\mu_E(x), \mu_F(x))}{\sum_{x \in X} \mu_E(x)}, \qquad (3.9)$$

where $\top$ stands for a triangular norm. Expression (3.9) confers a quantitative (as opposed to logical) nature on the obtained degree. When the "minimum" is taken as the norm $\top$ in Expression (3.9), the grades associated with E play the role of a *threshold*. If an element x attains this value in F ($\mu_F(x) \geq \mu_E(x)$), the contribution of x to the overall degree of inclusion is maximal (the case of elements a and b in Example 3.10). Analogously, the choice of the "product" leads to:

$$deg(E \subseteq F) = \frac{\sum_{x \in X} \mu_E(x) * \mu_F(x)}{\sum_{x \in X} \mu_E(x)},$$

which corresponds to a weighted mean where the degrees $\mu_E(x)$ are the weights and play the role of a *level of importance* assigned to x.

In general, if E is included in F in the sense of Zadeh (Expression (3.6)), the degree of inclusion does not equal 1 except if the norm used in Expression (3.9) is the minimum (see Example 3.10).

Example 3.10. Consider the fuzzy sets $E = \{0.4/a, 0.6/b\}$ and $F = \{0.5/a, 1/b\}$, which satisfies $E \subseteq F$. Using Expression (3.9) with the norm "minimum", one has:

$$deg(E \subseteq F) = \frac{min(0.4, 0.5) + min(0.6, 1)}{0.4 + 0.6} = 1,$$

whereas with the product, one obtains:

$$deg(E \subseteq F) = \frac{(0.4 * 0.5) + (0.6 * 1)}{0.4 + 0.6} = 0.8.\diamond$$

Logical view of graded inclusion. It is also possible to adopt a logical approach to graded inclusion starting with Expression (3.2), which extends to fuzzy sets as follows:

$$deg(E \subseteq F) = min_{x \in X}(\mu_E(x) \Rightarrow_f \mu_F(x)), \tag{3.10}$$

$\Rightarrow_f$ being a fuzzy implication (see Section 3.4.1).

It turns out that the nature of the inclusion obtained differs depending on the type of fuzzy implication used in Expression (3.10). In particular, if E is included in F according to Zadeh (Expression (3.6)), the degree of inclusion is 1 for any R-implication (or its contraposition), but it is less than 1 when an S-implication is used. For instance, with the Kleene–Dienes or Reichenbach implication, degree 1 is obtained if and only if the support of E is included in the core of F, as it is for a non-graded inclusion defined in Expression (3.8).

Example 3.11. Consider the following fuzzy sets:

$$E_1 = \{0.4/a, 0.7/b\}, E_2 = \{1/a, 0.9/b, 0.2/c\}, F = \{1/a, 1/b, 0.9/c\}.$$

According to Expression (3.10), for $i = 1$ or 2, we have:

$$deg(E_i \subseteq F) = min(\mu_{E_i}(a) \Rightarrow_f \mu_F(a), \mu_{E_i}(b) \Rightarrow_f \mu_F(b), \mu_{E_i}(c) \Rightarrow_f \mu_F(c)),$$

which, for the Kleene–Dienes implication, leads to:

$$deg(E_1 \subseteq F) = min(0.4 \Rightarrow_{KD} 1, 0.7 \Rightarrow_{KD} 1) = 1,$$
$$deg(E_2 \subseteq F) = min(1 \Rightarrow_{KD} 1, 0.9 \Rightarrow_{KD} 1, 0.2 \Rightarrow_{KD} 0.9) = 0.9,$$

while using Gödel's implication, one obtains:

$$deg(E_1 \subseteq F) = min(0.4 \Rightarrow_{Gd} 1, 0.7 \Rightarrow_{Gd} 1) = 1,$$
$$deg(E_2 \subseteq F) = min(1 \Rightarrow_{Gd} 1, 0.9 \Rightarrow_{Gd} 1, 0.2 \Rightarrow_{Gd} 0.9) = 1.\diamond$$

Difference-based view of graded inclusion. A third type of expression for the inclusion of A in B relies of the set difference operation:

$$A \subseteq B \Leftrightarrow (A - B) = \emptyset,$$

which extends to two fuzzy sets E and F as follows:

$$deg(E \subseteq F) = 1 - h(E - F), \tag{3.11}$$

where $h(G)$ denotes the height of the fuzzy set G, i.e., the highest degree of membership attached to its elements. If one uses the "standard" definition of the difference given in Expression (3.1), one obtains:

$$deg(E \subseteq F) = 1 - max_{x \in X} \top(\mu_E(x), 1 - \mu_F(x)))$$
$$= min_{x \in X} 1 - \top(\mu_E(x), 1 - \mu_F(x))$$
$$= min_{x \in X} \bot(1 - \mu_E(x), \mu_F(x)).$$

This last expression is exactly that of the degree of inclusion given by Expression (3.10) when $\Rightarrow_f$ is replaced by an S-implication. This proves that the logical approach based on S-implications also captures the semantics of a degree of inclusion built from the "standard" difference between fuzzy sets.

Example 3.12. Consider the two fuzzy sets $E = \{1/a, 0.6/b, 0.3/c\}$ and $F = \{0.7/a, 0.4/b, 1/c\}$. The degree of inclusion of E in F using

Reichenbach's implication $(P \Rightarrow_{Rb} Q = 1 - p + pq)$ in Expression (3.10) is:

$$deg(E \subseteq F) = min(1 \Rightarrow_{Rb} 0.7, 0.6 \Rightarrow_{Rb} 0.4, 0.3 \Rightarrow_{Rb} 1)$$
$$= min(0.7, 0.64, 1)$$
$$= 0.64.$$

The difference of E and F with the norm "product" in Expression (3.1) is $\{0.3/a, 0.36/b\}$ and $h(E - F) = 0.36$. The degree of inclusion founded on Expression (3.11) then equals $(1 - 0.36) = 0.64$ as obtained before.◊

3.4.2.4 *Graded equality of fuzzy sets*

The equality of two sets is usually expressed as either the equality of their respective characteristic functions or their mutual inclusion. Based on Expression (3.7), the first approach extends to fuzzy sets, but its result is binary (0/1 or alternatively *false/true*). As we did with the inclusion, it may be convenient to define the notion of degree of equality of two sets as:

$$deg(E = F) = \top(deg(E \subseteq F), deg(F \subseteq E)),$$

where $\top$ stands for a norm, and the two degrees of inclusion are obtained using Expressions (3.9) or (3.10).

Example 3.13. Let E and F be the sets $E = \{1/a, 0.4/b, 0.6/c\}$ and $F = \{0.4/a, 0.7/b, 0.5/c\}$. Using Expression (3.9) with the norm "minimum", one has:

$$deg(E \subseteq F) = \frac{min(1, 0.4) + min(0.4, 0.7) + min(0.6, 0.5)}{1 + 0.4 + 0.6} = 0.65$$

$$deg(F \subseteq E) = \frac{min(1, 0.4) + min(0.4, 0.7) + min(0.6, 0.5)}{0.4 + 0.7 + 0.5} = 0.8125$$

and finally:

$$deg(E = F) = min(0.65, 0.8125) = 0.65.$$

With the norm "product", the grades would be:

$$deg(E \subseteq F) = \frac{(1 * 0.4) + (0.4 * 0.7) + (0.6 * 0.5)}{1 + 0.4 + 0.6} = 0.49$$

$$deg(F \subseteq E) = \frac{(1 * 0.4) + (0.4 * 0.7) + (0.6 * 0.5)}{0.4 + 0.7 + 0.5} = 0.6125$$

$$deg(E = F) = min(0.49, 0.6125) = 0.38.$$

The fact that elements a and c somewhat violate the inclusion of E in F has a limited impact in both cases, due to the compensation which takes place in these formulas. This would hold even with elements in total contradiction with the inclusion. On the contrary, the use of Expression (3.10), where a norm occurs, will lead to a quite different behavior. Indeed, a low value resulting from the implication for a given element x will become an upper bound for the degree of inclusion, then that of equality. For instance, using Gödel's implication in Expression (3.10), one obtains:

$$deg(E \subseteq F) = min(1 \Rightarrow_{\text{Gd}} 0.4, 0.1 \Rightarrow_{\text{Gd}} 0.6, 0.6 \Rightarrow_{\text{Gd}} 0.5)$$

$$= min(0.4, 1, 0.5) = 0.4,$$

$$deg(F \subseteq E) = min(0.4 \Rightarrow_{\text{Gd}} 1, 0.6 \Rightarrow_{\text{Gd}} 0.1, 0.5 \Rightarrow_{\text{Gd}} 0.6)$$

$$= min(1, 0.1, 1) = 0.1,$$

$$deg(E = F) = min(0.4, 0.1) = 0.1. \diamond$$

3.4.2.5 *Tolerant inclusion*

An alternative extension of inclusion is based on some tolerance of exceptions. This can be understood in two different ways depending on the nature of the exceptions, which can be either quantitative or qualitative. More details on tolerant inclusions can be found in Bosc and Pivert (2006, 2008), especially regarding their properties.

Quantitative tolerant inclusion. Some tolerance may be introduced on the basis of a number of exceptions with respect to the universal quantifier implicitly present in Expression (3.10). The definition of a quantitative exception-tolerant inclusion is based on ignoring the fact that some elements of E are not sufficiently, or even not at all, included in F (depending on the fuzzy implication taken). In other words, a certain number of values of E can be more or less ignored depending on the desired level of relaxation. The principle adopted is to weaken the universal quantifier into a relaxed quantifier *"almost all"*; see Kerre and Liu (1998), Zadeh (1983). In the following, the quantifier *"almost all"* induces grades defined as follows:

- $\mu_{almost\ all}(0) = w_n = 0$,
- $\mu_{almost\ all}(1) = w_0 = 1$,
- $\mu_{almost\ all}(1 - \frac{i}{n}) = w_i$.

Grade w_i expresses the degree of satisfaction when i out of the n elements are ignored. If we denote:

$$k_1 = max\{j \mid w_j = 1\}, k_2 = max\{j \mid w_j > 0\},$$

the quantifier *"almost all"* allows for the *total ignoring* of k_1 exceptions and the *partial ignoring* of up to k_2 exceptions. Basically, the idea is to search for the best compromise such that k elements of E are included in F and k is compatible with *"almost all"*, which leads to the following definition:

$$deg(E \subseteq_{\text{qttol}} F) = max_{k \in [1,n]} \, min(\alpha_k, w_{k-1})$$
$$= min_{k \in [1,n]} max(\alpha_k, w_k), \qquad (3.12)$$

where α_k is the kth smallest implication degree ($\mu_E(x) \Rightarrow_f \mu_F(x)$) and $w_k = \mu_{almost \; all}(1 - \frac{k}{n})$ is the degree of ignoring generated by the quantifier *"almost all"* for E whose support has n elements, i.e., n implication values intervene in Expression (3.12). It is worth noting that:

- Expression (3.10) is recovered from Expression (3.12) when the universal quantifier is used ($w_0 = 1, w_1 = \cdots = w_n = 0$), i.e., when no exception is admitted,
- as expected the result obtained is at least equal to that returned by the non-tolerant inclusion,
- Expression (3.12) establishes a clear connection with Expression (3.10) since, when w_i is 1, total ignoring takes place, whereas for $w_i = 0$, the associated element is completely taken into account as it stands.

Example 3.14. Consider the quantifier *"almost all"* defined as:

$$\mu_{almost \; all}(f) = \begin{cases} 0 \text{ if } f \in [0, 0.75], \\ 1 \text{ if } f \in [0.95, 1], \\ \text{linearly increasing if } f \in [0.75, 0.95]. \end{cases}$$

Moreover, let

$$E = \{1/a, 0.9/b, 0.9/c, 0.9/d, 0.9/f, 0.8/g, 0.7/h, 0.4/i, 0.2/j, 0.1/k\}$$

and

$$F = \{0.1/b, 0.2/c, 0.5/d, 0.7/e, 0.9/f, 1/g, 1/h, 0.2/i, 0.5/j\}.$$

The degrees generated by the above quantifier are $w_0 = 1, w_1 = 0.75, w_2 = 0.25, w_3 = \cdots = w_{10} = 0$, since E contains 10 tuples. The non-tolerant graded inclusion of E in F using Gödel's implication leads to the degree 0, since a is missing in F. On the contrary, when the tolerant inclusion is performed with Expression (3.12), the grade obtained is:

$$min(max(0, 0.75), max(0.1, 0.25), max(0.2, 0), max(0.5, 0),$$

$$max(0.7, 0), max(1, 0), \ldots, max(1, 0))$$

$$= max(min(0, 1), min(0.1, 0.75), min(0.2, 0.25), min(0.5, 0),$$

$$min(0.7, 0), min(1, 0), \ldots, min(1, 0)) = 0.2.$$

The two lowest implication values 0 and 0.1 are ignored thanks to w_1 and w_2.$\diamond$

Qualitative tolerant inclusion.   In the previous case, the quantitative inclusion of E in F expresses the idea that *"almost all* elements of E are included in F according to the chosen implication". If a qualitative view is adopted, the inclusion operator expresses the idea that "all elements of E are *almost included* in F according to the chosen implication". Exceptions are then taken into account according to the idea of "almost inclusion". In other words, the idea is to (more or less) compensate for the initial value of the implication when it expresses a sufficiently *low-intensity* exception.

The principle is to consider exceptions with respect to the inclusion in the following sense: if one looks for the inclusion of E in F, compensation takes place for an element x such that $\mu_E(x)$ and $\mu_F(x)$ are sufficiently close to the case of "full" inclusion. It seems reasonable to consider that closeness is a matter of degree; for instance, one may think that if we must be close to a, $a \pm 0.1$ is totally acceptable, but a shift beyond 0.3 cannot be tolerated, and the compensation is linear in between. Of course, this does not make sense for regular sets, for which exceptions correspond to the case where $\mu_E(x)$ equals 1 and $\mu_F(x)$ is 0: this is definitely not a case of low-intensity exception.

Using any R-implication, the intensity of an exception depends on the difference between $\mu_E(x)$ and $\mu_F(x)$. Intuitively, if this difference is positive but "small enough", we are in the presence of a low-intensity exception, which is somewhat tolerable. Here, the compensation is based on a change in the computation of the implication degree itself, where the conclusion part may be upgraded in the presence of a low-intensity exception. The definition of the qualitative exception-tolerant inclusion is then very similar in form to Expression (3.10), namely:

$$deg(E \subseteq_{\text{qltolR}} F) = min_{x \in X}(\mu_E(x) \Rightarrow_{\text{R}} (\mu_F(x)) + \delta) \qquad (3.13)$$

where

$$\delta = \begin{cases} 0 \text{ if } \mu_E(x) - \mu_F(x) \geq \beta, \beta \in [0,1], \\ \mu_E(x) - \mu_F(x) \text{ if } \mu_E(x) - \mu_F(x) \leq \alpha, \alpha \in [0,1] \text{ and } \alpha < \beta, \\ \text{linear in between.} \end{cases}$$

Example 3.15. Consider $E = \{1/a, 0.1/b, 0.6/c\}$ and $F = \{0.7/a, 0.4/c\}$. The degree of inclusion of these two sets using Gödel's implication in Expression (3.10) is 0, due to the absence of element b in F. If the qualitative exception-tolerant inclusion (Expression (3.13)) is performed with $\alpha = 0.1$ and $\beta = 0.3$, the result is:

$$min(1 \Rightarrow_{\text{Gd}} 0.7, 0.1 \Rightarrow_{\text{Gd}} 0 + 0.1, 0.6 \Rightarrow_{\text{Gd}} 0.4 + 0.05) = min(0.7, 1, 0.45)$$

$$= 0.45.$$

With Goguen's implication, the degree would be $min\left(0.7, 1, \dfrac{0.45}{0.6}\right) = 0.7.\diamond$

In the case of an S-implication ($P \Rightarrow_S Q$), the idea is to say that if p is "small enough" or q is "high enough", then a low-intensity exception occurs and the implication value can be upgraded to 1. On the other hand, if p is "not at all small enough" and q is "not at all high", then no compensation should take place, since the element is too big an exception. In between these two extreme situations, some partial compensation can take place.

If α and β denote two thresholds ($0 < \alpha < \beta$), the interval $[0, \alpha]$ represents "small enough" and the interval $[\alpha, \beta]$ corresponds to "somewhat small", then $[1-\alpha, 1]$ represents "high enough" and $[1-\beta, 1-\alpha]$ represents "somewhat high".

In this context, the definition of the qualitative exception-tolerant inclusion is analogous to Expression (3.13), i.e.:

$$deg(E \subseteq_{\text{qltolS}} F) = min_{x \in X} ((\mu_E(x) - \delta_1) \Rightarrow_S (\mu_F(x)) + \delta_2), \quad (3.14)$$

where

$$\delta_1 = \begin{cases} \mu_E(x) \text{ if } \mu_E(x) \leq \alpha, \\ 0 \text{ if } \mu_E(x) \geq \beta, \\ \left(\dfrac{\alpha}{\beta - \alpha}\right) * (\beta - \mu_E(x)) \text{ in between,} \end{cases}$$

$$\delta_2 = \begin{cases} 1 - \mu_F(x) \text{ if } \mu_F(x) \geq 1 - \alpha, \\ 0 \text{ if } \mu_F(x) \leq 1 - \beta, \\ \left(\dfrac{\alpha}{\beta - \alpha}\right) * (\mu_F(x) + \beta - 1) \text{ in between.} \end{cases}$$

Example 3.16. Take the two sets $E = \{0.7/a, 0.9/b, 0.1/c, 0.3/d\}$ and $F = \{0.8/a, 0.85/b, 0.2/c, 0.75/d\}$. With the Kleene–Dienes implication, the degree of inclusion of E in F according to Expression (3.10) is:

$$min(max(0.3, 0.8), max(0.1, 0.85), max(0.9, 0.2), max(0.7, 0.75)) = 0.75.$$

Using the qualitative tolerant inclusion in Expression (3.14), based on the Kleene–Dienes implication, and the thresholds $\alpha = 0.2$, $\beta = 0.45$, one obtains the degree:

$$min(max(1 - (0.7 - 0), 0.8 + 0.2), max(1 - (0.9 - 0), 0.85 + 0.15),$$

$$max(1 - (0.1 - 0.1), 0.2 + 0), max(1 - (0.3 - 0.12), 0.75 + 0.16))$$

$$= min(max(0.3, 1), max(0.1, 1), max(1, 0.2), max(0.82, 0.91)) = 0.91.$$

$\diamond$

3.5   Fuzzy Measures and Integrals

3.5.1   *Introduction*

This section deals with the notion of measure of the subsets of a finite universe X. In the usual theory, it is considered that measure is an additive notion (e.g., the measure of probability). Furthermore, the Lebesgue integral allows for the extension of the notion of measure to a function f defined over X. This integral calculates the surface delimited by a stepwise function; its value represents the extension of the concept of distance to the set of points defined by the function. However, it is possible to call the additivity hypothesis into question, since this may sometimes be too strong. This leads to the introducing of fuzzy measures (which should better be called *non-additive measures*), then fuzzy integrals which make use of such measures.

3.5.2   *Fuzzy measures*

A fuzzy measure over a finite universe X is a function defined as:

$$m : \mathscr{P}(X) \longrightarrow [0, 1],$$

where $\mathscr{P}(X)$ is the power set of X. It complies with the following three axioms:

- $m(X) = 1$,
- $m(\emptyset) = 0$,
- $\forall A, B$ such that $A \subseteq B, m(A) \le m(B)$ (monotonicity).

The last axiom weakens the additivity property, which may be written as:

$$\text{if } A \cap C = \emptyset, m(A \cup C) = m(A) + m(C).$$

Indeed, letting $B = A \cup C$ ($C \ne \emptyset$), it follows that $m(B) > m(A)$, which states that an additive measure is a fuzzy measure while the converse is not true.

Example 3.17. Consider the work associated with five tasks denoted respectively by a, b, c, d and e, assumed to be independent and without any constraint as to their order of execution. The work is complete when the five tasks are done. The measure of the work that has been accomplished at a given time depends on the tasks that are finished (taken in the universe $X = \{a, b, c, d, e\}$) and is given by:

$$m : \mathscr{P}(X) \longrightarrow [0, 1].$$

Thus, $m(A)$ is the state of the work if the tasks belonging to A are finished. For instance, $m(\{b, c\}) = 0.7$ means that 70% of the total work is executed if tasks b and c are over. It is easy to check that m is a fuzzy measure (i.e., that it complies with the previous three axioms) since the work is finished when all the tasks are done ($m(X) = 1$) and is not at all executed as long as a task is not done ($m(\emptyset) = 0$). In addition, when the number of finished tasks increases, the satisfaction cannot decrease then $A \subseteq B$ entails $m(A) \le m(B)$. If all the tasks are equally important and they contribute equally to the final result, the measure is additive and the measure m_1 is defined as:

- $m_1(\{a\}) = m_1(\{b\}) = m_1(\{c\}) = m_1(\{d\}) = m_1(\{e\}) = 0.2$,
- $m_1(A) = \sum_{x \in A} m_1(\{x\})$.

Conversely, if all the tasks contribute to the final result in a non-additive fashion, the following measure m_2 can be used:

- for singletons:

$$m_2(\{a\}) = m_2(\{b\}) = 0.3,$$

$$m_2(\{c\}) = m_2(\{d\}) = m_2(\{e\}) = 0.2,$$

- for subsets of two elements:

$$
\begin{cases}
\text{if } A = \{a, b\}, m_2(A) = 0.6, \\
\text{otherwise }
\begin{cases}
\text{if } a \text{ or } b \text{ belongs to } A, m_2(A) = 0.4, \\
\text{otherwise } m_2(A) = 0.3,
\end{cases}
\end{cases}
$$

- for subsets of three elements:

$$
\begin{cases}
\text{if } \{a, b\} \subseteq A, m_2(A) = 0.8, \\
\text{otherwise }
\begin{cases}
\text{if } a \text{ or } b \text{ belongs to } A, m_2(A) = 0.6, \\
\text{otherwise } m_2(A) = m_2(\{c, d, e\}) = 0.5,
\end{cases}
\end{cases}
$$

- for subsets of four elements:

$$
\begin{cases}
\text{if } \{a, b\} \subseteq A, m_2(A) = 0.9, \\
\text{otherwise } m_2(A) = 0.7. \diamond
\end{cases}
$$

3.5.3 *Fuzzy integrals*

Integration with respect to a fuzzy measure may be performed using several operators (i.e., several integrals), the most usual being the Choquet fuzzy integral (Murofushi and Sugeno, 1989) and the Sugeno fuzzy integral (Sugeno, 1974). The calculus of the Choquet integral consists of using the fuzzy measure in the same way as an additive measure, which leads to:

$$
C_m(\mu_A) = \sum_{i=1}^{n} \mu_A(x_i) * (m(A_i) - m(A_{i+1})),
$$

where the elements $\{x_1, \ldots, x_n\}$ are ranked in increasing order of their degree of membership of A $(\mu_A(x_1) \leq \ldots \leq \mu_A(x_n))$, $A_i = \{x_i, \ldots, x_n\}$ and $A_{n+1} = \emptyset$. This corresponds to the Lebesgue integral when the measure is actually an additive one.

The Sugeno integral of function μ from X to $[0, 1]$ is given by:

$$
S_m(\mu_A) = max_{\alpha \in [0,1]} \, min(\alpha, m(A_\alpha)),
$$

where A_α denotes the cut of level α of the fuzzy set A. Letting X be the set of elements $\{x_1, \ldots, x_n\}$ ranked in increasing order of their degree of membership to A, one obtains:

$$
S_m(\mu_A) = max_{i \in [1,n]} min(\mu_A(x_i), m(A_i)),
$$

with $A_i = \{x_i, \ldots, x_n\}$. When A represents a property (or predicate) and m is a measure of satisfaction, the value $S_m(\mu_A)$ expresses the extent to which there is a satisfactory set E (in the sense of m) such that all of its elements have the property:

$$S_m(\mu_A) = max_{E \in \mathscr{P}(X)}min(m(E), t(E)),$$

with $t(E) = min_{x \in E}\mu_A(x)$ expressing the fact that every element of E satisfies property A.

Example 3.18. Consider again the context of the previous example. Function μ from $\{a, b, c, d, e\}$ to the unit interval expresses the percentage of the overall work performed by each task, and the measure m states the percentage of the overall work completed depending on the tasks that have been finished. The assessment of the overall work achieved so far takes into account both μ and m, considering the most favorable set of tasks:

$$max_{E \in \mathscr{P}(X)}min(m(E), t(E)),$$

with $t(E) = min_{x \in E}\mu(x)$. This assessment is exactly the Sugeno integral $S_m(\mu)$. Taking the values $\mu(a) = 0.8, \mu(b) = 0.7, \mu(c) = 0.3, \mu(d) = 0.2, \mu(e) = 0.1$, one obtains:

$$S_m(\mu) = max(min(\mu(e), m(e, d, c, b, a)), min(\mu(d), m(d, c, b, a)),$$
$$min(\mu(c), m(c, b, a)), min(\mu(b), m(b, a)), min(\mu(a), m(a))).$$

If the measure m_1 is chosen (tasks equally important), it follows that:

$$S_{m_1}(\mu) = max(min(0.1, 1), min(0.2, 0.8), min(0.3, 0.6),$$
$$min(0.7, 0.4), min(0.8, 0.2))$$
$$= max(0.1, 0.2, 0.3, 0.4, 0.2) = 0.4,$$

whereas with measure m_2, the result is:

$$S_{m_2}(\mu) = max(min(0.1, 1), min(0.2, 0.9), min(0.3, 0.8),$$
$$min(0.7, 0.6), min(0.8, 0.3))$$
$$= max(0.1, 0.2, 0.3, 0.6, 0.3) = 0.6. \diamond$$

3.6 The Extension Principle

In some situations, a fuzzy set may be considered to be an imperfect representation of a given quantity. Although manipulating a quantity by means of operations is fairly easy when it is perfectly known, it raises the question of using these operators in the presence of an imprecise value. A typical example is that of real numbers which can be added: one can ask what happens for the addition of two imprecise numbers, also called fuzzy numbers (see Dubois and Prade, 1980). The extension principle defined by Zadeh (1975b,c) proposes an answer to this question.

Consider an application from a set X to a set Y, which maps an element x of X onto an element y of Y. This application is used to define the image of a fuzzy set X according to the following intuitive idea: if x belongs to the fuzzy set A of X with the degree d, one associates the fuzzy set B of Y with A in such a way that y (the image of x) belongs to B with a degree at least equal to d. Formally, if f is an application from X to Y, the extension principle maps a fuzzy set A of X to the fuzzy set B of Y as follows:

$$\forall y \in Y, \mu_B(y) = \begin{cases} sup_{x \in X \mid y=f(x)}\mu_A(x) & \text{if } f^{-1}(y) \neq \emptyset, \\ 0 & \text{otherwise.} \end{cases} \tag{3.15}$$

In the particular case where A reduces to the singleton x_0, the extension principle maps it into the non-fuzzy set B composed of the sole element $f(x_0)$.

Example 3.19. Let f_1 be the function defined as $f_1(x) = y = |3x - 6|$ where $|v|$ stands for the absolute value of v. The calculus of that function extends to imprecise (fuzzy) values according to Expression (3.15). The characteristic function of the image of any fuzzy set A equals 0 for any negative value y, since it cannot be an absolute value. For instance, with the input set $A = \{0.4/(-1), 1/1.5, 0.7/2.4, 0.9/3, 0.2/3.3, 0.6/5\}$, the image of A through f_1 is $B = \{0.6/9, 1/1.5, 0.7/1.2, 0.9/3, 0.2/3.9\}$. The value 9 has two antecedents (-1 and 5) whose degrees of membership are 0.4 and 0.6 respectively, and 9 is assigned the degree $max(0.4, 0.6)$.◇

The extension principle may also apply to the case where X is a Cartesian product of sets, as shown in Example 3.20 related to (fuzzy) arithmetics.

Example 3.20. Consider the addition of two imprecise integers represented as two fuzzy sets n_1 and n_2. The regular addition extends to such numbers using the extension principle, and Expression (3.15) becomes:

$$\forall z \in \mathbb{N}, \mu_{n_3}(z) = sup_{(x,y) \mid x \in \mathbb{N}, y \in \mathbb{N}, x+y=z} min(\mu_{n_1}(x), \mu_{n_2}(y)). \tag{3.16}$$

With $n_1 = \{0.2/5, 0.6/6, 0.8/7, 1/8\}$ and $n_2 = \{1/2, 0.4/3\}$, applying Expression (3.16) returns n_3, the sum of n_1 and n_2 defined as $n_3 = \{0.2/7, 0.6/8, 0.8/9, 1/10, 0.4/11\}$. Here, values 8, 9, 10 are obtained in two ways and their associated degree is the largest of the grades obtained in each case. For instance, the degree $max(min(0.8, 1), min(0.6, 0.4)) = 0.8$ is assigned to value 9. The resulting fuzzy set is normalized, inasmuch as the fuzzy sets representing the inputs are normalized, as happens with the data in this example.◇

3.7 Fuzzy Quantified Propositions

3.7.1 *Fuzzy linguistic quantifiers*

Fuzzy linguistic quantifiers were introduced by Zadeh (1983) (see also Kerre and Liu, 1998) in order to extend the usual quantifiers, among which the most used are the universal quantifier ($\forall$) and the existential quantifier ($\exists$). It is possible to distinguish between *absolute* quantifiers expressing a quantity (a number) such as *"a dozen"* or *"about 6"*, and *relative* quantifiers which refer to a proportion, such as *"a small half"* or *"almost all"*. An absolute quantifier QA is modeled as:

$$\mu_{QA} : \mathbb{N}(\text{or } \mathbb{R}) \longrightarrow [0, 1],$$

whereas a relative QR is represented as:

$$\mu_{QR} : [0, 1] \longrightarrow [0, 1].$$

The value $\mu_{QA}(n)$ (resp. $\mu_{QR}(p)$) expresses the adequation of number n (resp. proportion p) with respect to the considered quantifier. Quantifiers can be divided into three classes depending on the type of their characteristic function:

- increasing (e.g., *at least about* 5, *almost all, most of*),
- decreasing (e.g., *at most about* 10, *a few*),
- increasing–decreasing (e.g., *around* 7, *more or less a dozen*).

3.7.2 *Quantified propositions*

Fuzzy quantifiers act inside expressions where they aggregate a set of values generated by fuzzy predicates; they are called fuzzy quantified propositions. The scope of this section is restricted to propositions involving a single increasing absolute quantifier and a fuzzy set A, in the context of the evaluation of the proposition "$Q\,X$ *are* A" which is used in Chapter 6. The objective is to assess the extent to which the number of elements of the referential X satisfying the (fuzzy/gradual) property A is in adequation with the quantifier Q.

The presentation given here is limited to a general view, with the aim of providing an intuitive interpretation for a casual user. Determining the truth value of "$Q\,X$ *are* A" relies on the idea that this expression has as many interpretations as there are distinct α-cuts for A. Each level-cut plays the role of a more or less demanding representative of A. It is worth noting that this approach does not seek to compute the cardinality of A, but rather to assess the truth value of "$Q\,X$ *are* A" when A is a regular set. Due to the nesting of α-cuts, and to the monotonicity property of the considered quantifier Q (which is increasing), when α diminishes, $\mu_Q(card(A_\alpha))$ cannot decrease. So it seems reasonable to look for the best trade-off between the quality of the representative chosen for A and its adequation with respect to Q. This leads to the following truth value v for "$Q\,X$ *are* A":

$$v = max_\alpha\, min(\alpha, \mu_Q(card(A_\alpha))),$$

which ensures that: $\forall \alpha \in [0, v], \mu_Q(card(A_\alpha)) \geq v$. It appears that this expression corresponds to a Sugeno integral (see Section 3.5.3) of the characteristic function of set A with the fuzzy measure $Q(card(-))$. This measure is non-additive in general, i.e.:

$$(card(A \cup B)) \neq Q(card(A)) + Q(card(B)),$$

as illustrated by Example 3.21. Nevertheless, it obeys the monotonicity requirement of fuzzy measures, since the quantifier (Q) is increasing.

Example 3.21. Let Q be the absolute quantifier "*at least 5*" defined as:

$$\mu_{at\ least\ 5}(v) = 0 \text{ if } v < 3, \mu_{at\ least\ 5}(3) = 0.4, \mu_{at\ least\ 5}(4) = 0.7,$$

$$\mu_{at\ least\ 5}(v) = 1 \text{ if } v > 4.$$

Assume that $A = \{a, b\}$ and $B = \{c, d, e\}$ are two fuzzy sets. Then:

$$\mu_{at\ least\ 5}(card(A)) = \mu_{at\ least\ 5}(2) = 0$$

$$\mu_{at\ least\ 5}(card(B)) = \mu_{at\ least\ 5}(3) = 0.4$$

$$\mu_{at\ least\ 5}(card(A \cup B)) = \mu_{at\ least\ 5}(5) = 1.$$

Thus:

$$\mu_{at\ least\ 5}(card(A \cup B)) \neq \mu_{at\ least\ 5}(card(A)) + \mu_{at\ least\ 5}(card(B)),$$

$$\mu_{at\ least\ 5}(card(A \cup B)) > \mu_{at\ least\ 5}(card(A)),$$

$$\mu_{at\ least\ 5}(card(A \cup B)) > \mu_{at\ least\ 5}(card(B)).\diamond$$

In addition, this approach generalizes the following two special cases:

- if A is a regular set, the truth value of "$Q\,X$ *are* A" is given by $\mu_Q(card(A))$,
- if Q is a non-fuzzy quantifier such as "*at least p*" (which is increasing), by analogy with the existential quantifier, the truth value of "$Q\,X$ *are* A" is defined as the pth largest value among the membership degrees to set A.

Furthermore, everything that has just been said for an absolute increasing quantifier can also be adapted for an absolute decreasing quantifier. The case of an increasing–decreasing quantifier Q is dealt with by decomposing it into an increasing part QI and a decreasing part QD, and then aggregating the truth values obtained for "$QI\,X$ *are* A" and "$QD\,X$ *are* A". Finally, this approach also applies to relative quantifiers.

Chapter 4

Non-Fuzzy Approaches to Preference Queries: A Brief Overview

4.1 Introduction

The past two decades have witnessed an increasing interest in expressing preferences inside database queries. The motivations for this are manifold; see Hadjali *et al.* (2008). First, it has become desirable to offer more expressive query languages that are more faithful to what a user intends to say. Second, the introduction of preferences in queries provides a basis for rank-ordering the retrieved items, which is especially valuable in cases where large sets of items satisfy a query. Third, while a classical query may have an empty set of answers, a relaxed (and thus less restrictive) version of the query might be matched by items in the database.

The approaches to database preference queries may be classified into two categories according to their qualitative or quantitative nature (Hadjali *et al.*, 2008). In the latter case, preferences are expressed quantitatively by a monotone scoring function (the overall score is positively correlated with partial scores), often taken as a weighted linear combination of attribute values (which therefore have to be numerical). Since the scoring function associates each tuple with a numerical score, tuple t_1 is preferred to tuple t_2 if the score of t_1 is higher than the score of t_2. In the qualitative approach, preferences are defined through binary preference relations.

In this chapter, we briefly review the main approaches proposed in the literature.

4.2   Quantitative Approaches

4.2.1   *Distances and similarity*

In this approach, preferences are integrated into elementary conditions by means of a similarity (or resemblance) operator, denoted by $\approx$, which extends strict equality. An elementary condition $A \approx v$ (resp. $A \approx B$) is interpreted in the context of a distance defined over the domain of attribute A (resp. of attributes A and B). For a condition of the type $A \approx v$, the idea is that v is the ideal value, but that other values are acceptable even though they are not as preferred. The greater the distance between the values of A and v, the less the satisfaction, and if the distance between A and v is over a predefined threshold, the condition is considered not at all fulfilled. This type of approach can be seen as a refinement of the nearest-neighbors technique (Friedman *et al.*, 1975) where the similarity operator is implicit. The systems ARES (Ichikawa and Hirakawa, 1986) and VAGUE (Motro, 1988) are both founded on such an approach.

Example 4.1. In ARES, the user attaches a threshold to every preference condition. The different atomic conditions may be combined only in a conjunctive way. The interpretation of the query:

$$(A_1 \approx v_1, t_1) \text{ and } \cdots \text{ and } (A_n \approx v_n, t_n)$$

involves two steps:

(1) expression of a Boolean selection condition involving distances and the user-specified thresholds:

$$dist(A_1, v_1) \leq t_1 \text{ and } \cdots \text{ and } dist(A_n, v_n) \leq t_n,$$

(2) aggregation of the distances in order to compute a global distance which is used to rank-order the previously selected elements:

$$g\text{-}dist = \sum_i dist(A_i, v_i) \quad \left(\leq \sum_i t_i \right).$$

Consider relation *Emp* depicted in Table 4.1, and the query:

$$(salary \approx 2500, \; threshold = 2) \text{ and } (age \approx 41, \; threshold = 1).$$

With the distance relations specified in Table 4.2, employees Dupont, Martin and Dubois are selected (Durant and Lorant are discarded because

Table 4.1   Extension of the relation *Emp*

num	name	salary	age	city
17	Dupont	3,500	42	Lyon
76	Martin	3,000	40	Paris
26	Durant	2,500	37	Lyon
12	Dubois	2,500	39	Lyon
55	Lorant	3,500	35	Lyon

Table 4.2   Distances defined on salaries (left) and ages (right)

$|sal_1 - sal_2|$	d	$|age_1 - age_2|$	d
0	0	0	0
500	1	1	1
1,000	2	2	1
1,500	2	3	2

of their age). The global distances computed for these elements are: 3 $(2+1)$ for Dupont, 2 $(1+1)$ for Martin, and 1 $(0+1)$ for Dubois, which yields the order: Dubois $\succ$ Martin $\succ$ Dupont.$\diamond$

4.2.2   Linguistic preferences

In this approach, the idea is to associate preference terms with the Boolean conditions involved in a query. In the system MULTOS (Rabitti and Savino, 1990), it is also possible to use linguistic weights to express the importance of the elementary conditions. For instance, to specify that the conditions on age and salary can be more or less satisfied, and that the condition on age is more important than that on salary, one may write:

$(((age = 40)$ **ideal**, $(age = 41$ **or** $age = 39)$ **good**),
$((age \leq 46$ **and** $age \geq 42)$ **or**
$(age \geq 34$ **and** $age \leq 38))$ **acceptable**) [**high**];
$((salary \leq 2500)$ **ideal**,
$(salary > 2500$ **and** $salary < 3300)$ **acceptable**) [**medium**].

The terms "ideal", "good", and "acceptable" define preferences over the values taken by the attributes, whereas "high" and "medium" reflect importances. The evaluation of such a query relies on a two-step process:

(1) a selection based on the more-or-less acceptable values for each attribute,
(2) an ordering of the elements selected by the previous step, based on a numerical translation of the linguistic labels into grades in the unit interval.

Each elementary condition

$$((X_k = v_{k,1})p_{k,1}, \ (X_k = v_{k,2})p_{k,2}, \ldots, (X_k = v_{k,n_k}) \ p_{k,n_k})i_k,$$

where X_k denotes an attribute, $v_{k,m}$ is a value whose preference is $p_{k,m}$, and i_k is the importance of the term concerning attribute X_k, is assigned a selection value: *true* if X_k takes one of the values $v_{k,j}$, *false* otherwise, and a ranking value: $p_{k,j} \times i_k$ if $X_k = v_{k,j}$, 0 otherwise. A disjunction (resp. conjunction) of such terms is associated with the highest value (resp. the sum of the values) obtained for the elementary conditions involved.

4.2.3   *Explicit scores attached to entities*

The approach proposed by Agrawal and Wimmers (2000) allows a user to express his/her preference for an entity, either by attaching a score in $[0, 1]$ to that entity, or by expressing a veto (by means of the special symbol $\natural$), or by an indifference statement (default case) regarding that entity. An entity is described by a tuple in which the value of a field either belongs to the domain of the corresponding attribute, or equals $*$ (a special symbol which represents every domain value). In order to illustrate these notions, consider a relation *fridge* (*model, color, price*) describing different models of refrigerators. A user expressing the preferences $\{(\langle 123, \text{red}\rangle, 0.4), (\langle 123, *\rangle, \natural), (\langle 234, \text{green}\rangle, \natural), (\langle 456, \text{white}\rangle, 0.8)\}$ indicates that he/she has a strong preference for the model 456 in white, a much more moderate preference for the model 123 in red, and absolutely rejects the model 234 in green as well as every fridge of the model 123 in a color other than red. The authors also introduce a generic operator which makes it possible to combine preferences originating from different users.

The approach proposed by Koutrika and Ioannidis (2004) follows the same general philosophy but extends the approach introduced by Agrawal and Wimmers (2000) by considering a more general format for the user's preference profiles. Notably, it enables the expression of negative preferences (as in "I do not like action movies") and preferences regarding the absence of values (as in "I like movies without violence").

4.2.4   *Top-k queries*

The top-k query approach (Bruno *et al.*, 2002; Chaudhuri and Gravano, 1999), even though it uses the same general principles as systems based on the notions of distance and similarity, has some points in common with the fuzzy-set-based approach. In the top-k query framework, a user specifies ideal values for certain attributes as well as a number k of desired tuples. The distance between an attribute value and the ideal value is computed by means of a difference (absolute value), after a normalization step (which yields domain values between 0 and 1). The overall distance is calculated by aggregating the elementary distances using a function which can be the minimum, the sum, or the Euclidean distance. The steps in the computation are the following:

(1) using k, and taking into account both the chosen aggregation function and statistics about the considered relation, a threshold α over the global distance is deduced,

(2) a Boolean query computing the desired α-cut — i.e. the set of items whose score is at least equal to α — or a superset of this α-cut is determined,

(3) this query is processed and the score (the global distance) attached to every element of the result is calculated,

(4) if at least k tuples with a score greater than or equal to α have been obtained, the k best are returned to the user; otherwise the procedure is run again (from step 2) using a lower threshold α.

4.2.5   *Outranking*

Bosc *et al.* (2010d,e) introduce an approach to database preference queries based on the notion of outranking, initially proposed by Roy (1991) in a decision-making context. This approach, which uses a weighted majority rule, constitutes an alternative to using a Pareto-order-based approach (see Section 4.3.2) for handling incommensurable partial preferences. It assumes that a set of scoring functions translating the different partial preferences is available. The approach relies on an outranking measure which aggregates the numbers (weighted by importances) of partial preferences which are either concordant with, discordant with, or indifferent to a certain ordering between two tuples. Even though outranking does not define an order in the strict sense of the term, the authors describe a technique which yields a complete preorder, based on a global aggregation of the outranking degrees computed for each pair of tuples.

In Bosc *et al.* (2009e), a variant is presented, which aims at comparing each tuple with the profiles of predefined classes. In this way, instead of being compared pairwise as in a Pareto-order-based approach, tuples are compared with the acceptability profiles associated with the different user-defined classes, which is of course less computationally expensive. According to the satisfaction of the different partial preferences specified in the user query, a tuple is classified into a given class with a certain degree. An algorithm implementing this classification with linear data complexity is described in Bosc *et al.* (2009e).

4.3 Qualitative Approaches

4.3.1 *Secondary preference criterion*

In this type of approach, a query is made up of two parts: a Boolean selection condition C and a complementary component P aimed at specifying the preferences. A query is written as: "C; P" and its interpretation is: "find the elements which satisfy C and rank-order them according to P".

In the system called *Preferences* (Lacroix and Lavency, 1987), a preference is expressed by a set of Boolean conditions which can be combined by means of two operators: nesting (hierarchy of conditions) and juxtaposition (combining conditions which have the same priority). Starting from r_C, the subset gathering the tuples of a relation r satisfying condition C, the nesting of the preference clauses P_1 to P_n leads to construction of the sets H_i gathering the elements of r_C which satisfy the preference clauses P_1 to P_i but not P_{i+1}. H_0 is the subset of r_C whose elements do not satisfy P_1, and H_n is the subset of r_C whose elements satisfy all of the preference clauses P_1 to P_n. In a similar way, juxtaposing the preference clauses P_1 to P_n leads to construction of the sets J_i gathering the elements of r_C which satisfy i preference clauses ($i \in [0, n]$). The answer initially returned to the user is the non-empty set H_i (resp. J_i) whose index i is the highest (which corresponds to the best elements). The user can then browse less satisfactory sets if he/she wants to do so.

The major advantage of this system is that it avoids numerous successive formulations in order to reach the desired number of answers. However, one may find that the discrimination power is somewhat limited, since the number of satisfaction levels equals the number of preference clauses (since at most $(n + 1)$ distinct subsets are built).

Example 4.2. Consider again relation *Emp* from Table 4.1 and the query aimed at retrieving the employees who live in Lyon, if possible having a salary less than \$3,000 (P_1), and if possible older than 38 (P_2). This query involves the preference hierarchy $(P_1; P_2)$ and, with the extension from Table 4.1, one obtains:

$$H_0 = \{\text{Lorant, Dupont}\}, \quad H_1 = \{\text{Durant}\}, \quad H_2 = \{\text{Dubois}\}.$$

With the opposite hierarchy $(P_2; P_1)$, the result would be:

$$H_0' = \{\text{Lorant, Durant}\}, \quad H_1' = \{\text{Dupont}\}, \quad H_2' = \{\text{Dubois}\}.$$

If the juxtaposition (P_1, P_2) were used instead of a hierarchy, the result would be:

$$J_0 = \{\text{Lorant}\}, \quad J_1 = \{\text{Dupont, Durant}\}, \quad J_2 = \{\text{Dubois}\}.$$

Note that the second tuple from *Emp* does not belong to the result, since it does not satisfy the condition on attribute *city*.◇

4.3.2 *Pareto-order-based approaches*

In the past decade, many algorithms have been proposed for efficient computation of the non-dominated results of a query, in the sense of Pareto order. Seen as points in a multi-dimensional space, these answers constitute a so-called *skyline*. Some pioneering works in this domain have been done by Börzsönyi *et al.* (2001). First, we recall the general principle of Pareto-order-based approaches.

Let $\{G_1, G_2, \ldots, G_n\}$ be a set of atomic partial preferences. We denote by $t \succ_{G_i} t'$ (resp. $t \succeq_{G_i} t'$) the statement "tuple t satisfies preference G_i better than (resp. at least as well as) tuple t'". In the sense of Pareto order, a tuple t dominates another tuple t' if and only if

$$\forall i \in [1, n], \quad t \succeq_{G_i} t' \ \land \ \exists k \in [1, n], \quad t \succ_{G_k} t'.$$

In other terms, t dominates t' if and only if it is at least as good as t' regarding each preference, and it is strictly better than t' with respect to at least one preference.

Clearly, Pareto-order-based approaches do not require any assumption of commensurability between the satisfaction degrees pertaining to the different elementary preferences, in contrast to, for instance, the fuzzy-set-based approach. As a consequence, some points from the skyline (i.e., some tuples from the result) may represent very poor answers with respect to certain atomic conditions, whereas they are excellent regarding others; the skyline approach only yields a strict partial order while the fuzzy-set-based approach leads to a complete preorder. Kießling (2002) and Kießling and Köstler (2002) described the basis of a preference model founded on Pareto order for database systems. A preference algebra including an operator called *winnow* has also been proposed by Chomicki (2003) in order to integrate preference formulas inside a relational framework (and SQL). See also the work by Torlone and Ciaccia (2002), who introduced an operator called *Best* aimed at returning the non-dominated tuples of a relation. The following example uses the syntax of the language *Preference SQL* (Kießling and Köstler, 2002), which is a typical representative of a Pareto-order-based approach.

Example 4.3. Consider a relation *car* of schema (*#id, make, category, price, color, mileage*) whose extension is given in Table 4.3, and the query:

> **select** * **from** *car*
> **where** *color* ≠ "purple"
> **preferring** (*make* = "Opel" **else** *make* = "Ford")
>   **and** (*mileage* ≈ 40,000);

The preference condition on attribute *mileage* implies that a car whose mileage is 34,000 is better than a car whose mileage is 48,000, since 34,000 is closer to 40,000 than is 48,000. Tuple t_7 is discarded since it does not satisfy

Table 4.3   An extension of the relation *car*

#id	make	category	price	color	mileage
t_1	Opel	roadster	4,500	blue	19,000
t_2	Ford	SUV	4,000	red	35,000
t_3	VW	roadster	5,000	red	43,000
t_4	Fiat	roadster	5,000	red	19,000
t_5	VW	roadster	4,500	red	40,000
t_6	Ford	sedan	5,500	blue	51,000
t_7	Opel	sedan	2,500	purple	72,000

the selection condition from the **where** clause. Tuple t_4 is dominated by t_1 and is thus discarded. Tuple t_3 is dominated by t_5 whereas t_6 is dominated by t_2. On the other hand, t_1, t_2 and t_5 are incomparable and the final answer is $\{t_1, t_2, t_5\}$.◇

With this type of approach, when a query involves conditions on many attributes, there is a high risk of obtaining many incomparable tuples. Several techniques have been proposed to order two tuples t_1 and t_2 which are incomparable in the sense of skyline. These techniques exploit, for instance:

- the number of tuples that t_1 and t_2 (respectively) dominate (notion of k-representative dominance proposed by (Lin *et al.*, 2007)) or
- a preference order over the attributes; see for instance the notions of k-dominance introduced by Chan *et al.* (2006a), and k-frequency proposed by the same authors (Chan *et al.*, 2006b).

The issue of efficiently processing skyline queries has given rise to many research works, in particular Bartolini *et al.* (2008) and Chomicki *et al.* (2005).

4.3.3 *CP-nets*

The use of the structure called CP-net (network of conditional preferences) for modeling database preference queries has been suggested by Brafman and Domshlak (2004) — but this framework was initially developed in artifical intelligence (Boutilier *et al.*, 2004). A CP-net is a graphical representation of statements which express conditional preferences of the *ceteris paribus* type. The premise is that user preferences generally express the idea that, in a given context, a partially described state of affairs is strictly preferred to another partially described state of affairs, both states of affairs being mutually exclusive, in accordance with the *ceteris paribus* semantics, i.e., everything else being equal in the description of these states of affairs. By means of a CP-net, a user may describe how his/her preferences for the values of a variable depend on the values of other variables. For instance, a user may formulate the following statements:

s_1: I prefer minivans cars to sedan cars;

s_2: as to minivans, I prefer Chrysler to Ford;

s_3: for sedans, I prefer Ford to Chrysler;

s_4: in Ford cars, I prefer the black ones to the white ones;

s_5: in Chrysler cars, I prefer the white ones to the black ones.

In the CP-net approach applied to database preference queries (Brafman and Domshlak, 2004), a preference is represented by a binary relation over a relation schema (where the attributes are assumed to be binary). If r is a relation schema, then a preference query Q on r consists of a set $Q = \{s_1, ..., s_m\}$ of statements (usually between subtuples of r, relying on the *ceteris paribus* semantics). From Q, one induces a set of preference relations $\{>_{CP(1)}, \ldots, >_{CP(m)}\}$, from which one may derive a global preference relation $>_{CP(Q)}$ which defines a strict partial preorder between the tuples from r.

Example 4.4. Assume that black (b) jackets (resp. pants) are preferred to white (w) jackets (resp. pants), and that in case of jackets and pants of the same color, red (r) shirts are preferred to white ones; otherwise, white shirts are preferred. Only the colors mentioned are assumed to be available. Thus, we have three binary variables J, P, S corresponding to the colors of the jacket, the pants, and the shirt. See Figure 4.1 for the CP-net built on these variables. Thus, there are eight tuples corresponding to the relational schema jackets–pants–shirts: $bbr, bbw, bwr, bww, wbr, wbw, wwr, www$. The preferences associated with the induced CP-net, applying the *ceteris paribus* principle, are:

- $bPS >_{CP} \neg bPS, \forall P \in \{b, \neg b\}, \forall S \in \{r, \neg r\}$;
- $JbS >_{CP} J\neg bS, \forall J \in \{b, \neg b\}, \forall S \in \{r, \neg r\}$;
- $bbr >_{CP} bbw, wwr >_{CP} www, bww >_{CP} bwr, wbw >_{CP} wbr$.

Then the following partial order holds under the *ceteris paribus* assumption:

$$bbr >_{CP} bbw >_{CP} bww >_{CP} bwr >_{CP} wwr >_{CP} www$$
$$bbr >_{CP} bbw >_{CP} wbw >_{CP} wbr >_{CP} wwr >_{CP} www. \diamond$$

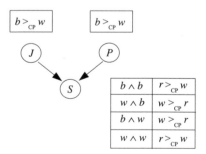

Fig. 4.1   CP-net for "evening dress: jacket, pants and shirt"

It is worth mentioning that the *ceteris paribus* semantics strongly differs from the *totalitarian* semantics, which is implicitly favored by authors from the database community (including those who advocate approaches based on Pareto order). Under the totalitarian semantics, when evaluating the preference clause of a query, the attributes which are not concerned with that clause are ignored. Obviously, with the *ceteris paribus* semantics, the number of incomparable tuples is in general much higher than with the totalitarian semantics.

4.3.4   *Domain linearization*

The approach proposed in Georgiadis *et al.* (2008) considers preferences defined as preorders over relational attributes and their respective domains. Let $R(\#i, A, F, L)$ be a table describing part of the content of a digital library, where $\#i$ is the identifier of a document, A corresponds to an author's name, F describes the format of the document, and L is the language in which the document is written. Then, an example of a preference query in the sense of Georgiadis *et al.* (2008) is made of the following statements:

(1) Joyce is preferred to Proust or Mann (preference P_A);
(2) ODT and DOC formats are preferred to PDF (P_F);
(3) English is preferred to French, which is itself preferred to German (P_L);
(4) Writer (W) is as important as format (F), whereas the writer–format combination is more important than language (L).

Such statements define binary preference relations: (1), (2) and (3) are defined over attribute domains, whereas (4) is defined over the set of attributes. Preference relations are required to be reflexive and transitive, i.e., they must be preorders. The authors propose a technique for linearizing the domains associated with these partial preorders (recall that a domain, in the sense of domain theory, is a partially ordered set). This way, one induces a block sequence (i.e., an ordered partition) of the result of the query. In such a sequence, each block contains preference-wise incomparable elements. The first block contains the most preferred elements, and in every other block, for each element, there exists a more preferred element in the preceding block.

   The algorithms proposed in Georgiadis *et al.* (2008) compute the block sequence that constitutes the answer to a preference query, without constructing the induced ordering of tuples. This is achieved by exploiting the semantics of a preference expression and, in particular, by linearizing the Cartesian product of all attribute terms appearing in the expression. In reality, one passes from a set of statements expressing partial preferences to a query lattice, from there to a lattice of query results, and finally to a block sequence that constitutes the answer.

With respect to Pareto-order-based approaches, the main originality of the approach described in Georgiadis *et al.* (2008) lies in its use of partial preorders instead of strict orders for modeling positive independent preferences. This makes it possible to distinguish between the notions of "equally preferred tuples" and "incomparable tuples".

4.3.5 *Possibilistic-logic-based approach*

In Hadjali *et al.* (2008), the authors present an approach to database preference queries based on possibilistic logic (Dubois and Prade, 2004) where the queries involve symbolic weights on a linearly ordered scale. These weights can be processed without assessing their precise values, which leaves the user free to not specify any priority among the preferences (in contrast to CP-nets, where a default priority ordering is induced by the structure of the preference graph). However, the user may also enforce a (partial) ordering between the priorities, if necessary.

In the case of binary preferences, the possibilistic encoding of the conditional preference "in context c, a is preferred to b" is a pair of possibilistic formulas: $\{(\neg c \lor a \lor b, 1), (\neg c \lor a, 1 - \alpha)\}$. In other words, if c is true, one should have a or b (the choice is only between a and b), and in context c, it is somewhat imperative to have a true. This encodes a constraint of the form $N(\neg c \lor a) \geq 1 - \alpha$, itself equivalent to a constraint on a conditional necessity measure $\Pi(\neg a|c) \leq \alpha$, where Π is the dual possibility measure associated with N. This constraint says that the possibility of *not* having a is upper-bounded by α, i.e., $\neg a$ is all the more impossible as α is small. To switch from necessity degrees to satisfaction levels (or possibility degrees), the authors use an order-reversing operator denoted by $1 - (.)$. Thus, the level of priority $1 - \alpha$ associated with a preference is changed into a satisfaction degree α when this preference is violated. Even if the values of the weights are unknown, a partial order between the different choices may be induced by a *leximin* ordering (Dubois *et al.*, 1997; see also Chapter 3).

This approach can be related to that based on fuzzy sets where the components of a query may be conditionally weighted in terms of importance. In fact, these approaches can be interfaced, which makes it possible to handle non-binary preferences.

In Hadjali *et al.* (2008), it is shown that the possibilistic-logic-based approach refines that proposed by Lacroix and Lavency (1987) (see also Section 4.3.1) as well as the operator *winnow* proposed by Chomicki (2003) and the operator *Best* introduced by Torlone and Ciaccia (2002) (see also Section 4.3.2).

4.4 Conclusion

Aspects related to implementation, in particular efficient query processing, have not been dealt with here since they are beyond the scope of this chapter, but they are of course crucial in a database context (where the volume of data handled is in general huge).

The interested reader may also find details of the way in which some quantitative approaches (as well as the approach that uses secondary preference criteria) may be modeled in a fuzzy-set-based framework, in Bosc and Pivert (1992).

Chapter 5

Simple Fuzzy Queries

5.1 Introduction

In this chapter, we present the main features of two languages aimed at expressing fuzzy queries to relational databases. First, we describe a complete extension of relational algebra, then we focus on the expression of simple fuzzy queries in an SQL-like language called SQLf (Bosc and Pivert, 1995b). By "simple queries", we mainly mean queries that do not involve any quantified statements or aggregates applied to fuzzy relations. These more complex queries, as well as bipolar fuzzy queries and division queries, are dealt with in subsequent chapters (Chapters 6, 7, and 8).

We first recall that gradual predicates (or conditions) can be associated with fuzzy sets (Zadeh, 1965; see also Chapter 3) aimed at describing classes of objects with vague boundaries, just as regular sets allow for the definition of Boolean predicates. Often, elementary fuzzy predicates correspond to adjectives of natural language, such as young, tall, cheap or well-paid. An elementary predicate can also compare two attributes using the usual operators (equality, superiority, etc.), but also gradual relational comparison operators such as "more or less equal" or "somewhat greater than".

It is possible to alter (weaken or strengthen) the meaning of a given predicate using a modifier which is generally associated with an adverb (e.g., very, more or less, relatively, really). For instance, "very cheap" is more restrictive than "cheap" and "fairly high" is less demanding than "high". It is possible to define the meaning of the predicate $mod\ P$ (where mod is a modifier and P is a fuzzy predicate) in a compositional way.

Different approaches have been advocated, among which are:

- $\mu_{modP}(x) = \mu_P(x)^n$,
- $\mu_{modP}(x) = \mu_P(x)\top \cdots \top \mu_P(x)$, where $\top$ is a non-idempotent triangular norm or co-norm,
- $\mu_{modP}(x) = \mu_P(x \pm a)$, where a is a constant.

The interested reader can find more detail about this topic in Bouchon-Meunier and Yao (1992) and Kerre and de Cock (1999).

As mentioned in Chapter 3, atomic and modified predicates can be involved in compound predicates which go far beyond those used in regular queries. Conjunction (resp. disjunction) is interpreted by means of a triangular norm $\top$ (resp. co-norm $\bot$), i.e., an operator which is associative, commutative, monotonically increasing with respect to both arguments, and whose neutral element is 1 (resp. 0), for instance the minimum or the product (resp. the maximum or the probabilistic sum):

$$\forall x, \mu_{P_1 \wedge P_2}(x) = \top(\mu_{P_1}(x), \mu_{P_2}(x))$$

$$\forall x, \mu_{P_1 \vee P_2}(x) = \bot(\mu_{P_1}(x), \mu_{P_2}(x))$$

Negation is interpreted by the complement to 1 of the degree:

$$\forall x, \mu_{\neg P}(x) = 1 - \mu_P(x).$$

The weighted conjunction and disjunction as well as weighted mean or OWA (Yager, 1988) can be used to assign a different importance to each of the predicates (see in particular Fodor and Yager, 2000, for a more complete presentation).

The basic idea behind the extensions of both relational algebra and SQLf is thus to authorize the use of (possibly compound) fuzzy predicates in selection or join conditions. The principal concept is that of a fuzzy relation, i.e., a relation r where each tuple t is attached a degree μ in the unit interval which expresses the extent to which t satisfies the fuzzy concept associated with r.

In this chapter, we first give definitions of the extended relational algebraic operators used in this framework (Section 5.2), then we describe the basic features of the SQLf language (Section 5.3). In Section 5.4, we deal with the definition of fuzzy terms and operators through an appropriate interface. Section 5.5 is devoted to a particular type of fuzzy query involving so-called contextual fuzzy predicates, i.e., predicates whose definition can be automatically derived from a certain context. Query processing aspects are tackled in the last section (5.6) of the chapter.

5.2 An Extended Relational Algebra

In the context of regular databases, a flexible query whose interpretation is based on fuzzy sets takes a set of regular relations as inputs and produces a result which is a weighted (type-1) fuzzy relation where the degree attached to each tuple depends on the satisfaction of fuzzy predicates involved in the query. Since a regular relation is a special case of a fuzzy relation (grades equal to 1), the compositionality principle is maintained. The extension of the three usual types of language (relational algebra, relational calculus, and SQL) has been addressed in Tahani (1977), Bosc *et al.* (1988), Wong and Leung (1990), Takahashi (1991), Lee and Kim (1993), and Bosc and Pivert (1995b). An extended relational algebra consists of the same operators as those usually employed (see Chapter 2), except that they are now defined over weighted (type-1) relations.

The Cartesian product $(r \times s)$ of two fuzzy relations r and s of respective universes X and Y is defined as:

$$r \times s = \{\mu/\langle u, v \rangle \mid u \in support(r) \wedge v \in support(s) \wedge \mu = min(\mu_r(u), \mu_s(v))\}.$$

If r and s are defined on the same universe X, the set operations union $(\cup)$, intersection$(\cap)$, and difference $(-)$ are defined as:

$$r \cup s = \{\mu/u \mid (u \in support(r) \wedge u \notin support(s) \wedge \mu = \mu_r(u)\} \cup$$
$$\{\mu/x \mid (u \in support(s) \wedge u \notin support(r) \wedge \mu = \mu_s(u)\} \cup$$
$$\{\mu/x \mid (u \in support(r) \wedge u \in support(s) \wedge \mu = max(\mu_r(u), \mu_s(u)\},$$
$$r \cap s = \{\mu/u \mid u \in support(r) \wedge u \in support(s) \wedge \mu = min(\mu_r(u), \mu_s(u))\},$$
$$r - s = \{\mu/u \mid u \in support(r) \wedge \mu = min(\mu_r(u), 1 - \mu_s(u))\}.$$

The algebraic operations, i.e., the selection $\sigma(r, \phi)$ where ϕ is a fuzzy predicate, the join $r[A\theta B]s$ where A is a subset of X, B is a subset of Y, θ is a fuzzy comparator (a binary fuzzy relation between the A-field value in the tuple x of r and the B-field value in the tuple y of s), and the projection $\pi_Y(r)$ where Y is a proper subset of X, are defined as follows:

$$\sigma(r, \phi) = \{\mu/u \mid u \in support(r) \wedge \mu = min(\mu_r(u), \mu_\phi(u))\},$$
$$r[A\,\theta\,B]s = \{\mu/\langle u, v \rangle \mid u \in support(r) \wedge v \in support(s) \wedge$$
$$\mu = min(\mu_r(u), \mu_s(v), \mu_\theta(u.A, v.B))\},$$
$$\pi_Y(r) = \{\mu/v \mid (\exists u \in support(r) \text{ s.t. } u.Y = v) \wedge$$
$$\mu = sup_{u \in support(r) \mid u.Y = v}\, \mu_r(u)\}.$$

Table 5.1   Extensions of the relations *Emp* (left) and *Dep* (right)

#e	name	salary	bonus	age	dep	#d	budget	city
19	Dupont	2,500 (0.1)	1,800	38	23			
76	Martin	4,000 (0.9)	2,600	42	23	17	200 (1)	Toulouse
26	Durant	3,000 (0.4)	1,500	37	23	23	150 (0.2)	Paris
12	Dubois	2,500 (0.1)	900	39	17			

The equivalence: $r[A \ \theta \ B]s = \sigma(r \times s, \ A \ \theta \ B)$ holds as in the usual case. Obviously, these operations may apply to regular relations to build fuzzy relations which are used as intermediate or final results.

Example 5.1. Consider the relations *Emp* (*#e, name, salary, bonus, age, dep*) and *Dep* (*#d, budget, city*) and the query: "find the departments (number) with a high budget where there is no employee less than 40 years old with a medium salary". This query can be stated as the following algebraic expression:

$$\pi_{\{\#d\}}(\sigma(Dep, \ budget \ \textbf{is} \ high)) -$$
$$\pi_{\{dep\}}(\sigma(Emp, \ age < 40 \ \textbf{and} \ salary \ \textbf{is} \ medium)).$$

With the extensions given in Table 5.1 (where the values associated with *salary* (resp. *budget*) denote the grades for the predicate *medium* (resp. *high*)), the result of this expression is: $\{1/17, 0.2/23\} - \{0.1/17, 0.4/23\} = \{0.9/17, 0.2/23\}.\diamond$

Beyond these operations, which are canonical extensions of the regular ones, the division of relations requires more attention. It will be dealt with in detail in Chapter 7.

5.3   An Overview of a Basic Version of SQLf

5.3.1   *Introduction*

The first fuzzy set-based extension of the language SEQUEL (Chamberlin *et al.*, 1976) was proposed in Bosc *et al.* (1988), which only allowed the expression of simple fuzzy queries (mainly projection–selection–join queries). The choice of SEQUEL was justified by the fact that it was, at that time, the most widely known relational database language. Following the arrival of standard SQL, a more complete extension, called SQLf (Bosc and Pivert, 1995b), was defined by studying some aspects previously not dealt with, particularly those which concerned the extension of nesting operators and also selection operators applying to sets of tuples, e.g. quantified statements. The aim was to make SQLf as similar to SQL as possible, particularly with regard to query equivalences (Bosc and Pivert, 1991). For each type of query, an investigation was made as to whether the equivalences between several formulations, which are valid in a Boolean context, remain when the relations derive from fuzzy restrictions, and when the used connectives themselves become fuzzy. The aim of this section is to present the main features of SQLf. First, we show the different forms that the multi-relation block in SQLf can take, and we provide the semantics of the considered fuzzy operations. The matter of "complex queries" is dealt with next by studying nesting and set-oriented operators. For each operator, we recall that in SQL several equivalent formulations exist, and we show which of these equivalences remain valid in an imprecise querying context. Then, we study the case of queries implying relation partitioning, in particular those that involve fuzzy quantifiers.

5.3.2 *The multiple relation base block*

In SQL, a projection–selection–join query can be expressed using a multi-relation block, without nesting. Such a block is written as:

$$\textbf{select } \langle\text{attributes}\rangle \textbf{ from } \langle\text{relations}\rangle \textbf{ where } \langle\text{condition}\rangle.$$

Its role is to select the tuples belonging to the Cartesian product of the specific relations which satisfy the requirement, and to project them onto the specified attributes. It is worth recalling that this projection is not exactly the usual relational projection, since duplicates are authorized (a multiset is obtained), unless otherwise specified (using the keyword *distinct*).

In SQLf, the select block remains fundamentally the same. The differences are essentially twofold. The first difference is related to the use of a parameter intended for the calibration of the result (either a number of desired responses denoted by n, or a qualitative threshold denoted by t, or both). The second difference concerns the nature of the authorized conditions, which are no longer solely Boolean. In SQLf, the new formulation of the select block is as follows:

$$\textbf{select } [n \mid t \mid n, t] \langle\text{attributes}\rangle$$
$$\textbf{from } \langle\text{relations}\rangle \textbf{ where } \langle\text{fuzzy condition}\rangle \qquad \text{(Q1)}$$

where ⟨relations⟩ corresponds to a list of usual (crisp) relations, and ⟨fuzzy condition⟩ may imply both fuzzy and Boolean basic conditions at the same time, linked by some connectives.

5.3.3   *Subqueries*

5.3.3.1   *Nesting with "in"*

In SQL, the operator *in* is used for the membership operation. In SQLf, some imprecision may appear at different levels inside queries of that kind: on the one hand, one may want to know whether an element belongs to a fuzzy relation, and on the other hand, one may want to check for fuzzy membership (to either a usual or a fuzzy relation).

Membership to a fuzzy relation.   In SQL, an example of a query involving the operator *in* is given by: "find the employees younger than 35 who work in a department whose budget is higher than \$100,000". It can be expressed as:

> **select** #*e* **from** *Emp* **where** *age* < 35 **and** #*dep* **in**
> (**select** #*d* **from** *Dep* **where** *budget* > 100,000).

In SQLf, since a block delivers a fuzzy relation, it is natural to extend the operator *in* in order to express membership to a fuzzy set. Fuzzy set theory makes it possible to determine the extent to which an element belongs to a certain category, by using the membership function associated with the set under consideration. In the present context, one has to deal with fuzzy relations likely to involve duplicates, since these may result from a projection. Thus, we are led to define the operator *in* as follows:

$$\mu_{in}(a, E) = sup_{b \in support(E)}(min(\mu_=(a, b), \mu_E(b))) \qquad (5.1)$$

where *a* is the element and *E* the considered (multi-) set. This semantics preserves the equivalences valid in SQL. For example, the query: "find the young employees who work in a high-budget department" may be expressed as:

> **select** #*e* **from** *Emp* **where** *age* **is** *young* **and** #*dep* **in**
> (**select** #*d* **from** *Dep* **where** *budget* **is** *high*),

and also, by means of a multi-relation block, as:

> **select** $\#e$ **from** *Emp, Dep* **where** *age* **is** *young* **and**
> *Emp.*$\#dep$ = *Dep.*$\#d$ **and** *budget* **is** *high.*

In this latter case, the grade of an employee e in the result res is given by:

$$min(\mu_{young}(e.sal), sup_{t \in Dep} min(\mu_{high}(budget), \mu_=(t.\#d, e.\#dep))).$$
$$(5.2)$$

In the former case, if SQ stands for the inner block, we have:

$$\mu_{res}(e) = min(\mu_{young}(e), min(e.\#dep, SQ)), \qquad (5.3)$$

and if we replace $min(e.\#dep, SQ)$ by its value according to Expression (5.1), one can see that both values obtained are the same. This means that, if $fc_1(r)$ (resp. $fc_2(s)$) denotes a fuzzy condition applying to relation r (resp. s), it remains possible to use either:

> **select** $r.*$ **from** r, s **where** $fc_1(r)$ **and** $fc_2(s)$ **and** $r.A = s.B$,

or:

> **select** $*$ **from** r **where** fc_1 **and** A **in** (**select** B **from** s **where** fc_2).

Symmetrically, using Expression (5.1), a straightforward way to define *not in* is:

$$\mu_{not\,in}(a, E) = 1 - \mu_{in}(a, E). \qquad (5.4)$$

Fuzzy membership. In the previous case, the transition from a multi-block query to a nested query corresponded to the presence of an equijoin clause in the query. It is also worth studying the case where the join clause relies on a closeness operator ($\approx$, *about*). For this purpose, SQLf offers the ability to express queries checking the membership to a set (fuzzy or not), by evaluating the extent to which an element of the set exists that is close to the considered element. To this end, a new constructor is necessary which will be denoted by in_f. For example, the query: "find the employees who work in a department whose budget is about 1,000 times their own salary" can be expressed by the multi-block query:

> **select** $\#e$ **from** *Emp, Dep* **where**
> *Emp.*$\#dep$ = *Dep.*$\#d$ **and** *Dep.budget* $\approx$ *Emp.salary* $*$ 1,000,

and, using an *in* nesting (replacement of the equijoin clause on the department):

> **select** #e **from** *Emp* **where** #dep **in**
> (**select** #d **from** *Dep* **where** $budget \approx Emp.salary$ * 1,000),

and also using the nesting operator in_f expressing the fuzzy membership of a set:

> **select** #e **from** *Emp* **where** $salary$ * 1000 **in**$_f$
> (**select** $budget$ **from** *Dep* **where** #$d = Emp.$#dep).

The resemblance between the considered element and those of the set must be taken into account when calculating the grade of membership. Therefore, in Expression (5.1), the equality degree is replaced by a closeness degree. The operator in_f is defined as:

$$\mu_{in_f}(a, E) = sup_{b \in support(E)}(min(\mu_{\approx}(a, b), \mu_E(b))). \qquad (5.5)$$

Note that operator *in* is a special case of in_f which corresponds to using the strict equality as a special case of the closeness operator $\approx$. This operator may be defined for example as:

$$\mu_{\approx}(x, y) = \begin{cases} 1 \text{ if } |x - y| \leq \delta_1, \\ 0 \text{ if } |x - y| \geq \delta_2, \\ \text{linear in between,} \end{cases} \qquad (5.6)$$

where δ_1 and δ_2 ($\delta_1 \leq \delta_2$) are two constants which may depend both on the attribute domain and the user.

It is possible to show that the equivalence between:

> **select** $r.$* **from** r, s **where** $fc_1(r)$ **and** $fc_2(s)$ **and** $r.A \approx s.B$

and

> **select** * **from** r **where** fc_1 **and** A **in**$_f$ (**select** B **from** s **where** fc_2)

is ensured by Expression (5.5). More precisely, this equivalence follows from the equality between:

$$sup_{y \in s} min(\mu_{\approx}(x.A, y.B), \mu_{fc_2}(y))$$

and

$$sup_{b \in support(sf)} min(\mu_{\approx}(x.A, b), \mu_{sf}(b)),$$

where *sf* is the result of the inner *select* block.

Operator *not in*$_f$ is defined in a way similar to *not in*; see Expression (5.4). As illustrated by the previous examples, it allows for queries which would be expressed as equijoins in relational algebra. Similarly, an extended equijoin operator can be associated with *in*$_f$. On the other hand, *not in*$_{(f)}$ can be associated with a non-standard relational operator called antijoin (Kim, 1982):

$$antijoin(r, s, \theta, A, B) = \{u \in r | \forall\, v \in s, \neg(u.A\theta v.B)\}.$$

A query such as:

select * **from** r **where** fc_1 **and** A **not in**$_f$
(**select** B **from** s **where** fc_2)

is expressed in relational algebra as:

$$antijoin(\sigma(r, fc_1), \sigma(s, fc_2), \approx, A, B),$$

where $\sigma(r, fc)$ denotes the fuzzy selection of relation r by condition fc.

The following example illustrates this kind of query: "find the young employees whose salary is close to none of the salaries of the employees having a large bonus". In SQLf it can be expressed as:

select #e **from** *Emp* **where** *age* **is** *young* **and** *salary* **not in**$_f$
(**select** *salary* **from** *Emp* **where** *bonus* **is** *large*).

5.3.3.2 *Nesting with "exists"*

A second type of nesting relies on the keyword *exists*, and is used in SQL to test the non-emptiness of a set (relation delivered by a subquery). In order to generalize this operator, we consider the case where it uses a fuzzy set as an argument. The objective is to calculate the extent to which a fuzzy set is not empty. At least two interpretations are possible:

- quantitative, based on the cardinality of the fuzzy set,
- qualitative, based on the extent to which at least one element belongs to the set; here, one is looking for the largest value α such that the α-cut of the set is not empty; in other words, the largest grade of membership is obtained (the height of this set), i.e:

$$\mu_{exists}(E) = sup_{x \in support(E)}\mu_E(x). \qquad (5.7)$$

This second interpretation is preferred since, on the one hand, it does not require any knowledge of a membership function applicable to the cardinality of the set, and on the other hand, it preserves the usual equivalences. In particular, one still has an equivalence between the expressions:

select * from r where A in$_f$ (select B from s)

and

select * from r where exists (select * from s where $B \approx r.A$).

In both cases, if r' denotes the resulting relation, we have:

$$\mu_{r'}(x) = sup_{y \in s}\mu_{\approx}(y.B, x.A).$$

The interpretation of *not exists* can be deduced canonically from that of *exists*:

$$\mu_{not\ exists}(E) = 1 - \mu_{exists}(E). \tag{5.8}$$

It should be mentioned that in SQLf, it is possible to express certain fuzzy equijoins using *exists* due to the equivalence between, on the one hand, this relational operator (equijoin) and the *in* (or *in$_f$*) construct, and, on the other hand, *exists* and *in* (or *in$_f$*) for these kinds of queries. For instance, the query: "find the employees who work in a department whose budget is about 1,000 times their own salary" can be expressed as:

select $\#e$ from Emp where exists
(select * from Dep where $\#d = Emp.\#dep$ and
$budget \approx Emp.salary$ * 1,000).

The operator *exists* can also be used for the expression of set difference, as we will see later.

5.3.3.3   *Nesting with "all" and "any"*

In SQL, quantified predicates are as follows: $A\ \theta\ \{$**all** $\mid$ **any**$\}\ SQ$, where A is an attribute, SQ is a subquery and θ is a comparator ($=, \neq, <$, etc). In the context of SQLf, two kinds of extension are possible. The first consists of extending these predicates in order to permit the use of fuzzy relational operators ($\approx$, *slightly greater*, etc.); the second aims at authorizing the use of fuzzy quantifiers (*around 3, almost all,...*) instead of only *all* and *any*. The first extension is presented here, while the second is discussed in Section 6.2.

Extension involving a fuzzy relational operator. An example of such a query is: "find the employees whose salary is much greater than that of any other employee in the same department". The objective is to adopt an interpretation such that the usual SQL equivalences remain valid. For instance, such an equivalence holds in SQL between the statements:

> **select * from** r **where** $A = $ **any (select** B **from** s ...)

and

> **select * from** r **where** A **in (select** B **from** s ...).

More generally, the evaluation of "$A\,\theta\,any\,E$" consists in checking whether there exists at least one value y from E such that $A\,\theta\,y$ is true. In other words, there is an equivalence between the expressions:

> **select * from** r **where** $A\,\theta$ **any (select** B **from** s **where** fc)

and

> **select * from** r **where exists (select** B **from** s **where** fc **and** $A\,\theta\,B$),

which leads us to interpret the generalized predicate $\theta\,any$ as:

$$\mu_{\theta any}(a, E) = sup_{b \in support(E)} min(\mu_E(b), \mu_\theta(a, b)). \qquad (5.9)$$

Similarly, the evaluation of "$A\,\theta\,all\,E$" comes down to assessing whether the statement "no element y from E is such that $A\,\theta\,y$" is false. We have an equivalence between the expressions:

> **select * from** r **where** $A\,\theta$ **all (select** B **from** s **where** fc)

and

> **select * from** r **where not exists**
> **(select** B **from** s **where** fc **and not** $(A\,\theta\,B)$).

One thus deduces the following interpretation of $\theta\,all$:

$$\mu_{\theta all}(a, E) = 1 - sup_{b \in support(E)} min(\mu_E(b), 1 - \mu_\theta(a, b)). \qquad (5.10)$$

For *all* as well as for *any*, the evaluation of the predicate consists of assessing the extent to which the result of the inner block satisfies the condition. The chosen interpretation is more qualitative than quantitative. It is worth mentioning that the extension suggested in Expressions (5.9) and (5.10) preserves the equivalence between "$= any$" and *in*, which is a natural consequence of the equivalence between *in* and *exists*.

5.3.3.4   *Nesting and scalar comparison*

As mentioned above, SQLf queries can involve fuzzy comparisons between values. This kind of mechanism can also be used to extend predicates involving a comparison between an attribute value and the result of an aggregate function returned by a regular nested block (here we only consider aggregates defined on crisp sets). The general form is:

select X **from** r **where** A θ (**select** $agg(B)$ **from** s),

where A and B are attributes defined on the same domain, θ is a comparison operator, and agg denotes an aggregate function. The semantics of such a query is given by the formula:

$$\mu_{res}(x) = sup_{t \in r \text{ and } t.X = x} \mu_\theta(t.A, v), \tag{5.11}$$

where *res* is the result of the query, and v is the value returned by the nested block. For example, "find the employees whose salary is much greater than the average of the salaries of the employees in the same department" can be expressed as:

select $\#e$ **from** *Emp* E **where** *salary* $\gg$
(**select** **avg**(*salary*) **from** *Emp* **where** $\#d = E.\#d$).

5.3.4   *Set-oriented operators*

In SQL, the only necessary set operator is the union; set difference and intersection can be expressed by means of other constructs. The *union* operator defines a relation resulting from the combination of the tuples of two other relations, after the clauses appearing in the *select* blocks have been applied. The extension of this operator to the case where the *select* blocks deliver fuzzy relations is straightforward. It is based on the usual definition of the union operator:

$$\mu_{r \cup s}(x) = max(\mu_r(x), \mu_s(x)). \tag{5.12}$$

In the general case, the intersection can be expressed using a join or an *exists* nesting, and the difference can be expressed with a *not exists* nesting. It is therefore worth checking whether the fuzzy extensions previously proposed for joins and *exists* preserve these equivalences according to the usual semantics of the fuzzy intersection (resp. difference). Their interpretation is usually given by:

$$\mu_{r \cap s}(x) = min(\mu_r(x), \mu_s(x)), \tag{5.13}$$

$$\mu_{r-s}(x) = min(\mu_r(x), 1 - \mu_s(x)). \tag{5.14}$$

Consider the difference and the query:

> (**select** $A_1, \ldots, A_n$ **from** r **where** fc_1)
> **minus**
> (**select** $A_1, \ldots, A_n$ **from** s **where** fc_2),

where A_i is an attribute of r and s. Let rf be the result of the first block, sf that of the second block, and res the global result. From Expression (5.14), we have:

$$\mu_{res}(a_1, \ldots, a_n) = min(\mu_{rf}(a_1, \ldots, a_n), 1 - \mu_{sf}(a_1, \ldots, a_n)),$$

where

$$\mu_{rf}(a_1, \ldots, a_n) = sup_{x \in r \wedge x.A_1 = a_1 \wedge \cdots \wedge x.A_n = a_n} \mu_{fc_1}(x)$$

and

$$\mu_{sf}(a_1, \ldots, a_n) = sup_{y \in s \wedge y.A_1 = a_1 \wedge \cdots \wedge y.A_n = a_n} \mu_{fc_2}(y).$$

The translation of the query using *not exists* leads to:

select $A_1, \ldots, A_n$ **from** r **where** fc_1 **and not exists**
  (**select** * **from** s **where** fc_2 **and** $A_1 = r.A_1$ **and** $\ldots$ **and** $A_n = r.A_n$).

According to the semantics of *not exists*, we obtain:

$$\mu_{res}(a_1, \ldots, a_n) =$$
$$sup_{x \in r \wedge x.A_1 = a_1 \wedge \cdots \wedge x.A_n = a_n} min(\mu_{fc_1}(x),$$
$$1 - sup_{y \in s} min(\mu_{fc_2}(y), \mu_{=}(y.A_1, a_1), \ldots, \mu_{=}(y.A_n, a_n))).$$

The equivalence of these two interpretations is straightforward. In the same way, it can be checked that the extensions of *join* and *exists* make it possible to express the intersection of fuzzy relations in accordance with Expression (5.13).

Intersection can also be translated with an "*in*" or "*= any*" nesting, whereas set difference is expressible with a "*not in*" or "*$\neq$ all*" nesting. For example, assuming the existence of a relation *Anc* of schema $(\#e, \#d, years)$, the query: "find the young employees who have never worked for more than three years in any department" may be expressed by:

(a) **select** $\#e$ **from** *Emp* **where** *age* **is** *young* **and not exists**
    (**select** * **from** *Anc* **where** $\#e = Emp.\#e$ **and** *years* > 3)

(b) **select** $\#e$ **from** *Emp* **where** *age* **is** *young* **and** $\#e$ **not in**
    (**select** $\#e$ **from** *Anc* **where** *years* > 3)

(c) **select** $\#e$ **from** *Emp* **where** *age* **is** *young* **and** $\#e \neq$ **all**
    (**select** $\#e$ **from** *Anc* **where** *years* > 3).

According to the preceding general result (the equivalence between difference and *not exists*), and due to the respective equivalences between these different nestings, one may assert that these formulations preserve the usual semantics of the set difference operator. A similar result can be obtained in the same way for the intersection.

5.3.5   *Relation partitioning*

In SQL, a relation may be partitioned into subrelations (groups) according to the values of one or several attributes (those specified in a *group by* clause). By doing so, each partition groups tuples which have the same value on this (these) considered attribute(s). This functionality is retained in SQLf, and in this context, the *having* clause can be used along with a fuzzy-set-oriented condition aimed at the selection of groups. In this subsection, we discuss the various possible conditions involving aggregate functions (*min*, *sum*, etc.). The case of more complex conditions involving fuzzy quantifiers is discussed in Section 6.2.

5.3.5.1   *Qualification of partitions by means of aggregate functions*

Like numerous other relational languages, SQL offers the possibility of evaluating numerical operators upon a set of tuples. This is performed by means of operators, called aggregate functions, among which are: *sum*, *count*, *avg*, *min*, and *max*. In the following, we limit the scope of the discussion to the case where aggregates apply to a crisp (non-fuzzy) relation. A more general situation is discussed in Section 6.3. An example of an SQL query involving an aggregate for selecting groups is: "find the departments where the average salary of the engineers is higher than \$3,500":

> **select** $\#dep$ **from** *Emp* **where** $job = $ "Engineer"
>
> **group by** $\#dep$ **having avg**($salary$) $\geq$ 3,500.

In SQLf, the process is similar but there is the additional possibility of using the result of an aggregate as an argument for fuzzy criteria. For example, the query: "find the departments where the average salary of the engineers is about \$3,500" is expressed in SQLf by:

> **select** $\#dep$ **from** *Emp* **where** $job = $ "Engineer"
>
> **group by** $\#dep$ **having avg**($salary$) $\approx$ 3,500.

Some equivalences concerning queries which involve aggregates inside a *having* clause exist in SQL. For instance, the previous SQL query may also be expressed using a particular nesting in which the inner block returns a single value (by means of an aggregate) which is part of a simple comparison term:

> **select** $\#dep$ **from** *Emp E* **where** $3500 \leq$
>   (**select avg**($salary$) **from** *Emp* **where** $\#dep = E.\#dep$ **and**
> $job = $ "Engineer").

This equivalence is valid since the condition $\#dep = E.\#dep$ does the same as a *group by*. More generally, with a regular (non-fuzzy) relation, it can be shown that the following SQLf queries are equivalent:

> **select** A **from** r **where** bc **group by** A
>
> **having** $fc_1(\ agg_1(B_1))$ **connective** $\cdots$ **connective** $fc_p(agg_p(B_p))$

and

> **select** A **from** $r\ r_1$ **where** bc **and**
>   (fc_1(**select** $agg_1(B_1)$ **from** r **where** $A = r_1.A$ **and** bc)
>   **connective** $\cdots$ **connective**
> fc_p(**select** $agg_p(B_p)$ **from** r **where** $A = r_1.A$ **and** bc)),

where agg_i stands for an aggregate function, bc denotes a Boolean condition and fc_i represents a fuzzy predicate.

5.4 Interface for User-Defined Terms and Operators

Since the semantics of a fuzzy term relies on its membership function, any fuzzy querying system must provide the users with a convenient way to define the membership functions of the fuzzy terms (and quantifiers, if any) that they wish to include in a query.

In practice, the membership function associated with a fuzzy set F is often chosen to be of a trapezoidal shape. F is then expressed by the quadruplet (A, B, a, b) where $core(F) = [A, B]$ and $supp(F) = [A - a, B + b]$; see Figure 5.1. If the function is a right (resp. left) shoulder, it can be encoded by $(A, k_2, a, 0)$ (resp. $(k_1, B, 0, b)$) where $[k_1, k_2]$ represents the domain of the attribute concerned.

In Kacprzyk and Zadrożny (1995) and Zadrożny and Kacprzyk (1996), the authors describe a fuzzy querying system built on top of the commercial DBMS Microsoft Access, where the definition of fuzzy predicates, fuzzy comparators and fuzzy quantifiers is performed through an appropriate graphical user interface. Goncalves and Tineo (2001a,b) introduce commands aimed at defining fuzzy predicates (**create fuzzy predicate**) and fuzzy comparators (**create comparator**) into SQLf.

For simple fuzzy queries — those without any fuzzy modifiers, quantifiers or comparators — another solution is to include the definitions of the fuzzy predicates in the query itself. Assuming that trapezoidal membership functions are used, when a fuzzy predicate concerns a numerical attribute one just has to specify its core (ideal values) and support (acceptable values):

- $att \leq u$ translates into: $\langle \mathbf{ideal} : att \leq u, \mathbf{acceptable} : att < u + v \rangle$,

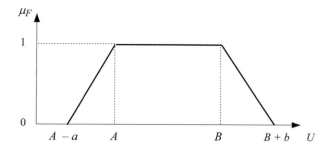

Fig. 5.1 Trapezoidal membership function

- $att \approx u$ translates into:

$$\langle \textbf{ideal} : att \in [u - v, u + v], \textbf{acceptable} : att \in]u - v - w, u + v + w[\rangle,$$

- $att \geq u$ translates into: $\langle \textbf{ideal} : att \geq u, \textbf{acceptable} : att > u - v \rangle$.

However, when a fuzzy predicate concerns a categorical attribute, it has to be given in extension.

Example 5.2. Consider a relation *cars* of schema (*make, category, price, color, mileage*). An example of a fuzzy query involving the definition of fuzzy terms is:

> **select** * **from** *cars* **where** (*color* **is** C_1) **and** (*make* **is** C_2) **and**
> (*category* **is** C_3) **and** (*price* **is** *low_P*) **and** (*mileage* **is** *low_M*)
> **with preferences**
> C_1: {1/blue, 1/black, 0.8/green, 0.7/gray, 0.5/red, 0.3/orange}
> C_2: {1/VW, 0.9/Audi, 0.7/BMW, 0.6/Seat, 0.6/Opel, 0.4/Ford}
> C_3: {1/sedan, 0.8/roadster, 0.7/coupe, 0.4/SUV}
> *low_P*: $\langle$**ideal:** *price* $\leq$ 4,000, **acceptable:** *price* $\leq$ 6,000$\rangle$
> *low_M*: $\langle$**ideal:** *mileage* $\leq$ 15,000, **acceptable:** *mileage* $\leq$ 20,000$\rangle$.◊

In Bodenhofer and Küng (2004), the authors suggest the use of *fuzzy orderings* in order to define the semantics of fuzzy predicates defined on numerical domains. They consider three comparison operators, namely *is at least*, *is at most*, and *is within*, that they make tolerant by means of a clause *tolerate up to*. For instance, the fuzzy predicate "*is at most q tolerate up to C*" may be associated with a membership function μ, based on the use of Łukasiewicz's t-norm, defined as follows:

$$\mu(x) = L_C(x, q)$$

where

$$L_C(u, v) = \begin{cases} 1 \text{ if } u \leq v \\ max\left(1 - \dfrac{1}{C} \cdot |u - v|, 0\right) \text{ otherwise.} \end{cases}$$

An example of the queries that the authors consider is:

> **select** * **from** *cars*
>
> **where** *make* = "Ford"
>
> **and** *price* **is at most** 20,000 **tolerate up to** 5,000
>
> **and** *mileage* **is at most** 30,000 **tolerate up to** 10,000;

It is also possible to weight the different atomic conditions involved in a (generalized) conjunction, by means of a clause *weighted by*.

5.5   Contextual Queries

In this section, we deal with the situation where the user is not aware of the content of the database that he/she wants to query, and thus is unable to define (fuzzy or non-fuzzy) selection predicates referring explicitly to some constants from the domains. Despite this absence of knowledge, the user may want to retrieve the best answers with respect to some relative conditions. As an example, consider a user who wants to move to a different country and aims at finding the "best" cities to settle in according to the following preferences: population between 50,000 and 100,000 (hard constraint), low average price per square meter, low crime rate, medium average annual temperature. We assume that the user does not know the values taken by the attributes "average price per square meter", "crime rate", "average annual temperature" in the country considered, but still wants to find the best solutions relative to the existing possibilities. Note that in the system *Preference SQL* (Kießling and Köstler, 2002), one may express conditions of the form "attribute A is as *high* (resp. *low*) as possible" — although not "A is *medium*" — but again, since it is based on Pareto order, one can only "combine" such conditions so as to obtain a partial order. In other words, Pareto-based approaches such as *Preference SQL* do not permit the expression of trade-offs between a predicate of the form "A *is low* (resp. *high*)" and other predicates. This seems desirable in many cases, however.

The idea that we advocate in the following is to use the fuzzy-set-based framework and to define the fuzzy predicates *high*, *medium* and *low* in a relative way, using the minimal, average and maximal values of the attribute values present in the associated query-defined context (in the example above: the cities whose population is between 50,000 and 100,000). There is a connection between this idea and the proposal by Tudorie *et al.* (2006) where a fuzzy predicate can be defined relative to the context created by another one. For example, in a query such as "find the inexpensive cars among the high-speed ones", the authors suggest adapting the definition of the fuzzy term *inexpensive* by taking into account the price values associated with high-speed cars. However, the authors do not formalize the notion of a context.

Even though the approach by Agrawal *et al.* (2006) deals with preferences and contexts, it does not have much in common with the idea developed here since; (i) it deals with preferences over categorical attributes whereas we consider numerical ones; (ii) it handles contexts and preferences which are given *explicitly* (and *statically*) by the user in the form of a set of conditions "*attribute = value*", whereas we deal with contexts which are specified *dynamically* by means of a specific clause in an extended SQL language, as well as with preferences which are expressed in an *implicit* and relative way; (iii) the approach proposed in Agrawal *et al.* (2006) does not combine contextual preferences with non-contextual ones, while the method presented here makes it possible to do so thanks to the commensurability assumption underlying the fuzzy-set-based model. As to the approaches of Holland and Kießling (2004), Stefanidis *et al.* (2007), and van Bunningen *et al.* (2006), they deal with a very different notion of context, namely the context in which the *user* is situated, which implies quite different issues.

In the following, we show how conditions of the form "*A is low* (resp. *medium, high*)" can be modeled in the framework of a fuzzy-set-based query language. The basic idea is to interpret these conditions relative to a given *context* specified in the user query. First, we clarify this latter notion.

Definition 5.1. A *query-defined context* is a referential of values returned by a (sub)query, on which a predicate can be defined in a relative manner.

For instance, if one has available a relation describing employees, one may define the predicate *young* (interpreted as "*age is low*") in the context of the *engineers'* ages, or the ages of those employees *whose monthly salary is less than $2,500*, and so on. Clearly, the *relative* meaning of *young* depends on the referential considered. First consider the simple case where a single context is given in the query.

5.5.1   *Queries with one level of context*

The syntax of the basic form of SQLf queries considered is as follows:

> **select** k X **from** r **where** $cond_1$ **and** *cfc*
>
> **context** {Boolean query | fuzzy query with a threshold α}.

In this query, k denotes a desired number of answers (the best ones), X is a set of attributes from relation r, $cond_1$ is a selection condition which may involve Boolean predicates and explicit fuzzy predicates (i.e., predicates whose membership function is user-defined), and *cfc* is a contextual fuzzy condition. Notice that contextual fuzzy terms can be altered by means of fuzzy modifiers such as *very*, *relatively*, etc., so as to express a great variety of nuanced contextual predicates.

The new clause introduced by the keyword *context* aims to define the referential of tuples that serves as a basis for constructing the fuzzy terms present in *cfc*. Two possibilities are offered; one may either use:

- a Boolean subquery (not only a selection–projection–join query, but any kind),
- a fuzzy query involving a qualitative threshold α.

A constraint is that the result of the context clause must include attributes of the same domains as those concerned by the contextual predicates. In the case of a fuzzy context query, the context is made of the tuples whose membership degree to the result of the fuzzy query is at least equal to α. Hence, the context is always defined as a *crisp set*.

Example 5.3. Consider a relation $FC(name, pop, crime, temp, univ)$ describing some French cities. Attribute *crime* corresponds to the crime rate and attribute *temp* to the annual average temperature in a given city, while *pop* gives the number of inhabitants. Attribute *univ* indicates whether there is a university in the city. Here are some examples:

(1) find the 10 best cities whose population is between 50,000 and 100,000, where a university is located, and where the crime rate is low relative to the set of French cities in the same range of population.

> **select** 10 *name* **from** FC
> **where** *pop* **between** 50k **and** 100k **and** *univ* = "yes" **and**
>   *crime* **is** *low*
> **context** (**select** * **from** FC **where** *pop* **between** 50k **and** 100k).

(2) find the 10 best cities whose population is large, where the annual average temperature is around 15 degrees, and where the crime rate is low relative to the set of French cities whose population fits the fuzzy predicate *large* at a degree at least equal to 0.7. Here, the fuzzy predicate *large* is assumed to be user-defined.

> **select** 10 *name* **from** *FC*
>
> **where** *pop* **is** *large* **and** *temp* **is** *around_15* **and** *crime* **is** *low*
>
> **context** (**select** 0.7 * **from** *FC* **where** *pop* **is** *large*).◇

As mentioned above, the idea is to define the membership functions of fuzzy predicates such as "*A is low*", "*A is medium*" and "*A is high*" in terms of the minimum, average and maximum *A*-values in the result of the query which defines the context. For interpreting *low*, *medium* and *high*, we propose the following default definitions (see also Figure 5.2):

- *lowA* decreases linearly from 1 to 0 when *A* moves from $min(A)$ to $avg(A)$.
- *mediumA* is represented by an isosceles triangle centered in $avg(A)$ and whose support is the interval $[avg(A) - \delta, avg(A) + \delta]$, where δ equals $min(avg(A) - min(A), max(A) - avg(A))$. This corresponds to interpreting *medium* as "close to the average".
- *highA* increases linearly from 0 to 1 when *A* moves from $avg(A)$ to $max(A)$.

It is of course possible to argue about these definitions. One could choose, for instance, to say that full satisfaction is assumed *around* the minimum (for *low*) or the average (for *medium*) or the maximum (for *high*). One could also imagine defining a partition of more than three implicit fuzzy predicates, and so on. In order to make the system more user-friendly, it is

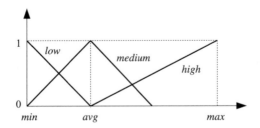

Fig. 5.2   Default definitions of implicit fuzzy terms

Table 5.2   Extension of the relation *FC*

name	pop	crime	temp
Montauban	53,300	4.8	20
Cannes	70,400	7.2	21
Rennes	210,200	4.3	14
Beauvais	54,100	2.4	12
Pau	82,500	5.3	18
...	...	...	...

of course conceivable to let the user personalize these membership functions through an appropriate interface. Note that the implicit assumption made here is that the context includes enough data to represent a statistically significant subset of the data (so as to be able to compute significant values for *min, avg* and *max*).

Example 5.4. Consider the (partial) extension of a relation *FC* describing French cities represented in Table 5.2, and the query:

> **select** 10 *name* **from** *FC*
>
> **where** (*pop* **between** 50k **and** 100k) **and** (*crime* **is** *low*) **and**
>
> (*temp* **is** *medium*)
>
> **context** (**select** * **from** *FC* **where** *pop* **between** 50k **and** 100k).

Suppose that the minimum (resp. average, resp. maximum) value for attribute *crime* over the set of cities in the specified population interval is 0.8 (resp. 4.1, resp. 11.3) and the minimum (resp. average, resp. maximum) value for attribute *temp* over the same set of cities is 8 (resp. 14, resp. 22). One can then define the fuzzy predicates low_{crime} and $medium_{temp}$ as described above, and the evaluation of the query on the first tuple (Montauban) provides the degrees 0.21 (for "*crime is low*") and 0.75 (for "*temperature is medium*"). If we assume that the conjunction is interpreted as a minimum, the first tuple receives an overall satisfaction degree of 0.21.◊

It is appropriate to mention the possibility of introducing a notion of *default context* so as to make the user's task easier. Informally, the *context default* clause corresponds to a query involving the Boolean part of the *where* clause from the original user query (i.e., the *where* clause without its fuzzy conditions, in particular those involving contextual predicates).

For instance, the query from Example 5.4 could be expressed more simply as:

> **select** 10 *name* **from** *FC*
> **where** (*pop* **between** 50k **and** 100k) **and** (*crime* **is** *low*) **and**
>   (*temp* **is** *medium*)
> **context default**.

5.5.2   *Queries with several levels of context*

We now extend the approach presented above, to consider several levels of context. An example is: "find the apartments with a medium price located in cities of less than 100,000 inhabitants with a low crime rate" where *low* is assumed to be defined with respect to the set of cities of less than 100,000 inhabitants, while *medium* is defined relative to the set of flats in the city where a given apartment is located. Consider the relations: *City* (*#id, name, pop, crime, temp*) and *Flat* (*#app, #city, category, price, surface*), and the query: "find the 10 best apartments of category F5 which have a medium price and are located in a city whose population is between 50,000 and 100,000 and whose crime rate is low". The term *low* — referring to the crime rate — is defined relative to the context of cities whose population is between 50,000 and 100,000, while the term *medium* — concerning the price — is defined in the context of the city where the considered apartment is located, for the category considered. In SQLf, this query can be expressed as:

select 10 *#app* **from** *Flat f1*
where *price* **is** *medium* **and** *category* = "F5" **and** *#city* **in**
  (**select** *#id* **from** *City*
    where *pop* **between** 50k **and** 100k **and** *crime* **is** *low*
    context default)
context
  (**select** * **from** *Flat* **where** *#city* = *f1. #city* **and** *category* = "F5").

It is also conceivable to jointly use contextual fuzzy predicates defined on different contexts. For instance, consider a relation *Emp* (*id, name, age, ed-level, salary*) describing the employees of a given company and the query: "find every employee who has a medium education level (relative to the entire set of employees) and a high salary (relative to the set of employees around his/her age at a degree at least equal to 0.7)". Expressing this query in SQLf involves extending the *context* clause introduced above so as to deal with different referentials. A possible formulation is:

> **select** *id, name* **from** *Emp e*
> **where** (*ed-level* **is** *medium*) **and** (*salary* **is** *high*)
> **context**
>   (*medium*: **default**;
>   *high*: (**select** 0.7 * **from** *Emp* **where** *age around e.age*)).

In this query, it is assumed that *around* is an explicit (i.e., user-defined) fuzzy comparator extending the equality.

Another extension consists of using the "top-k" mechanism in a nested manner. This allows restriction of the referential over which the contextual terms are defined to the most relevant elements only. For instance, in the preceding query about flats, one might choose to assess only the flats which are located in a city which is sufficiently satisfactory (e.g., among the 20 best) with respect to the criterion on crime. Yet another way of introducing nesting is to have a context clause which itself involves a context clause.

5.6   Evaluation of Simple Fuzzy Queries

In conventional DBMSs, the issue of query evaluation remains somewhat open since, given a query, the optimal evaluation plan cannot in general be determined. For fuzzy queries, the process becomes even more tricky, since access paths cannot be directly used. In this context, it appears useful to understand the connections which exist between properties tied to regular (Boolean) conditions and fuzzy ones, so that fuzzy query processing can be reduced to Boolean query processing (at least partly). An evaluation method, called derivation (Bosc and Pivert, 1993), exploiting such properties, is described in the following. The applicability of this method to the evaluation of different types of SQLf queries is discussed, as well as the integration of a derivation-based SQLf query interface on top of a regular relational DBMS.

5.6.1   *Derivation principle*

The strategy presented here assumes that a threshold α is associated with an SQLf query in order to retrieve the α-level cut of its answer set. The idea is to use an existing database management system which will process regular Boolean queries. An SQL query is derived from an SQLf expression in order to retrieve a superset of the α-level cut of its answer set. Then, the fuzzy query can be processed on this superset, thus avoiding an exhaustive scan of the whole database. The principle is to express the α-level cut in terms of a query involving only regular operators and expressions. The principal problem is to distribute the α-level cut operation applying to a selection expression into its constituent elements.

5.6.1.1 *Transformation of base predicates*

Consider a subset of base predicates of the form: (i) *"attribute is fuzzy term"*, (ii) *"attribute θ value"*, or (iii) *"attribute$_1$ θ attribute$_2$"* where θ is a fuzzy comparison operator (e.g., *age is young, quantity $\approx$ 150, qty$_1$ $\gg$ qty$_2$*). The objective is to replace such predicates with Boolean expressions, given a threshold α. In the first and second cases, the α-level cut of the initial expression is of the form *"attribute $\in [v_1, v_2]$"* if the characteristic function of the fuzzy term or the comparator (θ) has a trapezoidal shape. In the third case, the expression obtained may be defined as a function of the difference between (or the quotient of) the two attribute values.

Example 5.5. Consider the SQLf expression:

$$\textbf{select } 0.7 \ \#e, \ name \ \textbf{from } Emp \ \textbf{where } age \ \textbf{is } young.$$

If the membership function of *young* is that represented in Figure 5.3, one has:

$$\mu_{young}(x) \geq 0.7 \Leftrightarrow \text{age} \leq 30.$$

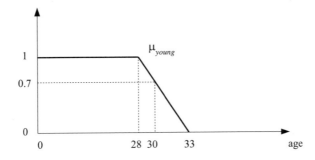

Fig. 5.3 Membership function of the fuzzy term *young*

In other terms:

$$DNC(age \text{ is } young, \geq, 0.7) = [age \leq 30],$$

where $DNC(fc, \geq, \alpha)$ denotes the derived necessary condition obtained from the condition $\mu_{fc}(s) \geq \alpha$ (in this example, as for any atomic predicate involving one attribute, the condition is necessary and sufficient, which is the ideal situation). The derived SQL query would then be:

select #*e*, *name* **from** *Emp* **where** *age* $\leq 30.\diamond$

It should be noted that predicates involving several attributes (e.g., the predicate *slim* involving the two attributes *height* and *weight*) cannot be derived in general. Nevertheless, it is worth noting that a non-derivable predicate can always be replaced by *true* in the final derived query.

5.6.1.2   *Single-block projection–selection–join queries*

First, we present the derived expressions tied to the usual connectives (and/or):

$$\mu_{P_1 \wedge \cdots \wedge P_n}(x) \geq \alpha \Leftrightarrow min(\mu_{P_1}(x), \ldots, \mu_{P_n}(x)) \geq \alpha$$
$$\Leftrightarrow \mu_{P_1}(x) \geq \alpha \wedge \cdots \wedge \mu_{P_n}(x) \geq \alpha.$$

Thus:

$$DNC(P_1 \text{ and } \cdots \text{ and } P_n, \geq, \alpha)$$
$$= DNC(P_1, \geq, \alpha) \text{ and } \ldots \text{ and } DNC(P_n, \geq, \alpha).$$

Similarly:

$$\mu_{P_1 \vee \cdots \vee P_n}(x) \geq \alpha \Leftrightarrow max(\mu_{P_1}(x), \ldots, \mu_{P_n}(x)) \geq \alpha$$
$$\Leftrightarrow \mu_{P_1}(x) \geq \alpha \vee \cdots \vee \mu_{P_n}(x) \geq \alpha.$$

Thus:

$$DNC(P_1 \text{ or } \cdots \text{ or } P_n, \geq, \alpha)$$
$$= DNC(P_1, \geq, \alpha) \text{ or } \cdots \text{ or } DNC(P_n, \geq, \alpha).$$

We also get the rules (useful when the negation is used):

$$DNC(P_1 \text{ and } \cdots \text{ and } P_n, <, \alpha)$$
$$= DNC(P_1, <, \alpha) \text{ or } \cdots \text{ or } DNC(P_n, <, \alpha)$$

and

$$DNC(P_1 \textbf{ or } \cdots \textbf{ or } P_n, <, \alpha)$$
$$= DNC(P_1, <, \alpha) \textbf{ and } \cdots \textbf{ and } DNC(P_n, <, \alpha).$$

Example 5.6. Consider the initial SQLf expression:

> **select** $0.8 \# e$, *name* **from** *Emp*
> **where** *age* **is** *young* **and** *salary* $\gg$ *bonus*.

If the characteristic functions for *young* and $\gg$ are those pictured in Figure 5.4, one obtains:

$$DNC(age \textbf{ is } young \textbf{ and } salary \gg bonus, \geq, 0.8)$$
$$= DNC(age \textbf{ is } young, \geq, 0.8) \textbf{ and } DNC(salary \gg bonus, \geq, 0.8)$$
$$= (age \leq 29) \textbf{ and } (salary - bonus) \geq 1{,}200).$$

The final SQL query is then:

> **select** $\# e$, *name* **from** *Emp*
> **where** $age \leq 29$ **and** $(salary - bonus) \geq 1{,}200.\diamond$

The above example corresponds to a case where the derivation process is exact, i.e., the derived query delivers the exact α-level cut of the initial fuzzy query. In some cases (e.g., predicates connected by mean operators), this can no longer be the case, and we only recover a superset of the desired α-level cut. The operators belonging to the class of means, denoted by mc,

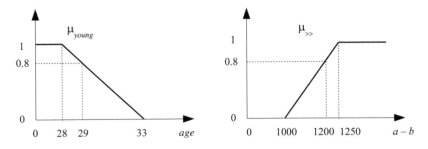

Fig. 5.4 Membership functions of *young* (left) and $\gg$ (right)

have two general properties. The first is:

$$min(\mu_{P_1}(x), \ldots, \mu_{P_n}(x)) \leq mc(\mu_{P_1}, \ldots, \mu_{P_n})(x)$$
$$\leq max(\mu_{P_1}(x), \ldots, \mu_{P_n}(x)).$$

As a consequence, two "weak" rules hold for any mean:

$$mc(P_1, \ldots, P_n) \geq \alpha \Rightarrow DNC(P_1, \geq, \alpha) \textbf{ or } \cdots \textbf{ or } DNC(P_n, \geq, \alpha),$$
$$mc(P_1, \ldots, P_n) < \alpha \Rightarrow DNC(P_1, <, \alpha) \textbf{ or } \cdots \textbf{ or } DNC(P_n, <, \alpha).$$

The second property is monotonicity:

$$\forall i, x_i \geq x_i' \Rightarrow \mu_{mc}(x_1, \ldots, x_n) \geq \mu_{mc}(x_1', \ldots, x_n').$$

Using this, one can point out some more specific rules for different mean operators (see Bosc and Pivert, 1995a). For example, to derive a query involving an arithmetic mean (am) connecting two fuzzy predicates P_1 and P_2, we would have to use the specific weak derivation rules:

$$am(P_1, P_2) \geq \alpha$$
$$\Rightarrow DNC(P_1, \geq, max(2\alpha - 1, 0)) \textbf{ and } DNC(P_2, \geq, max(2\alpha - 1, 0)),$$
$$am(P_1, P_2) < \alpha$$
$$\Rightarrow DNC(P_1, <, max(2\alpha - 1, 0)) \textbf{ and } DNC(P_2, <, max(2\alpha - 1, 0)).$$

We now consider the t-norm product $\otimes$. The derivation of a Boolean condition associated with $(\otimes(P_1, P_2) \geq \alpha)$ is possible thanks to the monotonicity of the product, and we obtain:

$$\otimes(P_1, P_2) \geq \alpha \Rightarrow DNC(P_1, \geq, \alpha) \textbf{ and } DNC(P_2, \geq, \alpha).$$

However, the property of monotonicity does not make it possible to derive a condition from $(\otimes(P_1, P_2) < \alpha)$. In such a situation, one can use exclusion cases, for instance:

$$(\mu_{P_1}(x) \geq \sqrt{\alpha} \wedge \mu_{P_2}(x) \geq \sqrt{\alpha}) \Rightarrow \mu_{\otimes(P_1,P_2)}(x) \geq \alpha,$$

from which we obtain the necessary condition:

$$\otimes(P_1, P_2) < \alpha \Rightarrow DNC(P_1, <, \sqrt{\alpha}) \textbf{ or } DNC(P_2, <, \sqrt{\alpha}).$$

5.6.1.3 *Nested queries*

We now review the Boolean expressions corresponding to the derivation of the subqueries presented in Section 5.3.3.

Recall that in SQLf, the operator *in* allows for testing whether the value of an attribute in the current tuple belongs to the (fuzzy) set of values returned by a subquery. The predicate "a **in** (**select** B **from** S **where** fc)" is defined by:

$$\mu_{in}(a, SQ) = sup_{b \in SQ \wedge b=a} \mu_{SQ}(b), \tag{5.15}$$

where SQ denotes the subquery returning a fuzzy bag of B-values from relation S. According to Expression (5.15), we have:

$$[a \textbf{ in } (\textbf{ select } B \textbf{ from } S \textbf{ where } fc)] \geq \alpha \Leftrightarrow$$

$$sup_{s \in S \wedge s.B=a} \mu_{fc}(s) \geq \alpha \Leftrightarrow$$

$$\exists s \in S \text{ such that } (s.B = a \wedge \mu_{fc}(s) \geq \alpha) \Leftrightarrow / \Rightarrow$$

$$a \textbf{ in } (\textbf{select } B \textbf{ from } S \textbf{ where } DNC(fc, \geq, \alpha)).$$

The final derivation step is strong if there exists a strong derivation rule for condition fc; it is weak otherwise.

In case of a negation, we have:

$$[a \textbf{ not in } (\textbf{select } B \textbf{ from } S \textbf{ where } fc)] \geq \alpha \Leftrightarrow$$

$$1 - sup_{s \in S \wedge s.B=a} \mu_{fc}(s) \geq \alpha \Leftrightarrow$$

$$sup_{s \in S \wedge s.B=a} \mu_{fc}(s) \leq 1 - \alpha \Leftrightarrow$$

$$\forall s \in S \text{ such that } s.B = a, \mu_{fc}(s) \leq 1 - \alpha.$$

Finally, the derived expression is:

$$a \textbf{ not in } (\textbf{select } B \textbf{ from } S \textbf{ where } DSC(fc, >, 1 - \alpha)),$$

where $DSC(fc, >, 1-\alpha)$ denotes the derived sufficient condition associated with fc. Because of the negation, one cannot use a necessary condition for the inner block. On the contrary, one needs a *sufficient* condition so as not to risk obtaining extra tuples from the inner block. Derived sufficient conditions can be obtained the same way as necessary conditions, using properties associated with the operators involved. For instance, one obtains the two general rules for any mean operator mc:

$$DSC(P_1, \geq, \alpha) \textbf{ and } \cdots \textbf{ and } DSC(P_n, \geq, \alpha) \Rightarrow mc(P_1, \ldots, P_n) \geq \alpha,$$

$$DSC(P_1, <, \alpha) \textbf{ and } \cdots \textbf{ and } DSC(P_n, <, \alpha) \Rightarrow mc(P_1, \ldots, P_n) < \alpha,$$

and based on the property of monotonicity, specific rules can be found. For instance, in the case of the arithmetic mean (am), we have:

$$DSC(P_1, \geq, 2\alpha) \textbf{ or } \cdots \textbf{ or } DSC(P_n, \geq, 2\alpha) \Rightarrow am(P_1, \ldots, Pn) \geq \alpha$$

$$DSC(P_1, <, 2\alpha - 1) \textbf{ or } \cdots \textbf{ or } DSC(P_n, <, 2\alpha - 1)$$
$$\Rightarrow am(P_1, \ldots, Pn) < \alpha.$$

For similar reasons, the condition "**exists (select** B **from** S **where** fc) $\geq \alpha$" can be transformed into:

$$\textbf{exists (select } B \textbf{ from } S \textbf{ where } DNC(fc, \geq, \alpha))$$

and its negation into:

$$\textbf{not exists (select } B \textbf{ from } S \textbf{ where } DSC(fc, >, 1 - \alpha)).$$

Example 5.7. To illustrate the transformation procedure, consider the query: "find the departments having a medium budget and no well-paid employees" written in SQLf:

select 0.5 #d **from** Dep **where** $budget$ **is** $medium$ **and not exists**
    (**select** * **from** Emp **where** $salary$ **is** $well\text{-}paid$ **and** #$dep = Dep.$#d).

Consider the fuzzy terms $medium$ and $well\text{-}paid$, represented in Figure 5.5. The 0.5-cut of the query can be calculated on the basis of the regular

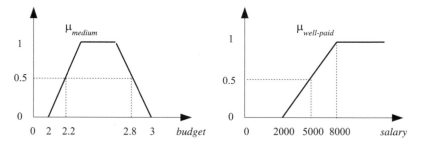

Fig. 5.5   Membership functions of $medium$ (left) and $well\text{-}paid$ (right)

SQL expression:

select $\#d$ **from** *Dep*
where *budget* ≥ 2.2 **and** *budget* ≤ 2.8 **and not exists**
 (**select** $\#dep$ **from** *Emp* **where** *salary* > 5000 **and** $\#dep = Dep.\#d$).

◇

5.6.2 *Derivation-based processing of SQLf queries*

5.6.2.1 *General strategy*

In this section, we study the possible architecture of a relational database system able to deal with fuzzy queries. There are two principal ways (and architectures) to process fuzzy queries, as described in Bosc and Pivert (2000):

- use a regular DBMS, and develop an additional layer playing the role of an interface, or
- build a completely new system including fuzzy query processing techniques (algorithms) in its kernel.

We focus on the first strategy which is strongly connected with the derivation method, since it implies a query transformation step: the basic principle is indeed to express the α-cut of a fuzzy query in terms of a query involving only regular (Boolean) expressions. It is then possible to use an existing relational DBMS to process the (derived) regular SQL query. By doing so, one can expect to take advantage of the implementation mechanisms of the DBMS to reach acceptable performances.

However, the problem is a bit more complex than that, since the derived query provides a regular (crisp) relation whereas we want to obtain a fuzzy relation, i.e., a relation containing weighted tuples. The computation of the final membership degrees can be performed by the DBMS during the processing of the derived SQL query, if the system allows for the inclusion of external functions in the query. If this is not the case, then the degrees must be computed by means of an external procedural program. We will make this assumption in the following, for the sake of generality.

Fuzzy query processing mainly reduces to a transformation procedure sitting on top of an existing DBMS, according to the architecture depicted in Figure 5.6. The translation mechanism generates a procedural evaluation program written in a host language, including one or more SQL queries obtained by applying the derivation principle to the initial fuzzy query,

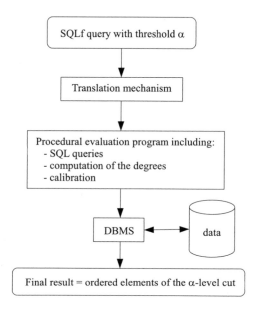

Fig. 5.6   Derivation-based processing strategy

and it also determines the expressions that allow for the computation of the degrees. The resulting program processes the SQL queries, computes the membership degrees, and calibrates the answer if necessary.

5.6.2.2   *Single-block selection–projection–join queries*

The general form of a single-block PSJ query is:

$$\textbf{select}\ ^{*}\ \textbf{from}\ R_1, \ldots, R_n\ \textbf{where}\ fc,$$

where fc is a condition that may involve fuzzy selections and fuzzy joins. Denote by X the set of attributes of $R_1, \ldots, R_n$. Below we show the external program, written in a host language, that can be used to evaluate such a query.

Algorithm 5.1.

declare c **cursor for select** * **from** $R_1, \ldots, R_n$ **where** DNC(fc, $\geq$, α);
open c;
fetch c **into** x;
while code(c) $\neq$ active_set_empty **do**

begin

  compute μ for the current tuple x;

  if $\mu \geq \alpha$ **then** result := result $+ \{\langle \mu/x \rangle\}$;

  fetch c **into** x;

 end;

close c;

Obviously, the test "$\mu \geq \alpha$" can be omitted in case of a strong derivation.

5.6.2.3 *Nested queries*

The evaluation method is based on the use of nested loops. In the case of a nested query, the computation of a final degree implies computation of a set of degrees generated by the inner block. The external program then involves several cursors, one for each level of nesting in the derived query. Since there is an equivalence between a query involving a [*not*] *in* nesting and a query involving a [*not*] *exists* nesting (Bosc and Pivert, 1995b), we only consider this latter case.

"Exists" nesting. The generic query format considered is:

  select * from R **where** fc_R **and exists**

  (**select * from** S **where** $S.B = R.A$ **and** fc_S). $\qquad$ (Q_{ex})

The final degree of a tuple t of relation R, i.e., its degree of membership to the resulting relation *res*, is expressed by:

$$\mu_{res}(t) = min(\mu_{fc_R}(t), \mu_{exists}(SQ(t))$$

where $\mu_{exists}(SQ(t)) = sup_{t' \in S \wedge t'.B=t.A}\mu_{fc_S}(t'))$.

  Since one wants to compute the α-cut of the initial query, one imposes the condition: $\mu_{res}(t) \geq \alpha$, with the two following pruning conditions:

$$\mu_{res}(t) \geq \alpha \Rightarrow \mu_{fc_R}(t) \geq \alpha \Rightarrow DNC(fc_R, \geq, \alpha)(t) \qquad \text{(H1)}$$

and:

$$\mu_{exists}(SQ(t)) \geq \alpha$$

$$\Leftrightarrow sup_{t' \in S \wedge t'.B=t.A \wedge DNC(fc_S,\geq,\alpha)(t')}\mu_{fc_S}(t')) \geq \alpha. \qquad \text{(H2)}$$

If Expression (H1) does not not hold, then computation of $\mu_{exists}(SQ(t)))$, as in Expression (H2), is not necessary. Equivalence (H2) holds because:

(1) $\mu_{exists}(SQ(t)) \geq \alpha \Leftrightarrow sup_{t' \in S \wedge t'.B=t.A \wedge \mu_{fc_S}(t') \geq \alpha}\mu_{fc_S}(t')) \geq \alpha$,

(2) the tuples t' that belong to the set

$$\{t'|t' \in S \wedge t'.B = t.A \wedge DNC(fc_S, \geq, \alpha)(t')\}$$

but not to

$$\{t'|t' \in S \wedge t'.B = t.A \wedge \mu_{fc_S}(t') \geq \alpha)\}$$

are such that $\mu_{fc_S}(t') < \alpha$.

Thus, the computation of $\mu_{exists}(SQ(t))$ only implies the calculation of $\mu_{fc_S}(t')$ for each tuple which belongs to the result of the query derived from the inner block.

The corresponding evaluation algorithm is as follows:

Algorithm 5.2.

```
declare c1 cursor for select * from R where DNC(fcR, ≥, α);
declare c2 cursor for select * from S where S.B = :a and
DNC(fcS, ≥, α);
open c1;
fetch c1 into t; a := t.A;
while code(c1) ≠ active_set_empty do
begin
   μ := fcR(t);
   if μ ≥ α then      /* useful in case of a weak derivation of fcR */
   begin
      open c2;
      fetch c2 into t';    /* t' = first tuple of the derived inner relation */
      μ' := 0;
      while code(c2) ≠ active_set_empty do
      begin
         μ' := max(μ', fcS(t'));   /* computation of the supremum */
         fetch c2 into t';
      end;
      close c2;
      μ := min(μ, μ');    /* computation of the final degree */
      if μ ≥ α then result := result + {⟨μ/t⟩};
end;
fetch c1 into t; a := t.A;
end;
close c1
```

Remark 5.1. Another possible evaluation strategy is based on the equivalence (see Bosc and Pivert, 1995b) between Q_{ex} and the query:

Q': **select** $R.*$ **from** R, S **where** fc_R **and** fc_S **and** $R.A = S.B$.

Then, one can use the evaluation method defined for single-block PSJ queries (see Section 5.6.2.2).

"Not exists" nesting. The generic form of the considered query is:

$$\text{select * from } R \text{ where } fc_R \text{ and not exists}$$
$$(\text{select * from } S \text{ where } S.B = R.A \text{ and } fc_S). \qquad (Q_{nex})$$

The final degree of a tuple t from relation R, i.e., its degree of membership to the resulting relation res, is now expressed by:

$$\mu_{res}(t) = min(\mu_{fc_R}(t), 1 - \mu_{exists}(SQ(t)).$$

Pruning condition H1 is still valid, since $\mu_{res}(t) \geq \alpha \Rightarrow DNC(fc_R, \geq, \alpha)(t)$. However, we have:

$$\mu_{res}(t) \geq \alpha \Rightarrow \mu_{exists}(SQ(t)) \leq 1 - \alpha$$
$$\Rightarrow sup_{t' \in S \wedge t'.B=t.A}\mu_{fc_S}(s) \leq 1 - \alpha,$$

thus we can use the following pruning condition H3:

$$E(t) = \{t'|t' \in S \wedge t'.B = t.A \wedge DSC(fc_S, >, 1 - \alpha)(t')\} \neq \emptyset$$
$$\Rightarrow \mu_{res}(t) < \alpha. \qquad (H3)$$

This condition can be used to detect a failure. However, if $E(t)$ is empty, one has to evaluate the condition: $\mu_{exists}(SQ(r)) \leq 1 - \alpha$, which implies calculation of $\mu_{fc_S}(s)$ for every tuple t' of S such that $t'.B = t.A$. Nevertheless, the scan of S can be stopped as soon as a tuple t' is encountered such that $\mu_{fc_S}(t') > 1 - \alpha$ (we are then in a failure case). This test, which is useful in case of a weak derivation of fc_S, corresponds to pruning condition H4:

$$\exists t' \in S \text{ s.t. } t'.B = t.A \wedge \mu_{fc_S}(t') > 1 - \alpha \Rightarrow \mu_{res}(t) < \alpha. \qquad (H4)$$

Finally, the evaluation algorithm is:

Algorithm 5.3.

declare c1 cursor for select * from R **where** DNC(fc_R, $\geq$, α);
declare c2 cursor for select * from S
      where $S.B$ = :a **and** DSC(fc_S, $>$, $1 - \alpha$);
declare c3 cursor for select * from S **where** $S.B$ = :a;
open c1;
fetch c1 **into** t; $a := t.A$;
while code(c1) $\neq$ active_set_empty **do**
begin
  $\mu := \mu_{fc_R}(t)$;
  if $\mu \geq \alpha$ **then**
  /* useful in case of a weak derivation of fc_R */
  begin
    open c2;
    fetch c2 **into** t';
    if code(c2) = active_set_empty **then**   /* condition H3 */
    begin
      open c3;
      fetch c3 **into** t';
      $\mu' := 0$;
      failure := **false**;
      while code(c3) $\neq$ active_set_empty **and not** failure **do**
      begin
        if $\mu_{fc_S}(t') \leq 1 - \alpha$ **then**
        /* useful in case of a weak derivation of fc_S */
        begin
          $\mu' := \max(\mu', \mu_{fc_S}(t'))$;   /* computation of the supremum */
          fetch c3 **into** t';
        end
        else failure := **true**;   /* condition H4 */
      end;
      close c3;
      if not failure **then**
      begin
        $\mu := \min(\mu, 1 - \mu')$;   /* computation of the final degree */
        result := result + $\{\langle \mu/t \rangle\}$;
      end

```
      end;
        close c2;
      end;
    fetch c1 into t; a := t.A;
  end;
close c1;
```

It is important to note that pruning condition H3 is useful only if the evaluation of the associated derived query (cf. the declaration of cursor c2) does not entail the scanning of relation S exhaustively. Otherwise, this condition must be removed from the algorithm in order to avoid scanning relation S twice (then, only two cursors are necessary, i.e., c1 and c3, and pruning condition H4 becomes more important).

Remark 5.2. In the presence of a *not exists* nesting, an evaluation method based on rewriting cannot be applied, since there is no equivalence between such a nested query and a single-block query.

5.6.2.4 *Efficiency of the derivation-based processing strategy*

Single-block PSJ queries. Depending on the connectors used in the initial SQLf query, the Boolean query obtained may deliver the exact α-cut or a superset (in which case extra elements must be removed, which implies an additional test on the degree). The proportion of additional tuples (which may be seen as an index of efficiency) is examined in Bosc and Pivert (1995a). It appears that this ratio is in general much less than 20% when two fuzzy predicates are aggregated by a mean operator, for instance, but it can reach 70% when four predicates are combined.

It is important to note that the derivation principle can also be used when the user does not specify a threshold α in the query. The derivation method is then applied with the threshold condition $\alpha > 0$, which allows the tuples which do not satisfy the query at all to be discarded. Of course, this is also true for nested queries.

Regarding this evaluation process, three types of single-block queries can be distinguished, according to the kind of derivation rules that can be used:

- exact derivation: queries involving predicates acting on single attributes and usual connectives (conjunction and disjunction interpreted respectively as *min* and *max*);

- weak derivation: queries involving mean operators; queries involving norms, co-norms other than *min* and *max*; queries involving at least one predicate that cannot be exactly derived;
- queries for which no derivation rules apply: in this case, the derivation method is useless. Alternative methods (specific algorithms) must be applied (see Chapters 6, 7, and 8).

Nested queries. In case of a weak derivation of the outer block, one can prevent useless evaluations of the inner block, thanks to the calibration performed at the outer level.

If the nesting operator is not negated, one can apply the derivation principle to the inner block, and the calibration operation can also be distributed onto the result of the inner derived query. This is especially interesting in the case of several levels of nesting.

If the nesting operator is negated, derivation of the inner block is not sufficient to allow for the computation of the final degrees. The derived query can only be used as a pruning condition to detect a failure case. In this case, even if the derivation of the inner query is exact, the evaluation method will not, in general, be as efficient as in the previous case.

5.7   Conclusion

In this chapter, we have presented the basic features of SQLf, an extension of SQL which makes it possible to express fuzzy queries to a classical relational database. The principle underlying this extension is to authorize fuzzy operators wherever it makes sense, while preserving, as much as possible, the syntactic and semantic characteristics of SQL (in particular when it comes to query equivalences). Even though SQLf is not the only language that has been proposed for database fuzzy querying (other proposals such as FSQL (Galindo *et al.*, 1998) and FQUERY for Access (Kacprzyk and Zadrożny, 1995) can be found in the literature), it constitutes the most complete fuzzy extension of SQL. It is also appropriate to mention that in SQLf, the satisfaction degrees are somewhat "transparent" to the user (who can only act on them through a global threshold), contrary to the case with FSQL, for instance, where the user may express conditions on the local degrees tied to atomic selection predicates, which, in our opinion, somewhat contradicts the philosophy of fuzzy sets and can make the semantics of a query difficult to grasp.

It is important to emphasize that the added value, in terms of expressivity, comes at a cost in terms of query elicitation: a flexible querying system implementing a language such as SQLf must include an appropriate interface through which the user can define fuzzy predicates and operators in a convenient way. We have seen that different philosophies can be considered for defining such interfaces.

An important fact, however, is that the price to pay in terms of query processing complexity remains limited (at least for the simple queries considered in this chapter), thanks in particular to a processing strategy (derivation) which takes advantage of the connections between properties tied to fuzzy conditions and Boolean ones, and makes it possible to exploit the capabilities of regular DBMSs for processing fuzzy queries.

Chapter 6

Fuzzy Queries Involving Quantified Statements or Aggregates

6.1 Introduction

In this chapter, we consider fuzzy queries of a more complex type than those studied in the previous chapter. More precisely, we focus on SQLf queries involving fuzzy quantified statements or aggregates applying to a fuzzy relation.

There are several ways to make use of fuzzy quantifiers in SQLf queries. First, they may appear inside a *where* clause in order to combine predicates in a less demanding way than can be expressed by a conjunction. An example is "find the employees who satisfy *most* of the properties among {to be young, to be well-paid, to have a high commission, to have a highly qualified job}". Second, fuzzy quantifiers generalize the quantifiers *all* and *any*, which are the only ones authorized in SQL, so they can be used as extended nesting operators. Third, they may appear in a *having* clause in order to qualify groups based on their compliance with a gradual cardinality-based condition. An example is "find the departments where *at least half* of the employees earn more than $3,000 a month". SQLf queries involving fuzzy quantified statements of the form "$Q\,X$ are A" (see Section 3.7) are studied in Section 6.2.

Note that a fuzzy quantified statement is just a special case of a condition matching an aggregate (namely *count*) to a fuzzy predicate. However, since much research work has been devoted to this particular case, and also because of its peculiarities, we believe fuzzy quantified statements deserve a specific section. As for other types of aggregates applying to a fuzzy relation, the corresponding generic query is of the form:

select X **from** r **where** *cond*
group by Y **having** $\{agg_1 \; \theta \; agg_2 \mid agg$ **is** $\psi\}$,

where $X \subseteq Y$, agg_1, agg_2, and agg denote aggregates, and both *cond* and ψ are fuzzy conditions. In other words, it is possible in SQLf to select a group by means of a condition which compares two aggregates or matches an aggregate to a fuzzy predicate, even in the situation where the underlying relation is fuzzy (because of condition *cond*). An α-cut-based interpretation of such queries is provided in Section 6.3.

6.2 Quantified Statements

6.2.1 *Introduction*

In this section, we are interested in introducing fuzzy quantifiers (Zadeh, 1983; see also Section 3.7) into SQLf queries. Such quantifiers can be used to express an intermediary attitude between conjunction ("all of the criteria must be satisfied") and disjunction ("at least one criterion must be satisfied"). They model linguistic expressions such as, "most of", "about a third", and are notably used to construct fuzzy predicates (with quantifications). For instance, the fuzzy quantifier "most of" can be used to define the quantified statement "most of the elements of set X satisfy criterion A". There are two types of quantified statements: those of the form "$Q \, X$ are A" ("most of the elements of X satisfy A") and those of the form "$Q \, X \, B$ are A" ("most of the elements of set X which satisfy B also satisfy A"). In the following, we only consider the first type, since the second one raises serious interpretation issues (in particular, in its way of dealing with situations where no — or almost no — element from X is B).

In this section, we show that the interpretation of fuzzy quantified statements can be based on Sugeno's or Choquet's integral. First, we present fuzzy quantifications and their connection with fuzzy integral theory. Then, we recall different propositions, respectively by Zadeh (1983), Prade (1990) and Yager (1988) for interpreting fuzzy quantifications. Since the use of the OWA operator in Yager (1988) is limited to the computation of increasing quantifications, we show how to extend its use to decreasing quantifications. We also show that the approaches advocated in Prade (1990) and in Yager (1988), when restricted to monotonous quantifiers, lead to the computation of fuzzy integrals.

6.2.2 Quantified statements and fuzzy integral theory

6.2.2.1 Introduction

Fuzzy quantifiers can be increasing (proportional) (Yager, 1988), which means that if the criteria are all entirely satisfied, then the statement "$Q\,X$ are A" is entirely true, whereas if the criteria are all entirely unsatisfied, then the statement "$Q\,X$ are A" is entirely false. Moreover, the transition between those two extremes is continuous and monotonous. Therefore, when Q is increasing (e.g., "most", "at least a half"), function μ_Q is increasing. Similarly, decreasing quantifiers (e.g., "at most two", "at most a half") are defined by decreasing functions. Zadeh (1983) distinguishes between absolute and relative quantifiers. Absolute quantifiers refer to a number while relative ones refer to a proportion. An example of an increasing relative quantifier is "at least half", while "at most three" illustrates the notion of a decreasing absolute quantifier.

An absolute quantifier is represented by a function μ_Q from an integer range to [0, 1] whereas a relative quantifier is a mapping μ_Q from [0, 1] to [0, 1]. In both cases, the value $\mu_Q(j)$ is defined as the truth value of the statement "$Q\,X$ are A" when exactly j elements from X fully satisfy A (where it is assumed that A is fully unsatisfied for the other elements). Here, we deal with absolute quantifiers, but the results are still valid for relative quantifiers, it is just necessary to turn every $\mu_Q(x)$ into $\mu_Q(x/n)$ in every formula, n being the cardinality of the crisp set X. The characteristics of monotonous fuzzy quantifiers are given in Table 6.1. Figure 6.1 gives examples of monotonous decreasing and increasing quantifiers. Calculating the truth degree of the statement "$Q\,X$ are A" raises the problem of determining the cardinality of the set of elements from X which satisfy A. If A is a Boolean predicate, this cardinality is a precise integer (k), and then the truth value of "$Q\,X$ are A" is $\mu_Q(k)$. If A is a fuzzy predicate, this cardinality cannot be established precisely, and computing the quantification corresponds to establishing the value of function μ_Q for an imprecise argument.

Table 6.1   Characteristics of monotonous fuzzy quantifiers

Increasing quantifier	Decreasing quantifier
$\mu_Q(0) = 0$	$\mu_Q(0) = 1$
$\exists k$ such that $\mu_Q(k) = 1$	$\exists k$ such that $\mu_Q(k) = 0$
$\forall a,\ b$, if $a > b$ then $\mu_Q(a) \geq \mu_Q(b)$	$\forall a,\ b$, if $a > b$ then $\mu_Q(a) \leq \mu_Q(b)$

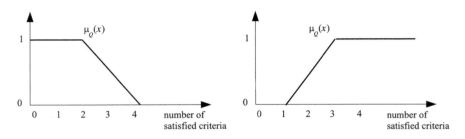

Fig. 6.1   Quantifier "at most 2" (left) and "at least 3" (right)

Table 6.2   A set of employees

#emp	#dep	salary
e_1	d_1	3,800
e_2	d_1	5,500
e_3	d_1	4,600
e_4	d_1	3,200
e_5	d_1	4,800

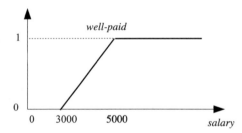

Fig. 6.2   The fuzzy predicate "well-paid"

Example 6.1. Let Q be the fuzzy quantifier "at least three" represented in Figure 6.1. Let X be the crisp set made up of the five employees from Table 6.2, and let A be the fuzzy predicate "well-paid" described by the fuzzy set from Figure 6.2. The satisfaction degrees related to the fuzzy predicate "well-paid" are given by the fuzzy set $\{0.4/e_1, 1/e_2, 0.8/e_3, 0.1/e_4, 0.9/e_5\}$. If we want to evaluate the quantification "at least three employees are well-paid", we face the problem of determining the value $\mu_Q(N)$, N being the number of well-paid employees. We can observe that the three largest satisfaction degrees are 1, 0.9 and 0.8, the others being 0.4 and 0.1. In this example, we can then consider that value N is "close to 3";

consequently, the evaluation of the statement "at least three employees are well-paid" should be close to 1 (since $\mu_Q(3)$ equals 1). This example illustrates the need to compute the value of μ_Q when the number of satisfied criteria is not perfectly known, i.e., when the set gathering the elements which satisfy A is fuzzy.◇

6.2.2.2 *Fuzzy integrals and increasing quantifiers*

In this subsection, we show that, given a measure defined on a regular set, both the Sugeno and Choquet fuzzy integrals (see Section 3.5) are tools enabling calculation of the value of the measure when its argument is a fuzzy set. Thus, if an increasing quantifier Q is defined as a measure, one has available a method for defining the truth value of the statement "$Q\,X$ are A".

Let $\mathcal{P}(X)$ denote the power set of $X = \{x_1, x_2, \ldots, x_n\}$. Recall that a fuzzy measure (Sugeno, 1974) on a finite, discrete regular set X is a function g from $\mathcal{P}(X)$ to the unit interval which satisfies the following three axioms:

(1) $g(X) = 1$,
(2) $g(\emptyset) = 0$,
(3) $\forall A,\ B$ such that $A \subseteq B$, $g(A) \leq g(B)$ (monotonicity).

Both the Sugeno (1974) and Choquet (see Murofushi and Sugeno, 1989) fuzzy integrals, respectively denoted by S_g and C_g in the following, define a characteristic of a function h (from a universe X to the unit interval) according to the measure g. Both are averaging operators over the values taken by h. Using the notation $h(x_i) = h_i$, and ordering the h_i's in an increasing way ($h_1 \leq h_2 \leq \cdots \leq h_n$), we have:

$$C_g(h) = \sum_{i=1}^{n} h_i \times (g(F_i) - g(F_{i+1})),$$

$$S_g(h) = sup_i\ min(h_i,\ g(F_i)),$$

where $F_i = \{x_i, x_{i+1}, \ldots, x_n\}$ and $F_{n+1} = \emptyset$. Moreover, $S_g(h)$ is a median (Kandel and Byatt, 1978), i.e., it delivers the nth element of an ordered list of $2n - 1$ elements. Consequently:

$$S_g(h) = sup_i min(h_i, g(F_i)) = med(h_1, h_2, \ldots, h_n, g(F_2), g(F_3), \ldots, g(F_n)).$$

In the following, we assume that the function h is a membership function of a fuzzy set denoted by H. Therefore a fuzzy integral can be viewed as a function defined on fuzzy sets.

Example 6.2. Consider a set X of five elements and a measure g such that $g(F) = |F|/5$, where $|F|$ denotes the usual cardinality of a crisp set F. If $h_1 = 0.1$, $h_2 = 0.4$, $h_3 = 0.8$, $h_4 = 0.9$, $h_5 = 1$, we obtain:

$$C_g(h) = 0.1 \times (1 - 4/5) + 0.4 \times (4/5 - 3/5) + 0.8 \times (3/5 - 2/5)$$
$$+ 0.9 \times (2/5 - 1/5) + 1 \times (1/5 - 0) = 0.64,$$
$$S_g(h) = sup(min(0.1, 1), min(0.4, 4/5), min(0.8, 3/5),$$
$$min(0.9, 2/5), min(1, 1/5)) = 0.6,$$

$$med(0.1, 1/5, 0.4, 2/5, 3/5, 0.8, 4/5, 0.9, 1) = 3/5 = 0.6.\diamond$$

If h and h' are the membership functions of two fuzzy sets H and H', both fuzzy integrals $C_g(h)$ and $S_g(h)$ satisfy the following properties (see Sugeno, 1974) (replacing I by C or S):

- if g is a fuzzy measure and H is a regular set, then $I_g(h) = g(H)$,
- if H and H' are such that $H' \subseteq H (\forall x, h'(x) \leq h(x))$ then, for any fuzzy measure g: $I_g(h') \leq I_g(h)$.

These properties show that g and C_g (resp. g and S_g) are identical when H is a regular set and that C_g (resp. S_g) complies with the property of monotonicity. We can therefore consider $C_g(h)$ and $S_g(h)$ as two possible values of g for the fuzzy set H (Grabisch *et al.*, 1992).

The definition of an increasing quantifier Q as a fuzzy measure g requires the definition of an underlying universe F:

$$g : \mathcal{P}(F) \to [0, 1] \text{ such that } g(E) = \mu_Q(|E|). \tag{6.1}$$

Since we need $g(F) = 1$, this definition requires:

$$\mu_Q(|F|) = 1. \tag{6.2}$$

When one wants to evaluate "$Q\,X$ are A", the satisfaction of Expression 6.2 entails taking F either as X (Q is increasing relative, or increasing absolute, and $\mu_Q(|X|) = 1$), or as X plus dummy elements which do not satisfy A at all (when $\mu_Q(|X|) < 1$). The dummy elements are added so that $\mu_Q(|F|)$ reaches 1, but of course they do not influence the evaluation of "$Q\,X$ are A" (for any dummy element z, $\mu_A(z) = 0$). By doing so, the meaning of "$Q\,X$ are A" is not altered.

Let E_A denote the set of elements from X satisfying predicate A. The set E_A is a (possibly fuzzy) subset of X and then of F. When E_A is a crisp set — the satisfaction degrees equal 0 or 1 — the truth value of

"$Q\,X$ are A" is $g(E_A) = \mu_Q(|E_A|)$. In the general case, E_A is a fuzzy set and the evaluation of "$Q\,X$ are A" requires the computation of g for the fuzzy set E_A, given by $C_g(E_A)$ or $S_g(E_A)$. Denoting by k the cardinality of universe F, these values are given by the following formulas, assuming that we order the membership degrees related to E_A increasingly:

$$C_g(E_A) = \sum_{i=1}^{k} \mu_{E_A}(x_i) \times (g(F_i) - g(F_{i+1}))$$

$$= \sum_{i=1}^{k} \mu_{E_A}(x_i) \times (\mu_Q(k - i + 1) - \mu_Q(k - i)),$$

$$S_g(E_A) = \sup_i \, min(\mu_{E_A}(x_i), g(F_i)),$$

where $F_i = \{x_i, x_{i+1}, \ldots, x_k\}$, $F_{k+1} = \emptyset$, and $\mu_{E_A}(x_1) \leq \mu_{E_A}(x_2) \leq \cdots \leq \mu_{E_A}(x_k)$.

It is important to note that, if $\mu_Q(n) \neq 1$, $(k - n)$ dummy elements have been added to X in order to build F.

Example 6.3. The quantifier "at least three", illustrated in Figure 6.1, may be represented using the measure g such that:

$$g(E) = \begin{cases} 0 \text{ if } |E| \leq 1, \\ 0.5 \text{ if } |E| = 2, \\ 1 \text{ if } |E| \geq 3. \end{cases}$$

Consider the quantified statement "at least three employees are well-paid" and the data from Example 6.1. The cardinality of X equals 5 and $\mu_Q(|X|) = 1$, therefore F is taken as X. After an appropriate ordering of the elements ($x_1 = e_4$, $x_2 = e_1$, $x_3 = e_3$, $x_4 = e_5$, $x_5 = e_2$), the satisfaction degrees are the following:

$$\mu_{E_A}(x_1) = 0.1, \mu_{E_A}(x_2) = 0.4, \mu_{E_A}(x_3) = 0.8, \mu_{E_A}(x_4) = 0.9, \mu_{E_A}(x_5) = 1.$$

The truth value of the quantified statement "at least three employees are well-paid" is given either by $C_g(E_A)$ or $S_g(E_A)$ (with $F_i = \{x_i, \ldots, x_5\}$ and $F_6 = \emptyset$):

$$C_g(E_A) = \sum_{i=1}^{5} \mu_{E_A}(x_i) \times (g(F_i) - g(F_{i+1}))$$

$$= \sum_{i=1}^{5} \mu_{E_A}(x_i) \times (\mu_Q(5 - i + 1) - \mu_Q(5 - i))$$

$$= (0.1 \times 0) + (0.4 \times 0) + (0.8 \times 0.5) + (0.9 \times 0.5) + (1 \times 0)$$

$$= 0.85,$$

$$S_g(E_A) = sup_i \, min(\mu_{E_A}(x_i), g(F_i)) = sup_i \, min(\mu_{E_A}(x_i), \mu_Q(|F_i|))$$

$$= sup_i \, min(\mu_{E_A}(x_i), \mu_Q(6 - i)) = 0.8.$$

These results confirm our intuition, which says that they should be "close to 1". We have considered the case where no dummy elements have been added, because the cardinality of X was 5 and $\mu_Q(5) = 1$. We now examine the case of the set $X = \{e_1, e_2\}$, where e_1 and e_2 are taken from the previous example. The fuzzy set of well-paid employees now becomes $\{0.4/e_1, 1/e_2\}$. In this case, the cardinality of X is not sufficient to represent μ_Q as a fuzzy measure g, since $g(|X|) = \mu_Q(2)$ is different from 1. This means that we need to add one dummy element e_3 that satisfies $\mu_A(e_3) = 0$. We can now take $F = \{e_1, e_2, e_3\}$ as the referential. After an appropriate ordering of the elements ($x_1 = e_3$, $x_2 = e_1$, $x_3 = e_2$), the satisfaction degrees are the following:

$$\mu_{E_A}(x_1) = 0, \quad \mu_{E_A}(x_2) = 0.4, \quad \mu_{E_A}(x_3) = 1.$$

The evaluation of the quantification is then given either by $C_g(E_A)$ or $S_g(E_A)$ (with $F_i = \{x_i, \ldots, x_3\}$ and $F_4 = \emptyset$):

$$C_g(E_A) = \sum_{i=1}^{3} \mu_{E_A}(x_i) \times (g(F_i) - g(F_{i+1}))$$

$$= \sum_{i=1}^{5} \mu_{E_A}(x_i) \times (\mu_Q(3 - i + 1) - \mu_Q(3 - i))$$

$$= (0 \times 0.5) + (0.4 \times 0.5) + (1 \times 0)$$

$$= 0.2,$$

$$S_g(E_A) = sup_i \, min(\mu_{E_A}(x_i), g(F_i))$$

$$= sup_i \, min(\mu_{E_A}(x_i), \mu_Q(|F_i|))$$

$$= sup_i \, min(\mu_{E_A}(x_i), \mu_Q(4 - i)) = 0.4.\diamond$$

6.2.3   *Interpretation of statements of the type "Q X are A"*

We now present different proposals from the literature for interpreting quantified statements of the type "$Q\,X$ are A", and we show that these approaches have strong connections with the Sugeno and Choquet fuzzy integrals when the quantifier is monotonous.

6.2.3.1 *Interpretation according to Zadeh*

Let X be the usual (crisp) set $\{x_1, x_2, \ldots, x_n\}$. Zadeh (1983) defines the cardinality of the set of elements of X which satisfy A, denoted by $\Sigma count(A)$, as:

$$\Sigma count(A) = \sum_{i=1}^{n} \mu_A(x_i).$$

The quantification "$Q\ X$ are A" is then evaluated by $\mu_Q(\Sigma count(A))$. It can be seen, however, that a large number of elements with a small degree $\mu_A(x)$ has the same effect as a small number of elements with a high degree $\mu_A(x)$, due to the definition of $\Sigma count$.

Example 6.4. Consider the following sets:

$$X_1 = \{0.9/x_1, 0.9/x_2, 0.9/x_3, 0.8/x_4, 0.8/x_5, 0.7/x_6, 0.6/x_7\},$$

$$X_2 = \{1/x_1, 1/x_2, 0.3/x_3, 0.2/x_4, 0.1/x_5, 0/x_6, 0/x_7\},$$

$$X_3 = \{1/x_1, 1/x_2, 1/x_3, 1/x_4, 1/x_5, 0.8/x_6, 0.3/x_7\}$$

and the quantifier "at least five" represented in Figure 6.3. The $\Sigma count(A)$ values associated with the sets X_1, X_2, and X_3 are 5.6, 2.6, and 6.1 respectively. The associated values of the quantification are 1, 0.2, and 1 respectively.◇

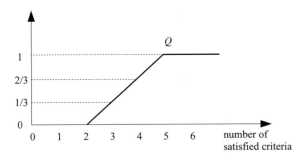

Fig. 6.3   The fuzzy quantifier "at least five"

6.2.3.2   *Interpretation according to Prade*

In Prade (1990), it is assumed that the elements from set X may be imprecise, but here we only consider the case where the elements of set X are
precisely known. The method proposed in Prade (1990) involves two steps:

(1) computation of the fuzzy cardinality π of the set E_A (gathering the
elements which satisfy A),
(2) evaluation of a degree of matching between this fuzzy cardinality π and
the quantifier Q viewed as a fuzzy predicate.

This matching degree corresponds to the truth value of the quantification.
Since E_A is a fuzzy set, its cardinality can be represented as a possibility
distribution π (Dubois and Prade, 1985a). This possibility distribution is
built from the number k of entirely satisfied criteria (possibly equal to 0)
according to the following definition:

$$\forall\, i < k, \ \pi(i) = 0,$$

$$\pi(k) = 1,$$

$$\forall\, j > k, \ \pi(j) \text{ is the } j\text{th largest value } \mu_A(x).$$

Note that the restriction of π to values greater or equal to k is decreasing.

    The second step of the process performs a fuzzy pattern matching
(Cayrol *et al.*, 1980; Dubois *et al.*, 1988) between the possibility distribution π obtained in the first step and the quantifier viewed as a predicate.
Consequently, it computes a pair of degrees: Π, the extent to which π possibly satisfies Q, and N, the extent to which π necessarily (certainly) satisfies
Q, according to the formulas:

$$\Pi = max_{u\,\geq\,k}\ min(\mu_Q(u),\ \pi(u)),$$

$$N = min_{u\,\geq\,k}\ max(\mu_Q(u),\ 1 - \pi(u)).$$

We can conclude that the truth value of the statement "$Q\ X$ are A" is
situated in the interval $[N,\ \Pi]$.

Example 6.5. Consider the sets X_1, X_2, X_3, and the quantifier "at least
five" from Example 6.4. Taking set X_3 first, we obtain the following possibility distribution for its imprecise cardinality:

$$\pi = 1/5 + 0.8/6 + 0.3/7.$$

The formulas above yield $\Pi = 1$ and $N = 1$, and we can therefore say that X_3 satisfies "at least five elements are A" with a degree of 1. Similar computations for X_1 and X_2 yield the intervals $[0, 0.8]$ and $[0, 0.3]$ respectively.◇

We now show that when Q is increasing (resp. decreasing), the quantified statement "QX are A" only requires the computation of π (resp. N), which is a Sugeno integral.

If Q is increasing, we can write that N equals $\mu_Q(k)$, k being the number of entirely satisfied criteria, since when $i > j \geq k$, $max(\mu_Q(i), 1 - \pi(i)) \geq max(\mu_Q(j), 1 - \pi(j))$. Indeed, since Q is increasing,

$$i > j \geq k \Rightarrow \mu_Q(i) \geq \mu_Q(j),$$

and since π is decreasing,

$$i > j \geq k \Rightarrow 1 - \pi(i) \geq 1 - \pi(j).$$

Thus, $N = min_{k \leq i} max(\mu_Q(i), 1 - \pi(i)) = \mu_Q(k)$. Hence, N is the truth value of the quantification if we consider only the entirely satisfied criteria. Q being an increasing quantifier, when the other criteria are taken into account, this truth value can only increase. The useful information is supplied by Π, whose value takes into account all of the $\mu_A(x)$'s. It has been shown in Prade (1990) and Yager (1984, 1991b) that, when Q is increasing, Π is given by the Sugeno fuzzy integral $S_g(E_A)$ (using the notation introduced in Section 6.2.2.2).

Similarly, when Q is decreasing, Π equals $\mu_Q(k)$, where k is the number of entirely satisfied criteria. When all the criteria are taken into account, the only changes affect N, which is still associated with a Sugeno integral, as follows:

$$N = min_{k \leq u} max(\mu_Q(u), 1 - \pi(u))$$

$$= 1 - max_{k \leq u} min(1 - \mu_Q(u), \pi(u)).$$

Defining g' as: $\forall E$, $g'(E) = 1 - \mu_Q(|E|)$, we obtain:

$$N = 1 - S_{g'}(E_A).$$

6.2.3.3   *Yager's competitive type aggregation*

The interpretation by decomposition described in Yager (1984) is limited to *increasing* quantifiers. The proposition "$Q\,X$ are A" is true if an ordinary subset C of X satisfies the conditions c_1 and c_2 given as

c_1: there are Q elements in C,
c_2: each element x of C satisfies A.

We emphasize that finding one such subset is sufficient, since the quantifier is increasing. The truth value of the proposition: "QX are A" is then defined as:

$$\mu(X) = sup_{C \subseteq X} \, min(\mu_{c_1}(C), \, \mu_{c_2}(C))$$

with

$$\mu_{c_1}(C) = \mu_Q(|C|)$$

and

$$\mu_{c_2}(C) = inf_{x \in C} \, \mu_A(x).$$

It has been shown in Yager (1984) that:

$$\mu(X) = sup_{1 \le i \le n} \, min(\mu_Q(i), \, \mu_A(x_i)), \tag{6.3}$$

where the elements of X are ordered in such a way that $\mu_A(x_1) \ge \cdots \ge \mu_A(x_n)$. As can be seen, Expression (6.3) corresponds to a Sugeno integral (see Sections 3.5.3, 3.7, and 6.2.2.2).

6.2.3.4 *Interpretation based on the OWA operator*

Yager (1988) considers the case of an increasing monotonous quantifier, and proposes an ordered weighted averaging operator (OWA) to evaluate quantifications of the type "QX are A". We first present this approach, then we show how it can be extended in order to evaluate decreasing quantifications (Bosc *et al.*, 1995). Finally, we show that this method boils down to using a Choquet fuzzy integral.

Case of an increasing quantifier. The OWA operator is defined in Yager (1988) as:

$$OWA(x_1, \ldots, x_n; w_1, \ldots, w_n) = \sum_{i=1}^{n} w_i \times x_{k_i}$$

where x_{k_i} is the ith largest value among the x_k's and $\sum_{i=1}^{n} w_i = 1$.

Let n be the crisp cardinality of X. The truth value of the statement "QX are A" is computed by an OWA of the n values $\mu_A(x_i)$. The weights w_i

involved in the calculation of the OWA are given by $w_i = \mu_Q(i) - \mu_Q(i-1)$. A value w_i corresponds to the increase in satisfaction when one moves from a situation where exactly $(i-1)$ elements totally satisfy A to a situation where exactly i elements totally satisfy A (assuming that the other elements do not satisfy A at all). The aggregated value which is calculated is:

$$OWA(\mu_A(x_1), \mu_A(x_2), \ldots, \mu_A(x_n); w_1, \ldots, w_n) = \sum_{i=1}^{n} w_i \times c_i$$

where c_i is the ith largest value among the $\mu_A(x_k)$'s.

Example 6.6. Consider the sets X_1, X_2, and X_3, and the quantifier "at least five" from Example 6.4. We have:

$$w_1 = 0, \ w_2 = 0, \ w_3 = 1/3, \ w_4 = 1/3, \ w_5 = 1/3, \ w_6 = 0, \ w_7 = 0.$$

We evaluate the statement "at least five elements of X_1 are A" and we obtain the degree 0.83 ($= 0.9 \times 1/3 + 0.8 \times 1/3 + 0.8 \times 1/3$). In the same way, we obtain the degrees 0.2 for X_2 and 1 for X_3.◇

Extension to a decreasing quantifier. We now describe a method for computing the truth value of a statement "$Q\ X$ are A" involving a decreasing quantifier Q by means of an OWA. We first give an introductory example which presents the interpretation of this type of quantification. Then, we point out the need to distinguish between statements involving a relative quantifier and those involving an absolute one. Finally, we show that computing the truth value of a statement "$Q\ X$ are A" when Q is decreasing boils down to computing a value $(1-\alpha)$, α being the truth value (computed by an OWA) of the quantified statement "$Q'\ X$ are $\neg A$", where Q' is another representation — defined on the proportion of unsatisfied criteria — of quantifier Q.

Consider the set $X = \{x_1, x_2, x_3, x_4\}$. Consider also the relative decreasing monotonous quantifier Q_1 and the quantifier Q'_1 defined by $\mu_{Q'_1}(x) = \mu_{Q_1}(1-x)$ (see Figure 6.4). The objective is to compute the truth value of the relative decreasing quantification "$Q_1\ X$ are A". If, among the four elements of X, there is one which totally satisfies A while the three remaining elements do not satisfy A at all, then the quantification is satisfied with a degree equal to $\mu_{Q_1}(1/4)$. Now, by definition, $\mu_{Q_1}(1/4) = \mu_{Q'_1}(3/4)$, and 3/4 is the proportion of criteria which are not satisfied. By extension, evaluating "$Q_1\ X$ are A" boils down to evaluating the relative increasing quantification "$Q'_1\ X$ are $\neg A$". This can be done, for

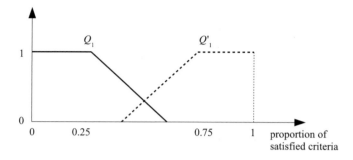

Fig. 6.4   Two related fuzzy quantifiers

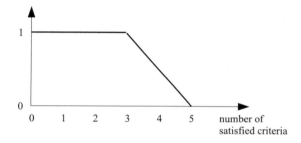

Fig. 6.5   The decreasing absolute quantifier "no more than three"

instance, using the OWA-based approach described above, replacing the satisfaction degrees $\mu_A(x_i)$ by the refutation degrees $(1 - \mu_A(x_i))$. Note, however, that interpretations other than the OWA-based one could be used too.

The generalization of this method to the case of an absolute quantification leads to the consideration of the particular situation illustrated by the following example. Consider the absolute decreasing quantifier "no more than three" from Figure 6.5. Consider the quantifier Q_2' — defined on the number of unsatisfied criteria — such that $\forall x$, $\mu_{Q_2'}(x) = \mu_{Q_2}(n - x)$, n being the cardinality of X. If n is greater than or equal to 5, then Q_2' is increasing monotonous and it is possible to evaluate "$Q_2\ X$ are A" by an OWA aggregating the refutation degrees. If n is smaller than 5, then Q_2' is not monotonous increasing — since $\mu_{Q_2'}(0) \neq 0$ — and it is therefore a special case. Note that this problem does not arise for *relative* quantifiers. This is why, in the following, we distinguish between *relative* decreasing and *absolute* decreasing monotonous quantifiers.

Decreasing relative quantifier. Let Q_{rd} be a decreasing relative quantifier and n the cardinality of X. One has:

$$\mu_{Q'_{rd}}\left(\frac{i}{n}\right) = \mu_{Q_{rd}}\left(1 - \frac{i}{n}\right).$$

Consequently, one can express the truth value of the decreasing relative quantification as the OWA aggregation of the refutation degrees $(1-\mu_A(x_i))$ with $w_i = \mu_{Q_{rd}}(1-\frac{i}{n}) - \mu_{Q_{rd}}(1-\frac{i-1}{n})$. Again, note that interpretations other than the OWA-based one (for instance, that relying on the competitive type aggregation presented in Section 6.2.3.3) could be used.

Example 6.7. Consider the decreasing relative quantifier "no more than a quarter" represented in Figure 6.6. Consider the following sets:

$$X_1 = \{0.6/x_1,\ 0.5/x_2,\ 0.4/x_3,\ 0.4/x_4,\ 0.3/x_5\},$$

$$X_2 = \{1/x_1,\ 0.1/x_2,\ 0.1/x_3,\ 0/x_4,\ 0/x_5\},$$

$$X_3 = \{0.9/x_1,\ 0/x_2,\ 0/x_3,\ 0/x_4,\ 0/x_5\}.$$

It is assumed that X_1 (resp. X_2, X_3) is a fuzzy subset which describes the elements of a crisp set $X = \{x_1,\ x_2,\ x_3,\ x_4,\ x_5\}$ which are A_1 (resp. A_2, A_3). Since the cardinality n of X equals 5, we get:

$$w_1 = \mu_{Q_1}(4/5) - \mu_{Q_1}(1) = 0, \qquad w_2 = \mu_{Q_1}(3/5) - \mu_{Q_1}(4/5) = 0,$$

$$w_3 = \mu_{Q_1}(2/5) - \mu_{Q_1}(3/5) = 0.4, \quad w_4 = \mu_{Q_1}(1/5) - \mu_{Q_1}(2/5) = 0.6,$$

$$w_5 = \mu_{Q_1}(0) - \mu_{Q_1}(1/5) = 0.$$

The OWA-based aggregation of the refutation degrees yields the truth value $0.54 (= 0.4 \times 0.6 + 0.6 \times 0.5)$ (resp. 0.9, 1) for the quantified statement "$Q_1 X$ are A_1" (resp. A_2, A_3).◊

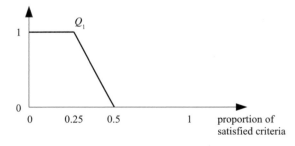

Fig. 6.6 The decreasing relative quantifier "no more than a quarter"

Decreasing absolute quantifier. We consider a decreasing absolute quantifier Q_{da} and we denote by m the smallest integer such that $\mu_{Q_{da}}(m) = 0$. First, we consider the case where the cardinality of X is smaller than m. A solution is to add $(m - n)$ dummy elements — which do not satisfy A at all — to X. By doing so, one can evaluate the absolute decreasing quantification as the OWA-based aggregation of the m degrees attached to the elements of X (completed).

Now we denote by n the cardinality ($\geq m$) of set X (possibly supplemented by dummy elements). In a context where $\forall i$, $\mu_A(x_i) \in \{0, 1\}$, $\mu_{Q_{da}}(n-i)$ is the degree of satisfaction attached to the quantification when there are $(n - i)$ totally satisfied criteria or, reciprocally, when there are i totally unsatisfied criteria. For the same reason, $\mu_{Q_{da}}(n - i + 1)$ is the degree of satisfaction in the case where there are $(i - 1)$ totally unsatisfied criteria. Thus, we can conclude that:

$$w_i = \mu_{Q_{da}}(n - i) - \mu_{Q_{da}}(n - i + 1)$$

is the increase in the satisfaction degree when one moves from a situation where $(i - 1)$ criteria are totally unsatisfied to a situation where i criteria are totally unsatisfied. In the general context where $\forall i$, $\mu_A(x_i) \in [0, 1]$, the truth value of a decreasing absolute quantification is therefore the OWA-based aggregation of the refutation degrees $(1 - \mu_A(x_i))$, using the weights w_i defined in the above expression. As in the case of decreasing relative quantifiers, approaches other than that based on OWA aggregation could be used to interpret the reformulated quantified statement.

Example 6.8. Consider the quantifier "no more than three" represented in Figure 6.5 (such that $m = 5$) and the following fuzzy sets:

$$X_1 = \{0.7/x_1, \ 0.8/x_2\},$$

$$X_2 = \{1/x_1, \ 1/x_2, \ 1/x_3, \ 0.1/x_4\},$$

$$X_3 = \{1/x_1, \ 1/x_2, \ 1/x_3, \ 0.7/x_4, \ 0.1/x_5\}.$$

We compute:

$$w_1 = \mu_{Q_2}(4) - \mu_{Q_2}(5) = 0.5, \qquad w_2 = \mu_{Q_2}(3) - \mu_{Q_2}(4) = 0.5,$$

$$w_3 = \mu_{Q_2}(2) - \mu_{Q_2}(3) = 0, \qquad w_4 = \mu_{Q_2}(1) - \mu_{Q_2}(2) = 0,$$

$$w_5 = \mu_{Q_2}(0) - \mu_{Q_2}(1) = 0.$$

The OWA-based aggregation of the refutation degrees yields the truth value 1 ($= 0.5 \times 1 + 0.5 \times 1$) (resp. 0.95 and 0.6) for X_1 (resp. X_2, X_3). $\diamond$

Relationship between an OWA-based quantifier and its negation. Consider an increasing (absolute or relative) quantifier Q and the decreasing quantifier $\overline{Q}$ defined as: $\forall x,\ \mu_{\overline{Q}}(x) = 1 - \mu_Q(x)$. It is possible to establish that, if a set X satisfies the quantification "$Q\,X$ are A" with a degree α, then it satisfies the quantification "$\overline{Q}\,X$ are A" with a degree $\beta = 1 - \alpha$.

Let n be the cardinality of X (considering the possible addition of dummy elements). The proof is based on the following points:

- the expression of both OWA-based computations use the same values $\mu_A(x_i)$ (recall that the dummy elements, if any, are such that $\mu_A(x_i) = 0$),
- we denote by w_i the weights used for evaluating "$Q\,X$ are A" and by $\overline{w}_i$ those used for evaluating "$\overline{Q}\,X$ are A". Then, $w_i = \overline{w}_{n-i+1}$. Thus:

$$
\alpha = \sum_{i=1}^{n} w_i \times \mu_A(x_i) = \sum_{i=1}^{n} \overline{w}_{n-i+1} \times \mu_A(x_i)
$$

$$
= 1 - \sum_{i=1}^{n} \overline{w}_{n-i+1} + \sum_{i=1}^{n} \overline{w}_{n-i+1} \times \mu_A(x_i)
$$

$$
= 1 - \sum_{i=1}^{n} \overline{w}_{n-i+1} \times (1 - \mu_A(x_i)) = 1 - \beta.
$$

Link with the Choquet fuzzy integral. In Section 6.2.2 we showed that, defining an increasing quantifier Q by a fuzzy measure g, the Choquet integral $C_g(E_A)$ is a method to compute the truth value of the quantified statement "$Q\,X$ are A". It is shown in Bosc *et al.* (1995) that if Q is increasing or decreasing, then the OWA-based evaluation of the quantification corresponds to computation of the Choquet fuzzy integral $C_g(E_A)$.

6.2.3.5   *Interpretation of quantifiers of the type "about S"*

We now describe an interpretation of quantified statements involving a quantifier of the type "about S", based on the decomposition of the quantifier into two monotonous ones.

Principle of the interpretation. We define a fuzzy quantifier Q of the type "about S" in the following way:

- $\mu_Q(S) = 1$ and $\exists t$ such that $\forall x \in [S - t,\ S + t],\ \mu_Q(x) = 1$ (t may equal 0),
- $\forall \alpha,\ \mu_Q(S + \alpha) = \mu_Q(S - \alpha)$ (symmetry).

The property of symmetry is not essential but corresponds to the intuitive definition of "about S". Such a quantifier can be absolute (if S is a number) or relative (if S is a proportion). The semantics of the quantifier suggests that, in the proximity of S completely satisfied criteria — the others being completely unsatisfied — the quantified statement "$Q\,X$ are A" is totally satisfied, and that the "damage" caused by an additional number α of satisfied criteria is the same as that caused by a lack of α satisfied criteria.

The quantified statement "about $S\,X$ are A" is equivalent to the statement "at least $S\,X$ are A and at most $S\,X$ are A". Therefore, computing the truth value attached to "about SX are A" boils down to computing the conjunction of the truth values attached respectively to "at least $S\,X$ are A" and to "at most $S\,X$ are A". The first step of the evaluation is thus to break down the quantifier "about S" into two quantifiers "at least S" and "at most S". The second step is to calculate the respective truth values α and β attached to the quantified statements "at least $S\,X$ are A" and "at most $S\,X$ are A". Finally, the truth value associated with "about $S\,X$ are A" is equal to $min(\alpha,\ \beta)$.

Example 6.9. Consider the following sets

$$X_1 = \{0.9/x_1,\ 0.9/x_2,\ 0.7/x_3,\ 0.1/x_4\},$$

$$X_2 = \{1/x_1,\ 1/x_2,\ 1/x_3,\ 0.3/x_4\},$$

$$X_3 = \{1/x_1,\ 1/x_2,\ 0.7/x_3,\ 0/x_4\},$$

$$X_4 = \{0.8/x_1,\ 0.5/x_2,\ 0/x_3,\ 0/x_4\}$$

and compute the truth value attached to the statement "about three Xs are A" using an OWA-based interpretation. Let Q be the quantifier "about three" represented in Figure 6.7. From Q, we can derive the quantifiers Q_1

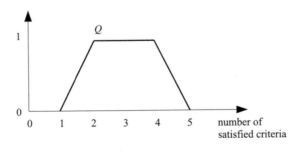

Fig. 6.7   The fuzzy quantifier "about three"

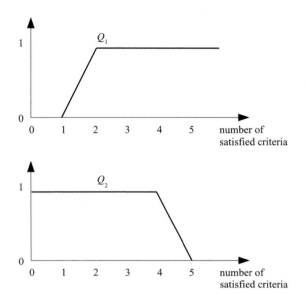

Fig. 6.8   The quantifiers "at least three" (Q_1, top) and "at most three" (Q_2, bottom)

and Q_2 represented in Figure 6.8, and evaluate the quantifications "at least three Xs are A" and "at most three Xs are A" for each set.

Computation of "at least three Xs are A". We have: $\mu_{Q_1}(0) = \mu_{Q_1}(1) = 0$, $\mu_{Q_1}(2) = 0.9$, and $\forall x \geq 3$, $\mu_{Q_1}(x) = 1$. Hence, $w_1 = 0$, $w_2 = 0.9$, $w_3 = 0.1$, and $\forall i > 3$, $w_i = 0$. The OWA-based evaluation of "at least three Xs are A" yields degree 0.88 ($= 0 \times 0.9 + 0.9 \times 0.9 + 0.1 \times 0.7$) for X_1, 1 for X_2, 0.97 for X_3, and 0.45 for X_4.

Computation of "at most three Xs are A". We have: $m = 5$, $\forall x \leq 3$, $\mu_{Q_2}(x) = 1$, $\mu_{Q_2}(4) = 0.9$, and $\forall x \geq 5$, $\mu_{Q_2}(x) = 0$. Hence, $w_1 = 0.9$, $w_2 = 0.1$, and $\forall i \geq 3$, $w_i = 0$. The OWA-based evaluation of "at most three Xs are A" yields degree 0.99 for X_1, 0.97 for X_2, 1 for X_3, and 1 for X_4.

Computation of "about three Xs are A". Finally, X_1 satisfies "about three Xs are A" to the degree 0.88 ($= min(0.88, 0.99)$), X_2 to the degree 0.97, X_3 to the degree 0.97, and X_4 to the degree 0.45.◇

6.2.4   Integration into SQLf

First, we consider that the fuzzy quantifier aggregates different satisfaction degrees related to a same tuple (horizontal quantification; see Kacprzyk and

Ziółkowski, 1986). An example of such a query is: "retrieve the employees satisfying most of the following predicates: *well-paid, young, . . . ,important position*". Second, we consider that the fuzzy quantifier applies to a set X of tuples (vertical quantification). An example of such a query is: "retrieve the departments where most of the employees are well-paid". Set X can be obtained by means of either a partitioning (*group by* clause in SQLf), or a block nesting.

6.2.4.1 *Horizontal quantification*

The format of an SQLf query involving horizontal quantification is:

$$\textbf{select * from } r \textbf{ where } Q\,(fc_1,\ fc_2,\ \ldots,\ fc_n). \tag{E1}$$

In this expression, r is a regular relation, Q is a fuzzy quantifier and $\{fc_1, \ldots, fc_n\}$ is a set of n fuzzy conditions. This query retrieves the tuples satisfying Q conditions among $\{fc_1,\ fc_2,\ \ldots,\ fc_n\}$. Therefore, the satisfaction degree obtained by a tuple t of r (with respect to query E1) is the truth value of the statement "$Q\,X$ are A" where $X = \{fc_1,\ fc_2,\ \ldots,\ fc_n\}$ and $A =$ "to be satisfied by t" ($\forall\,fc_i,\ \mu_A(fc_i) = \mu_{fc_i}(t)$).

Considering a relation $Emp(\#e,\ \#dep,\ salary,\ position,\ age,\ address)$ describing employees of a company, the query: "retrieve the employees fulfilling at least two conditions among *well-paid, high commission, young*" is expressed by the following SQLf query (format E1):

select $\#e$ **from** Emp
where at_least_2 (*salary* **is** *well-paid, commission* **is** *high, age* **is** *young*).

6.2.4.2 *Nested queries (extension of any and all)*

An interesting feature of SQL is that it allows the nesting of query blocks to an arbitrary depth. In particular, two *select* blocks can be connected by means of the existential ($\exists$) or the universal quantifier ($\forall$) using the keywords *any* or *all* (see Chapter 2). In this case, the internal block (subquery) is seen as a set, and a comparison between the value of the current tuple and the values of that set is performed. For instance, the query "find the employees whose salary is not smaller than that of any engineer" can be expressed:

> **select** $\#e$ **from** Emp **where** $salary \geq$ **all**
> (**select** $salary$ **from** Emp **where** $position =$ "engineer").

The objective in SQLf is to authorize fuzzy quantifiers in addition to *all* and *any* as well as any fuzzy comparator (*much greater, more or less equal*, etc.). The general form of such SQLf queries is:

> **select * from** r
> **where** att_1 θ Q (**select distinct** att_2 **from** s **where** bc),   (E2)

where θ is a fuzzy comparator, att_1 (resp. att_2) is an attribute of relation r (resp. s), Q is a fuzzy quantifier, and bc is a *Boolean* condition. To help define its semantics, we reformulate this query in the form of a fuzzy statement "Q X are A". Note that the quantifier Q applies to the set made of values x for att_2 appearing in tuples (belonging to s) which satisfy bc. The use of the keyword *distinct* in the inner block ensures that it delivers a set and not a multiset. The degree to which a tuple t' of r with value u on att_1 belongs to the result is the truth value of the statement "Q X are A", where $X = \{t.att_2 \mid t \in s \wedge bc(t)\}$, and A is the predicate $\theta(u, x)$ (i.e., $\mu_A(x) = \mu_\theta(u, x)$). The query "find the employees whose salary is greater than that of almost all the employees over 30 years old" can be written as:

> **select * from** *Emp* **where** *salary* > *almost_all*
> (**select distinct** *salary* **from** *Emp* **where** *age* > 30).

6.2.4.3 *Quantified statement in the having clause*

We now consider the partitioning of relations and the use of vertical quantification. Just as in SQL, the partitioning is expressed in SQLf using the keyword *group by*. The SQLf expression which can be associated with this kind of query is as follows:

> **select** att **from** r **where** bc_1
> **group by** att **having** $Q(bc_2)$ **are** A,   (E3)

where bc_1 and bc_2 denote Boolean conditions. This query splits relation r into subsets (partitions) according to the value of attribute att. The degree to which a value x of attribute att is an answer to query E3 is the truth value of the statement "Q X are A", where X is the group made of those tuples satisfying conditions bc_1 and bc_2, and sharing the value x for attribute att.

An equivalent expression for query E3 is:

select *att* **from** *r* **where** bc_1 **and** bc_2

group by *att* **having** Q **are** A.   (E4)

The query "retrieve the departments where at least two employees over 30 years old are well-paid" may be expressed by the following SQLf queries:

select #*dep* **from** *Emp* **group by** #*dep*

having at_least_2 (*age* > 30) **are** (*salary* **is** *well-paid*),   (format E3)

select #*dep* **from** *Emp* **where** *age* > 30

group by #*dep* **having** at_least_2 **are** (*salary* **is** *well-paid*). (format E4)

6.2.5   *Evaluation of SQLf queries involving quantified statements*

In this section, we describe algorithms which make it possible to determine whether, for a given set X, the satisfaction degree attached to the quantified statement "Q X are A" is above a user-specified threshold α (a case of qualitative calibration). Suppose that the number of elements in set X is known, but that X is assumed not to be sorted on the satisfaction degrees (its elements are accessed in a random order). The objective is to find conditions for stopping the calculus as soon as possible. Generally speaking, the loop that governs data access can stop in two situations:

- when it is certain that X cannot reach the desired level α,
- when it is certain that X will reach the desired level, but one does not need to know the precise value of the satisfaction degree attached to X.

This reasoning is very similar to that in the design of "trial and error" or "branch and bound" algorithms, where some pruning conditions are used for trimming the search tree, i.e., the number of candidates to be examined.

6.2.5.1   *Zadeh's interpretation*

According to Zadeh (1983), the evaluation of the quantification "Q X are A" for a set $X = \{x_1,\, x_2,\, \ldots,\, x_n\}$ is

$$\mu_Q \left(\sum_{i=1}^{n} \mu_A(x_i) \right).$$

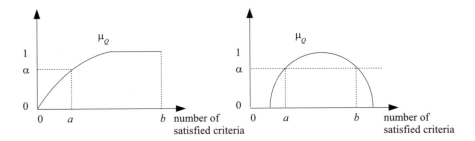

Fig. 6.9 α-cut of (left) an increasing and (right) an increasing–decreasing quantifier

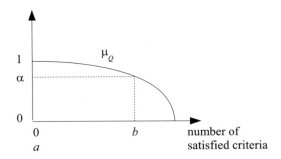

Fig. 6.10 α-cut of a decreasing quantifier

Using a threshold α, the problem is thus to determine the sets X which satisfy $\mu_Q(\sum_{x_i \in X} \mu_A(x_i)) \geq \alpha$. Depending on the type of quantifier Q involved (increasing, decreasing, or increasing–decreasing), three cases may be considered (see Figures 6.9 and 6.10), which can be captured by the following common expression:

$$a \leq \mu_Q \left(\sum_{x_i \in X} \mu_A(x_i) \right) \leq b.$$

Note that values a and b can reach respectively 0 (for a decreasing quantifier) and 1 (increasing relative quantifier). Thus, we have to characterize the sets $X = \{x_1, x_2, \ldots, x_n\}$ such that:

$$a \leq \mu_Q \left(\sum_{x_i \in X} \mu_A(x_i) \right) \leq b. \tag{6.4}$$

Naïve algorithm. The straightforward algorithm works by performing an exhaustive scan of set $X = \{x_1, x_2, \ldots, x_n\}$. We write $S_k = \sum_{i=1}^{k} \mu_A(x_i)$. We aim to obtain and then test the value S_n, which corresponds to the satisfaction degree attached to set X with respect to the quantification "Q X are A". This "naïve" method is encoded by Algorithm 6.1.

Algorithm 6.1.

$S_0 := 0$;
for $i := 1$ **to** n **do** $S_i := S_{i-1} + \mu_A(x_i)$ **enddo**;
if $S_n \in [a, b]$ **then** X is an answer **else** X is not qualified;

Improved algorithm. The idea is to modify the naïve algorithm using pruning conditions which enable us to decide whether or not the set will comply with the requirement in Expression (6.4). Letting $k \in [0, n-1]$, we have $S_n - S_k = \sum_{i=k+1}^{n} \mu_A(x_i)$. Now, $\forall i$, $\mu_A(x_i) \in [0, 1]$, which implies that $0 \leq S_n - S_k \leq (n-k)$. We can thus write:

$$\forall k \in [0, 1], \ S_k \leq S_n \leq S_k + (n-k).$$

Therefore, two pruning conditions can be used to stop the algorithm at iteration k:

- If $S_k \in [a, b]$ and if $S_k + (n-k) \in [a, b]$, then it is certain that $S_n \in [a, b]$. In this case, X is certainly an answer.
- If $S_k > b$ or $S_k + (n-k) < a$, then it is certain that $S_n \notin [a, b]$. In this case, we know for sure that X is not an answer.

This improved method is encoded by Algorithm 6.2.

Algorithm 6.2.

$S_0 := 0$;
for $i := 1$ **to** n **do**
   $S_k := S_{k-1} + \mu_A(x_k)$;
   if $S_k > b$ **or** $S_k + (n-k) < a$ **then exit**(failure)
   else if $S_k \in [a, b]$ **and** $S_k + (n-k) \in [a, b]$ **then exit**(success);
enddo;
exit success: X is an answer (it satisfies "Q X are A" to a degree $\geq \alpha$);
exit failure: X is not an answer;

The algorithm for evaluating a quantification involving a relative fuzzy quantifier would be the same, except that each expression $\mu_A(x_k)$ and $(n-k)$ would have to be divided by n, i.e., the cardinality of set X.

6.2.5.2   *Interpretation based on Sugeno's integral*

Recall that the value of "$Q \, X$ are A" is given by (see Section 6.2.2.2):

$$S_g(E_A) = med(\mu_{E_A}(x_1), \ldots, \mu_{E_A}(x_k), \mu_Q(k-1), \mu_Q(k-2), \ldots, \mu_Q(1)).$$

In this formula, k denotes the cardinality of X' where X' is either X itself, or X completed with dummy elements. One thus has:

- if $n < k$ then $\forall j \in [1, k-n]$, $\mu_{E_A}(x_j) = 0$, n being the cardinality of X,
- the other values $\mu_{E_A}(x_j)$ are the satisfaction degrees of the elements of X with respect to A.

Moreover, the values $\mu_Q(1), \ldots, \mu_Q(k-1)$ are constant for a given quantifier Q and are computed once and for all at the beginning of the algorithm.

The algorithm consists mainly of a loop accessing the elements of X. Consider the situation at the end of the ith iteration. At that point, $(n-i)$ values are still missing in the computation of $S_g(E_A)$. If we assume these missing values to be zeros and $S_g(E_A)$ is already greater than α, due to the monotonicity of Sugeno's integral we can conclude that whatever the missing values, the actual $S_g(E_A)$ will be over α. Similarly, if we assume these values to be ones and $S_g(E_A)$ is less than α, then we can conclude that whatever the degrees of the missing elements, $S_g(E_A)$ will be less than α. These two remarks form the basis of the pruning conditions used in the algorithm.

The implementation requires two sorted arrays MI and MS of $(2k-1)$ elements. At the ith iteration, MI contains the previously treated elements $\mu_A(x)$, the values $\mu_Q(1), \ldots, \mu_Q(k-1)$, and $(n-i)$ zeros for the remaining elements (not yet accessed). MS contains the previously treated elements $\mu_A(x)$, the values $\mu_Q(1), \ldots, \mu_Q(k-1)$, and $(n-i)$ values set to 1 (the elements which are still missing are assumed to have the maximal degree). When moving from step i to step $i+1$, a new satisfaction degree $\mu_A(x_i)$ for the current element x_i will replace a zero (resp. 1) in MI (resp. MS).

Let $MI[k]_i$ (resp. $MS[k]_i$) be the value of the median element $MI[k]$ (resp. $MS[k]$) at iteration i. Then:

$$\forall \, i, \; MI[k]_i \leq S_g(E_A) \leq MS[k]_i, \tag{6.5}$$

$$MI[k]_n = MS[k]_n = S_g(E_A). \tag{6.6}$$

Expression (6.5) relies on the fact that S_g is monotonic, which implies that:

$$S_g(y_1, \, y_2, \ldots, y_n) \geq S_g(y_{i_1}, y_{i_2}, \ldots, y_{i_j}, \, 0, \ldots, 0)$$

and

$$S_g(y_1, y_2, \ldots, y_n) \leq S_g(y_{i_1}, y_{i_2}, \ldots, y_{i_j}, 1, \ldots, 1),$$

where $\{i_1, i_2, \ldots, i_j\}$ is any subset of $\{1, 2, \ldots, n\}$. Expression (6.6) is based on the fact that, at the end of the iterations $(i = n)$, the contents of MI and MS are equal and $S_g(E_A)$ is their median element. The evaluation procedure is encoded by Algorithm 6.3.

Algorithm 6.3.

for $i := 1$ **to** k **do begin** $MI[i] := 0$; $MS[i] := 0$ **end**;
for $i := k + 1$ **to** $2k - 1$ **do** $MI[i] := \mu_Q(i - k)$;
for $i := 2k - n$ **to** $2k - 1$ **do** $MS[i] := 1$;
for $i := k - n + 1$ **to** $2k - n - 1$ **do** $MS[i] := \mu_Q(i - k + n)$;
for $i := 1$ **to** n **do**
　　if $MI[k] \geq \alpha$ **then exit**(success) **else if** $MS[k] < \alpha$ **then exit**(failure);
　　ordered insertion of $\mu_A(x_i)$ into MI　　/* $\mu_A(x_i)$ replaces a zero */
　　ordered insertion of $\mu_A(x_i)$ into MS　　/* $\mu_A(x_i)$ replaces a 1 */
enddo;
exit success: X is an answer (it satisfies "$Q\,X$ are A" to a degree $\geq \alpha$);
exit failure: X is not an answer;

We now consider the use of a decreasing quantifier Q. Recall that in this case, the value of "$Q\,X$ are A" is given by $1 - S_{g'}(E_A)$ where $\forall E$, $g'(E) = 1 - \mu_Q(|E|)$. We define the increasing quantifier Q' as:

$$\forall i, \ \mu_{Q'}(i) = 1 - \mu_Q(i).$$

Measure g' is computed from $\mu_{Q'}$ using Expressions 6.1 and 6.2. To compute $S_{g'}(E_A)$ in an efficient way, we introduce pruning conditions which take advantage of the fact that only the Xs sought for are such that the degree of "$Q\,X$ are A" is over a threshold α. Since one has:

$$\forall i, \ MI_i[k] \leq S_{g'}(E_A) \leq MS_i[k],$$

the property

$$\forall i, \ 1 - MS_i[k] \leq 1 - S_{g'}(E_A) \leq 1 - MI_i[k]$$

holds and may be used to prune the search space. Algorithm 6.3 is modified the following way:

$$\textbf{if } MI[k] \geq \alpha \textbf{ then exit}(\text{success})$$
$$(\text{resp. } \textbf{if } MS[k] < \alpha \textbf{ then exit}(\text{failure}))$$

is replaced by:

$$\textbf{if } (1 - MS[k]) \geq \alpha \textbf{ then exit}(\text{success})$$
$$(\text{resp. } \textbf{if } (1 - MI[k]) < \alpha \textbf{ then exit}(\text{failure})).$$

6.2.5.3 *Interpretation based on Choquet's integral*

We now deal with the OWA-based evaluation of a quantified statement "QX are A" in the case where Q is a monotonic quantifier. First, we present a straightforward algorithm, then we show that the properties of the OWA operator can be used to design a more efficient algorithm.

Naïve algorithm. The "naïve" algorithm performs the evaluation of the OWA-based aggregation by scanning the entire set X considered. It is assumed that W is the vector that describes the weights of the OWA operator (recall that the $W[i]$'s are derived from μ_Q). We denote by n the cardinality of X and the result of the aggregation by GV. The procedure is encoded by Algorithm 6.4.

Algorithm 6.4.

for each x_i **in** X **do** $V[i] := \mu_A(x_i)$ **enddo**;
$V' := \text{rank-order } (V)$;
compute vector W;
$GV := 0$;
for $i := 1$ **to** n **do** $GV := GV + V'[i] \times W[i]$ **enddo**;
if $GV \geq \alpha$ **then** set X is qualified and its satisfaction degree equals GV;

The straightforward algorithm in the case where Q is decreasing is the same except that the final degree is $1 - GV$, where GV is the OWA-based evaluation of "$\overline{Q} X$ are A" with $\overline{Q}$ defined as $\forall x, \mu_{\overline{Q}}(x) = 1 - \mu_Q(x)$.

Some properties of the OWA operator. The OWA operator has the following interesting properties (for any given vector of weights W):

$$OWA(x_1, \ldots, x_n) \leq OWA(x_1, \ldots, x_i, 1, \ldots, 1), \qquad (6.7)$$

$$OWA(x_1, \ldots, x_n) \geq OWA(x_1, \ldots, x_i, 0, \ldots, 0), \qquad (6.8)$$

$$1 - OWA(x_1, \ldots, x_n) \geq 1 - OWA(x_1, \ldots, x_i, 1, \ldots, 1), \qquad (6.9)$$

$$1 - OWA(x_1, \ldots, x_n) \leq 1 - OWA(x_1, \ldots, x_i, 0, \ldots, 0). \qquad (6.10)$$

These properties are related to the monotonicity of mean operators, and to the fact that $\forall i$, $x_i \in [0, 1]$. From these basic properties, one can derive conditions bearing on the x_i's which are necessary for the satisfaction of the global condition:

$$OWA(x_1, \ldots, x_n) \geq \alpha.$$

From Expressions (6.7) and (6.8), we have:

$$OWA(x_1, \ldots, x_i, 1, \ldots, 1) < \alpha \Rightarrow OWA(x_1, \ldots, x_n) < \alpha, \quad (6.11)$$

$$OWA(x_1, \ldots, x_i, 0, \ldots, 0) \geq \alpha \Rightarrow OWA(x_1, \ldots, x_n) \geq \alpha. \quad (6.12)$$

From Expressions (6.9) and (6.10), we have:

$$1 - OWA(x_1, \ldots, x_i, 1, \ldots, 1) \geq \alpha \Rightarrow 1 - OWA(x_1, \ldots, x_n) \geq \alpha, \quad (6.13)$$

$$1 - OWA(x_1, \ldots, x_i, 0, \ldots, 0) < \alpha \Rightarrow 1 - OWA(x_1, \ldots, x_n) < \alpha. \quad (6.14)$$

These conditions can be used for computing partial evaluations of an OWA-based aggregation, as we see below.

Improved algorithm. We first consider the case where quantifier Q is increasing. The algorithm relies on the properties in Expressions (6.11) and (6.12). We assume that we have already accessed k elements of set X (elements x_1 to x_k), and the values $v_i = \mu_A(x_i)$ for $i \in [1, k]$ are known. If we also assume that the $(n - k)$ missing values equal 1 and the result of the OWA-based evaluation remains smaller than α, according to Expression (6.11), we can be certain that set X will never reach the desired level α. We compute the aggregation:

$$OWA(v_1, \ldots, v_k, 1, \ldots, 1) = \sum_{i=1}^{n-k} w_i + \sum_{i=1}^{k} w_{n-k+i} \times v_{j_i},$$

where v_{j_i} is the ith largest value among the v_j's. This computation only requires that the values $V[1]$ to $V[k]$ are sorted. In addition, the expression does not have to be recalculated from scratch when one moves from step k to step $k + 1$, since the first part can be computed incrementally. Once again, it is possible to express a condition that is likely to stop the outer loop before it is complete:

> insert $\mu_A(x_k)$ into $V[i : k]$;
> compute $A = \sum_{i=1}^{n-k} W[i] + \sum_{i=1}^{k} W[n - k + i] \times V[i]$;
> **if** $A < \alpha$ **then exit**(failure);

When $k = n$ (last element of set X), the value of A corresponds to the overall degree GV associated with set X.

If one is only interested in knowing whether X qualifies or not (but does not care about its precise satisfaction degree), one can also use Expression (6.12). If k elements (x_1 to x_k) have already been accessed and the result of the OWA-based aggregation already exceeds α, assuming that the $(n - k)$ missing values equal zero, then set X qualifies for sure. One has to compute the aggregation:

$$OWA(v_1, \ldots, v_k, 0, \ldots, 0) = \sum_{i=1}^{k} w_i \times v_{k_i}.$$

Here again, one only has to sort the values $V[1]$ to $V[k]$. The related pruning condition can be inserted into the algorithm in the following way:

> insert $\mu_A(x_k)$ into $V[i : k]$;
> compute $B = \sum_{i=1}^{k} W[i] \times V[i]$;
> **if** $B \geq \alpha$ **then exit**(success);

Again, when $k = n$, the value of B equals that of A and corresponds to the overall satisfaction degree GV associated with set X.

The final evaluation procedure is given in Algorithm 6.5.

Algorithm 6.5.

compute vector W;
for each x_k **in** X **do**
 insert $\mu_A(x_k)$ into $V[1 : k]$;
 $A = \sum_{i=1}^{n-k} W[i] + \sum_{i=1}^{k} W[n - k + i] \times V[i]$;
 if $A < \alpha$ **then exit**(failure);

$B = \sum_{i=1}^{k} W[i] \times V[i];$
  if $B \geq \alpha$ **then exit**(success);
enddo;
exit success: X is an answer;
exit failure: X is not an answer;

When quantifier Q is decreasing, the properties in Expressions (6.13) and (6.14) can be used. The definitions of A and B become, respectively:

$$A = 1 - \left(\sum_{i=1}^{n-k} W[i] + \sum_{i=1}^{k} W[n-k+i] \times V[i] \right)$$

and

$$B = 1 - \sum_{i=1}^{k} W[i] \times V[i].$$

The previous algorithm must then be modified the following way:

if $A < \alpha$ **then exit**(failure)
(resp. **if** $B \geq \alpha$ **then exit**(success))

is replaced by:

if $A \geq \alpha$ **then exit**(success)
(resp. **if** $B < \alpha$ **then exit**(failure)).

6.3   Aggregates

6.3.1 *Introduction*

In SQLf, as in SQL, it is possible to consider aggregates (such as cardinality, sum, maximum or average) which are functions applying to a set of items. Aggregates can be integrated into SQLf queries as in the following example calling on the aggregate average (avg):

select $\#dep$ **from** *Emp* **group by** $\#dep$
having avg(*salary*) **is** *high*.

The underlying relation $Emp(\#e, \#dep, age, salary)$ describes employees, and this query aims at retrieving departments where the average salary is high. A department is all the more satisfactory as it satisfies the fuzzy condition: "the average salary of its employees is high". In this example, the aggregate *avg* applies to a crisp set of salaries and, for each department, the average salary is computed and matched against the fuzzy condition *high*. However, when the items to be aggregated are attached a satisfaction degree, the interpretation becomes more tricky since the aggregate applies to a fuzzy referential. This is the case of the query aimed at the retrieval of departments where "the average salary of young employees is high" which could be expressed in SQLf as:

> **select** #*dep* **from** *Emp* **where** *age* **is** *young*
> **group by** #*dep* **having avg**(*salary*) **is** *high.*

This query is difficult to interpret, since the aggregate — here, the average — applies to the fuzzy set of salaries of young employees. The objective of this section is to describe a sound technique for interpreting (and computing) queries where an aggregate applies to a fuzzy set.

A condition in which the value of an aggregate is matched to a fuzzy predicate is written "$agg(A)$ *is* C" for short (e.g., "$avg(A)$ *is high*", where A is the fuzzy set of salaries of young employees).

In the context of SQLf, a unique degree of satisfaction for "$agg(A)$ *is* C" (denoted by $truth[agg(A)$ *is* $C]$) is needed in order to be consistent with other predicates. In this section, we describe an interpretation of conditions of type "$agg(A)$ *is* C" in terms of a single degree (Bosc and Liétard, 2008) and we define SQLf structures devoted to such conditions. We do not deal with the case where the aggregate is *count*, since this corresponds to interpreting a fuzzy quantified proposition, which has already been discussed in the preceding section.

6.3.2 *The case of monotonic predicates and aggregates*

This section presents a generalization of the Sugeno-integral-based approach that was presented in Section 6.2 in a context of fuzzy quantified propositions. The objective is to extend this approach so as to evaluate conditions of the form "$agg(A)$ *is* C" when the aggregate *agg* and the fuzzy condition C are monotonic in the same way (i.e., both increasing or decreasing). The idea is to consider that the more numerous the interpretations of set A (i.e., its α-cuts) with a high satisfaction for the condition "the aggregate is C", the higher the truth value for "$agg(A)$ *is* C". Examples of monotonic aggregates are *max*, *min*, and *count*, but also *sum* if the values to be added are either all positive or all negative.

The evaluation relies on the set-oriented function m defined as follows (over a crisp set E onto which the aggregate applies):

$$m(E) = \mu_C(agg(E)).$$

Obviously, when A is a crisp set:

$$truth[agg(A) \ is \ C] = C(agg(A)) = m(A),$$

and this function satisfies the following property of monotonicity (since the aggregate and C are assumed to be monotonic in the same way):

$$E \subseteq F \Rightarrow m(E) \leq m(F).$$

For two crisp sets E and F, this property of monotonicity can be rewritten:

$$(E \subseteq F) \Rightarrow truth[agg(E) \ is \ C] \leq truth[agg(F) \ is \ C]. \qquad (6.15)$$

This expression is the starting point for the evaluation of $truth[agg(A) \ is \ C]$ when A is fuzzy. In this case, the right-hand part of the implication can be read as "the higher $truth[agg(E) is \ C]$ is for a crisp set E included in A, the higher $truth[agg(A) \ is \ C]$ should be". This leads to the following definition (where $truth[agg(E) \ is \ C]$ is given by $m(E)$):

$$truth[agg(A) \ is \ C] = max_{E \in S} \ min(min_{x \in E} \ \mu_A(x), \ m(E))$$
$$= max_{E \in S} \ min(min_{x \in E} \ \mu_A(x), \ \mu_C(agg(E))),$$

where S is the power set of the support of A restricted to sets onto which the aggregate applies. In this definition:

- $min_{x \in E} \ \mu_A(x)$ is the extent to which the crisp set E is included in A,
- $\mu_C(agg(E))$ is the value of $truth[agg(E) \ is \ C]$,
- as before, the operators max and min are respectively a generalized existential quantifier and a generalized conjunction.

Because of the monotonicity property of function m, $truth[agg(A) \ is \ C]$ can be rewritten:

$$truth[agg(A) \ is \ C] = max_{\alpha_i \in D} \ min(\alpha_i, \ m(A_{\alpha_i}))$$
$$= max_{\alpha_i \in D} \ min(\alpha_i, \ \mu_C(agg(A_{\alpha_i}))), \qquad (6.16)$$

where D is the set made of the actual different membership degrees in A.

In the particular case where m is a fuzzy measure, Expression (6.16) is nothing but a Sugeno fuzzy integral.

Example 6.10. Consider the aggregate "maximum" and the statement "$max(A)$ *is high*" with the following fuzzy set A:

$$A = \{0.1/100, \ 0.3/105, \ 0.8/670, \ 1/120\}.$$

We have:

$$truth[max(A) \ is \ high] = max(min(0.1, \ \mu_{high}(670)), \ min(0.3, \ \mu_{high}(670)),$$
$$min(0.8, \ \mu_{high}(670)), \ min(1, \ \mu_{high}(120))).$$

If we assume that $\mu_{high}(670) = 1$ and $\mu_{high}(120) = 0.2$, we obtain 0.8 as the truth value of "$max(A)$ *is high*". This result agrees with our intuition, since 670 represents a good trade-off between two aspects: i) to be the maximum value of the fuzzy set A (with $\mu_A(670) = 0.8$), and ii) to satisfy *to be high* ($\mu_{high}(670) = 1$).$\diamond$

This approach defines $truth[agg(A) \ is \ C]$ as the highest level β for which each α-level cut A_α, with $\alpha \in [0, \ \beta]$, satisfies the expression "$agg(A) \ is \ C$" at least to the degree β (Bosc and Liétard, 2005):

$$truth[agg(A) \ is \ C] = max\{\beta \mid \forall \alpha \in [0, \ \beta], \ \mu_C(agg(A_\alpha)) \geq \beta\}.$$

Referring to the previous example, any level α in $[0, \ 0.8]$ is such that the α-cut of A satisfies "the maximum is *high*" at least to the degree 0.8. When $truth[agg(A) \ is \ C]$ equals 1, each α-cut of A (i.e., each interpretation of set A) is such that the value of the aggregate fully satisfies C. As mentioned above, according to this view, the more numerous the interpretations of set A (i.e., its α-cuts) with a high satisfaction for the condition "the aggregate is C", the higher the truth value for "$agg(A) \ is \ C$". The number of interpretations of A is measured by the length of an interval of levels (interval of type $[0, \ \beta]$) with the meaning: the larger the interval, the higher the number of interpretations.

Obviously, when the satisfaction of "the value of the aggregate is C" is high for a large interval of levels α, we obtain a high value for $truth[agg(A) \ is \ C]$ (for example 0.8 when: $\forall \alpha \in [0, \ 0.8]$, $\mu_C(agg(A_\alpha)) \geq 0.8$). On the contrary, a low value for $truth[agg(A) \ is \ C]$ means that each α-cut (or at least each α-cut with a significant level) satisfies "the value of the aggregate is C" only poorly. This behavior is due to the monotonicity of both the aggregate and the predicate. These two points make it legitimate to consider $truth[agg(A) \ is \ C]$ as a suitable measure of the global satisfaction of the α-cuts; they also provide an interpretation in terms of α-cuts for $truth[agg(A) \ is \ C]$.

Although sound, this approach remains restricted to monotonic aggregates and predicates. In the next section, we propose a generalization in which the constraint of monotonicity is not imposed. This generalization maintains the meaning introduced in this section, namely: the more numerous the interpretations of set A (i.e., its α-cuts) with a high satisfaction for the constraint "the aggregate is C", the higher the truth value for "$agg(A)$ is C".

6.3.3   *Dealing with the general case*

In this section, a technique to compute $truth[agg(A)\ is\ C]$ in the general case is introduced. First, it is shown in Section 6.3.3.1 that a straightforward adaptation of the interpretation introduced in Section 6.3.2 (Expression (6.16)) is inappropriate. Then, a new approach is introduced in Section 6.3.3.2 which is also based on the interpretation in terms of α-cuts introduced in Section 6.3.2. Finally, Section 6.3.3.3 focuses on the relationship between "$agg(A)$ *is* C" and "$agg(A)$ *is* $\neg C$", which differs from the usual case.

6.3.3.1   *A straightforward interpretation*

In the general case, the main drawback of using Expression (6.16) is that a low value for $truth[agg(A)\ is\ C]$ does not necessarily mean that every α-cut (or at least, every α-cut with a significant level) poorly satisfies "the aggregate is C". More precisely, we may have a low result for $truth[agg(A)\ is\ C]$ when a unique α-level cut with a low level poorly satisfies "the aggregate is C", even when the others (including all significant α-cuts) strongly satisfy "the aggregate is C".

To overcome this problem, it is necessary to design other generalizations that discard α-cuts with low level and poor satisfaction with respect to the condition. As a consequence, instead of considering an interval of type $[0, \beta]$, the idea is to consider any kind of interval. A first generalization is to look for an interval of levels α that is as large as possible, where $\mu_C(agg(A_\alpha))$ is as large as possible:

$$truth[agg(A)\ is\ C] = max\{(\beta - \lambda) \mid \forall \alpha \in [\lambda,\ \beta],\ \mu_C(agg(A_\alpha)) \geq (\beta - \lambda)\}.$$

Obviously, the higher $truth[agg(A)\ is\ C]$ becomes, the larger the interval of levels with a higher $\mu_C(agg(A_\alpha))$ should be. When $truth[agg(A)\ is\ C]$ equals 1, it means that for each α-cut (i.e., for each interpretation of set A), the value of the aggregate fully satisfies predicate C. The main drawback of this approach appears when a high satisfaction for "the aggregate is C" is obtained for many α-cuts but over small intervals (since only a few levels may have a low satisfaction). In this case, we would expect a rather high result for $truth[agg(A)$ *is* $C]$ but this generalization leads to a low result, as illustrated in the next example.

Example 6.11. The condition "$avg(A)$ *is around 600*" is considered along with the following fuzzy set A:

$$A = \{0.38/1197, 0.39/3, 0.4/600, 1/600\}.$$

If we assume that:

$$\mu_{around\,600}(600) = 1 \quad \text{and} \quad \mu_{around\,600}(401) = 0.2,$$

then we obtain the result represented in Table 6.3. According to this generalization:

$$truth[avg(A) \text{ } is \text{ } around \text{ } 600] = max\{(0.38 - 0), (1 - 0.4)\} = 0.6.$$

A higher value for "$avg(A)$ *is around 600*" is expected, since $\mu_{around\,600}$ $(avg(A_\alpha))$ differs from 1 only when α lies within $]0.38, 0.39]$.◇

This drawback is mainly due to the fact that a unique interval of levels is considered in these generalizations. Another way is to take several intervals into consideration and to integrate the contribution of each of them. When referring to the previous example, the two intervals $]0, 0.38]$ and $]0.39, 1]$ could be taken into account. Such a generalization is introduced below.

6.3.3.2 *The proposed interpretation*

The interpretation proposed in this section defines $truth[agg(A)$ *is* $C]$ as the highest β which satisfies the *gradual* condition "for each level α in $[0, 1]$, $\mu_C(agg(A_\alpha))$ is at least equal to β". We emphasize that "for each" is seen here as a fuzzy expression. So we need to maximize a conjunction expressing

Table 6.3 The truth values of "$avg(A_\alpha)$ *is around 600*"

α	0.38	0.39	0.4	1
$avg(A_\alpha)$	600	401	600	600
$\mu_{around\,600}(avg(A_\alpha))$	1	0.2	1	1

the idea that β is high and "for each level α in $[0, 1]$, $\mu_C(agg(A_\alpha))$ is at least equal to β":

$$truth[agg(A) \ is \ C] = max_{\beta \in [0, 1]} \ min(\beta, \ each(\beta)), \qquad (6.17)$$

where $each(\beta)$ is a degree expressing that $\mu_C(agg(A_\alpha)) \geq \beta$ for each interpretation A_α of A with α in $[0, 1]$.

Obviously, this definition depends on $each(\beta)$ and, as was pointed out above, a solution is to sum up the lengths of the intervals (of levels) where the threshold β is reached:

$$each(\beta) = \sum_{]\alpha_i, \alpha_j] \ \text{s.t.} \ \forall \alpha \in]\alpha_i, \alpha_j], \ agg(A_\alpha) \ \text{is defined} \ \wedge \ \mu_c(agg(A_\alpha)) \geq \beta} (\alpha_j - \alpha_i).$$

$$(6.18)$$

The higher $each(\beta)$, the more numerous the levels α for which $\mu_C(agg(A_\alpha)) \geq \beta$. In particular, $each(\beta)$ equals 1 when for each level α in $[0, 1]$, $\mu_C(agg(A_\alpha))$ is larger than (or equal to) β.

A priori, the computation of Expression (6.17) needs to handle an infinity of values for β. However, it is possible to restrict computations to values for β belonging to the set of "effective" $\mu_C(agg(A_\alpha))$ values (Bosc and Liétard, 2005) in the spirit of Expression (6.16):

$$truth[agg(A) \ is \ C] = max_{\beta \in D} \ min(\beta, \ each(\beta)), \qquad (6.19)$$

where $D = \{\beta \mid \exists \alpha \ \text{such that} \ \beta = \mu_C(agg(A_\alpha))\}$.

Example 6.12. The statement "*avg(A) is high*" is considered with the following fuzzy set A:

$$A = \{0.49/4050, \ 0.5/103, \ 0.5/14, \ 0.5/12, \ 0.5/25, \ 0.5/16, \ 0.5/20,$$
$$0.5/10, \ 0.51/700, \ 0.8/500, \ 1/600\}.$$

If we assume that:

$$\mu_{high}(200) = 0, \quad \mu_{high}(550) = 0.9 \quad \text{and} \quad \mu_{high}(600) = 1,$$

we obtain the values represented in Table 6.4. From Table 6.4 we have: $D = \{0, 0.9, 1\}$ which leads to: $each(0) = 1$, $each(0.9) = 0.99$ and $each(1) = 0.21$.

Table 6.4   The truth values of "$avg(A_\alpha)$ *is high*"

α	0.49	0.5	0.51	0.8	1
$avg(A_\alpha)$	550	200	600	550	600
$\mu_{high}(avg(A_\alpha))$	0.9	0	1	0.9	1

According to Expression (6.19), we obtain:

$$truth[avg(A) \ is \ high] = max(min(0,1), min(0.9, 0.99), min(1, 0.21)) = 0.9.$$

The statement "$avg(A)$ *is high*" is rather true (to the degree 0.9), since most of the interpretations of fuzzy set A strongly satisfy "the average is high". Note that the gap between the levels 0.49 and 0.5 does not have a significant impact on the result, since it represents very few α-cuts. In that respect, this behavior differs from that illustrated in Example 6.11.◇

The next proof shows that this approach is a generalization of that introduced in Section 6.3.2 for monotonic aggregates and predicates. In other words, when the aggregate and the predicate are monotonic in the same sense, Expression (6.19) boils down to Expression (6.16).

Proof. Recall that Expression (6.19) is:

$$truth[agg(A) \ is \ C] = max_{\beta \in D} \ min(\beta, \ each(\beta)),$$

where $D = \{\beta \mid \exists \alpha \ \text{such that} \ \beta = \mu_C(agg(A_\alpha))\}$. This can be rewritten:

$$truth[agg(A) \ is \ C] = max_{\alpha_i \in D} \ min(\mu_C(agg(A_{\alpha_i})), \ each(\mu_C(agg(A_{\alpha_i})))),$$

where D is the set made up of the different membership degrees in A. When the aggregate and C are monotonic in the same sense, $each(\mu_C(agg(A_{\alpha_i})))$ can be replaced by α_i:

$$truth[agg(A) \ is \ C] = max_{\alpha_i \in D} \ min(\alpha_i, \ \mu_C(agg(A_{\alpha_i}))),$$

and we recover Expression (6.16).   ∎

6.3.3.3   *Algebraic properties related to negation*

This subsection is devoted to the property valid in the crisp case stating that "$agg(A)$ *is* C" is the negation of "$agg(A)$ *is* $\neg C$" and vice versa. We start with the case where the aggregate is defined for the empty set, or the fuzzy set A is normalized (in this latter case, the aggregate is always applicable since the fuzzy set A is not at all empty). This leads to the following Proposition 6.1 (the interested reader can find its proof in Bosc and Liétard, 2006).

Proposition 6.1. *When the aggregate agg is defined for the empty set, or when the fuzzy set, A, is normalized, one has*:

$$truth[agg(A) \ is \ C] = 1 - truth[agg(A) \ is \ \neg C].$$

In particular, this property holds for the statement "*card(A) is high*", as well as for the statement "*max(A) is high*", provided that fuzzy set A is normalized, since the aggregate *maximum* is not defined on the empty set.

In the general case (i.e., both A and C are fuzzy), we show that this property does not hold when A is not normalized and the aggregate is not defined for the empty set. In this situation, fuzzy set A is more or less empty (A being not normalized) which implies that the aggregate more or less does not apply (the aggregate being undefined for the empty set). As a consequence, the following property holds (a proof of which can be found in Bosc and Liétard, 2008).

Proposition 6.2. *When the aggregate agg is not defined for the empty set and A is a non-normalized fuzzy set, one has*:

$$truth[agg(A) \ is \ C] \leq sup_{x \ \in \ support(A)} \ \mu_A(x).$$

In other words, the truth value of "*agg(A) is C*" is bounded by the height of the fuzzy set A, which indeed reflects that the aggregate is somewhat inapplicable (fuzzy set A being more or less empty). As illustrated in the next example, due to this property, "*agg(A) is C*" cannot be the negation of "*agg(A) is* $\neg C$", i.e., their truth values are not complementary.

Example 6.13. Consider the fuzzy set A:

$$A = \{0.1/100, \ 0.1/10, \ 0.1/20000, \ 0.2/300\},$$

and the statement "*max(A) is high*". The fuzzy set A is close to the empty set, and *maximum* does not apply to the empty set. Consequently, $truth[max(A) \ is \ high]$ and $truth[max(A) \ is \ not \ high]$ cannot be expected to be high, and more precisely, neither of them can be over 0.2 (due to Proposition 6.2). This result agrees with intuition, and as a consequence, we cannot have $truth[max(A) \ is \ not \ high] = 1 - truth[max(A) \ is \ high]$. This example shows that the property stating that "*agg(A) is C*" is the negation of "*agg(A) is* $\neg C$" does not hold in the particular case where A is not normalized and the aggregate is not defined for the empty set.◇

6.3.4 *SQLf queries involving aggregates*

We now describe how the SQLf language can be extended by authorizing conditions which involve aggregates computed on fuzzy sets. The approach to evaluating such conditions advocated in the previous subsection is convenient in SQLf, since it delivers a unique degree of truth. In addition, no particular assumption is made as to its applicability, e.g., in terms of monotonicity.

It is worth mentioning that queries aimed at delivering the value of an aggregate as a final result are outside of the scope of this approach. This is the case, for instance, with the query: "for each department, retrieve the average salaries of young employees", which does not reduce to evaluating a condition of the type "$agg(A)$ is C".

Throughout this section, examples are based on the relation $Emp(\#e,$ *salary, age, nationality, children, distance,* $\#dep)$ which describes employees and whose key is $\#e$. For a given employee, the value of the attribute *distance* is the distance between his or her home and workplace, the value of the attribute *children* is the number of children he/she has. We first describe the use of aggregates in queries involving a partitioning of relations, then we deal with aggregates in the context of nested queries.

6.3.4.1 *Aggregates in the having clause*

In the basic version of SQLf (see Chapter 5), the partitioning is limited to a crisp relation (the application of aggregates being limited to crisp sets). Since the proposition introduced in the previous subsection allows the application of an aggregate to a fuzzy set, it becomes possible to partition a fuzzy relation and to deal with fuzzy subsets. As a consequence, a fuzzy predicate may appear in the *where* clause, and a more general pattern is now available:

> **select** ⟨calibration⟩ ⟨set$_1$ of attributes⟩ **from** ⟨relations⟩
> **where** ⟨fuzzy predicate⟩ **group by** ⟨set$_2$ of attributes⟩
> **having agg**(att) **is** C.

As in SQL, ⟨*set$_1$ of attributes*⟩ must be a subset of ⟨*set$_2$ of attributes*⟩ for the query to make sense. The result is obtained by means of a procedure which, from a conceptual point of view, consists of the following five-step process:

Step 1: The Cartesian product of the relations mentioned in the *from* clause is performed and the rows fulfilling the fuzzy condition mentioned in the *where* clause are retained (a fuzzy set of rows is obtained).

Step 2: Rows are gathered according to their values in $\langle set_2 \ of \ attributes \rangle$. This step delivers different fuzzy sets of rows (fuzzy relations) which are denoted by p hereafter.

Step 3: For each fuzzy relation p resulting from the partitioning, the aggregate *agg* is applied to its (fuzzy) projection $p[att]$ onto the attribute *att*. This projection is defined by:

$$\forall x \in support(p)[att], \ \mu_{p[att]}(x) = max_{t \in support(p) \ | \ t.att = x} \ \mu_p(t).$$

Each fuzzy relation p is then associated with the degree $truth[agg(p[att])$ *is* $C]$ which expresses its satisfaction with respect to the set condition mentioned in the *having* clause.

Step 4: The fuzzy set *res* of answers is delivered. The support of *res* is made of values of $\langle set_1 \ of \ attributes \rangle$ appearing in the fuzzy subsets p:

$$support(res) = \cup_p \ support(p)[\langle set_1 \ \text{of attributes} \rangle].$$

For a given fuzzy relation p, $((support(p))[\langle set_1 \ of \ attributes \rangle])$ is a singleton (the value of $\langle set_1 \ of \ attributes \rangle$ being unique for each fuzzy set p, since $\langle set_1 \ of \ attributes \rangle$ is included in the set of attributes mentioned in the *group by* clause). Each element a in $support(res)$ is an answer to the query to a degree given by:

$$\mu_{res}(a) = max_{p \ | \ a = support(p)[\langle set_1 \ of \ attributes \rangle]} truth[agg(p[att]) \ \text{is} \ C].$$

This last expression can be simplified in the particular case where $\langle set_1 \ of \ attributes \rangle = \langle set_2 \ of \ attributes \rangle$. In this case, for a given value a, there exists a unique fuzzy relation p where the value of $\langle set_1 \ of \ attributes \rangle$ equals a. In this case, we have:

$$\mu_{res}(a) = truth[agg(p[att]) \ \text{is} \ C],$$

where p is the fuzzy relation where $support(p)[\langle set_1 \ of \ attributes \rangle] = \{a\}$.

Step 5: A quantitative or a qualitative calibration is performed depending on $\langle calibration \rangle$. If no value appears in $\langle calibration \rangle$, the entire fuzzy set of answers is delivered to the user.

Example 6.14. The query: "retrieve the departments where the average salary of young employees is high" involves an aggregate function (the average) which applies to each fuzzy set made of young employees from the same department. This query is expressed in SQLf as follows:

> **select** #*dep* **from** *Emp* **where** *age* **is** *young*
> **group by** #*dep*
> **having avg**(*salary*) **is** *high*.

Relation *Emp* is partitioned into fuzzy subsets, we consider the subset *p* associated with department 100, as given in Table 6.5. This fuzzy relation is associated with the degree *truth*[*avg*(*A*) *is high*] where *A* is the result of the projection of *p* onto the attribute *salary*:

$$A = \{0.2/51000, \ 0.8/3000, \ 0.9/1000, \ 1/8000, \ 1/12000\}.$$

If it is assumed that $\mu_{high}(15000) = 1$, $\mu_{high}(6000) = 0.3$, $\mu_{high}(7000) = 0.5$, and $\mu_{high}(10000) = 1$, the results associated with each α-cut are those given in Table 6.6. From this table, we obtain the set of values $D = \{0.3, 0.5, 1\}$, which leads to $each(0.3) = 1$, $each(0.5) = 0.4$, $each(1) = 0.3$. Finally, we obtain:

$$truth[avg(A) \ is \ high] = max(min(0.3, 1), min(0.5, 0.4), min(1, 0.3)) = 0.4.$$

From Table 6.6, it can be checked that few α-cuts strongly satisfy "to have a high average salary". Consequently, the interpretation delivers a rather low result (degree 0.4) for the condition "the average salary of young employees is high".◇

Table 6.5   *Young* employees of department 100

#*e*	*salary*	*age*	*nationality*	*children*	*distance*	#*dep*	*young*
12	3,000	34	French	3	20	100	0.8
21	12,000	18	French	1	190	100	1
23	8,000	24	French	0	200	100	1
42	51,000	40	German	2	80	100	0.2
46	1,000	30	French	1	110	100	0.9

Table 6.6   The truth values of "$avg(A_\alpha)$ *is high*"

α	0.2	0.8	0.9	1
$avg(A_\alpha)$	15,000	6,000	7,000	10,000
$\mu_{high}(avg(A_\alpha))$	1	0.3	0.5	1

We now imagine that, in Table 6.5, several employees have the same salary. This is a particular case where several occurrences of the same value are aggregated. As a consequence, the aggregate applies to a fuzzy multiset instead of a fuzzy set, and the interpretation of $truth[agg(A)$ *is* $C]$ is slightly changed (since A is a fuzzy multiset instead of a fuzzy set). However, as shown in the next example, the approach still works, the only change being in the nature of the α-cuts, which become crisp multisets. As to partitioning, it is necessary to revise the projection so as to keep duplicate values (i.e., the projection delivers a fuzzy multiset).

Example 6.15. The query: "retrieve the departments where the average salary of young employees is around 2,500" is considered:

> **select** #*dep* **from** *Emp* **where** *age* **is** *young*
> **group by** #*dep* **having avg**(*salary*) **is** *around_2500*.

We consider the subset p of tuples associated with department 100 where three employees (13, 29, 32) have the same salary (3,000) (see Table 6.7). Fuzzy relation p (i.e., department 100) is associated with the degree $truth[avg(A)$ *is around* 2500], where A is the fuzzy projection of p onto the attribute *salary*. Since several employees have the same salary of 3,000 (employees 13, 29, 32) this salary is attached to several degrees of satisfaction with respect to the condition *to be young*. As a consequence, in this particular case, the projection delivers a fuzzy multiset of salaries (duplicate salary values are retained):

$$A = \{0.2/51000,\ 0.8/3000,\ 0.9/1000,\ 1/3000,\ 1/3000\}.$$

Assuming that:

$$\mu_{around\ 2500}(2500) = 1, \qquad \mu_{around\ 2500}(2333) = 0.8,$$
$$\mu_{around\ 2500}(3000) = 0.2, \qquad \mu_{around\ 2500}(12200) = 0,$$

Table 6.7   *Young* employees of department 100

#*e*	*salary*	*age*	*nationality*	*children*	*distance*	#*dep*	*young*
13	3,000	34	French	3	200	100	0.8
29	3,000	18	German	1	100	100	1
32	3,000	24	Italian	0	220	100	1
4	51,000	40	German	2	380	100	0.2
47	1,000	30	French	1	10	100	0.9

Table 6.8   The truth values of "$avg(A_\alpha)$ is *around 2500*"

α	0.2	0.8	0.9	1
$avg(A_\alpha)$	12,200	2,500	2,333	3,000
$\mu_{arnd2500}(avg(A_\alpha))$	0	1	0.8	0.2

the results associated with each α-cut (which is a multiset) are those represented in Table 6.8. From this table, we have the set of values $D = \{0.2, 0.8, 1\}$ which leads to $each(0.2) = 0.8$, $each(0.8) = 0.7$, $each(1) = 0.6$. Finally, we obtain:

$$truth[avg(A) \text{ is } around \text{ } 2500]$$
$$= max(min(0.2, \text{ } 0.8), \text{ } min(0.8, \text{ } 0.7), \text{ } min(1, \text{ } 0.6)) = 0.7.$$

This result confirms our intuition, since most of the α-cuts strongly satisfy "to have an average around 2,500".◇

6.3.4.2   *Nested queries*

As in SQL, it is possible in SQLf to build predicates calling on subqueries and to compare the value of an attribute with the value of an aggregate delivered by a subquery. The simplest case is when a unique value is returned by the subquery; in SQLf such a condition is written:

⟨attribute⟩ θ_f
(**select** agg(att) **from** ⟨relations⟩ **where** ⟨Boolean condition⟩),

where θ_f is a usual comparator in $\{>, <, =, \neq, \geq, \leq\}$ or a fuzzy one (e.g., *much larger than*). A restriction in the first version of SQLf made it impossible to consider a fuzzy predicate in the *where* clause of the inner selection block, since the application of aggregates was restricted to crisp sets. Thanks to the approach described above, a more general pattern can be used:

⟨attribute⟩ θ_f (**select** agg(att) **from** ⟨relations⟩ **where** ⟨fuzzy condition⟩).

This condition states that the value of the attribute is in relation θ_f with the aggregate returned by the inner selection block. The approach described above makes it possible to evaluate such a condition without evaluating the inner selection block, as is done in the regular case. The aggregate applies to the projection $r[att]$, where r is the fuzzy relation made of rows of the Cartesian product of ⟨relations⟩ satisfying ⟨fuzzy condition⟩. The truth value of this condition is $truth[agg(r[att])$ *is* $C]$, where C means "to be in relation θ_f^{-1} with the value of $\langle$attribute$\rangle$".

Example 6.16. The query: "retrieve the employees whose salary is *around* the average salary of their *young* colleagues" is expressed in SQLf by:

> **select** $\#e$ **from** *Emp E1*
> **where** *salary* $\approx$
>   (**select avg**(*salary*) **from** *Emp E2*
>   **where** $E1.\#dep = E2.\#dep$ **and** $E2.age$ **is** *young* **and**
> $E1.\#e \neq E2.\#e)$.

This query involves two copies of relation *Emp* (namely *E1* and *E2*) and the fuzzy comparator $\approx$, which stands for *around* and can be defined, e.g., as:

$$\mu_\approx(x, y) = 1 - min\left(\frac{|x-y|}{2000}, 1\right) \text{ for any pair of real values } (x, y).$$

Consider employee 23 of department 100 (see Table 6.5) whose salary is 8,000. The truth value of the condition:

$salary \approx$ (**select avg**(*salary*) **from** *Emp E2* **where** $E1.\#dep = E2.\#dep$
        and $E2.age$ **is** *young* **and** $E1.\#e \neq E2.\#e)$,

is given by $truth[avg(A)$ *is* $C]$, where A is the fuzzy set of salaries tied to his/her young colleagues given in Table 6.9, and condition C is defined by:

$$\mu_C(y) = \mu_\approx(8000, y) = 1 - min\left(\frac{|8000 - y|}{2000}, 1\right).$$

The results obtained for each α-cut are reported in Table 6.10. From this table, we see that the set of values to be considered in the computation of

Table 6.9   Salaries of the *young* colleagues of employee 23

salary	*young*
3,000	0.8
12,000	1
51,000	0.2
1,000	0.9

Table 6.10   The truth values of "$avg(A_\alpha)$ *is* C"

α	0.2	0.8	0.9	1
$avg(A_\alpha)$	16,750	5,333.3	6,500	12,000
$\mu_C(avg(A_\alpha))$	0	0	0.25	0

the final degree is $D = \{0.25\}$. As $each(0.25) = 0.1$, we obtain:

$$truth[avg(A) \ is \ C] = min(0.25, \ 0.1) = 0.1.$$

The satisfaction degrees attached to the α-cuts are very low and, as a consequence, a low result is obtained for the degree of satisfaction of the considered query.◇

The keyword *all* (resp. *any*) can be used when the inner selection block returns several values. The condition is then:

⟨attribute⟩ θ_f **all** (resp. **any**) (**select** agg(att) **from** ⟨relations⟩
where ⟨fuzzy condition⟩
group by ⟨set of attributes⟩).

For a given value v of ⟨attribute⟩, the evaluation of a nested condition involving *all* or *any* is equivalent to the following three-step process:

Step 1: The partition defined in the nested query is performed (each fuzzy relation thereby obtained is denoted by p hereafter).

Step 2: The truth value of the comparison is computed for each fuzzy relation p. Each fuzzy relation p is associated with the degree $truth[agg(p[att])$ *is* $C]$ — where C stands for θ_f^{-1} — of v ($\mu_C(x) = \mu_{\theta_f}(v, \ x)$).

Step 3: The overall degree of satisfaction is computed. When the keyword *all* (resp. *any*) is used, this degree expresses the fact that all (resp. at least one) fuzzy relations satisfy the comparison. It is defined as the smallest (resp. largest) value $truth[agg(p[att])$ *is* $C]$.

As before, the process to evaluate this condition does not entail the computation of the value returned by the inner selection block. More details can be found in Bosc and Liétard (2008).

6.3.5   *Evaluation of SQLf queries involving aggregates*

6.3.5.1   *Queries involving aggregates over fuzzy sets*

We now deal with the evaluation of SQLf queries involving conditions of
the type "$truth[agg(A)$ is $C]$". We first present a generic algorithm suited
to the processing of such queries, then we discuss its different variations
corresponding to the various ways in which such conditions can be used.

A generic algorithm. In the general case, Expression (6.19) is used to
compute $truth[agg(A)$ is $C]$ whose definition is:

$$truth[agg(A) \text{ is } C] = max_{\beta \in D} \, min(\beta, \, each(\beta)),$$

where $D = \{\beta \mid \exists \alpha \text{ such that } \beta = \mu_C(agg(A_\alpha))\}$ and:

$$each(\beta) = \sum_{\substack{]\alpha_i, \alpha_j] \text{ s.t. } \forall \alpha \in \,]\alpha_i, \alpha_j], \, agg(A_\alpha) \text{ is defined } \wedge \, \mu_c(agg(A_\alpha)) \geq \beta}} (\alpha_j - \alpha_i).$$

The algorithm which computes $truth[agg(A)$ is $C]$ needs to access the different values β (in an outer loop) and to compute $each(\beta)$ (in an inner
loop) for each of them. It is assumed, first, that the n levels of α-cuts are
increasingly ranked:

$$\alpha_0 = 0 < \alpha_1 < \alpha_2 < \cdots < \alpha_n$$

and stored in the array A: $\forall \, i \in [0, n]$, $A[i] = \alpha_i$.
    A second assumption concerns the values $\mu_C(agg(A_\alpha))$, which are pre-
computed and stored in the array B:

$$\forall \, i \in \{1, 2, \ldots, n\}, \, B[i] = \mu_C(agg(A_{\alpha_i})).$$

The final algorithm is based on an outer loop which scans B in order to
retrieve the largest value $min(B[i], \, each(B[i]))$. Obviously:

$$each(B[i]) = \sum_{j \text{ such that } B[j] \geq B[i]} (A[j] - A[j-1]).$$

The different values $each(B[i])$ are dynamically computed during the
processing in an inner loop, and stored in the variable E. We obtain
Algorithm 6.6:

Algorithm 6.6.

$res := 0;$
for $i := 1$ **to** n **do**
    $E := 0;$

```
for j := 1 to n do
   if B[j] ≥ B[i] then E := E + (A[j] − A[j − 1]);
enddo;
res := max(res, min(B[i], E));
enddo;
```

It is shown in the following how the previous algorithm can be used to evaluate SQLf queries calling on aggregates. The two cases of Section 6.3.4 (aggregates in the *having* clause, nesting) are dealt with in turn. We point out that the generation of the inputs to the algorithm (the two arrays A and B) can generally be performed in a reasonable time.

Aggregates in the having clause. In this case, the query is written (see Section 6.3.4.1):

> **select** ⟨calibration⟩ ⟨set$_1$ of attributes⟩ **from** ⟨relations⟩
> **where** ⟨fuzzy predicate⟩
> **group by** ⟨set$_2$ of attributes⟩
> **having** agg(att) **is** C

where ⟨set$_1$ of attributes⟩ is a subset of ⟨set$_2$ of attributes⟩. In this query, the fuzzy set of tuples satisfying the condition mentioned in the *where* clause is partitioned into several fuzzy subsets.

It is necessary to compute the degree of satisfaction with respect to the set condition mentioned in the *having* clause of each fuzzy subset p resulting from the partitioning. This degree is given by $truth[agg(p[att])$ is $C]$ and can be obtained using Algorithm 6.6, which implies that arrays A and B (which represent the inputs) must be appropriately initialized.

The values α in array A represent the different membership degrees appearing in the fuzzy set p resulting from the partitioning. It is assumed that they are increasingly ranked, i.e.:

$$\alpha_0 = 0 < \alpha_1 < \alpha_2 < \cdots < \alpha_n$$

and:

$$\forall i \in [0, n], \ A[i] = \alpha_i.$$

Array B contains the values $\mu_C(agg(p[att]_\alpha))$:

$$\forall i \in \{1, 2, \ldots, n\}, \ B[i] = \mu_C(agg(p[att]_{\alpha_i})).$$

These two arrays can be computed by scanning the fuzzy set p resulting from the partitioning.

In terms of processing time, the main cost of the evaluation comes from the partitioning, since it is necessary to access each tuple of the considered relation. If it is assumed that each fuzzy set resulting from the partitioning can be stored in main memory (this can be done using an index on the attributes mentioned in the *group by* clause, or else the partitioning can be entirely made in main memory), the additional cost conferred by the proposed algorithm remains quite reasonable.

Example 6.17. Consider the query: "retrieve the departments where the average salary of young employees is high" from Example 6.14, which can be expressed in SQLf as:

> **select** #*dep* **from** *Emp* **where** *age* **is** *young*
> **group by** #*dep*
> **having avg**(*salary*) **is** *high*.

As described in Example 6.14, relation *Emp* is partitioned into fuzzy subsets (made of young employees), each of them containing the employees working in the same department (a fuzzy set p describes the young employees of a given department). Relation *Emp* is partitioned into fuzzy subsets, and we consider the subset p associated with department 100 as given in Table 6.11. This fuzzy relation is associated with the degree $truth[avg(A) \text{ is } high]$, where A is the fuzzy projection of p onto the attribute *salary*:

$$A = \{0.2/51000,\ 0.8/3000,\ 0.9/1000,\ 1/8000,\ 1/12000\}.$$

If it is assumed that:

$$\mu_{high}(15000) = 1, \quad \mu_{high}(6000) = 0.3,$$
$$\mu_{high}(7000) = 0.5, \quad \mu_{high}(10000) = 1,$$

Table 6.11   *Young* employees of department 100

#*e*	*salary*	*age*	*nationality*	*children*	*distance*	#*dep*	*young*
12	3,000	34	French	3	20	100	0.8
21	12,000	18	French	1	190	100	1
23	8,000	24	French	0	200	100	1
42	51,000	40	German	2	80	100	0.2
46	1,000	30	French	1	110	100	0.9

then the results associated with each α-cut are those given in Table 6.12. Array A contains the different levels of α-cuts:

$$A[1] = 0.2, \ A[2] = 0.8, \ A[3] = 0.9, \ A[4] = 1,$$

while array B contains the different satisfactions of the α-cuts of A with respect to the condition "average is high" ($B[i] = \mu_C(agg(A_{\alpha_i})$ where $\alpha_i = A[i]$):

$$B[1] = 1, \ B[2] = 0.3, \ B[3] = 0.5, B[4] = 1.$$

It is then possible to apply the algorithm for the computation of Expression 6.19. Table 6.13 shows the evolution of computation (the indicated values for E and *res* are those obtained at the end of the iteration). At the end of the processing, the final result (in variable *res*) is 0.4, which, again, is in accordance with that obtained in Example 6.14.◇

Table 6.12   The truth values of "$avg(A_\alpha)$ is *high*"

α	0.2	0.8	0.9	1
$avg(A_\alpha)$	15,000	6,000	7,000	10,000
$\mu_{high}(avg(A_\alpha))$	1	0.3	0.5	1

Table 6.13   Evolution of the computation of $truth[avg(A)$ is *high*]

# iteration	i	j	E	*res*
1	1	1	0.2	0
2		2	0.2	0
3		3	0.2	0
4		4	0.3	0.3
5	2	1	0.2	0.3
6		2	0.8	0.3
7		3	0.9	0.3
8		4	1	0.3
9	3	1	0.2	0.3
10		2	0.2	0.3
11		3	0.3	0.3
12		4	0.4	0.4
13	4	1	0.2	0.4
14		2	0.2	0.4
15		3	0.2	0.4
16		4	0.3	0.4

Nested queries. When the aggregate appears in the *select* clause of a subquery, the following fuzzy predicate is defined (see Section 6.3.4.2):

⟨attribute⟩ θ_f
(**select** agg(att) **from** ⟨relations⟩ **where** ⟨fuzzy condition⟩),

where θ_f is a usual comparator in $\{>, <, =, \neq, \geq, \leq\}$ or a fuzzy relational operator (e.g., *much larger than*). The truth value of this condition is $truth[agg(r[att])$ is $C]$ where C means "to be in relation θ_f^{-1} with the value of ⟨attribute⟩" and r is the fuzzy relation made of the rows of ⟨relations⟩ satisfying ⟨fuzzy condition⟩.

From a processing point of view, the *where* clause of the subquery must be evaluated first, since it produces a fuzzy relation r. The projection of r onto *att* is then performed and $truth[agg(R[att])$ is $C]$ can be computed using Algorithm 6.6. The first step is then to build the two arrays A and B by scanning the fuzzy relation $r[att]$. The values in array A are the different membership degrees in $r[att]$ (satisfaction degrees of tuples from ⟨relations⟩ with respect to ⟨fuzzy condition⟩). Array B is such that:

$$B[i] = \mu_C(agg(r[att]_{\alpha_i})),$$

where $\alpha_i = A[i]$.

Example 6.18. We consider the query "retrieve the employees whose salary is *around* the average salary of their *young* colleagues" from Example 6.16:

>   **select** #*e* **from** *Emp E1*
>   **where** *salary* ≈
>   (**select avg**(*salary*) **from** *Emp E2*
>   **where** *E1.#dep* = *E2.#dep* **and** *E2.age* **is** *young* **and**
>   *E1.#e* ≠ *E2.#e*).

This query involves two copies of relation *Emp* (namely *E1* and *E2*) and the fuzzy comparator ≈, which stands for *around* and can be defined as:

$$\mu_{\approx}(x, y) = 1 - min\left(\frac{|x - y|}{2000}, 1\right) \text{ for any pair of real values } (x, y).$$

We consider employee 23 of department 100 (see Table 6.14) whose salary is 8,000. The truth value of the condition:

salary ≈ (**select avg**(*salary*) **from** *Emp E2* **where** *E1.#dep* = *E2.#dep*
and *E2.age* **is** *young* **and** *E1.#e* ≠ *E2.#e*)

Table 6.14 *Young* employees of department 100

#e	salary	age	nationality	children	distance	#dep	young
12	3,000	34	French	3	20	100	0.8
21	12,000	18	French	1	190	100	1
23	8,000	24	French	0	200	100	1
42	51,000	40	German	2	80	100	0.2
46	1,000	30	French	1	110	100	0.9

Table 6.15 Salaries of the *young* colleagues of employee 23

salary	young
3,000	0.8
12,000	1
51,000	0.2
1,000	0.9

is given by $truth[avg(A) \text{ is } C]$, where A is the fuzzy set of salaries tied to the employee's young colleagues (see Table 6.15).

Because the inner selection block is evaluated first, the relation represented in Table 6.15 is stored in main memory. It is scanned to fill in arrays A and B. Array A contains the different levels of α-cuts:

$$A[1] = 0.2, \quad A[2] = 0.8, \quad A[3] = 0.9, \quad A[4] = 1,$$

while array B contains the satisfaction degrees associated with the different α-cuts of $r[salary]$ with respect to the condition "≈ 8000" ($B[i] = \mu_C(avg (r[att]_{\alpha_i}))$, where $\alpha_i = A[i]$ and $\mu_C(y) = \mu_{\approx}(8000, y) = 1 - min(\frac{|8000-y|}{2000}, 1)$):

$$B[1] = 0, \ B[2] = 0, \ B[3] = 0.25, \ B[4] = 0. \diamond$$

As mentioned above, when the keyword *all* (resp. *any*) is used, the condition becomes:

⟨attribute⟩ θ_f **all** (resp. **any**) (**select** agg(att) **from** ⟨relations⟩
where ⟨fuzzy condition⟩
group by ⟨set of attributes⟩).

For a given value v of ⟨attribute⟩, Algorithm 6.6 can be used to evaluate a nested condition involving *all* or *any*. The processing consists of the following three steps:

(1) The partition mentioned in the inner selection block is built. Each fuzzy set p resulting from the partitioning is assumed to be either in main memory or accessible via an index.
(2) The truth value of the comparison is performed for each fuzzy relation p. The algorithm applies successively to each fuzzy relation p in order to compute $truth[agg(p[att])$ is $C]$ where C means "to be in relation θ_f^{-1} with v" ($\mu_C(x) = \mu_{\theta_f}(v, x)$). Array A contains the different levels of satisfaction appearing in $p[att]$, while array B is such that $B[i] = \mu_C(agg(p[att]_{\alpha_i}))$ where $\alpha_i = A[i]$.
(3) The overall degree of satisfaction is computed. It is defined as the smallest (resp. largest) $truth[agg(p[att])$ is $C]$ value.

6.4   Conclusion

In this chapter, we have discussed the expression, interpretation and evaluation of SQLf queries involving quantified statements or aggregates.

In the case of quantified statements, we have shown that such a construct can be used in SQLf queries for:

(1) aggregating atomic fuzzy predicates inside a *where* clause,
(2) expressing a condition at the level of a group of tuples inside a *having* clause,
(3) generalizing the nesting operators *all* and *any*.

Two interpretations of fuzzy quantified propositions have been pointed out, one based on Sugeno's integral, the other on Choquet's. We have limited the scope of the study to quantified statements of the type "*Q X are A*", since the more general form, namely "*Q X B are A*" raises serious interpretation problems. In particular, the aforementioned fuzzy-integral-based interpretations do not satisfy the following property: "If Q is an increasing quantifier, and if all the degrees $\mu_B(x)$ tend toward 0, then the truth value of the statement "*Q X B are A*" should tend toward 0". For the form "*Q X are A*", it has been shown that query processing algorithms can take advantage of some properties associated with Sugeno's and Choquet's fuzzy integrals in order to allow for early termination.

Conditions involving aggregates applied to fuzzy relations can be seen as a generalization of fuzzy quantified statements, in the sense that *count* is just a special case of aggregate (which has the nice property of being monotonic). The problems introduced by this generalization have been pointed out, and an interpretation based on an extension of Sugeno's fuzzy integral has been described. It must be noted, however, that this approach makes it possible to evaluate conditions *comparing* an aggregate to another aggregate or to a constant, or *matching* it against a fuzzy predicate, but does not provide a way of *computing the value* of an aggregate over a fuzzy set (which is a rather tricky issue; see Dubois and Prade, 1990). The integration of this latter functionality into SQLf is still a matter for future research.

Chapter 7

Division and Antidivision
of Fuzzy Relations

7.1 Introduction

It turns out that the division and antidivision operators, presented in Sections 2.2.2 and 2.3.4, are rich from a semantic point of view, as they convey the idea of association between concepts of a given domain. For instance, consider a database containing the two relations *curriculum (c)* and *profile (p)* with respective schemas $C(cand, skill, level)$ and $P(skill, importance)$. Tuple $\langle c, s, l \rangle$ of *curriculum* states that candidate c possesses skill s with level l, while tuple $\langle s, i \rangle$ of *profile* means that for the considered position, skill s has importance i. The query to look for candidates with at least level 2 for all the skills of importance 3 can be written by means of the division:

$$div(c\text{-}n2, \ p\text{-}i3, \ \{skill\}, \ \{skill\}),$$

where $c\text{-}n2 = project(select(c, \ level \geq 2), \ \{emp, \ skill\})$, and
$\quad \ p\text{-}i3 = select(p, \ importance = 3)$.

Now, assume that a user would like to retrieve the candidates who master all the "highly important" skills of the profile with a level "close to 5". A solution is to translate the two terms "highly important" and "close to 5", e.g., as "level greater than 8" and "importance in the interval [4, 6]", but it should be noted that a small change in these choices may have a significant impact on the result delivered. A more gradual behavior might help, by introducing preferences in the query such that:

- "highly important" and "close to 5" are fuzzy predicates,
- a division operating on fuzzy relations is made available.

Such a *division of fuzzy relations* is presented in Section 7.2. Similarly, imagine the case where the divisor relation $(p\text{-}i3)$ is made of 20 elements $(s_1, \ldots, s_{20})$ and that the dividend relation $(c\text{-}n2)$ contains the tuples (pairs):

$$\{\langle e_1, s_1 \rangle, \langle e_1, s_6 \rangle, \langle e_1, s_{20} \rangle, \langle e_2, s_1 \rangle, \langle e_2, s_2 \rangle, \ldots,$$
$$\langle e_2, s_{19} \rangle, \langle e_3, s_1 \rangle, \langle e_3, s_2 \rangle, \ldots, \langle e_3, s_{18} \rangle\}.$$

Neither e_1, nor e_2, nor e_3, is satisfactory for the initial query. However, it seems legitimate to think that if e_1 is definitely unsatisfactory, e_2 and e_3 are *almost* satisfactory (with an advantage for e_2) as they are associated with 19 and 18 of the required skills, respectively. The ability to discriminate between these three candidates may be desirable, and it is a matter of tolerance to exceptions. Such a mechanism is provided through the *tolerant division* discussed in Section 7.3.

A quite different extension of division can also be envisaged in order to deal with divisors where preferences are not assigned to tuples individually but to subsets of tuples. For example, suppose a user is interested in candidates who possess the skills $\{s_2, s_4, s_9\}$ and if possible $\{s_1, s_6\}$ and if possible $\{s_{15}\}$. In such a context, the ordering of candidates takes into account the fact that the sets of skills are hierarchically ordered, which will allow for production of a discriminated set of answers, as is the case in the two previous extensions. The notion of *stratified division* is dealt with in Section 7.4, while stratified antidivision queries and stratified queries mixing a division and an antidivision constitute the subject of Section 7.5.

7.2   Division of Fuzzy Relations

7.2.1   *Principles*

The division of fuzzy relations (as well as the extensions presented in the forthcoming sections) raises the question of rationality or legitimacy. We consider that the resulting operator deserves to be called a division if and only if its result may be characterized in terms of a quotient, i.e., the largest relation according to some inclusion criterion. Although some researchers (Cubero *et al.*, 1994; Dubois and Prade, 1996; Mouaddib, 1993; Yager, 1991a) have proposed extended divisions, the above point is most often absent, and we concentrate on approaches defining "sound" extensions.

The extension of division to fuzzy relations is based on an adaptation of the expression defining the original division (see Expression (2.2)):

$$div(r, s, A, B) = \{x \mid project(s, B) \subseteq \Gamma_r^{-1}(x)\},$$

where:

- the regular inclusion is replaced by a fuzzy one (i.e., a degree of inclusion in the spirit of Section 3.4),
- the two operands are fuzzy relations instead of regular ones.

If the dividend r and the divisor s have the respective schemas $R(A, X)$ and $S(B)$, this yields:

$$\forall x \in project(supp(r, X)), \ \mu_{div(r, s, A, B)}(x) = deg(s \subseteq \Gamma_r^{-1}(x)),$$

with $\mu_{\Gamma_r^{-1}(x)}(a) = \mu_r(a, x)$, $project(supp(r, X))$ representing the domain of X restricted to those values appearing in the dividend (relation r). Several types of degrees of inclusion exist (see for example Section 3.4.2) and they may be used in the above formula, provided that the result obtained is a quotient. To assess the fact that the result t of the extended division is a quotient entails an adaptation of the double characterization given in Section 2.2.2 for the regular division, which yields:

$$\forall x, \ (x \in project(supp(r), X)) \Rightarrow (cartprod(s, \mu_t(x)/\langle x \rangle)) \subseteq r, \qquad (7.1)$$

$$\forall x, \ (x \in project(supp(r), X)) \Rightarrow (\forall d_1 > \mu_t(x), \ cartprod(s, d_1/\langle x \rangle) \not\subseteq r). \qquad (7.2)$$

It is then necessary to specify the Cartesian product as well as the inclusion used in these two expressions. It is of interest to consider a generalized version of the Cartesian product (with respect to that introduced in Section 3.3.3) whose general format is:

$$\mu_{cartprod(r, s)}(uv) = cnj(\mu_r(u), \mu_s(v)),$$

where cnj denotes an extended conjunction operator. As for the inclusion, it is based on the crisp inclusion of fuzzy sets (Expression (3.6)) as this property is satisfied or not. In Bosc *et al.* (2007b,d), it is shown that the extension based on a logical view of the inclusion, i.e.:

$$\forall x \in project(supp(r, X)), \mu_{div(r, s, A, B)}(x) = \\ min_s(\mu_s(a) \Rightarrow_f \mu_r(a, x)), \qquad (7.3)$$

returns a resulting relation t which is a quotient provided that:

- if an R-implication ($\Rightarrow_R$) is used in Expression (7.3), the Cartesian product used in Expressions (7.1) and (7.2) is based on the generative norm of $\Rightarrow_R$ (e.g., the minimum for Gödel's implication, the product for Goguen's implication),
- if an S-implication ($\Rightarrow_S$) is used in Expression (7.3), the Cartesian product used in Expressions (7.1) and (7.2) is based on the noncommutative conjunction associated with $\Rightarrow_S$ (see Section 3.4.1).

Example 7.1. Consider the fuzzy relations:

$$r = \{0.7/\langle a_1,\, x\rangle,\, 0.4/\langle a_2,\, x\rangle,\, 1/\langle a_3,\, x\rangle,\, 1/\langle a_1,\, y\rangle,\, 0.6/\langle a_2,\, y\rangle,\, 0.2/\langle a_3,\, y\rangle\}$$

and

$$s = \{1/a_1,\, 0.5/a_2,\, 0.3/a_3\},$$

whose respective schemas are $R(A, X)$ and $S(B)$. The result t of the division of r by s according to Expression (7.3) is successively computed for three implications. With Gödel's implication, the result yields:

$$\mu_t(x) = min(1 \Rightarrow_{Gd} 0.7,\, 0.5 \Rightarrow_{Gd} 0.4,\, 0.3 \Rightarrow_{Gd} 1) = 0.4,$$

$$\mu_t(y) = min(1 \Rightarrow_{Gd} 1,\, 0.5 \Rightarrow_{Gd} 0.6,\, 0.3 \Rightarrow_{Gd} 0.2) = 0.2.$$

When performing the Cartesian product of s and t with the norm minimum, one obtains the relation:

$$\{0.4/\langle a_1,\, x\rangle,\, 0.4/\langle a_2,\, x\rangle,\, 0.3/\langle a_3,\, x\rangle,\, 0.2/\langle a_1,\, y\rangle,\, 0.2/\langle a_2,\, y\rangle,\, 0.2/\langle a_3,\, y\rangle\},$$

which is strictly included in r; thus Expression (7.1) holds. It is easy to check that Expression (7.2) holds as well, because of the presence of the tuples $\langle a_2,\, x\rangle$ and $\langle a_3,\, y\rangle$ whose grades equal those they have in r.

Similarly, with the Kleene–Dienes implication, the result t of the division of r by s is such that:

$$\mu_t(x) = min(1 \Rightarrow_{KD} 0.7,\, 0.5 \Rightarrow_{KD} 0.4,\, 0.3 \Rightarrow_{KD} 1) = 0.5,$$

$$\mu_t(y) = min(1 \Rightarrow_{KD} 1,\, 0.5 \Rightarrow_{KD} 0.6,\, 0.3 \Rightarrow_{KD} 0.2) = 0.6.$$

When performing the Cartesian product of s and t with the appropriate noncommutative conjunction ($nccl(a, b) = 0$ if $a + b \leq 1$, b otherwise), one obtains: $\{0.5/\langle a_1,\, x\rangle, 0.6/\langle a_1, y\rangle, 0.6/\langle a_2, y\rangle\}$, which is strictly included in r.

Relation t is maximal, because if 0.5 (resp. 0.6) is increased to 0.5^+ (resp. 0.6^+), the value $nccl(0.5, 0.5^+)$ (resp. $nccl(0.5, 0.6^+)$) leads to assignment of the degree 0.5^+ (resp. 0.6^+) to $\langle a_2, x \rangle$ (resp. $\langle a_2, y \rangle$) which is over 0.4 (resp. 0.6), and Expression (7.2) holds as well.

Last, we use Łukasiewicz's implication. The result of the division is:

$$t = \{0.7/x, \ 0.9/y\}.$$

When performing the Cartesian product of s and t with the associated norm $\top(a, b) = max(a + b - 1, 0)$, one obtains:

$$\{0.7/\langle a_1, x \rangle, \ 0.2/\langle a_2, x \rangle, \ 0.9/\langle a_1, y \rangle, \ 0.4/\langle a_2, y \rangle, \ 0.2/\langle a_3, y \rangle\},$$

which is included in r. In addition, it can easily be checked that t is maximal and once again, the characterization Expressions (7.1) and (7.2) hold.◇

As mentioned in Section 3.4.2, the use of an S-implication also accounts for a difference-based inclusion degree using Expression (3.11). As to the cardinality-based inclusion (see Expression (3.9)) for the division of fuzzy relations, it is shown in Bosc *et al.* (2007d) that no conjunction (neither norm nor noncommutative conjunction) can be found that characterizes the result of the division as a maximal relation. Indeed, it turns out that:

- the smallest Cartesian product of the divisor and the smallest result of a division may lead to a relation which is not included in the dividend,
- the largest result of a division may not be maximal.

7.2.2 *On the choice of implication*

The division of fuzzy relations constitutes an enrichment of database query languages which, in addition, turns out to be sound from a theoretical point of view, provided that R-implications or S-implications are used. To illustrate the impact of the choice of a given type of fuzzy implications, we will consider the application context with the two relations *curriculum* and *profile* previously introduced. We consider queries of the form: "find the candidates with a high level in all the skills of the considered (fuzzy) profile". Depending on whether an R-implication or an S-implication is chosen, the meaning of this query will vary significantly. With an R-implication, the levels of the skills in the profile play the role of thresholds (according to the meaning of R-implications). The profile is seen as a prototype, i.e., the description of an employee with the minimal levels of skills required to be completely satisfactory. Any actual candidate is penalized as soon as he/she has (at least) one skill with a level below the objective appearing in the prototype. The choice of different R-implications impacts the result when the threshold is not reached. When an S-implication is used, the profile accounts for the importance of each skill, or alternatively, the extent to which a skill is considered more or less critical. As a consequence, any non-completely important skill will confer a guaranteed degree of satisfaction, whatever the level attained by the candidate.

Example 7.2. Consider the relations:

$$curriculum = \{1/\langle John,\ s_1 \rangle,\ 0.6/\langle John,\ s_2 \rangle,\ 0.4/\langle John,\ s_3 \rangle,$$

$$0.8/\langle Peter,\ s_1 \rangle,\ 0.6/\langle Peter,\ s_2 \rangle\},$$

$$profile = \{1/s_1,\ 0.8/s_2,\ 0.2/s_3\}.$$

The division of *curriculum* by *profile* using Gödel's (resp. Goguen's) implication returns $\{0.6/John\}$ (resp. $\{0.75/John\}$), whereas the use of the Kleene–Dienes (resp. the Reichenbach) implication leads to $\{0.6/John, 0.8/Peter\}$ (resp. $\{0.68/John, 0.8/Peter\}$). In this example, a candidate who is eliminated with an R-implication (here *Peter* does not possess skill s_3 at all and he is discarded using either of the two considered R-implications), might be the best one with an S-implication (*Peter* is only somewhat penalized, since competence s_3 is not considered highly important in this context).◇

7.2.3   *Primitivity of the extended division operator*

We saw in Section 2.2.2 that regular division is a non-primitive operator which can be rewritten as an algebraic expression calling on difference, projection and Cartesian product operators; see Expression (2.3). One may wonder about the primitivity (or not) of the extended division defined by Expression (7.3). This question was investigated in Bosc (1998) and the main result achieved is the following. The division of fuzzy relations initially expressed using Expression (7.3), i.e., according to a logical view of the inclusion based on R-implications or S-implications, can be reformulated as:

$$div(r,\ s,\ A,\ B) =$$

$$differ(project(supp(r),\ X), \tag{7.4}$$

$$project(differ(supp(r),\ cartprod(project(r,\ X),\ s)),\ X)),$$

provided that:

- the Cartesian product is performed with the norm minimum,
- the conjunction intervening in the difference is the noncommutative conjunction associated with the implication when an R-implication is used for the division, or the norm associated with the implication if the division is done with an S-implication.

It should be noted that relation r must be replaced by its support in its first two occurrences (in the previous formula), which is intended to define the referential of X-values of interest.

Example 7.3. Consider the relations:

$$r = \{1/\langle a_1, x \rangle, 0.5/\langle a_2, x \rangle, 0.8/\langle a_1, y \rangle\}, \quad s = \{1/a_1, 0.6/a_2\},$$

whose respective schemas are $R(A, X)$ and $S(B)$. Using the definition based on an implication, as in Expression (7.3), we, obtain:

$$div(r, s, A, B) = \{0.5/x\} \text{ for Gödel's implication,}$$
$$div(r, s, A, B) = \{0.5/x, 0.4/y\} \text{ for the Kleene–Dienes implication,}$$
$$div(r, s, A, B) = \{0.9/x, 0.4/y\} \text{ for Łukasiewicz's implication.}$$

Now, we compute the result of the algebraic expression of division (Expression (7.4)) for the set difference operators corresponding to the conjunctions associated with these three implications. The components that do not depend on the difference are:

$$project(supp(r)) = \{x, y\},$$
$$cartprod(project(supp(r)), s) = \{1/\langle a_1, x \rangle, 0.6/\langle a_2, x \rangle,$$
$$1/\langle a_1, y \rangle, 0.6/\langle a_2, y \rangle\}.$$

With the noncommutative conjunction $ncc1(a, b) = 0$ if $(a + b) \leq 1$, b otherwise, associated with Gödel's implication, the inner difference yields $\{0.5/\langle a_2, x \rangle, 1/\langle a_1, y \rangle\}$ as $ncc1(1, 0) = 0$, $ncc1(0.6, 0.5) = 0.5$, $ncc1(1, 0.2) = 0.2$, $ncc1(0.6, 1) = 1$, and the final result is $\{0.5/x\}$.

With the norm $\top(a, b) = min(a, b)$ associated with the Kleene–Dienes implication, the inner difference returns $\{1/\langle a_1, x \rangle, 0.5/\langle a_2, x \rangle, 0.6/\langle a_2, y \rangle\}$ as $min(1, 0) = 0$, $min(0.6, 0.5) = 0.5$, $min(1, 0.2) = 0.2$, $min(0.6, 1) = 0.6$, and the final result is $\{0.5/x, 0.4/y\}$.

Finally, with the norm $\top(a, b) = max(a + b - 1, 0)$ associated with Łukasiewicz's implication, the inner difference delivers $\{0.1/\langle a_2, x \rangle,$

$0.2/\langle a_1, y \rangle$, $0.6/\langle a_2, y \rangle\}$, and the final result is $\{0.9/x, 0.4/y\}$. Observe that the two methods of computation lead to the same results for the three implications considered.◇

7.2.4   *Expressing extended division in SQLf*

From a practical point of view, it is necessary to express division queries in a user-oriented language such as SQLf (see Section 2.3). Recall that there are two ways of expressing a division in SQL: one based on relation partitioning and a transformation of set inclusion into a cardinality constraint, and another one calling on nested predicates (see Section 2.3.4). It turns out (see Bosc *et al.* (2007b,d) for details) that none of these approaches works for the division of fuzzy relations. The adopted formulation is based on the introduction of a set containment operator, in the spirit of that initially present in SEQUEL2 (Chamberlin *et al.*, 1976). This operator, generically denoted by "$F\,contains\,E$", delivers the degree of inclusion of E in F. Thus, the division of $r(A, X)$ by $s(B, Y)$ is written as:

> **select** X **from** r **where** *fuzzy-condition-1*
> **group by** X
> **having set**(A) **contains**[*implication*]
>   (**select** B **from** s **where** *fuzzy-condition-2*).

The degree of inclusion is computed using Expression (3.10) with the implication whose name is given as a parameter ("KD" for Kleene–Dienes, "Gd" for Gödel, "Lu" for Łukasiewicz, and so on).

Example 7.4. Consider the query to look for candidates who master all the "highly important" skills of the profile with a level "close to 5", addressed to the database containing the two relations *curriculum* and *profile* introduced previously. Using Reichenbach's implication, this query is expressed as:

> **select** *cand* **from** *curriculum* **where** *level* **is** *close_to_5*
> **group by** *cand*
> **having set**(*skill*) **contains**[*Rb*]
>   (**select** *skill* **from** *profile* **where** *importance* **is** *high*),

where the fuzzy terms "close_to_5" and "high" are user-defined predicates.◇

7.3 Tolerant Division

As mentioned in the introduction to this chapter, defining tolerant divisions may be appealing when it is necessary to discriminate between situations where division represents too high a demand with the risk of returning no answer. Two approaches to the design of tolerant divisions are reviewed below.

7.3.1 *Exception-based tolerant division*

The first approach to extension relies on replacement of the inclusion at the basis of the division of regular or fuzzy relations (Expressions (2.2) and (7.3)) by a tolerant inclusion in the sense of Section 3.4.2.5. Of course, the semantics of such a division depends on the choice of a quantitative or a qualitative tolerant inclusion.

7.3.1.1 *Quantitative tolerant division*

Quantitative tolerant division makes use of the quantifier *"almost all"* which is a softened version of the universal quantifier ($\forall$) from which the grades:

- $\mu_{almost\ all}(0) = w_n = 0$,
- $\mu_{almost\ all}(1) = w_0 = 1$,
- $\mu_{almost\ all}(1 - \frac{i}{n}) = w_i$ for $1 < i < n$

are issued, and where w_i expresses the degree of satisfaction when i out of the n elements of the referential are ignored. Algebraically, the tolerant division of $r(A, X)$ by $s(B)$ can be written as:

$$\mu_{qt\text{-}tol\text{-}div(r,\ s,\ A,\ B)}(x)$$
$$= max_{k\ \in\ [1,\ n]}\ min(\alpha_k,\ w_{k-1}) = min_{k\ \in\ [1,\ n]}\ max(\alpha_k,\ w_k), \quad (7.5)$$

where α_k is the kth smallest implication degree ($\mu_s(a) \Rightarrow_f \mu_r(a,\ x)$) and $w_k = \mu_{almost\ all}\ (1 - \frac{k}{n})$ assuming that the support of relation s involves n elements. Bosc *et al.* (2007b) showed that the result of this tolerant division with any R- or S-implication used in the calculus of the α_j's in Expression (7.5) is a quotient, provided that:

- an appropriate tolerant Boolean inclusion is used in the characterization formulas,

- either the divisor is a normalized relation (i.e., at least one element has the maximal degree 1), or else the relaxed quantifier "*almost all*" is non-fuzzy.

In SQLf, the expression of this division is similar to that given previously:

> **select** X **from** r **where** *fuzzy-condition-1*
> **group by** X
> **having set**(A) **qt-tol-contains**[*implication, almost all*]
>   (**select** B **from** s **where** *fuzzy-condition-2*).

The set comparison operator becomes "*qt-tol-contains*", whose arguments are the implication used and the user-defined softened quantifier "*almost all*".

7.3.1.2   *Qualitative tolerant division*

If qualitative tolerant inclusion is used, the division obtained allows for *low-intensity* exceptions, i.e., some compensation takes place when the situation is close to *full inclusion* (see Section 3.4.2.5). The technical aspects of such inclusions are dealt with in Section 3.4.2.5; here, we simply give the algebraic expression of the tolerant division of r by s according to the implication used. This expression is a direct adaptation of Expressions (3.13) and (3.14), both calling on two parameter values α and β in the unit interval. For an R-implication, we have:

$$\mu_{qlR\text{-}tol\text{-}div(r,\,s,\,A,\,B)}(x) = min_{x\,\in\,X}\;(\mu_s(a) \Rightarrow_R (\mu_r(a,\,x)) + \delta),$$

where

$$\delta = \begin{cases} 0 \text{ if } \mu_s(a) - \mu_r(a,\,x) \geq \beta,\, \beta \in [0,\,1], \\ \mu_s(a) - \mu_r(a,\,x) \text{ if } \mu_s(a) - \mu_r(a,\,x) \leq \alpha,\, \alpha \in [0,\,1] \text{ and } \alpha < \beta, \\ \text{linear in between.} \end{cases}$$

It is easy to see that it is possible to characterize the resulting relation t of such a tolerant division as a quotient, provided that the characterization accounts for the tolerance introduced in the division as follows:

$$\forall x,\, (x \in project(supp(r),\, X)) \Rightarrow (cartprod(s,\, \mu_t(x)/\langle x \rangle)) \subseteq r', \quad (7.6)$$

$$\forall x,\, (x \in project(supp(r),\, X)) \Rightarrow \\ (\forall d_1 > \mu_t(x),\, cartprod(s,\, d_1/\langle x \rangle) \not\subseteq r'), \quad (7.7)$$

with the Cartesian product performed with the generative norm of the R-implication considered for the division and r' such that $\mu_{r'}(u) = \mu_r(u) + \delta$.

Example 7.5. Consider the relations $s = \{1/a, \ 0.1/b, \ 0.6/c\}$ and $r = \{0.7/\langle a, \ x\rangle, \ 0.4/\langle c, \ x\rangle\}$. Element x does not belong to the result of the non-tolerant division of r by s using Gödel's implication. However, with $\alpha = 0.1$, $\beta = 0.3$, qualitative exception-tolerant division assigns x the degree 0.45. The Cartesian product of s and $0.45/x$ delivers $\{0.45/\langle a, \ x\rangle, \ 0.1/\langle b, \ x\rangle, \ 0.45/\langle c, \ x\rangle\}$, which is included in $r' = \{0.7/\langle a, \ x\rangle, \ 0.1/\langle b, \ x\rangle, \ 0.45/\langle c, \ x\rangle\}$. The degree 0.45 cannot be upgraded, as it would lead to a tuple $\langle c, \ x\rangle$ in the Cartesian product with a degree strictly greater than that it has in r' (0.45), and we can conclude that the result obtained is maximal.$\diamond$

For an S-implication, qualitative tolerant division can be written as:

$$\mu_{qlS\text{-}tol\text{-}div}(r, \ s, \ A, \ B)(x) = min_{x \ \in \ X} \ ((\mu_s(a) - \delta_1) \Rightarrow_S (\mu_r(a, \ x)) + \delta_2)),$$

where

$$\delta_1 = \begin{cases} \mu_s(a) \text{ if } \mu_s(a) \leq \alpha, \\ 0 \text{ if } \mu_s(a) \geq \beta, \\ \left(\dfrac{\alpha}{\beta - \alpha}\right) * (\beta - \mu_s(a)) \text{ in between}, \end{cases}$$

$$\delta_2 = \begin{cases} 1 - \mu_r(a, \ x) \text{ if } \mu_r(a, \ x) \geq 1 - \alpha, \\ 0 \text{ if } \mu_r(a, \ x) \leq 1 - \beta, \\ \left(\dfrac{\alpha}{\beta - \alpha}\right) * (\mu_r(a, \ x) + \beta - 1) \text{ in between}. \end{cases}$$

The result delivered in this case can also be characterized as a quotient thanks to:

$$\forall x, \ (x \in project(supp(r), \ X)) \Rightarrow (cartprod(s', \ \{\mu_t(x)/x\})) \subseteq r',$$
$$\forall x, \ (x \in project(supp(r), \ X)) \Rightarrow (\forall d_1 > \mu_t(x), \ cartprod(s', \ \{d_1/x\}) \not\subseteq r'),$$

where the Cartesian product is performed with the noncommutative conjunction associated with the S-implication chosen in the tolerant division. Relations r' and s' are such that $\mu_{r'}(u) = \mu_r(u) + \delta_2, \mu_{s'}(u) = \mu_s(u) - \delta_1$.

Example 7.6. Consider the relations $s = \{0.7/a, \ 0.9/b, \ 0.18/d\}$ and $r = \{1/\langle a, \ x\rangle, \ 1/\langle b, \ x\rangle, \ 0.2/\langle c, \ x\rangle, \ 0.85/\langle d, \ x\rangle\}$. Using the

Kleene–Dienes implication, non-tolerant division assigns x the grade 0.75. Using qualitative tolerant inclusion along with the thresholds $\alpha = 0.2$, $\beta = 0.45$, one obtains the degree 0.91 for x. The (modified) relations r' and s' are respectively $s' = \{0.7/a,\ 0.9/b,\ 0.1/c,\ 0.3/d\}$ and $r' = \{1/\langle a,\ x\rangle,\ 1/\langle b,\ x\rangle,\ 0.2/\langle c,\ x\rangle,\ 0.91/\langle d,\ x\rangle\}$. The Cartesian product of s' and $0.91/x$ yields $\{0.91/\langle a,\ x\rangle,\ 0.91/\langle b,\ x\rangle,\ 0.91/\langle d,\ x\rangle\}$, which is included in r'. If 0.91 is increased, tuple $\langle d,\ x\rangle$ in the Cartesian product receives a degree strictly greater than 0.91, and the inclusion no longer holds. Here again, the result obtained by qualitative tolerant division is maximal.◇

In SQLf, the expression of qualitative tolerant division does not significantly differ from that of the quantitative tolerant form. It is written as:

> **select** X **from** r **where** *fuzzy-condition-1*
> **group by** X
> **having set**(A) **ql-tol-contains**[*implication, α, β*]
>   (**select** B **from** s **where** *fuzzy-condition-2*).

7.3.2   *Resemblance-based tolerant division*

We now consider a tolerant division based on the use of a resemblance relation. In order to recover a superset of the result of the original division, the principle is to replace the dividend relation r by an enlarged relation r', obtained by composing r with a resemblance relation saying that values of the domain common to the dividend and divisor relations $(dom(A) = dom(B))$ may be somewhat close. In the Boolean context, an equivalence relation (reflexive, symmetric, and transitive) would be used for transforming the dividend. In the fuzzy framework, a similarity relation, where transitivity is replaced by:

$$\forall x,\ y,\ z \in X,\ sim(x,\ y) \geq sup_z\ min(sim(x,\ z),\ sim(z,\ y)),$$

or a proximity relation if transitivity is skipped, can be used. Whatever the type of resemblance relation used (denoted later by rsb), the dividend r is dilated, in the sense that the elements of the referential that are somewhat close to an element initially present in r are added to r. One considers that an element $\langle a, x\rangle$ that is missing in the dividend, can be replaced by another $\langle b, x\rangle$ which is present and such that b is close to (resembles) a. The mechanism suggested here produces *resemblance-based tolerant division*.

If r and s are two fuzzy relations of respective schemas $R(A, X)$ and $S(B)$, the resemblance-based tolerant division of r by s is defined as follows:

$$\mu_{rsb\text{-}tol\text{-}div(r, s, A, B)}(x) = min_{a \in supp(s)}\ \mu_s(a) \Rightarrow_f \mu_{dil(r)}(a, x), \qquad (7.8)$$

where $dil(r)$ is a dilated variant of r obtained using the resemblance relation rsb, i.e.:

$$\mu_{dil(r)}(a, x) = sup_{b \in dom(A)} \top(\mu_r(b, x), \mu_{rsb}(a, b)),$$

where $\top$ denotes a triangular norm. It is worth noting that, if a value initially absent can be added to the dividend r (with a given degree of membership), the degree of a value initially present can also be increased. The approximate division of $r(A, X)$ by $s(B)$ looks for the X-values associated in r with all the elements of the divisor or their neighbors (or substitutes). The less demanding the norm used, the larger the final dividend obtained, and the greater the result of the tolerant division.

By its very nature, resemblance-based tolerant division returns a quotient. Indeed, one may observe that this division reduces to a non-tolerant division where the dividend is not the initial one, but the one stemming from the use of the resemblance relation. The result t obtained can be characterized as a quotient thanks to Expressions (7.6) and (7.7), where the relation called r' becomes $dil(r)$.

Example 7.7. We consider:

- the proximity relation defined over colors $simcol$ = {$1/(red,\ red)$, $0.7/(red,\ carmine)$, $0.2/(red, vermillion)$, $1/(carmine,\ carmine)$, $1/(vermillion,\ vermillion)$, $0.8/(vermillion,\ orange)$, $1/(orange,\ orange)$},
- the dividend relation r = {$1/\langle carmine,\ p_1\rangle$, $0.6/\langle red,\ p_1\rangle$, $1/\langle red,\ p_2\rangle$, $0.6/\langle vermillion,\ p_1\rangle$, $0.4/\langle orange,\ p_2\rangle$},
- the divisor relation s = {$1/carmine$, $0.3/orange$}.

It is assumed that the tuple $d/\langle c,\ p\rangle$ of r means that color c is present in painting p with the level of significance d. The two tuples of s represent reference colors which are of interest to the user. Non-tolerant division of r by s using Gödel's implication delivers an empty result. The dilation of r with the norm minimum (the largest one) yields:

$$dil(r) = \{1/\langle carmine,\ p_1\rangle,\ 0.7/\langle red,\ p_1\rangle,\ 0.6/\langle vermillion,\ p_1\rangle,$$
$$0.6/\langle orange,\ p_1\rangle,\ 1/\langle red,\ p_2\rangle,\ 0.7/\langle carmine,\ p_2\rangle,$$
$$0.4/\langle orange,\ p_2\rangle,\ 0.4/\langle vermillion,\ p_2\rangle\},$$

and resemblance-based tolerant division of r by s with Gödel's implication in Expression (7.8) returns the relation $t = \{1/p_1, 0.7/p_2\}$. The Cartesian product of s and $\{1/p_1\}$ using the conjunction $\top(a, b) = min(a, b)$, which is the generative norm of Gödel's implication, is: $\{1/\langle carmine, p_1\rangle,$ $0.3/\langle orange, p_1\rangle\}$, which is included in $dil(r)$. Moreover, since 1 is the maximal grade, the grade assigned to p_1 cannot be increased. Similarly, the product of s and $\{0.7/p_2\}$ is $\{0.7/\langle carmine, p_2\rangle, 03/\langle orange, p_2\rangle\}$, which is also included in $dil(r)$ and is maximal.◇

7.4 Stratified Division

7.4.1 *Introduction*

The key idea behind the stratified division is to split the divisor into subsets organized hierarchically. By so doing, ordinal preferences are attached to the divisor, which is called a "stratified divisor". The general approach is to consider that the degree of satisfaction assigned to an element x of the dividend depends on the number of subsets S_i of the divisor with which it is connected. Three quite natural meanings can be distinguished, depending on the role allotted to the divisor seen as a hierarchical set:

- a direct extension of the division in a conjunctive way, where the first layer of the divisor is mandatory and the following layers are considered only desirable: find the elements x connected with S_1 *and if possible ... and if possible* S_n,
- a disjunctive view where x is all the more satisfactory as it is connected with all the values of a highly preferred (sub)set of the divisor: find the elements x connected with S_1 *or else ... or else* S_n,
- an intermediate approach where x is all the more highly ranked as it is connected with numerous and preferred (sub)sets of the divisor: find the elements x connected with S_1 *and-or ... and-or* S_n.

These three types of queries can be expressed in an SQL-like style, where the dividend may be any intermediate relation and the stratified divisor is either explicitly given by the user or results from a series of subqueries. Here also, we use a syntax based on a containment operator:

select top k X from r [**where** condition]
group by X
having set(A)
    contains $\{v_{1,1}, \ldots, v_{1,j_1}\}$ *connective ... connective* $\{v_{n,1}, \ldots, v_{n,j_n}\}$,

where "connective" stands for either "and if possible", or "or else", or "and-or". Such a statement induces an ordering over the divisor, namely $(S_1 = \{v_{1,1}, \ldots, v_{1,j_1}\}) \succ \cdots \succ (S_n = \{v_{n,1}, \ldots, v_{n,j_n}\})$, where $a \succ b$ denotes preference of a over b. Associated with this preference relation is an ordinal scale L with labels l_i (such that $l_1 > \cdots > l_n > l_{n+1}$) which is used to assign levels of satisfaction to elements pertaining to the result of a stratified division (l_1 corresponds to the highest satisfaction and l_{n+1} expresses rejection; they are the counterparts of 1 and 0 in the unit interval). Clearly, the framework considered is purely ordinal, and the user just has to specify a stratified divisor.

Example 7.8. First, consider the case of a user looking for wineshops offering Saint Emilion Grand Cru, Pomerol, and Margaux, and if possible Gewurztraminer Vendanges Tardives and Chablis Premier Cru, and if possible Pommard and Chambertin, assuming that a database involving the relation *wineshops(shop-name, wine)* is available. This query can be written as:

> **select top** 6 *shop-name* **from** *wineshops*
> **group by** *shop-name*
> **having set**(*wine*) **contains** {Saint Emilion Grand Cru,
> Pomerol, Margaux}
> **and if possible** {Gewurztraminer Vendanges Tardives,
> Chablis Premier Cru}
> **and if possible** {Pommard, Chambertin},

and induces the scale $L = l_1 > l_2 > l_3 > l_4$.

We next move to the context of medical diagnosis, and we illustrate the use of subqueries to build the stratified divisor. Consider relation *disease(name, symptom, frequency)* which describes the symptoms associated with some diseases as well as the frequency with which a given symptom appears for a given disease, and relation *patient(p-name, symptom)* which gives the symptoms shown by some patients. The following stratified division query looks for the patients who have all of the 100% frequent symptoms of influenza, and if possible all of the symptoms whose frequency is above 80%, and if possible all of the symptoms whose frequency is above 50%:

> **select top** 10 *p-name from patient*
> **group by** *p-name*
> **having set** (*symptom*) **contains**

> (**select** *symptom* **from** *disease*
> **where** *name* = "flu" **and** *frequency* = 100)
> **and if possible**
> (**select** *symptom* **from** *disease*
> **where** *name* = "flu" **and** *frequency* **between** 80 **and** 99)
> **and if possible**
> (**select** *symptom* **from** *disease*
> **where** *name* = "flu" **and** *frequency* **between** 50 **and** 79).

Here also, the scale is $L = l_1 > l_2 > l_3 > l_4$ since the divisor is composed of three strata.◇

7.4.2   The queries

The three types of queries, called conjunctive (CJ), disjunctive (DJ), and full-discrimination-based (FD), are the following:

- find the best k elements associated with S_1 *and if possible* ... *and if possible* S_n (CJ),
- find the best k elements associated with S_1 *or else* ... *or else* S_n (DJ),
- find the best k elements associated with S_1 *and-or* ... *and-or* S_n (FD),

and it is assumed that the schema of relation r is (A, X).

7.4.2.1   *Conjunctive queries (CJ)*

In CJ queries, to be qualified an element x must be connected with all the elements having the maximal importance (S_1). In this respect, this type of stratified query is strongly related to bipolar queries, a topic developed in Chapter 8. In addition, as soon as it ceases to be connected with all the elements of a set S_k, its association with the values in any set S_{k+p} does not matter for its final ranking. An element x is all the more preferred as it is associated with all the values of the succession of sets S_1 to S_i where i is large (if possible n for "perfection"). In other words, x is preferred to y if x is associated with all the values of the sets S_1 to S_p and y is associated with a shorter list of sets. More formally, we denote:

$$I(x) = \{i \mid S_i \not\subseteq \Gamma_r^{-1}(x)\} \text{ and if } I(x) \neq \emptyset, \, imin(x) = min(I(x)),$$

where, as before, $\Gamma_r^{-1}(x)$ stands for the set of A-values associated with x in relation r, i.e.:

$$\Gamma_r^{-1}(x) = \{a \mid \langle a, \, x \rangle \in r\}.$$

The grade of satisfaction $sat(x)$ obtained by x is expressed thanks to the scale L stemming from the stratified divisor as follows:

$$sat(x) = \begin{cases} l_1 \text{ if } I(x) = \emptyset, \\ l_{n+2-imin(x)} \text{ otherwise.} \end{cases} \tag{7.9}$$

By doing this, the satisfaction is seen to be a composition of the results of the division of the dividend with each of the layers of the divisor.

An alternative way of modeling CJ queries stems from the extension of Expression (7.3) by:

- dealing with the preferences applying to the divisor,
- using a symbolic/ordinal implication.

Indeed, we may use an augmented relational framework where each tuple of a relation rel is assigned a (symbolic) level of preference taken from the scale L, denoted by $pref_{rel}(t)$, and any tuple can be written $pref_{rel}(t)/t$. Since the dividend relation is not concerned with explicit preferences, its tuples are assigned the maximal level l_1, while the tuples which are absent are (virtually) assigned the lowest level l_{n+1}. The level of preference attached to a tuple of the divisor is directly induced from the place of the corresponding element in the hierarchy provided by the user. The implication can be chosen from among the fuzzy implications (Fodor and Yager, 2000) provided that:

- it is compatible with an ordinal context,
- it conveys the semantics of importance associated with the layered divisor.

It turns out that the implication defined as:

$$s_1 \Rightarrow_o s_2 = max(rev(s_1), \, s_2), \tag{7.10}$$

where s_1, s_2 are two symbols of an ordinal scale and rev denotes order reversal, meets the above requirements. With the scale $L = l_1 > \cdots > l_{n+1}$, one has: $\forall i \in [1, n], \, rev(l_i) = l_{n+2-i}$. Thus equipped, if V denotes the values of the divisor, the stratified division is defined as follows:

$$sat(x) = min_{v \in V} \, pref_s(v) \Rightarrow_o pref_r(v, \, x). \qquad (7.11)$$

As a consequence, if x is associated with all the values of the entire divisor, the maximal level of preference l_1 is obtained, and as soon as an association $<v, x>$ is missing in the dividend, the level of preference of x decreases all the more as v is highly preferred.

Example 7.9. Consider the divisor: $\{a, b\} \succ c \succ \{d, e\}$ and the dividend relation:

$$r = \{\langle a, x_1 \rangle, \langle b, x_1 \rangle, \langle c, x_1 \rangle, \langle d, x_1 \rangle), \langle a, x_2 \rangle), \langle b, x_2 \rangle),$$

$$\langle a, x_3 \rangle, \langle b, x_3 \rangle, \langle d, x_3 \rangle, \langle e, x_3 \rangle, \langle e, x_4 \rangle, \langle b, x_5 \rangle, \langle d, x_5 \rangle\}.$$

One has: $n = 3$, $I(x_1) = \{3\}$, $imin(x_1) = 3$ and, according to Expression (7.9), $sat(x_1) = l_2$; similarly, $sat(x_2) = sat(x_3) = l_3$, $sat(x_4) = sat(x_5) = l_4$, and the final result is: $x_1 \succ \{x_2, x_3\}$.

Now, referring to Expression (7.11), one has:

$$sat(x_1) = min(pref_s(a) \Rightarrow_o pref_r(a, x_1), \, pref_s(b) \Rightarrow_o pref_r(b, x_1),$$
$$pref_s(c) \Rightarrow_o pref_r(c, x_1), \, pref_s(d) \Rightarrow_o pref_r(d, x_1), \, pref_s(e) \Rightarrow_o$$
$$pref_r(e, x_1)) = min(l_1 \Rightarrow_o l_1, \, l_1 \Rightarrow_o l_1, \, l_2 \Rightarrow_o l_1, \, l_3 \Rightarrow_o l_1, \, l_3 \Rightarrow_o l_4)$$
$$= min(l_1, \, l_1, \, l_1, \, l_1, \, l_2) = l_2.$$

Similarly, one has:

$$sat(x_2) = min(l_1, l_1, l_3, l_2, l_2) = l_3, sat(x_3) = min(l_1, l_1, l_3, l_1, l_1) = l_3,$$

$$sat(x_4) = min(l_4, l_4, l_3, l_2, l_1) = l_4, sat(x_5) = min(l_4, l_1, l_3, l_1, l_2) = l_4.$$

As expected, these results coincide with those obtained previously with Expression (7.9).◇

7.4.2.2 *Disjunctive queries (DJ)*

While CJ queries have a conjunctive behavior, DJ queries are intentionally disjunctive instead, and S_1 is no longer a mandatory subset. Here, the order of the subsets is taken according to the user's preferences, so that element x is all the more preferred as it is connected with all the values of S_k and k is small (ideally 1 for "perfection"). In this case again, the associations with the subsets of higher index ($> k$), and then lower importance, do not play any role in the discrimination strategy. In other words, x is preferred to y if x is associated with all the values of the set S_k (and no S_j with $j < k$) and y is associated with S_p (and no S_m with $m < p$) and $p > k$. We denote:

$$I'(x) = \{i \mid S_i \subseteq \Gamma_r^{-1}(x)\} \text{ and if } I'(x) \neq \emptyset, \; ipmin(x) = min(I'(x)).$$

The grade of satisfaction attached to x is expressed as:

$$sat(x) = \begin{cases} l_{n+1} & \text{if } I'(x) = \emptyset, \\ l_{ipmin(x)} & \text{otherwise.} \end{cases} \tag{7.12}$$

The satisfaction is still a combination of the results of the division of the dividend with each of the layers of the divisor.

Example 7.10. Consider the divisor: $\{a, b\} \succ c \succ \{d, e\}$ and the dividend:

$$r = \{\langle a, x_1 \rangle, \langle d, x_1 \rangle, \langle e, x_1 \rangle, \langle c, x_2 \rangle, \langle d, x_2 \rangle, \langle e, x_2 \rangle,$$
$$\langle a, x_3 \rangle, \langle b, x_3 \rangle, \langle c, x_3 \rangle, \langle d, x_3 \rangle, \langle e, x_3 \rangle, \langle c, x_4 \rangle, \langle b, x_5 \rangle\}.$$

One has: $n = 3$, $I'(x_2) = \{2, 3\}$, $ipmin(x_2) = 2$, and $sat(x_2) = l_2$; similarly, $sat(x_1) = l_3$, $sat(x_3) = l_1$, $sat(x_4) = l_2$, $sat(x_5) = l_4$, and then the final result is: $x_3 \succ \{x_2, x_4\} \succ x_1.\diamond$

7.4.2.3 *Full discrimination-based queries (FD)*

Queries of type FD are designed to counter the common inability of CJ and DJ queries to distinguish between elements which are equally ranked because additional associations are not taken into account (e.g., x_2 and x_4 in the above example). Therefore, the principle when interpreting FD queries is to consider all the layers for which a complete association occurs. An element is all the more preferred as it is associated with a set S_i highly preferred; this same point of view applies when breaking ties. In this case, the grade of satisfaction for x may be expressed by using a vector $V(x)$ of dimension n, where $V(x)[i] = 1$ if x is associated with all the values of S_i, 0 otherwise. Ordering the elements boils down to comparing such vectors according to the lexicographic order ($\succ_{\text{lex}}$):

$$x \succ y \Leftrightarrow V(x) \succ_{\text{lex}} V(y) \Leftrightarrow$$
$$\exists k \in [1, n] \text{ such that } \forall j < k, \; V(x)[j] = V(y)[j] \text{ and } V(x)[k] > V(y)[k].$$

In this view, the scale L is not used directly even if the order of the elements of the vectors reflects it, in the sense that, if $i < j$, $V(x)[i]$ is more important than $V(x)[j]$ as $l_i > l_j$. It is, however, possible to use a scale to perform the comparison of elements in the context of FD queries, although this scale is not the initial one and is much larger (2^n levels instead of $(n + 1)$ in the original one). Consider the function which maps a vector V onto an integer score s as follows:

$$sat(x) = \sum_{i=1,\ldots,n} V(x)[i] * 2^{n-i}. \tag{7.13}$$

It is straightforward to prove that the preference of x over y as defined above is equivalent to $sat(x) > sat(y)$. In addition, from a calculus point of view, dealing with such scores is easier than comparing vectors.

Example 7.11. Consider the divisor: $\{a, b\} \succ c \succ \{d, e\}$ and the dividend:

$$r = \{\langle a, x_1\rangle, \langle d, x_1\rangle, \langle e, x_1\rangle, \langle c, x_2\rangle, \langle d, x_2\rangle, \langle e, x_2\rangle,$$
$$\langle a, x_3\rangle, \langle b, x_3\rangle, \langle d, x_3\rangle, \langle c, x_4\rangle, \langle b, x_5\rangle\}.$$

One has:

$$V(x_1) = (0, 0, 1), V(x_2) = (0, 1, 1), V(x_3) = (1, 0, 0), V(x_4) = (0, 1, 0),$$
$$V(x_5) = (0, 0, 0).$$

According to Expression (7.13):

$$sat(x_1) = 1, sat(x_2) = 3, sat(x_3) = 4, sat(x_4) = 2, sat(x_5) = 0,$$

and then the final result is: $x_3 \succ x_2 \succ x_4 \succ x_1.\diamond$

Relationship with the lexicographic order. As has been indicated, FD queries potentially use all the layers of the divisor in order to discriminate between the elements returned by a query; they are also founded on the lexicographic order. It turns out that the other two types of queries can also be thought of in this way. Interpreting any CJ or DJ query can be done through a vector accounting for the association with the values of each complete stratum of the divisor, as is done for FD queries. For CJ queries:

$sat(x) = l_{n-k+2}$ where k is the smallest index such that $V(x)[k] = 0$ ($k = n + 1$ if none).

In other words, the comparison of x and y can be based on a modified vector V' obtained from V by propagating the first 0 to the right, which yields the equivalence:

$$(sat(x) > sat(y)) \Leftrightarrow (V'(x) \succ_{\text{lex}} V'(y)).$$

Similarly, for DJ queries:

$sat(x) = l_k$ where k is the smallest index such that $V(x)[k] = 1$ ($k = n + 1$ if none).

Here also, the comparison of x and y can be based on a modified vector V'' obtained from V by propagating the first 1 to the right, which yields:

$$(sat(x) > sat(y)) \Leftrightarrow (V''(x) \succ_{\text{lex}} V''(y)).$$

Example 7.12. Consider again the data of Example 7.11, in particular the vectors V obtained there. From them, we obtain the modified vectors:

$$V'(x_1) = (0,0,0), V'(x_2) = (0,0,0), V'(x_3) = (1,0,0),$$
$$V'(x_4) = (0,0,0), V'(x_5) = (0,0,0),$$

which leads us to keep only x_3 as the result of the conjunctive stratified query. Similarly, the modified vectors V'' are:

$$V''(x_1) = (0,0,1), V''(x_2) = (0,1,1), V''(x_3) = (1,1,1),$$
$$V''(x_4) = (0,1,1), V''(x_5) = (0,0,0),$$

and the result of the disjunctive stratified query is: $x_3 \succ \{x_2, x_4\} \succ x_1$. These two results are exactly those obtained with Expressions (7.9), (7.11) and (7.12).◇

7.4.3   *Quotient property of the result delivered*

We now show that the result delivered by the three types of queries is a quotient. We specify a characterization in the spirit of Expressions (7.1) and (7.2) for each type of stratified query, which says that the result obtained is a maximal relation (with respect to the satisfaction levels (l_i's) assigned to its elements). For CJ queries, if it is assumed that x is assigned the grade l_i ($i \in [1, n]$) the following property holds:

$$\forall k \in [1, n - i + 1], \ S_k \times \{x\} \subseteq r, \tag{7.14}$$

$$\text{if } i > 1, \ S_{n-i+2} \times \{x\} \not\subseteq r. \tag{7.15}$$

In addition, any value x which is not (at all) in the result (grade of satisfaction l_{n+1}) is such that: $S_1 \times \{x\} \not\subseteq r$, which expresses the fact that its grade cannot even be increased from l_{n+1} to l_n.

Example 7.13. Consider the data of Example 7.9 where $n = 3$ and $sat(x_1) = l_2$. One has: $S_1 \times \{x_1\} = \{\langle a, x_1 \rangle, \langle b, x_1 \rangle\} \subseteq r$, and $S_2 \times \{x_1\} = \{\langle c, x_1 \rangle\} \subseteq r$, whereas $S_3 \times \{x_1\} = \{\langle d, x_1 \rangle, \langle e, x_1 \rangle\} \not\subseteq r$.

The same situation occurs for x_2.

Similarly, for x_3 one has: $S_1 \times \{x_3\} = \{\langle a, x_3 \rangle, \langle b, x_3 \rangle\} \subseteq r$, whereas $S_2 \times \{x_3\} = \{\langle c, x_3 \rangle\} \not\subseteq r$.

Finally, for $i = 4$ and 5: $S_1 \times \{x_i\} = \{\langle a, x_i \rangle, \langle b, x_i \rangle\} \not\subseteq r$.

This illustrates the validity of Expressions (7.14) and (7.15).◇

Similarly, for DJ queries, if x is assigned the grade of satisfaction l_i, letting $S_{n+1} = \emptyset$, one has:

$$S_i \times \{x\} \subseteq r \tag{7.16}$$

$$\text{if } i > 1, \ \forall k \in [1, i-1], \ S_k \times \{x\} \not\subseteq r. \tag{7.17}$$

Example 7.14. Consider the data of Example 7.10 where $n = 3$. One has: $sat(x_1) = l_3$ and $S_3 \times \{x_1\} = \{\langle d, x_1 \rangle, \langle e, x_1 \rangle\} \subseteq r$, whereas both $S_2 \times \{x_1\} = \{\langle c, x_1 \rangle\} \not\subseteq r$ and $S_1 \times \{x_1\} = \{\langle a, x_1 \rangle, \langle b, x_1 \rangle\} \not\subseteq r$.

Similarly, for $i = 2$ and 4, $sat(x_i) = l_2$, and $S_2 \times \{x_i\} = \{\langle c, x_i \rangle\} \subseteq r$ and $S_1 \times \{x_i\} = \{\langle a, x_i \rangle, \langle b, x_i \rangle\} \not\subseteq r$.

For x_3, $sat(x_3) = l_1$ and $S_1 \times \{x_3\} = \{\langle a, x_3 \rangle, \langle b, x_3 \rangle\} \subseteq r$.

Finally, $sat(x_5) = l_4$ and $S_4 \times \{x_5\} = \emptyset \subseteq r$ on the one hand, and $S_3 \times \{x_5\} = \{\langle d, x_5 \rangle, \langle e, x_5 \rangle\} \not\subseteq r$, $S_2 \times \{x_5\} = \{\langle c, x_5 \rangle\} \not\subseteq r$, $S_1 \times \{x_5\} = \{\langle a, x_5 \rangle, \langle b, x_5 \rangle\} \not\subseteq r$ on the other hand.

It turns out that Expressions (7.16) and (7.17) hold.◇

Turning to FD queries, recall that the grade of satisfaction of x is simply expressed as a function of the values of the vector V stating whether x is connected or not with all the values of the different layers of the divisor (see Expression (7.13)). The following property holds:

$$\forall i \in [1, n] \text{ such that } V(x)[i] = 1, S_i \times \{x\} \subseteq r, \qquad (7.18)$$
$$\forall i \in [1, n] \text{ such that } V(x)[i] = 0, S_i \times \{x\} \not\subseteq r, \qquad (7.19)$$

which means that if the grade $sat(x)$ is increased, some inclusion constraint(s) of the type seen in Expression (7.18) will be violated.

Example 7.15. Consider again Example 7.11. $V(x_1) = (0, 0, 1)$ and $S_1 \times \{x_1\} = \{\langle a, x_1 \rangle, \langle b, x_1 \rangle\} \not\subseteq r$, $S_2 \times \{x_1\} = \{\langle c, x_1 \rangle\} \not\subseteq r$, and $S_3 \times \{x_1\} = \{\langle d, x_1 \rangle, \langle e, x_1 \rangle\} \subseteq r$.

$$V(x_2) = (0, 1, 1) \text{ and } S_1 \times \{x_2\} = \{\langle a, x_2 \rangle, \langle b, x_2 \rangle\} \not\subseteq r, S_2 \times \{x_2\}$$
$$= \{\langle c, x_2 \rangle\} \subseteq r, \text{ and } S_3 \times \{x_2\} = \{\langle d, x_2 \rangle, \langle e, x_2 \rangle\} \subseteq r.$$
$$V(x_3) = (1, 0, 0) \text{ and } S_1 \times \{x_3\} = \{\langle a, x_3 \rangle, \langle b, x_3 \rangle\} \subseteq r, S_2 \times \{x_3\}$$
$$= \{\langle c, x_3 \rangle\} \not\subseteq r, \text{ and } S_3 \times \{x_3\} = \{\langle d, x_3 \rangle, \langle e, x_3 \rangle\} \not\subseteq r.$$
$$V(x_4) = (0, 1, 0) \text{ and } S_1 \times \{x_4\} = \{\langle a, x_4 \rangle, \langle b, x_4 \rangle\} \not\subseteq r, S_2 \times \{x_4\}$$
$$= \{\langle c, x_4 \rangle\} \subseteq r, \text{ and } S_3 \times \{x_4\} = \{\langle d, x_4 \rangle, \langle e, x_4 \rangle\} \not\subseteq r.$$
$$V(x_5) = (0, 0, 0) \text{ and } S_1 \times \{x_5\} = \{\langle a, x_5 \rangle, \langle b, x_5 \rangle\} \not\subseteq r, S_2 \times \{x_5\}$$
$$= \{\langle c, x_5 \rangle\} \not\subseteq r, \text{ and } S_3 \times \{x_5\} = \{\langle d, x_5 \rangle, \langle e, x_5 \rangle\} \not\subseteq r.$$

This is an illustration of the fact that Expressions (7.18) and (7.19) hold.⋄

7.5 Queries Mixing Division and Antidivision

7.5.1 *Motivation*

Most of what has been said about extending the division operator also holds for the antidivision operator, i.e., it is possible to define the antidivision of fuzzy relations, a tolerant antidivision and a stratified antidivision. Moreover, in each case the result obtained can be characterized as an anti-quotient (see Section 2.2.2). For instance, consider the case of a consumer who wants food products (e.g., noodles or vegetable oil) without certain additive substances. In the presence of the relation *Products(p-name, add-s)* describing which additives (*add-s*) are involved in products, a possible antidivision query is to search for products from which some prioritized substances are absent:

> **select top** 6 *p-name* **from** *Products* **group by** *p-name*
> **having set**(*add-s*) **contains-none** { "AS27", "BT12", "C3" }
> **and if possible none** { "AS5", "D2" } **and if possible none** { "D8" }.

The keyword "contains-none" is the counterpart of "contains" in a stratified division query. "*F contains-none E*" returns *true* if and only if $\forall x \in X$, $x \in E \Rightarrow x \notin F$. As with stratified division queries, an ordinal scale stems from the hierarchical divisor specified by the user.

    Now consider a user who would like to retrieve elements both connected with more or less necessary values and not connected with some more or less rejected values. Such queries constitute a new family of queries of interest which have both a stratified division component and an antidivision component. Although this new family is applicable to disjunctive and/or full discrimination stratified queries, we only deal with conjunctive queries in the rest of this section.

7.5.2   *Mixed stratified queries*

Here, we start with a stratified division or antidivision of a relation r whose schema is (A, X) by a relation s defined over B with A and B compatible (sets of) attributes. The scale L derived from the stratified divisor is used to attach a preference level to each value a of the divisor s, denoted by $pref_s(a)$. Since the dividend relation r is not concerned with preferences, its tuples are assigned the maximal level l_1 (if necessary, tuples absent from it receive the lowest level l_{n+1}). Letting V denote the values of the divisor s, the definition of stratified division and antidivision is as follows:

$$pref_{strat\text{-}div(r, s, A, B)}(x) = min_{v \in V}\ pref_s(v) \Rightarrow_o pref_r(v,\ x))$$
$$= min_{v \in V}\ max(rev(pref_s(v)), pref_r(v,\ x))$$

$$pref_{strat\text{-}antidiv(r, s, A, B)}(x)$$
$$= min_{v \in V}\ pref_s(v) \Rightarrow_o rev(pref_r(v,\ x)))$$
$$= min_{v \in V}\ max(rev(pref_s(v)), rev(pref_r(v,\ x))).$$

As a consequence, if x is associated with all (resp. none) of the values of the entire divisor, the maximal level of preference l_1 is obtained, and as soon as an association $\langle v,\ x \rangle$ is missing (resp. found) the level of preference of x decreases all the more as v is highly preferred (resp. unwanted).

A starting view of mixed stratified queries would be to consider them as made of two components, one "positive" expressing a stratified division, another "negative" issued from an antidivision, according to the following pattern:

select top k X **from** r **where** *condition*
group by X
having set(A) **contains**
$\{v_{1,1}, \ldots, v_{1,j_1}\}$ **and if possible** ... **and if possible** $\{v_{n,1}, \ldots, v_{n,j_n}\}$
and contains-none
$\{w_{1,1}, \ldots, w_{1,k_1}\}$ **and if possible none** ... **and if possible none**
$\{w_{p,1}, \ldots, w_{p,k_p}\}$.

This means that the query refers to two scales: $L_1 = l_1 > \cdots > l_{n+1}$ for the positive part, and $L_2 = l'_1 > \cdots > l'_{p+1}$ for the negative part. The overall satisfaction of a given x would then require the combination of two symbols (one from each scale), which raises a serious problem.

To overcome this difficulty, a solution is to build mixed queries in such a way that only a single scale ever comes into play. Each level of the scale used in a query will be assigned a set of desired values (contributing the positive part) and a set of unwanted values (the negative part), one of them being possibly empty. A mixed stratified query is then expressed according to the following pattern:

select top k X **from** r **where** *condition*
group by X
having set(A) **contains** [**pos:** $\{v_{1,1}, \ldots, v_{1,j_1}\}$, **neg:** $\{w_{1,1}, \ldots, w_{1,k_1}\}$]
and if possible ... **and if possible**
[**pos:** $\{v_{n,1}, \ldots, v_{n,j_n}\}$, **neg:** $\{w_{n,1}, \ldots, w_{n,k_n}\}$]

where "pos: S" (resp. "neg: S") denotes the positive (resp. negative) part associated with a set of desired (resp. unwanted) values at a given level of importance (layer), with which x must be (resp. not be) associated. In addition, note that it is possible to have "pos: {}" or "neg: {}", i.e. an empty positive or negative set, but not both, at each layer. Moreover, the absence of an element of the positive part or the presence of an element of the negative part leads to the non-satisfaction of the associated layer. Obviously, the scale behind this query is $L = l_1 > \cdots > l_{n+1}$.

The above type of query can be interpreted in a straightforward manner as follows. To be somewhat satisfactory, element x:

- must be associated with all the values $\{v_{1,1}, \ldots, v_{1,j_1}\}$ and none of the values $\{w_{1,1}, \ldots, w_{1,k_1}\}$,
- receives a level of satisfaction ($pref$) all the larger as it satisfies the association with all the values $\{v_{2,1}, \ldots, v_{2,k_2}\}, \ldots, \{v_{j,1}, \ldots, v_{j,k_j}\}$ and none of the values of $\{w_{2,1}, \ldots, w_{2,p_2}\}, \ldots, \{w_{j,1}, \ldots, w_{j,p_j}\}$, with j taking a high value ($j = n$ for the maximal level l_1).

In other words, x is preferred to y if x is connected with $\{v_{1,1}, \ldots, v_{1,k_1}\}, \ldots, \{v_{i,1}, \ldots, v_{i,k_i}\}$ and none of $\{w_{1,1}, \ldots, w_{1,p_1}\}, \ldots, \{w_{i,1}, \ldots, w_{i,p_i}\}$, while y is associated with $\{v_{1,1}, \ldots, v_{1,k_1}\}, \ldots, \{v_{j,1}, \ldots, v_{j,k_j}\}$ and none of $\{w_{1,1}, \ldots, w_{1,p_2}\}, \ldots, \{w_{j,1}, \ldots, w_{j,p_j}\}$ and $i > j$. Formally, we denote by $s = \{V_1, \ldots, V_n\}$ the different layers of the divisor where each V_i is made of a positive part P_i and a negative part N_i. Alternatively, s can be written as (P, N), its positive and negative parts. The mixed stratified division is defined as:

$$
\begin{aligned}
pref_{mix\text{-}strat\text{-}div(r, s, A, B)}&(x) \\
= min_{i \in [1, n]} \, min(&min_{v \in P_i} pref_s(v) \Rightarrow_o pref_r(v, x)), \\
&min_{w \in N_i} pref_s(w) \Rightarrow_o rev(pref_r(w, x))) \\
= min_{i \in [1,n]} \, min(&min_{v \in P_i} max(rev(l_i), pref_r(v, x)), \\
&min_{w \in N_i} max(rev(l_i), rev(prefr(w, x)))) \\
= min(&min_{v \in P} max(rev(pref_s(v)), pref_r(v, x)), \\
&min_{w \in N} max(rev(pref_s(w)), rev(pref_r(w, x)))).
\end{aligned}
$$

By construction, the result delivered by the above operation is a quotient, in the sense that it is a maximal relation.

Example 7.16. The following query in the context of non-weighted document retrieval illustrates the idea of mixed queries:

> **select top** 4 *title* **from** *books* **where** *year* > 2007 **group by** *title*
> **having set**(*terms*) **contains** [**pos**: $\{t_1, t_2, t_3\}$, **neg**: $\{t_4, t_5\}$]
>   **and if possible**
> [**pos**: $\{t_6\}$, **neg**: $\{\}$] **and if possible** [**pos**: $\{\}$, **neg**: $\{t_7\}$].

Here, the user wants books about t_1, t_2, and t_3, but neither t_4 nor t_5; in addition, dealing with t_6 is appreciated and to a lesser extent not dealing with t_7. In the presence of the following documents:

- d_1 indexed by t_1, t_2, t_6, t_{12}, t_{23},
- d_2 indexed by t_1, t_2, t_4, t_5, t_{10}, t_{14},
- d_3 indexed by t_1, t_2, t_3, t_4, t_{13}, t_{20}, t_{21},
- d_4 indexed by t_1, t_2, t_3, t_7, t_{11},
- d_5 indexed by t_1, t_2, t_3, t_6, t_7, t_{15},
- d_6 indexed by t_1, t_2, t_3, t_6, t_8, t_9

the degrees of satisfaction $(pref)$ assigned to these documents are:

$$pref(d_1) = min(min(l_1, l_1, l_4, l_1), min(l_1, l_1, l_1)) = l_4,$$
$$pref(d_2) = min(min(l_1, l_1, l_4, l_1), min(l_4, l_4, l_1)) = l_4,$$
$$pref(d_3) = min(min(l_1, l_1, l_1, l_3), min(l_4, l_1, l_1)) = l_4,$$
$$pref(d_4) = min(min(l_1, l_1, l_1, l_3), min(l_1, l_1, l_2)) = l_3,$$
$$pref(d_5) = min(min(l_1, l_1, l_1, l_1), min(l_1, l_1, l_2)) = l_2,$$
$$pref(d_6) = min(min(l_1, l_1, l_1, l_1), min(l_1, l_1, l_1)) = l_1,$$

which leads to the final result: $d_6 \succ d_5 \succ d_4$, since the first three documents are totally unsatisfactory (term t_3 is missing in documents d_1 and d_2, whereas document d_3 contains the definitely rejected term t_4).⬦

7.6 Evaluation of Division Queries

We first present strategies for processing the division over fuzzy relations. Subsequently, the evaluation of tolerant and stratified division queries is examined.

7.6.1 *Processing the division of fuzzy relations*

In Bosc *et al.* (1999b), three methods for the processing of regular (i.e., non-tolerant) division of fuzzy relations have been devised and compared:

- translation of the original division query into an SQL query involving a comparison of cardinalities, and a user-defined function to calculate the satisfaction degrees,
- translation of the original division query into an SQL query involving an inclusion, and a user-defined function to calculate the satisfaction degrees,
- compilation of the original division query into a processing algorithm encoded in a procedural language such as Pro*C or PL/SQL.

It appears that the third technique is by far the most efficient. For example, some experimental measures we have made, using the Oracle DBMS, show that for a dividend relation made of 60,000 tuples and a divisor made of 1,000 tuples, the processing time is 62 s for the cardinality-based approach, 36 s for the inclusion-based approach, and only 18 s for the approach based on a compiled algorithm. Another interesting result is that a similar division query addressed to crisp (instead of fuzzy) relations takes 15 s instead of 18 s to be processed. The additional cost introduced by the fuzziness of the relations under study is thus only around 20%. Hereafter, we describe the principle of the algorithm implementing the division of relation r of schema $R(A, X, \mu)$ by relation s of schema $S(B, \mu)$, where μ denotes in both cases the membership degree associated with each tuple. Recall that the evaluation of the division is based on Expression (7.3), i.e.:

$$\forall x \in project(supp(r,\ X)),\ \mu_{div(r,\ s,\ A,\ B)}(x) = min_s(\mu_s(a) \Rightarrow_f \mu_r(a,\ x)).$$

The idea is to use two nested loops. The first loop scans the different X-values present in relation r. For a given x, the inner loop scans the B-values b in the divisor, checks by means of a selection query whether $\langle b, x \rangle$ is in the dividend (and if so, with which degree), and updates the satisfaction degree associated with x in the result. In the algorithm, "impl" ($\Rightarrow_f$ in the above formula) denotes the fuzzy implication underlying the division (recall that either R-implications or S-implications are possible, which makes the division a parameterized operator).

If r (resp. s) is the fuzzy dividend (resp. divisor) relation and λ is the user-specified threshold (if the user does not specify one, $\geq \lambda$ can be replaced by > 0), we obtain Algorithm 7.1 as follows:

Algorithm 7.1.

define $cursX = $ **select distinct** X **from** r;
define $cursB = $ **select** μ, B **from** s;
$div \leftarrow \emptyset$;
for all x **in** $cursX$ **do**
begin
   $val\_imp \leftarrow 1$;
   for all $\langle mu_1, b \rangle$ **in** $cursB$ **and** $val\_imp > 0$ **do**
      select mu **into** mu_2 **from** r **where** $X = x$ **and** $A = b$;
      — it is assumed that if $\langle b,\ x \rangle$ is not in r, μ takes the value 0 —
      $val\_imp \leftarrow min(val\_imp,\ impl(mu_1,\ mu_2))$;
   end;
   if $val\_imp \geq \lambda$ **then** $div \leftarrow div \cup \{\langle val\_imp/x \rangle\}$ **endif**;

end;

rank-order(div) according to the satisfaction degrees val_imp.

7.6.2 *Processing the tolerant divisions of fuzzy relations*

The method associated with Algorithm 7.1 serves as the basis for implementing the various tolerant divisions.

7.6.2.1 *Quantitative exception-tolerant division*

In order to deal with this type of tolerant division, this algorithm has to go through a few modifications. First, it is no longer possible to calculate val_imp "incrementally" since the implication degrees attached to a given X-value x must be ranked in order to apply the weights w_i (see Section 7.3.1) appropriately. Consequently, it is necessary to store the different implication degrees attached to a given x. As for the weights, they depend on the cardinality of the divisor and on the fuzzy quantifier *"almost all"*. Therefore, they can be computed before entering the outer loop of the previous algorithm. Considering that val_imp can no longer be computed incrementally, it is not possible to stop the inner loop as soon as one obtains a zero implication degree (for a certain value b from s). However, it is still possible in some cases to stop that loop before scanning s entirely. We denote by k the number of w_i's greater than zero. As soon as more than k implication values equal to zero have been found (for a given x), one can conclude that x does not belong to the result. In the case where the user specifies a threshold λ (> 0), this pruning criterion can be refined in the following way. Let k' denote the number of w_i's greater than or equal to λ. As soon as more than k' implication degrees lower than λ are found (for a given x), one can conclude that x is not an answer. Compared to the reference algorithm suited to the classical division of fuzzy relations, the additional cost is related to: i) the necessity of scanning relation s once in order to compute its cardinality and then the weights w_i, ii) the fact that the inner loop cannot be stopped as often. The pruning condition is not as favorable in the tolerant case, but this does not change the nature of the worst case that can be encountered (and thus the maximal complexity of the algorithm).

7.6.2.2 *Qualitative exception-tolerant division*

Here, the impact on Algorithm 7.1 is more limited. One just has to replace the calls $impl(\mu_1, \mu_2)$ with $relaxed\_impl(\mu_1, \mu_2)$ which takes the thresholds α and β (see Section 7.3.1) into account. The extra cost is thus practically negligible, since the number of accesses to the relevant relations remains the same.

7.6.2.3   *Resemblance-based tolerant division*

Let $Prox(A_1, A_2, \mu)$ denote the proximity relation used (it is assumed that this relation is stored in the database). The basic idea is to retrieve, for a given x of the dividend r and a given b of the divisor s, the best substitute b' for b (in the sense of $Prox$), i.e., the value b' such that:

$$min(\mu_{Prox}(b', b), \mu_r(b', x)) = sup_{h \in domain(B)}\ min(\mu_{Prox}(h, b), \mu_r(h, x)).$$

The processing algorithm becomes:

Algorithm 7.2.

define $cursX$ = **select distinct** X **from** r;
define $cursB$ = **select** mu, B **from** s;
$div \leftarrow \emptyset$;
for all x **in** $cursX$ **do**
  $val\_imp \leftarrow 1$;
  for all $\langle mu_1, b \rangle$ **in** $cursB$ **and** $val\_imp > 0$ **do**
    $mu_2 \leftarrow$ highest degree attached to $\langle x, b' \rangle$ **in** r
    where b' is a possible substitute for b;
    $val\_imp \leftarrow min(val\_imp, impl(mu_1, mu_2))$
  enddo;
  if $val\_imp \geq \lambda$ **then** $div \leftarrow div \cup \langle val\_imp/x \rangle$ **endif**;
enddo;
rank-order(div) according to the satisfaction degrees val_imp.

The computation of the highest degree attached to $\langle x, b' \rangle$ in r where b' is a possible substitute for b is performed the following way:

Algorithm 7.3.

define $cursP$ = **select** μ, A_1 **from** $Prox$ **where** $A_2 = b$ **and** $\mu > 0$;
$d \leftarrow 0$;
for all $\langle \mu, a_1 \rangle$ **in** $cursP$ **do**
  select mu **into** μ' **from** r **where** $X = x$ **and** $A = a_1$;
  — it is assumed that if $\langle a_1, x \rangle$ is not in r, mu takes the value zero —
  $d \leftarrow max(min(\mu, \mu'), d)$;
enddo;
return d.

As an improvement, the definition of $cursP$ can be replaced by the following sequence:

select mu **into** μ **from** r **where** $X = x$ **and** $A = b$;
define $cursP$ = **select** mu, A_1 **from** $Prox$ **where** $A_2 = b$ **and** $mu > \mu$;

Indeed, for a given b, only the elements which are close to b at a degree higher than the degree of membership of $\langle x, b \rangle$ to r can possibly upgrade the final satisfaction degree attached to x.

The extra cost is due to the fact that, for each $\langle x, b \rangle$, one has to scan a subset of the possible substitutes to b. Let k_b denote the cardinality of that subset. One performs k_b selections on r instead of one in the inner loop (plus the k_b accesses to $Prox$ associated with b). The extra cost is thus equal to:

$$n * m * \left(2 \left[\sum_{b \in project(s, B)} k_b \right] - 1 \right)$$

where n (resp. m) denotes the cardinality of r (resp. s). This extra cost is not negligible and can even be seriously penalizing if the number of substitutes for each element of the divisor is high.

7.6.3 *Processing the conjunctive stratified division*

We now tackle implementation issues related to stratified divisions. We focus on CJ queries which give a good flavor of what can be done in this domain. The objective is to suggest some algorithms which are suited to a reasonably efficient evaluation of such queries, and to assess the extra cost with respect to queries involving no preferences.

7.6.3.1 *Principle of the algorithms*

Three algorithms implementing Expression (7.11) are described in turn. The first algorithm, called SSD, is based on a sequential scan of the dividend relation r. The idea is to access the tuples from the dividend "in gusts", i.e., by series of tuples which share the same X-attribute value (in the spirit of what is performed by a "group by" clause). Moreover, inside a cluster the tuples $\langle x, a \rangle$ are ordered increasingly on A. This is performed by the query:

select * **from** r **order by** X, A.

Thanks to a table which gives, for each value $(val\text{-}A)$ of the divisor, the layer to which it belongs $(str\text{-}A)$, one can update the number of values from each layer which are associated with the current element x, while scanning the result of the query above. At the end of a group of tuples, the layers are checked in decreasing order of their importance. The process stops as soon as the current element x is no longer associated with all of the values from a layer S_i. Three cases can occur:

- x is associated with all of the values from all the layers of the divisor and it gets the preference level l_1,
- the stop occurs while checking layer S_i whose importance is not maximal $(i > 1)$ and x is assigned the preference level $rev(l_i) = l_{n+2-i}$,
- the stop occurs while checking layer S_1 and x is assigned the level l_{n+1}, meaning that it is rejected.

In the second algorithm, called AGD, data accesses are guided by the divisor relation s. Thus, instead of scanning the dividend exhaustively and then checking the layers satisfied by a given x by means of the aforementioned table, the X-values are first retrieved from the dividend, and for each such x, the associations with the different layers are checked by means of an SQL query involving the aggregate *count*. Again, a layer is checked only if the layers of higher importance had all of their values associated with x. The first step is to retrieve the distinct values of attribute X present in r by means of the query:

select distinct X from r.

Then, for each value x returned, the A-values from S_1 which are associated with x in r are counted, by means of the query:

select count(*) from r where $X = x$ and A in (select A from S_1).

If the value returned equals the cardinality of S_1, layer S_2 is checked by means of a similar query, and so on. The loop stops as soon as a missing association with the current layer is detected. The preference level assigned to x is computed according to the same principle as in the previous algorithm.

The last strategy, called SRD, relies on a series of regular division queries. It consists of two steps:

- process as many regular division queries as there are layers in the divisor,
- merge the different results and compute the final preference degrees.

This algorithm has the following general shape:

(1) for each layer S_i of the divisor, process a division query which retrieves the x's which are associated in r with all of the values from S_i. The layers are examined in decreasing order of importance, and an element x is checked only if it belongs to the result of the query related to the previous layer.

(2) the results $T_1, \ldots, T_n$ of the previous division queries are merged by taking them in decreasing order of the corresponding layers. An element x which belongs to T_i (the result of layer S_i) but not to T_{i+1} is assigned the preference level l_{n-i+1} (assuming an empty table T_{n+1}). In the queries of this step, the algorithm used relies on an outer join.

7.6.3.2 *Experiments and results*

The main objective of the experimentation is to assess the additional processing cost related to the handling of preferences, and to compare the performances of the algorithms presented above. The experimentation was performed with the DBMS Oracle™ Enterprise Edition Release 8.0.4.0.0 running on an Alpha server 4000 bi-processor with 1.5 GB memory. A generic stratified division query was run on dividend relations of 300, 3,000 and 30,000 tuples, and a divisor including five layers made of respectively 3, 2, 1, 2 and 2 values. The query taken as a reference was the analogous division query without preferences, where the divisor is made of the sole first layer of the divisor. By doing this, we were able to assess the extra cost related only to the "preference part" of the query, i.e., to the presence of the non-mandatory layers. The reference division query was evaluated using three methods:

- sequential scan of the dividend (i.e., algorithm SSD without preferences, denoted by REF1),
- access guided by the divisor (i.e., algorithm AGD without preferences, denoted by REF2),
- algorithm REF3 based on a query involving a "group by" clause and a counting, as in the first step of algorithm SRD.

Moreover:

- we used synthetic data generated in such a way that the selectivity of each value b from the divisor relative to any x from the dividend was equal to 75% in the case of a division query (for a given value b from the

Table 7.1   Results from the division experiments
of Section 7.6.3.2

Size of the dividend	300	3,000	30,000
REF1	15.8	144.6	1451
REF2	49.7	570	15536
REF3	11.4	40.5	361.9
SSD	99	1011	10451
AGD	84	1035	29927
SRD	89	332	2923
Number of answers	15	172	1693

divisor and a given x from the dividend, tuple $\langle x, b \rangle$ had three chances out of four to be present in the dividend),

- each algorithm was run eight times so as to avoid any bias introduced by the load of the machine,
- the time unit equals 1/60 second.

The results obtained for the division are reported in Table 7.1. It can be seen that:

- among the reference methods for non-stratified operations, by far the most efficient is REF3. This is because it is based on a single query involving a "group by" clause, which is very efficiently optimized by the system,
- the processing time of the algorithms based on a sequential scan of the dividend (i.e., SSD and REF1) vary linearly with respect to the size of the dividend, in contrast to those from the second family (REF2 and AGD); in the case of algorithm SRD (implemented with an outer join), its complexity shows some linearity as soon as the size of the dividend is above a certain threshold (which means that there is a fixed cost attached to it, which depends on the number of layers of the divisor),
- algorithm SSD becomes better than AGD as soon as the size of the dividend is over 1,000 tuples. But the best algorithm is SRD (implemented with an outer join), which outperforms all the others as soon as the dividend contains more than 300 tuples. It is worth noting that the ratio between SRD and REF3 is almost constant (around eight), which is due to the fact that SRD performs one query of type REF3 per layer (of which there are five in this case), plus the combination of the intermediate results.

In summary, it appears that algorithm SRD based on an outer join is the most efficient, except for very small sizes of dividend where AGD is slightly better. However, the extra cost of SRD with respect to the most efficient reference algorithm, namely REF3, is still significant (the multiplicative factor is around eight). What all these measures show is somewhat predictable: the best way to process a division (stratified or not) is to express it by means of a single query that can be efficiently handled by the optimizer of the system, and not by external programs which usually introduce a significant overhead. Consequently, if stratified division functionality were to be integrated into a commercial DBMS, it is clear that it would have to be handled by the optimizer at an internal level, and processed as one query, according to the format given in Section 7.4.2.1 and in such a way that the evaluation of a given x is done in one step.

7.7 Conclusion

This chapter has been devoted to the division operation, which turns out to be rich from a semantic point of view. The original operator of the relational algebra is intended to retrieve those values of a binary dividend relation that are connected with at least all the elements of another relation called divisor. Its extension in order to introduce preferences (and therefore graduality) has been considered according to various points of view:

- the operands become fuzzy (graded) relations and, depending on the type of fuzzy implication used to generalize the non-fuzzy operator, the division operator obtained conveys different meanings,
- some tolerance is introduced into the checking of the connection between elements of the divisor and dividend relations; here also, diverse semantics are available depending on whether the tolerance is of a quantitative or qualitative nature, or is a consequence of some similarity between the values of the domain serving to pair dividend and divisor relations,
- the divisor is stratified, i.e., it is composed of diverse subsets corresponding to values more or less required/desired; in this context, queries calling on both a positive and negative divisor, i.e., an ordered list of desired and unwanted elements, have been proposed, thus mixing division and antidivision operations.

We have focused on "elementary" extensions; one might think of composing some of them, for instance both softening the universal quantifier and having a stratified divisor.

Two central questions have been dealt with for the diverse approaches to extension: i) the quotient property of the delivered result, which makes it legitimate to call the extended operator a division, and ii) the rewriting of the extended operator in terms of primitive operations as is the case for the original division.

Incidentally, note the relationship between the division of fuzzy relations and quantified statements of the form "QXB **are** A", where Q is a quantifier, X is a regular set of elements, and A, B are fuzzy predicates. Indeed, to find the extent to which "each store has ordered almost all *cheap* products in a *moderate* quantity" corresponds to evaluating the proposition "almost all *cheap* products are *ordered in a moderate quantity*".

Finally, it is worth mentioning that the query/document matching process in information retrieval is based on the inclusion operation, as is the case for the division (see Expressions (2.1) and (2.2)). In Bosc *et al.* (2009b), the authors investigate the use of a graded inclusion (see Section 3.4.2.3) in textual information retrieval. In this context, documents and queries are represented by fuzzy sets, which are matched using a tolerant inclusion based on fuzzy implications and triangular norms. Some insights on the practical use of this graded inclusion in information retrieval are provided. Experiments show that, with appropriate settings (fuzzy operators and weighting schemes), it is possible for the fuzzy-set-based model to mimic classical systems and to provide results close to those returned by state-of-the-art systems.

Chapter 8

Bipolar Fuzzy Queries

8.1 Introduction

A complementary concept to flexible preferences is that of bipolarity, and especially its application to queries in the context of databases and information systems. Bipolarity refers to the propensity of the human mind to reason and make decisions on the basis of positive and negative effects (Dubois and Prade, 2002, 2008b). Positive statements express what is possible, satisfactory, permitted, desired, or considered as being acceptable. Negative statements, however, express what is impossible, rejected, or forbidden (De Tré *et al.*, 2010). Negative preferences correspond to *constraints*, since they specify which values or objects have to be rejected (i.e., those that do not satisfy the constraints), while positive preferences correspond to *wishes*, as they specify which objects are more desirable than others (i.e., satisfy user wishes) without rejecting those that do not meet the wishes.

Several types of bipolarity have been described (Dubois and Prade, 2008a). In this chapter, asymmetric (also called heterogeneous) bipolarity is considered, where positive and negative poles refer to potentially different notions (attributes). More precisely, we deal with queries made up of two poles, one meant as a constraint — denoted by C — and the other acting as a wish — denoted by W — where a pair (C, W) is interpreted as: "C and if possible W". In the situation considered later on, the two components of a query, although they can be assessed on the same scale (true/false or the unit interval), are not of the same nature, and it is convenient to specify how any pair of elements (tuples or objects) are compared depending on their scores with respect to the constraint and the wish. Recall, however, that in a complex constraint (resp. wish), the fuzzy-set-based approach requires the elementary preferences to be commensurable.

A commonly made choice (see in particular Dubois and Prade, 2008a) for interpreting a bipolar condition consists of discriminating between two objects x and y using first the constraint, and then, if needed (i.e., if x and y are not distinguishable on the constraint), using the wish. In this chapter, this point of view is chosen and a lexicographic order is used. If $(C(x), W(x))$ and $(C(y), W(y))$ denote the scores of x and y with respect to the constraint C and the wish W, one has:

$$x \succ y \Leftrightarrow (C(x) > C(y)) \text{ or } (C(x) = C(y) \text{ and } W(x) > W(y))$$

$$(8.1)$$

where $x \succ y$ means that x is preferred to y. A consequence is that an object which is beaten on the constraint cannot win even if it is much better on the wish.

In this chapter, we describe an extension of relational algebra (Bosc *et al.*, 2010a) which provides a querying framework capable of handling bipolar fuzzy queries and relations. The set of operators defined in the following generalizes the "fuzzy relational algebra" that has been previously proposed for handling non-bipolar fuzzy queries and relations (see, e.g., Bosc *et al.*, 1999a and Chapter 5), which is itself a generalization of classical relational algebra.

8.2   Preliminaries

8.2.1   *About bipolarity*

In the following, we denote by $\mu(u)$ (resp. $\eta(u)$) the degree reflecting the extent to which an element u satisfies a constraint C (resp. a wish W). When C and W concern the same attribute, two consistency conditions may be considered (Dubois and Prade, 2008a):

- Strong consistency, as for twofold fuzzy sets (Dubois and Prade, 1987):

$$sup_u min(\eta(u), 1 - \mu(u)) = 0, \qquad (8.2)$$

which states that the support of the wish must be included in the core of the constraint. Then the wish can only discriminate between the tuples which have degree 1 for the constraint. As noted in Dubois and Prade (2008a), the pair (W, C) under the condition in Expression (8.2) is a twofold fuzzy set, since $support(W) \subseteq core(C)$.

- Weak consistency in the spirit of intuitionistic fuzzy sets (Atanassov, 1986):

$$\forall u, \eta(u) \leq \mu(u) \qquad (8.3)$$

which states that the wish must be included in the constraint (in the sense of Zadeh). The wish can then be used to discriminate between these tuples that somewhat satisfy the constraint. As noted in Dubois and Prade (2008a), the pair $(\overline{C}, W)$ under the condition in Expression (8.3) is an intuitionistic fuzzy set in the sense of Atanassov (1986).

When C and W concern different attributes, the weak consistency of the wish with the constraint can be recovered by replacing (C, W) with $(C, C \wedge W)$, as suggested in Dubois and Prade (2008a). In the following, we will interpret the conjunction (in $C \wedge W$) by means of the t-norm product so as not to lose any discrimination power (which would be the case if *min* were chosen).

From now on only weak consistency is enforced. We define a bipolar relation (in the database sense) as a relation where each tuple t is associated with two degrees $\mu(t)$ and $\eta(t)$ in the unit interval, expressing the extent to which the tuple satisfies the constraint (resp. wish) that has been used to produce the relation. A tuple will be denoted by $(\mu, \eta)/t$. In base relations, $\mu(t) = \eta(t) = 1, \forall t$. It is assumed that tuples such that $\mu = 0$ do not appear in the relation (they do not belong to it at all). We denote by r a bipolar *base relation* and by (C, W) the constraint/wish pair that is applied to r in order to build a *bipolar fuzzy relation* r'. One has:

$$r' = \{(\mu, \eta)/t | \mu = \mu_C(t) \wedge \eta = \eta_W(t)\}. \qquad (8.4)$$

When no constraint is expressed, Dubois and Prade (2008a) suggest to use $C = true$. Note that this case is unlikely to be very useful in practice, since it corresponds to the situation where all the tuples from the queried relation are considered equally acceptable. The wish just allows a "bonus" to be given to some items; for example, "I prefer red cars, but if there are none, any car will do". Reciprocally, when no wish is expressed (the case of a non-bipolar — fuzzy or not — condition), we use $W = false$. In this case, the condition acts as a regular selection expression, i.e., it discards the items which do not satisfy the constraint at all (and ranks the others, if the constraint is fuzzy).

We introduce the operators *lmin* and *lmax*, which play a major role in defining the conjunction (and intersection) and the disjunction (and union):

$$lmin((\mu,\eta),(\mu',\eta')) = \begin{cases} (\mu,\eta) \text{ if } \mu < \mu' \text{ or } (\mu = \mu' \text{ and } \eta < \eta'), \\ (\mu',\eta') \text{ otherwise.} \end{cases}$$

$$lmax((\mu,\eta),(\mu',\eta')) = \begin{cases} (\mu,\eta) \text{ if } \mu > \mu' \text{ or } (\mu = \mu' \text{ and } \eta > \eta'), \\ (\mu',\eta') \text{ otherwise.} \end{cases}$$

It is straightforward to prove that *lmin* (resp. *lmax*) is commutative, associative, idempotent, monotonic, has $(1, 1)$ (resp. $(0, 0)$) as a neutral element, and $(0, 0)$ (resp. $(1, 1)$) as an absorbing element. These properties make it legitimate to use *lmin* and *lmax* as conjunction and disjunction operators respectively (in the spirit of triangular norms and co-norms).

Note that Expression (8.4) can also be written:

$$r' = \{(\mu,\eta)/t|\mu = lmin((\mu_C(t),\eta_W(t)),(\mu_r(t),\eta_r(t)))\}, \qquad (8.5)$$

since r is a *base* relation (where $\mu_r(t) = \eta_r(t) = 1, \forall t$).

8.3 Extended Algebraic Operators

In this section, we review the operators from classical relational algebra, and we give an extended version of them in the framework of bipolar fuzzy relations. For each operator, the starting point is its usual definition; we generalize that by stating how the pairs of degrees attached to every tuple of a bipolar relation must be taken into account. In the following, we use as an example the case of a user who wants to buy a used car. We consider the relation *Car* of schema (*#id, make, model, mileage, years, price, color*).

8.3.1 *Intersection*

The straightforward definition of intersection is:

$$inter(r,s) = \{(\mu'',\eta'')/t|(\mu,\eta)/t \in r \wedge (\mu',\eta')/t \in s \\ \wedge(\mu'',\eta'') = lmin((\mu,\eta),(\mu',\eta'))\}. \qquad (8.6)$$

Example 8.1. The query "find the cars that meet both John's and Peter's needs/preferences" may be expressed as $inter(Car_J, Car_P)$, where $Car_J = select(Car, (C_1, W_1))$, $Car_P = select(Car, (C_2, W_2))$, and (C_1, W_1) (resp. (C_2, W_2)) represents John's (resp. Peter's) bipolar requirement.

Table 8.1   An instance of relation Car_J

#id	make	model	mileage	years	price	μ	η
1	Ford	Mondeo	35,000	2008	22,000	0.7	0.2
2	Seat	Altea	50,000	2007	17,000	0.6	0.4
3	VW	Golf	39,000	2008	21,000	0.8	0.8
4	Toyota	Corolla	60,000	2006	18,000	0.9	0.4
5	VW	Passat	75,000	2004	16,000	0.8	0.1
6	Opel	Zafira	58,000	2007	15,000	1	0.5

Table 8.2   An instance of relation Car_P

#id	make	model	mileage	years	price	μ	η
2	Seat	Altea	50,000	2007	17,000	0.9	0.3
4	Toyota	Corolla	60,000	2006	18,000	0.7	0.7
5	VW	Passat	75,000	2004	16,000	0.8	0.6
7	Renault	Laguna	18,000	2008	25,000	0.3	0.1

Table 8.3   The result of $inter(Car_J, Car_P)$

#id	make	model	mileage	years	price	μ	η
2	Seat	Altea	50,000	2007	17,000	0.6	0.4
4	Toyota	Corolla	60,000	2006	18,000	0.7	0.7
5	VW	Passat	75,000	2004	16,000	0.8	0.1

Note: the selection operator on bipolar fuzzy relations is formally defined in Section 8.3.6. With the extensions of Car_J and Car_P given in Tables 8.1 and 8.2 respectively, one obtains the result represented in Table 8.3.◇

8.3.2   *Union*

The definition of the union of fuzzy bipolar relations is:

$$
\begin{aligned}
union(r, s) = & \\
\{((\mu'', \eta'')/t| & \\
(\exists(\mu, \eta)/t \in r & \wedge \exists(\mu', \eta')/t \in s \wedge \\
& (\mu'', \eta'') = lmax((\mu, \eta), (\mu', \eta')))\vee \\
(\exists(\mu, \eta)/t \in r & \wedge \not\exists(\mu', \eta')/t \in s \wedge (\mu'', \eta'') = (\mu, \eta))\vee \\
(\not\exists(\mu, \eta)/t \in r & \wedge \exists(\mu', \eta')/t \in s \wedge (\mu'', \eta'') = (\mu', \eta'))\}.
\end{aligned}
\tag{8.7}
$$

Table 8.4   Result of *union* (Car_J, Car_P)

#id	make	model	mileage	years	price	μ	η
1	Ford	Mondeo	35,000	2008	22,000	0.7	0.2
2	Seat	Altea	50,000	2007	17,000	0.9	0.3
3	VW	Golf	39,000	2008	21,000	0.8	0.8
4	Toyota	Corolla	60,000	2006	18,000	0.9	0.4
5	VW	Passat	75,000	2004	16,000	0.8	0.6
6	Opel	Zafira	58,000	2007	15,000	1	0.5
7	Renault	Laguna	18,000	2008	25,000	0.3	0.1

Example 8.2. The query "find the cars that meet John's or Peter's needs/preferences" may be expressed as *union*(Car_J, Car_P). With the extensions of Car_J and Car_P given in Tables 8.1 and 8.2 respectively, one obtains the result represented in Table 8.4.◇

8.3.3   *Cartesian product*

The straightforward definition of the Cartesian product of bipolar fuzzy relations is:

$$cartprod(r, s) = \{(\mu'', \eta'')/t \oplus t'|(\mu, \eta)/t \in r \wedge (\mu', \eta')/t' \in s$$
$$\wedge(\mu'', \eta'') = lmin((\mu, \eta), (\mu', \eta'))\}, \tag{8.8}$$

where $\oplus$ denotes concatenation.

8.3.4   *Negation*

Even though it does not appear very useful in practice to negate a bipolar condition involved in a selection clause, the negation operator plays a crucial role in defining the set difference, as we will see later. Several ways of defining the negation of a bipolar condition can be envisaged *a priori*. We denote $(C', W') = \neg(C, W)$. We consider three requirements for the negation of bipolar fuzzy conditions. Operator $\neg$ must be:

- order-reversing (R1):

$$\forall t_1, t_2, (\mu_C(t_1), \eta_W(t_1)) <_{\text{lex}} (\mu_C(t_2), \eta_W(t_2))$$
$$\Leftrightarrow (\mu_{C'}(t_2), \eta_{W'}(t_2)) <_{\text{lex}} (\mu_{C'}(t_1), \eta_{W'}(t_1)),$$

where $<_{\text{lex}}$ denotes lexicographic order,
- consistency-preserving (R2): $\forall t, \eta_{W'}(t) \leq \mu_{C'}(t)$,
- involutive (R3): $\neg(\neg(C, W)) = (C, W)$.

8.3.4.1 *Approach inspired by twofold fuzzy sets*

The definition of the negation proposed by Dubois and Prade (1987) in the framework of twofold fuzzy sets is:

$$\neg(C, W) = (\neg W, \neg C), \tag{8.9}$$

where $\neg$ is a standard fuzzy negation. However, using it *as such* in the context of bipolar fuzzy conditions is debatable for two reasons:

- first, this definition does not preserve the equivalence between a bipolar condition involving an empty wish and a non-bipolar condition, which induces the constraint $\neg(C, false) = (\neg C, false)$. Indeed, with Expression (8.9), one has: $\neg(C, false) = (true, \neg C)$. A solution is to represent a bipolar condition involving an empty wish as (C, C) instead of $(C, false)$ — note that this choice preserves weak consistency. Then $\neg(C, C) = (\neg C, \neg C)$, and the aforementioned equivalence holds.
- second, this definition assumes that the negation of a constraint (resp. a wish) is a wish (resp. a constraint), whereas this is not so obvious in the case where C and W concern different attributes. Indeed, in general, the wish makes sense (i.e., is relevant) only when the constraint is satisfied. A typical example is: "I want a Volkswagen and if possible a black one". With the definition above, the bipolar condition becomes "I do not want a black car, and if possible not a Volkswagen", which does not appear to be a very intuitive negation of the initial statement.

In fact, when C and W concern different attributes, the solution is to replace (C, W) by $(C, W \wedge C)$ — as proposed in Dubois and Prade (2008a) — to enforce the consistency condition. Then, adapting Expression (8.9), we obtain:

$$\neg(C, W) = (\neg(C \wedge W), \neg C), \tag{8.10}$$

and the second problem mentioned above disappears. The negation of "I want a Volkswagen and if possible a black one" is now "a black Volkswagen is out of the question, and if possible I would like a car which is not a Volkswagen".

Unfortunately, this negation is not order-reversing.

8.3.4.2 *Counter-example*

Consider the bipolar condition $Q = (C, W)$ — where C and W are assumed to concern the same attribute — and a relation r containing the tuples t_1

and t_2 such that:

$$\mu_C(t_1) = 0.8, \eta_W(t_1) = 0,$$
$$\mu_C(t_2) = 0.6, \eta_{W_1}(t_2) = 0.6.$$

We have:

$$\mu_{C'}(t_1) = 1, \eta_{W'}(t_1) = 0.2,$$
$$\mu_{C'}(t_2) = 0.4, \eta_{W'}(t_2) = 0.4,$$

and we have both

$$(\mu_C(t_1), \eta_W(t_1)) >_{\text{lex}} (\mu_C(t_2), \eta_W(t_2))$$

and

$$(\mu_{C'}(t_1), \eta_{W'}(t_1)) >_{\text{lex}} (\mu_{C'}(t_2), \eta_{W'}(t_2)).\diamond$$

Note that viewing a bipolar requirement (C, W) as an intuitionistic fuzzy set $(\neg C, W)$ (see Section 8.2.1) leads to the same problem. Indeed, since the standard negation of an intuitionistic fuzzy set (E, F) is defined as (F, E), one obtains the bipolar requirement $(\neg W, \neg C)$ — corresponding to the intuitionistic fuzzy set $(W, \neg C)$ — as the negation of (C, W), i.e., the same as that obtained with the twofold fuzzy set view.

8.3.4.3   *From "and if possible" to "or else"*

Another approach that can be thought of has its starting point in the idea that, since (C, W) has a conjunctive nature ("*C and if possible W*"), its negation should be of a disjunctive nature and could be expressed as "W' *or else* C'". A straightforward definition of (W', C') is:

$$W' = \neg C \quad \text{and} \quad C' = \neg W.$$

The initial consistency condition then leads to $\forall x, \eta_{W'}(x) \geq \mu_{C'}(x)$, and when C and W concern different attributes, $C' = \neg W$ must be replaced by $C' = \neg(C \wedge W)$. However, this view raises important problems of compositionality, since it leads to mixing in the same relation — resulting from a compound bipolar condition — of pairs of degrees with different semantics, as illustrated in the following example.

Example 8.3. Consider the compound bipolar condition $Q = (C_1, W_1) \wedge \neg(C_2, W_2)$, where C_i and W_i are assumed to concern the same attribute, and a relation r containing the tuples t_1 and t_2 such that:

$$\mu_{C_1}(t_1) = 0.8, \eta_{W_1}(t_1) = 0.6,$$
$$\mu_{C_1}(t_2) = 0.4, \eta_{W_1}(t_2) = 0.3,$$
$$\mu_{C_2}(t_1) = 0.2, \eta_{W_2}(t_1) = 0,$$
$$\mu_{C_2}(t_2) = 0.7, \eta_{W_2}(t_2) = 0.1.$$

We have:

$$(\mu_Q(t_1), \eta_Q(t_1)) = lmin((0.8, 0.6), (0.8, 1)) = (0.8, 0.6),$$
$$(\mu_Q(t_2), \eta_Q(t_2)) = lmin((0.4, 0.3), (0.3, 0.9)) = (0.3, 0.9).$$

In one case (t_1), the pair of degrees has the semantics "and if possible", whereas in the other (t_2) it has the meaning "or else", which makes the result very difficult to interpret.◇

8.3.4.4 *An approach based on product and division*

We start from the following definition:

$$\neg(C, W) = (C', W') \quad \text{with}: \quad \mu_{C'} = 1 - \mu_C \quad \text{and}$$

$$\eta_{W'} = \begin{cases} (1 - \mu_C) \cdot \left(1 - \dfrac{\eta_W}{\mu_C}\right) & \text{if } \mu_C \neq 0, \\ 1 & \text{otherwise.} \end{cases} \qquad (8.11)$$

This definition trivially satisfies properties (R1) and (R2), but requirement (R3), which expresses the involutivity property, is not perfectly satisfied, as illustrated by the example below.

Example 8.4. We use the notations: $\neg(C, W) = (C', W')$ and $\neg(C', W') = (C'', W'')$. Table 8.5 illustrates that, in most cases, the involutivity property holds, i.e., $(C, W) = (C'', W'')$. In fact, the only case where it does not hold is when $\mu_C = 1$ and $\eta_W \neq 1$ (illustrated by the row in bold in the table). Indeed $(1, b \neq 1)$ becomes $(0, 0)$ through negation, which itself becomes $(1, 1)$.◇

A solution to this problem of imperfect involutivity is to tolerate the presence of pairs of the type $(0, b > 0)$ in a bipolar fuzzy relation — which represents a slight exception to the consistency requirement — considering that, when the constraint is entirely false, one does not care about the value

Table 8.5   Imperfect involutivity of the negation

	μ_C	η_W	$\mu_{C'}$	$\eta_{W'}$	$\mu_{C''}$	$\eta_{W''}$
t_1	1	1	0	0	1	1
t_2	1	0.6	0	0	1	1
t_3	0.8	0.8	0.2	0	0.8	0.8
t_4	0.8	0.5	0.2	0.075	0.8	0.5
t_5	0.8	0.2	0.2	0.15	0.8	0.2
t_6	0.8	0	0.2	0.2	0.8	0
t_7	0.7	0.7	0.3	0	0.7	0.7
t_8	0.6	0.6	0.4	0	0.6	0.6
t_9	0.6	0.1	0.4	0.33	0.6	0.1
t_{10}	0.6	0	0.4	0.4	0.6	0
t_{11}	0.2	0.2	0.8	0	0.2	0.2
t_{12}	0.1	0.1	0.9	0	0.1	0.1
t_{13}	0.1	0	0.9	0.9	0.1	0
t_{14}	0	0	1	1	0	0

of the wish anyway. This can be done by changing the previous definition into:

$$\neg(C, W) = (C', W') \text{ with: } \mu_{C'} = 1 - \mu_C \text{ and}$$

$$\eta_{W'} = \begin{cases} 1 - \eta_W & \text{if } \mu_C \in \{0, 1\}, \\ (1 - \mu_C) * \left(1 - \dfrac{\eta_W}{\mu_C}\right) & \text{otherwise.} \end{cases} \tag{8.12}$$

However, while building a bipolar relation by means of a pair (C, W) that concerns different attributes, one must then:

- not replace (C, W) by $(C, C \wedge W)$ when $\mu_C = 0$,
- also store the elements whose pair of degrees is of the type $(0, b \neq 0)$ in the bipolar relation,

so as not to disrupt the computation of set difference. In fact, instead of replacing (C, W) by $(C, C \wedge W)$, one must replace (C, W) by:

$$(C, W \wedge (C \vee (1 \Rightarrow_{RG} \neg C))),$$

where $\Rightarrow_{RG}$ denotes the Rescher–Gaines implication.

However, instead of tolerating exceptions to the consistency requirement, one may instead choose to accept the slight twist to the involutivity property, inasmuch as:

- involutivity is not so crucial in the context considered, i.e. that of database querying,

Table 8.6 Involutivity of the negation

	μ_C	η_W	$\mu_{C'}$	$\eta_{W'}$	$\mu_{C''}$	$\eta_{W''}$
t_1	1	1	0	0	1	1
t_2	1	0.6	0	0.4	1	0.6
t_3	0.8	0.8	0.2	0	0.8	0.8
t_4	0.8	0.5	0.2	0.075	0.8	0.5
t_5	0.8	0.2	0.2	0.15	0.8	0.2
t_6	0.8	0	0.2	0.2	0.8	0
t_7	0.7	0.7	0.3	0	0.7	0.7
t_8	0.6	0.6	0.4	0	0.6	0.6
t_9	0.6	0.1	0.4	0.33	0.6	0.1
t_{10}	0.6	0	0.4	0.4	0.6	0
t_{11}	0.2	0.2	0.8	0	0.2	0.2
t_{12}	0.1	0.1	0.9	0	0.1	0.1
t_{13}	0.1	0	0.9	0.9	0.1	0
t_{14}	0	0	1	1	0	0

- the exception concerns a very specific situation,
- defining set difference with Expression (8.11) instead of (8.12) amounts to assigning the bipolar grade $(0,0)$ instead of $(0, b > 0)$ to some elements in the result of the difference; but these elements are considered totally rejected anyway since their degree with respect to the constraint is zero.

Example 8.5. Table 8.6 illustrates that, with the definition in Expression (8.12), the involutivity property holds in all cases.$\diamond$

Proof of involutivity.

- Case where $\mu_C = 1$: $(\mu_C, \eta_W) = (1, b)$.
  $\mu_{C'} = 1 - 1 = 0, \eta_{W'} = (1 - \eta_W) = (1 - b)$
  $\mu_{C''} = 1 - 0 = 1, \eta_{W''} = 1 - \eta_{W'} = b$
  Finally: $(\mu_{C''}, \eta_{W''}) = (1, b) = (\mu_C, \eta_W)$.
- Case where $\mu_C = 0$: $(\mu_C, \eta_W) = (0, b)$.
  $\mu_{C'} = 1 - 0 = 1, \eta_{W'} = (1 - \eta_W) = (1 - b)$
  $\mu_{C''} = 1 - 1 = 0, \eta_{W''} = 1 - \eta_{W'} = b$
  Finally: $(\mu_{C''}, \eta_{W''}) = (0, b) = (\mu_C, \eta_W)$.
- General case: $(\mu_C, \eta_W) = (a \in]0, 1[, b)$.
  $\mu_{C'} = 1 - a, \eta_{W'} = (1 - a) \times (1 - \frac{b}{a})$
  $\mu_{C''} = 1 - (1 - a) = a,$
  $\eta_{W''} = a \times (1 - \frac{(1-a) \times (1 - \frac{b}{a})}{1-a}) = a \times (1 - (1 - \frac{b}{a})) = b$
  Finally: $(\mu_{C''}, \eta_{W''}) = (a, b) = (\mu_C, \eta_W)$. ∎

It is straightforward to prove that with the definitions in Expressions (8.11) and (8.12), the De Morgan laws hold (using *lmin* and *lmax* for the conjunction and the disjunction respectively).

8.3.4.5   *Negation based on antonymy*

Another view of the "negation" is based on the use of antonyms (Trillas and Riera, 1981; Ovchinnikov, 1981; Trillas *et al.*, 2008). For instance, it might make sense to say that the negation of "I want a car whose price is at most \$20,000 and if possible at most \$15,000" is "I want a car whose price is over \$20,000 and if possible over \$25,000"; or, in the case of different attributes for the constraint and the wish, the negation of: "I want to find a person who is well-paid and if possible young" could be "I want to find a person who is not well-paid and if possible old". In the first example, ">\$25,000" is the condition obtained from "≤\$15,000" by symmetry with respect to "≤\$20,000". Formally, this corresponds to the definition:

$$\neg(C, W) = (\neg C, W') \quad \text{with } W' = ant(W, C). \tag{8.13}$$

In the second case, the fuzzy term *old* is assumed to be an antonym of *young*, and in Expression (8.13), $W' = ant(W, C)$ may be replaced by $W' = ant(W)$, since here the definition of the antonym of W does not depend on C. As usual, when C and W concern different attributes, $(\neg C, W')$ must be understood as $(\neg C, \neg C \wedge W')$.

Several ways for defining antonyms are possible, but as noted in Trillas *et al.* (2008), the inequality $\mu_{ant(P)} \leq \mu_{\neg P}$ should be respected, and shows $\neg P$ as a limit case for any possible antonym of P.

Expression (8.13) preserves consistency and is involutive (provided that $ant(ant(W, C), \neg C) = W$), but is not order-reversing in general. Note also that the antonym of a predicate P does not necessarily exist. This is the case in particular when P concerns a categorical attribute, for instance "color is red".

8.3.5   *Difference*

8.3.5.1   *A logical view of difference*

We first recall the definition of difference in the context of classical relational algebra:

$$differ(r, s) = \{t | t \in r \wedge t \notin s\}. \tag{8.14}$$

The most commonly used definition of the difference between two unipolar fuzzy relations r and s is:

$$\mu_{differ(r,s)}(t) = min(\mu_r(t), \mu_{\bar{s}}(t)) = min(\mu_r(t), 1 - \mu_s(t)). \qquad (8.15)$$

In the case of a bipolar fuzzy relation, one may also consider a definition of difference based on negation. The straightforward negation-based definition of the difference of bipolar fuzzy relations is then as follows:

$$\begin{aligned}(\mu_{differ(r,s)}&(x), \eta_{differ(r,s)}(x)) \\ &= lmin((\mu_r(x), \eta_r(x)), (\mu_{\bar{s}}(x), \eta_{\bar{s}}(x))).\end{aligned} \qquad (8.16)$$

An example of a relational algebraic query involving a difference between two bipolar fuzzy relations is given below.

Example 8.6. The query "find the cars that meet John's needs/preferences but not Peter's" may be expressed as:

$$differ(Car_J, Car_P),$$

where Car_J and Car_P represent two bipolar fuzzy relations resulting from two bipolar selection queries on Car issued respectively by John and Peter, as in Example 8.1. With the extensions of Car_J and Car_P from Tables 8.1 and 8.2, and using Expression (8.11) to interpret the negation, one obtains the result shown in Table 8.7.◇

8.3.5.2 *A non-logical view of the difference*

Another way to define difference is to take a set-oriented point of view. One of the corresponding usual definitions is: $E - F =$ the smallest set that must be added to $E \cap F$ so as to obtain E. This point of view leads to

Table 8.7   Result of $differ(Car_J, Car_P)$

#id	make	model	mileage	years	price	μ	η
1	Ford	Mondeo	35,000	2008	22,000	0.7	0.2
2	Seat	Altea	50,000	2007	17,000	0.1	0.07
3	VW	Golf	39,000	2008	21,000	0.8	0.8
4	Toyota	Corolla	60,000	2006	18,000	0.3	0
5	VW	Passat	75,000	2004	16,000	0.2	0.05
6	Opel	Zafira	58,000	2007	15,000	1	0.5

the definition:

$$E - F = \cap\{G | G \cup (E \cap F) = E\}, \tag{8.17}$$

which implies:

$$(\mu_{E-F}(x), \eta_{E-F}(x)) = \begin{cases} (0,0) \text{ if } (\mu_E(x), \eta_E(x)) \leq_{\text{lex}} (\mu_F(x), \eta_F(x)), \\ (\mu_E(x), \eta_E(x)) \text{ otherwise,} \end{cases}$$

where $\leq_{\text{lex}}$ denotes lexicographic order. However, this definition is not very satisfactory from a semantic viewpoint. Consider an element x such that $(\mu_E(x), \eta_E(x)) = (0.9, 0.7)$ and $(\mu_F(x), \eta_F(x)) = (0.8, 0.6)$. With the definition above, one obtains:

$$(\mu_{E-F}(x), \eta_{E-F}(x)) = (0.9, 0.7),$$

which means that x clearly belongs to $E - F$ whereas it also clearly belongs to F.

Another solution is to extend the notion of bounded difference $\ominus$ defined by Zadeh (1975a) for fuzzy sets:

$$\mu_{E \ominus F}(x) = max(0, \mu_E(x) - \mu_F(x)).$$

In the case of bipolar fuzzy relations, one could use:

$$(\mu_{E-F}(x), \eta_{E-F}(x)) = (\mu_{E \ominus F}(x), \eta_{E \ominus F}(x)). \tag{8.18}$$

Consider again an element x such that $(\mu_E(x), \eta_E(x)) = (0.9, 0.7)$ and $(\mu_F(x), \eta_F(x)) = (0.8, 0.6)$. With the latter definition, one obtains:

$$(\mu_{E-F}(x), \eta_{E-F}(x)) = (0.1, 0.1).$$

Expression (8.17) satisfies 15 out of the 17 main properties of regular set difference (Suppes, 1972). The only two which do not hold are:

- $(E - F = E) \Leftrightarrow (E \cap F = \emptyset)$,
- $(E - F) = (E \cup F) \Leftrightarrow (F = \emptyset)$,

but this is already the case with regular fuzzy sets.

On the other hand, with Expression (8.18), the following seven properties are lost:

- $(E - F) - H = (E - F) \cap (E - H)$,
- $E - (F - H) = (E - F) \cup (E \cap H)$,
- $(E - F) \cup H = (E \cup H) - (F - H)$,
- $(E \cap F) - H = E \cap (F - H)$,

- $(E \cap F) - H = (E - H) \cap (F - H)$,
- $(E \cup F) - H = (E - H) \cup (F - H)$,
- $E - (F \cap H) = (E - F) \cup (E - H)$.

The basic reason why these properties no longer hold in the fuzzy bipolar case is that the bounded difference involves an arithmetic difference between the degrees, whereas the union and intersection operators, which are based on the lexicographic order, do not modify the original degrees.

8.3.5.3 *Counter-example (first property).*

Consider the bipolar fuzzy relations $E = \{(0.7, 0.1)/x\}$, $F = \{(0.3, 0.3)/x\}$, and $H = \{(0.2, 0)/x\}$. From Expression (8.18), we have:
$(\mu_{(E-F)-H}, \eta_{(E-F)-H})/x = (0.2, 0)/x$ whereas:
$(\mu_{(E-F) \cap (E-H)}, \eta_{(E-F) \cap (E-H)})/x = (0.4, 0)/x.\diamond$

8.3.5.4 *Conclusion*

It appears that the definition of the difference of bipolar fuzzy relations relying on Expressions (8.16) and (8.12) looks the most satisfactory, since this definition does not have any major semantic drawbacks.

8.3.6 *Selection*

The straightforward definition of selection is:

$$select(r, (C, W)) = \{(\mu', \eta')/t | (\mu, \eta)/t \in r \wedge$$
$$(\mu', \eta') = lmin((\mu, \eta), (\mu_C(t), \eta_W(t)))\}, \qquad (8.19)$$

where $\mu_C(t)$ (resp. $\eta_W(t)$) denotes the satisfaction degree of t with respect to C (resp. W).

Example 8.7. The query "find the cars among those preferred by Paul (in the sense of the bipolar requirement that was used to build the relation Car_{Paul}) which are less than \$20,000 and if possible have a mileage less than 60,000" may be expressed as:

$$select(Car_{Paul}, (price \; is \; lt\_20k, \; mileage \; is \; lt\_60k)).$$

Table 8.8   An instance of relation Car_{Paul}

#id	make	model	mileage	years	price	μ	η
1	Ford	Mondeo	35,000	2008	22,000	0.7	0.2
2	Seat	Altea	65,000	2007	21,000	0.9	0.3
3	VW	Passat	66,000	2008	23,000	0.8	0.8
4	Toyota	Corolla	60,000	2006	26,000	0.9	0.4
5	VW	Passat	75,000	2004	16,000	0.8	0.6
6	Seat	Altea	58,000	2007	15,000	1	0.5
7	Toyota	Corolla	18,000	2008	25,000	0.3	0.1

Table 8.9   Result of the bipolar selection on the relation Car_{Paul}

#id	make	model	mileage	years	price	μ	η
1	Ford	Mondeo	35,000	2008	22,000	0.6	0.6
2	Seat	Altea	65,000	2007	21,000	0.8	0.4
3	VW	Passat	66,000	2008	23,000	0.4	0.16
5	VW	Passat	75,000	2004	16,000	0.8	0.6
6	Seat	Altea	58,000	2007	15,000	1	0.5

Assume that the fuzzy predicates lt_20k and lt_60k are defined as follows:

$$\mu_{lt\_20k}(x) = \begin{cases} 1 \text{ if } x \leq 20,000, \\ 0 \text{ if } x > 25,000, \\ \dfrac{25,000 - x}{5000} \text{ otherwise;} \end{cases}$$

$$\mu_{lt\_60k}(x) = \begin{cases} 1 \text{ if } x \leq 60,000, \\ 0 \text{ if } x > 70,000, \\ \dfrac{70,000 - x}{10,000} \text{ otherwise.} \end{cases}$$

Using the data from Table 8.8, the result of the selection is represented in Table 8.9 (recall that the t-norm product is used for interpreting the conjunction when W has to be replaced by $C \wedge W$ in order to preserve weak consistency).◇

In Expression (8.19), C and/or W can be a complex condition expressing an aggregation (e.g., involving conjunctions and/or disjunctions) of atomic predicates. However, it is important to note that, in general:

- $(C_1 \wedge C_2, W_1 \wedge W_2) \neq (C_1, W_1) \wedge (C_2, W_2)$,
- $(C_1 \vee C_2, W_1 \vee W_2) \neq (C_1, W_1) \vee (C_2, W_2)$.

8.3.6.1 *Counter-example*

Consider a tuple t such that $\mu_1(t) = 0.8$, $\eta_1(t) = 0.3$, $\mu_2(t) = 0.7$, and $\eta_2(t) = 0.4$. Interpreting $\wedge$ as *min* and $\vee$ as *max* in the left-hand part of the previous inequalities, we have:

$$(min(0.8, 0.7), min(0.3, 0.4)) = (0.7, 0.3) \text{ whereas}$$
$$lmin((0.8, 0.3), (0.7, 0.4)) = (0.7, 0.4),$$
$$(max(0.8, 0.7), max(0.3, 0.4)) = (0.8, 0.4) \text{ whereas}$$
$$lmax((0.8, 0.3), (0.7, 0.4)) = (0.8, 0.3). \diamond$$

Therefore, the user must employ the appropriate formulation when expressing his/her query. One may suppose that a formulation of the type $(C_1, W_1) \wedge \cdots \wedge (C_n, W_n)$ — where the C_i's and W_i's are atomic conditions — will be chosen when each atomic bipolar condition involved concerns a specific attribute, as in: "find the cars which cost less than \$20,000 (C_1) and if possible less than \$15,000 (W_1), and which are less than 5 years old (C_2) and if possible less than 3 years old (W_2)". However, in a bipolar condition (C, W) where C and/or W are composite, the set of attributes involved in the constraint and the wish respectively will be disjoint in general. An example is: "find the German cars whose price is less than \$20,000, and if possible recent and powerful".

8.3.7 *Projection*

We start from the usual definition of projection, i.e.:

$$project(r, X) = \{x | \exists t \in r \text{ such that } t.X = x\}.$$

In the case of bipolar fuzzy relations, the existential quantifier is naturally interpreted by means of operator *lmax*, and so we obtain the definition:

$$project(r, X) = \{(\mu, \eta)/x | (\exists t \in r \text{ s.t. } t.X = x) \wedge$$
$$(\mu, \eta) = lmax_{t \in r \text{ s.t. } t.X = x}(\mu(t), \eta(t))\}. \tag{8.20}$$

Example 8.8. The query "find the pairs (make, model) corresponding to the cars that meet Paul's needs/preferences" may be expressed as:

$$project(select(Car, (C_1, W_1)), \{make, model\}),$$

where (C_1, W_1) represents Paul's bipolar requirement. Assume that $Car_{Paul} = select(Car, (C_1, W_1))$ is the relation represented in Table 8.8. The result of the projection is represented in Table 8.10. $\diamond$

Table 8.10 $project(Car_{Paul}, \{make, model\})$

make	model	μ	η
Ford	Mondeo	0.7	0.2
Seat	Altea	1	0.5
VW	Passat	0.8	0.8
Toyota	Corolla	0.9	0.4

8.3.8   *Join*

The straightforward definition of the join operation is:

$$
\begin{aligned}
join(r, s, (C(X, Y), W(Z, T))) = \\
\{(\mu'', \eta'')/t \oplus t' | (\mu, \eta)/t \in r \wedge (\mu', \eta')/t' \in s \wedge \\
(\mu'', \eta'') = lmin(lmin((\mu, \eta), (\mu', \eta')), \\
(\mu_C(t.X, t'.Y), \eta_W(t.Z, t'.T)))\},
\end{aligned}
\tag{8.21}
$$

where X, Y, Z, and T denote sets of attributes, and X and Y (resp. Z and T) are compatible. Condition $C(X, Y)$ (resp. $W(Z, T)$) is of the form $X\theta_1 Y$ (resp. $Z\theta_2 T$), where θ_1 and θ_2 are (fuzzy or not) comparators ($=, <, \leq, >, \geq, \neq, \approx, <<$, etc.). As usual, in the case of a Boolean equijoin, only one occurrence of the join attribute is kept (which implies the addition of a final projection to the definition above). For instance, if $C(X, Y)$ is written as "$X = Y$", only X is kept — the same applies for W. The above definition straightforwardly preserves the usual equivalence between a join and a Cartesian product followed by a selection:

$$
\begin{aligned}
join(r, s, (C(X, Y), W(Z, T))) \\
= select(cartprod(r, s), (C(X, Y), W(Z, T))).
\end{aligned}
$$

Example 8.9. Assume the existence of two relations $Dealer_1$ and $Dealer_2$, with the same schema as Car. An example of a bipolar join query is "find the cars (*make, model*) which are sold both by $Dealer_1$ and $Dealer_2$ preferably in the same range of price". This query can be expressed as:

$$
\begin{aligned}
join(Dealer_1, Dealer_2, (make_1 = make_2 \text{ and} \\
model_1 = model_2, price_1 \approx price_2).\diamond
\end{aligned}
$$

8.3.9   *Division*

8.3.9.1   *Reminder about "classical" division*

We assume that the dividend relation r has the schema (A, X), while that of the divisor relation s is (B), where A and B are compatible sets of attributes. The division of relation r by relation s is classically defined (Section 2.2.2) as:

$$div(r, s, A, B) = \{x \in r[X] | \forall a, a \in s \Rightarrow (x, a) \in r\}, \qquad (8.22)$$

where $r[X]$ denotes the projection of r over X. In other words, an element x belongs to the result of the division of r by s if and only if it is associated in r with at least all the values a appearing in s.

Example 8.10. Consider a database involving the two relations order (o) and product (p) with respective schemas $O(np, store, qty)$ and $P(np, price)$. Tuples $\langle n, s, q \rangle$ of o and $\langle n, pr \rangle$ of p state that product n has been ordered from store s in quantity q and that its price is pr. Retrieving the stores from which all the products priced under \$127 have been ordered in a quantity greater than 35, can be expressed thanks to a division as: $div(o_{g35}, p_{u127}, np, np)$, where relation o_{g35} corresponds to pairs $\langle n, s \rangle$ such that product n has been ordered from store s in a quantity over 35, and relation p_{u127} gathers products whose price is under \$127. From the extensions of relations o_{g35} and p_{u127} given as:

$$o_{g35} = \{\langle p_{15}, s_{32} \rangle, \langle p_{12}, s_{32} \rangle, \langle p_{34}, s_{32} \rangle, \langle p_{26}, s_{32} \rangle, \langle p_{12}, s_7 \rangle, \langle p_{26}, s_7 \rangle,$$
$$\langle p_{15}, s_{19} \rangle, \langle p_{12}, s_{19} \rangle, \langle p_{26}, s_{19} \rangle\},$$
$$p_{u127} = \{\langle p_{15} \rangle, \langle p_{12} \rangle, \langle p_{26} \rangle\},$$

the result of the division is $\{\langle s_{32} \rangle, \langle s_{19} \rangle\}$.◇

8.3.9.2   *Reminder about the division of fuzzy relations*

When the relations involved are fuzzy (i.e., contain graded tuples), Expression (8.22) becomes (see Chapter 7):

$$\mu_{div(r,s,A,B)}(x) = min_s \mu_s(a) \Rightarrow_f \mu_r(x, a) \qquad (8.23)$$

where $\Rightarrow_f$ denotes a fuzzy implication (Dubois *et al.*, 2000).

Example 8.11. Consider again the relations from Example 8.10 and two fuzzy conditions "quantity is around 30" and "price is around \$100" applied to O and P respectively, leading to two fuzzy relations o_{a30} and p_{a100} whose extensions are given as:

$$o_{a30} = \{0.4/\langle p_{11}, s_{32}\rangle, 1/\langle p_{17}, s_{32}\rangle, 0.7/\langle p_{29}, s_{32}\rangle, 0.8/\langle p_{11}, s_{7}\rangle,$$
$$0.6/\langle p_{29}, s_{7}\rangle, 1/\langle p_{11}, s_{19}\rangle, 0.3/\langle p_{17}, s_{19}\rangle, 0.9/\langle p_{42}, s_{19}\rangle\},$$
$$p_{a100} = \{1/\langle p_{11}\rangle, 0.8/\langle p_{17}\rangle, 0.6/\langle p_{29}\rangle\}.$$

The division of o_{a30} by p_{a100} based on Lukasiewicz's implication ($p \Rightarrow_{Lu} q = 1$ if $q \geq p$, $1 - p + q$ otherwise) returns $\{0.6/\langle s_{32}\rangle, 0.2/\langle s_{7}\rangle, 0.4/\langle s_{19}\rangle\}$.◇

8.3.9.3　*Bipolar division of bipolar fuzzy relations*

When two bipolar fuzzy relations r and s (assumed to be consistent) come into play, Expression (8.23) can be used to compute four degrees:

$$\mu(x) = min_s \eta_s(a) \Rightarrow_f \mu_r(x, a) \tag{8.24}$$

$$\eta(x) = min_s \mu_s(a) \Rightarrow_f \eta_r(x, a) \tag{8.25}$$

$$\mu'(x) = min_s \mu_s(a) \Rightarrow_f \mu_r(x, a) \tag{8.26}$$

$$\eta'(x) = min_s \eta_s(a) \Rightarrow_f \eta_r(x, a) \tag{8.27}$$

Because of the monotonicity of fuzzy implications, and the consistency condition between the constraint and the wish used to generate each bipolar relation, one has:

$$\forall x, \eta(x) \leq \mu'(x) \leq \mu(x)$$

and

$$\forall x, \eta(x) \leq \eta'(x) \leq \mu(x).$$

In order for the result also to be a consistent bipolar relation, the only possible choices are (μ, η), (μ, μ'), (μ, η'), (μ', η), and (η', η). It seems natural to choose (μ, η) for the following reasons:

- it captures the two extreme cases: $\mu(x)$ expresses the extent to which every "somewhat ideal" element of the divisor is associated in a somewhat necessary fashion with x (the lax view, corresponding to the constraint aimed at retrieving the acceptable elements), whereas $\eta(x)$ is the extent to which every "somewhat necessary" element of the divisor is associated in a somewhat ideal fashion with x (the drastic view, corresponding to the wish aimed at retrieving the ideal elements);

- it keeps its discrimination power intact in the particular cases where r and/or s is a non-bipolar relation; this is not true with the other pairs (when r is unipolar, one has $\mu(x) = \eta'(x)$ and $\eta(x) = \mu'(x)$, and when s is unipolar, one has: $\mu(x) = \mu'(x)$ and $\eta(x) = \eta'(x)$).

Note that Expressions (8.24) and (8.25) can serve as the basis for the definition of a (graded) bipolar fuzzy-implication-based inclusion between bipolar fuzzy sets.

We denote by *birel* the operation, not part of the query language itself, that builds a bipolar fuzzy relation from two consistent (in the sense of weak consistency) regular fuzzy relations:

$$
\begin{aligned}
birel(r,s) = \\
\{(\mu,\eta)/t | t \in support(r) \wedge \mu_r(t) = \mu \wedge \\
t \in support(s) \wedge \mu_s(t) = \eta\} \\
\cup \{(\mu,0)/t | t \in r \wedge \mu_r(t) = \mu \wedge t \notin support(s)\},
\end{aligned}
\tag{8.28}
$$

where $\mu_r(t)$ (resp. $\mu_s(t)$) denotes the membership degree associated with tuple t in the regular fuzzy relation r (resp. s). The definition of the division of bipolar fuzzy relations can be rewritten as:

$$
div(r, s, A, B) = birel(div(r_C, s_W, A, B), div(r_W, s_C, A, B)),
\tag{8.29}
$$

where rel_C (resp. rel_W) denotes the fuzzy relation obtained by keeping only the degrees μ (resp. η) attached to the tuples from the bipolar fuzzy relation *rel*.

Example 8.12. Consider relations r and s from Table 8.11. Using Lukasiewicz's implication, and denoting by *res* the bipolar relation resulting

Table 8.11   Relations r (left) and s (right)

X	A	μ	η
x_1	a_1	0.2	0
x_1	a_2	0.6	0.3
x_1	a_3	1	0.6
x_2	a_2	1	1
x_2	a_3	0.1	0

B	μ'	η'
a_1	0.7	0.4
a_2	1	0.6
a_3	0.3	0

from the division, one obtains:

$$\mu_{res}(x_1) = min(0.4 \Rightarrow_{Lu} 0.2, 0.6 \Rightarrow_{Lu} 0.6, 0 \Rightarrow_{Lu} 1)$$
$$= min(0.8, 1, 1) = 0.8,$$

$$\eta_{res}(x_1) = min(0.7 \Rightarrow_{Lu} 0, 1 \Rightarrow_{Lu} 0.3, 0.3 \Rightarrow_{Lu} 0.6)$$
$$= min(0.3, 0.3, 1) = 0.3,$$

$$\mu_{res}(x_2) = min(0.4 \Rightarrow_{Lu} 0, 0.6 \Rightarrow_{Lu} 1, 0 \Rightarrow_{Lu} 0.1) = min(0.6, 1, 1) = 0.6,$$

$$\eta_{res}(x_2) = min(0.7 \Rightarrow_{Lu} 0, 1 \Rightarrow_{Lu} 1, 0.3 \Rightarrow_{Lu} 0) = min(0.3, 1, 0.7) = 0.3.$$

The result is the bipolar relation: $\{(0.8, 0.3)/\langle x_1 \rangle, (0.6, 0.3)/\langle x_2 \rangle\}$, and we have $\langle x_1 \rangle \succ \langle x_2 \rangle$ according to lexicographic order.$\diamond$

In practice, it is likely that either the divisor or the dividend will be bipolar but not both, since the meaning of the query then becomes rather complex; Expressions (8.24)–(8.25) nevertheless make it possible to deal with the general case where both divisor and dividend are bipolar.

Example 8.13. Consider again the relations O and P from Example 8.12. Assume that a bipolar relation O_b is built from O using the twofold condition: (C_O: qty **is** *higher_than_10*, W_O: qty **is** *higher_than_15*), where *higher_than_10* and *higher_than_15* are assumed to be fuzzy predicates. An example of a division query involving a bipolar dividend is: "find the stores which have ordered at least 10 occurrences of each product, and if possible at least 15 occurrences of each product".

Now assume that a bipolar relation P_b is built from P using the twofold condition: (C_P: price **is** *less_than_200*, W_P: price **is** *less_than_150*), where *less_than_200* and *less_than_150* are fuzzy predicates. An example of a division query involving a bipolar divisor is: "from which all of the products priced at less than \$200 and if possible all of those priced at less than \$150 have been ordered".$\diamond$

8.3.9.4 *About the quotient property*

As mentioned in Section 2.2.2, the justification of the term "division" assigned to this operation relies on the fact that a property similar to that of the quotient of integers holds. Indeed, the resulting relation *res* obtained with Expression (8.22) has the double characteristic of a quotient:

$$\forall t \in res, cartprod(s, \{t\}) \subseteq r, \tag{8.30}$$

$$\forall t \notin res, cartprod(s, \{t\}) \not\subseteq r. \tag{8.31}$$

Expressions (8.30) and (8.31) state that the relation *res* resulting from the division is the largest relation whose Cartesian product with the divisor returns a result smaller than or equal to the dividend (according to set inclusion).

Considering the definition given in the previous section, processing a division $div(r, s, A, B)$ of two bipolar fuzzy relations r and s comes down to processing two divisions of non-bipolar fuzzy relations, namely $div(r_C, s_W, A, B)$ and $div(r_W, s_C, A, B)$ — see Expression (8.29). Since it has been proven that the result of the division of two fuzzy relations is a quotient, provided that the conjunction operator used for the Cartesian product is appropriately chosen (Bosc *et al.*, 2007b), the result of a division of bipolar fuzzy relations can be characterized as a twofold quotient. However, when the implication used is an S-implication, the quotient property can only be guaranteed if the divisor is normalized. In the context of bipolar relations, this means that both s_C and s_W have to contain a tuple whose associated degree equals 1.

Example 8.14. Consider the relations from Example 8.12. Relation r is equivalent to $birel(r_C, r_W)$ where

$$r_C = \{0.2/\langle x_1, a_1 \rangle, 0.6/\langle x_1, a_2 \rangle, 1/\langle x_1, a_3 \rangle, 1/\langle x_2, a_2 \rangle, 0.1/\langle x_2, a_3 \rangle\},$$
$$r_W = \{0.3/\langle x_1, a_2 \rangle, 0.6/\langle x_1, a_3 \rangle, 1/\langle x_2, a_2 \rangle\},$$

and relation s is equivalent to $birel(s_C, s_W)$ where

$$s_C = \{0.7/\langle a_1 \rangle, 1/\langle a_2 \rangle, 0.3/\langle a_3 \rangle\},$$
$$s_W = \{0.4/\langle a_1 \rangle, 0.6/\langle a_2 \rangle\}.$$

The result of $div(r_C, s_W, A, B)$ using Lukasiewicz's implication is:

$$res_C = \{0.8/\langle x_1 \rangle, 0.6/\langle x_2 \rangle\},$$

whereas the result of $div(r_W, s_C, A, B)$ is:

$$res_W = \{0.3/\langle x_1 \rangle, 0.3/\langle x_2 \rangle\},$$

and $birel(res_C, res_W)$ is equivalent to the result obtained in Example 8.12. It is useful to check that res_C is a quotient. Interpreting the Cartesian product by means of Lukasiewicz's t-norm ($\perp_{\text{Lu}}(a, b) = max(a + b - 1, 0)$), one obtains:

$$cartprod(s_W, \{0.8/\langle x_1 \rangle\}) = \{0.2/\langle x_1, a_1 \rangle, 0.4/\langle x_1, a_2 \rangle\} \subseteq r_C \quad \text{and}$$
$$cartprod(s_W, \{0.6/\langle x_2 \rangle\}) = \{0.2/\langle x_2, a_2 \rangle\} \subseteq r_C.$$

On the other hand, if the degree attached to $\langle x_1 \rangle$ in res_C is upgraded to 0.8^+ (i.e., to a value slightly greater than 0.8), one has:

$$cartprod(s_W, \{0.8^+/\langle x_1 \rangle\}) = \{0.2^+/\langle x_1, a_1 \rangle, 0.4^+/\langle x_1, a_2 \rangle\} \not\subseteq r_C.$$

Similarly, if the degree attached to $\langle x_2 \rangle$ in res_C is upgraded to 0.6^+, one obtains:

$$cartprod(s_W, \{0.6^+/\langle x_2 \rangle\}) = \{0^+/\langle x_2, a_1 \rangle, 0.2^+/\langle x_2, a_2 \rangle\} \not\subseteq r_C.$$

In the same way, it can be checked that res_W is also a quotient.◇

8.3.9.5 *About the non-primitivity of the operator*

As mentioned in Section 2.2.2, when considering regular (non-fuzzy) relations, the division operator can also be defined in terms of other relational operators (which shows its non-primitivity). The division comes down to discarding from $r[X]$ all x's from $r[X]$ such that $\exists a \in s, \langle x, a \rangle \notin r$. It is expressed as:

$$div(r, s, A, B) = differ(project(r, X),$$
$$project(differ(cartprod(project(r, X), project(s, B)), r), X)). \tag{8.32}$$

In this formula, the expression $differ(cartprod(project(r, X), s), r)$ determines the tuples that associate those values of attributes X and B that are missing in r. The X-values present in this set must then be discarded from the final result, as is done by the outermost difference.

Bosc *et al.* (1997) showed that the division of fuzzy relations is also a non-primitive operator, and can be rewritten in a similar way to Expression (8.32)

$$div(r, s, A, B) = differ(sproject(r, X),$$
$$project(gdiffer(cartprod(sproject(r, X), project(s, B)), r), X)), \tag{8.33}$$

where the operation denoted by $sproject(r, X)$ returns the support of the projection of relation r on the set of attributes X, and $gdiffer$ is a difference based on the triangular norm or the noncommutative conjunction underlying the implication present in Expression (8.23). Since $div(r, s, A, B)$ can be rewritten as the combination of two divisions of regular fuzzy relations — as in Expression (8.29) — one has:

$$div(r,s,A,B) =$$
$$birel(differ(sproject(r_C,X),$$
$$project(gdiffer(cartprod(sproject(r_C,X),$$
$$project(s_W,B)),r_C),X)),$$
$$differ(sproject(r_W,X),$$
$$project(gdiffer(cartprod(sproject(r_W,X),$$
$$project(s_C,B)),r_W),X))).$$

Example 8.15. Consider the relations from Examples 8.12 and 8.13, and check that

$$res_C =$$
$$differ(sproject(r_C,X),$$
$$project(gdiffer(cartprod(sproject(r_C,X),$$
$$project(s_W,B)),r_C),X)).$$

One has:

$$sproject(r_C,X) = \{\langle x_1 \rangle, \langle x_2 \rangle\}$$

and

$$cartprod(sproject(r_C,X), project(s_W,B)) =$$
$$\{0.4/\langle x_1,a_1 \rangle, 0.6/\langle x_1,a_2 \rangle, 0.4/\langle x_2,a_1 \rangle, 0.6/\langle x_2,a_2 \rangle\}.$$

Using

$$\mu_{gdiffer(E,F)}(x) = max(\mu_E(x) + (1 - \mu_F(x)) - 1, 0)$$
$$= max(\mu_E(x) - \mu_F(x), 0),$$

one obtains:

$$gdiffer(cartprod(sproject(r_C,X), project(s_W,B)), r_C) =$$
$$\{0.2/\langle x_1,a_1 \rangle, 0.4/\langle x_2,a_1 \rangle\},$$
$$differ(sproject(r_C,X), \ project(gdiffer(cartprod(sproject(r_C,X),$$
$$project(s_W,B)),r_C),X)) =$$
$$\{1/\langle x_1 \rangle, 1/\langle x_2 \rangle\} \backslash \{0.2/\langle x_1 \rangle, 0.4/\langle x_2 \rangle\} = \{0.8/\langle x_1 \rangle, 0.6/\langle x_2 \rangle\},$$

which is indeed equal to res_C. In the same way, it can be checked that

$$res_W =$$
$$differ(sproject(r_W, X),$$
$$project(gdiffer(cartprod(sproject(r_W, X),$$
$$project(s_C, B)), r_W), X)).\diamond$$

8.4 Implementation Aspects

In terms of data representation, a regular DBMS can be used to handle bipolar queries, since the only modification with respect to the classical case concerns the schemas of those relations that must include two additional attributes for storing the degrees μ and η. In this section, the changes implied by the presence of bipolarity are discussed in terms of query processing for the different extended operators.

Intersection and union. These operations have the same data complexity as usual. It is necessary to do a nested scan of the relations involved, which can be optimized if indexes exist. With respect to an intersection (resp. union) of unipolar fuzzy relations, the only difference concerns the use of *lmin* (resp. *lmax*) instead of *min* (resp. *max*) — see Expressions (8.6) and (8.7).

Cartesian product. The situation is the same as for intersection and union: a nested scan of the relations involved is necessary. Again, *lmin* is used to compute the final twofold degree attached to a tuple of the result — see Expression (8.8).

Difference. For this operator too, the processing algorithm has a similar structure as in the classical case. The computation of $r - s$ implies a nested scan of the relations involved. Each tuple t in r is checked to see whether it is present in s or not. If t is in s, Expressions (8.16) and (8.12) are used to compute the final twofold degree attached to a tuple of the result. If t is not present in s, then it is in the result with the twofold degree $(\mu_r(t), \eta_r(t))$.

Selection. In the absence of any index of the attribute(s) concerned by the constraint C, the processing of a selection is similar as in the usual case: the relation concerned is sequentially scanned, and both conditions C and W are evaluated. If an index on the attribute(s) involved in C exists, one can take advantage of the derivation method proposed in Bosc and Pivert

(2000) for efficiently accessing the tuples t which belong to the support of C (i.e., those such that $\mu_C(t) > 0$). For each such tuple, W is then evaluated in order to compute the final twofold degree. In every case, the (linear) data complexity is the same as in the case of unipolar fuzzy queries.

Projection. Here too, the same type of algorithm as usual (e.g., based on a sort of the relation concerned) must be used. The only change concerns the elimination of duplicate, which entails computation of a twofold degree by means of $lmax$ (instead of max in the unipolar fuzzy case).

Join. If there are no indexes on the join attributes, a nested scan of the relations involved is necessary. The only difference with respect to the unipolar case is that the join condition is twofold; this does not imply any overhead in terms of data complexity, which remains in $\theta(|r| \cdot |s|)$ (where r and s denote the relations to be joined).

If the join condition in the constraint part C of the join condition is Boolean, this is evaluated first, following which the wish part of the join condition is computed by means of a (possibly fuzzy) selection.

On the other hand, if the join condition in the constraint part C of the join condition is fuzzy but concerns attributes on which indexes are available, the aforementioned derivation principle — described in Bosc and Pivert (2000) — can be used to evaluate it. The wish part W of the join condition is then evaluated by means of a selection on the result of the previous step.

In every case, the data complexity is as usual (between $|r| + |s|$ in the best case, when indexes are available, and $min(|r| \cdot (|s| + 1), |s| \cdot (|r| + 1))$ in the worst case).

Division. Here, it is necessary to process two divisions of unipolar fuzzy relations (Expression (8.29)), which means that the practical complexity is multiplied by two, but the class of data complexity stays the same. See Bosc *et al.* (1999b) and Section 7.6 for more details on the processing of a division of unipolar fuzzy relations.

To sum up, one can be reasonably optimistic about the data complexity of bipolar queries based on the extended relational algebra described here, and therefore about the performances of a "bipolar DBMS". Indeed, introducing bipolarity into relations and queries does not modify the complexity class of any algebraic operator (all of them remain in PTIME, and a naïve evaluation simply leads to a doubling of the cost with respect to an equivalent non-bipolar query).

8.5   Conclusion

In this chapter, we have defined an extension of relational algebra suited to the handling of bipolar fuzzy relations and conditions. This corresponds to a type of extension of database query languages which differs in nature from those considered in the other chapters of this book. Here, the goal was not to introduce some more sophisticated fuzzy conditions, but rather to take into account the fact that the human mind often makes decisions on the basis of both positive and negative information. Negative preferences correspond to *constraints*, since they specify those values or objects which have to be rejected (i.e., those that do not satisfy the constraints), while positive preferences correspond to *wishes*, as they specify those objects which are more desirable than others. The framework described in this chapter makes it possible for a user to express twofold requirements made of a (possibly complex) constraint and a (possibly complex) wish. The satisfaction of the constraint and of the wish can be used to order the tuples of the result by means of lexicographic order (with priority given to the constraint).

   To the best of our knowledge, this is the first complete algebraic framework aimed at handling bipolar fuzzy relations and conditions. We should mention, however, that a first step in that direction was made in Liétard *et al.* (2009) where the selection, projection and join operations were briefly tackled (but only a non-bipolar version of the join was considered, and the set-oriented operators were not formally defined). Zadrożny and Kacprzyk (2006) consider a specific interpretation of bipolar fuzzy *selection* queries. Instead of using the lexicographic order to combine constraints and wishes, they aim at generalizing the behavior of the *winnow* operator proposed by Chomicki (2003) in a framework of preference queries based on a dominance relation. Matthé and De Tré (2009) also deal with the interpretation of bipolar fuzzy selection queries. They define so-called satisfaction and dissatisfaction degrees following an approach closely related to Atanassov's intuitionistic fuzzy sets (the only difference with respect to Atanassov's approach is that the consistency condition is dropped). The authors discuss the operators needed for evaluating selection queries involving the standard logical operators conjunction, disjunction and negation, but do not attempt to define any bipolar relational algebra.

   We do not claim that the approach described in this chapter is the only one possible for handling bipolarity in a database context, but it does provide a *consistent* framework (contrary to any approach based on twofold fuzzy sets or intuitionistic fuzzy sets, because of the problem related to the negation in particular). If one wants to handle two separate degrees — which corresponds to a strict view of bipolarity — and obtain a total ordering of the results, lexicographic order looks like a rather straightforward choice, with a clear interpretation.

The bipolar fuzzy extension of relational algebra defined in this chapter can obviously be used as the basis for definition of a bipolar fuzzy SQL-like language, e.g., a bipolar extension of SQLf. However, it is still a matter for future research to investigate how those constructs that are specific to SQLf — for instance nesting operators, the relation partitioning mechanism, and group-oriented conditions — could be generalized in order to i) take bipolar fuzzy relations as inputs, ii) be endowed with bipolar behavior.

Chapter 9

Fuzzy Group By

9.1 Introduction

As noted in Silva *et al.* (2009), grouping capabilities have been extensively studied and implemented in data management systems. The standard *group by* operator has relatively good execution time and scalability properties. However, while its semantics are simple, it is also limited because it is based only on equality, i.e., all the tuples in a group have exactly the same values of the grouping attributes. In this chapter, we show how this core database operation can be extended by defining a "fuzzy grouping" mechanism. We do the following:

- introduce the *fuzzy group by* (FGB) operator, which extends standard group by to allow the formation of groups based on predefined fuzzy partitions of the attribute domains rather than equality of data,
- show how this mechanism makes it possible to perform some kind of data summarization "on demand",
- point out the relevance of the FGB operator to fuzzy association rule mining.

More precisely, the following section introduces the definition of the FGB operator and shows how fuzzy summaries can be obtained by means of appropriate aggregates applied to the fuzzy groups that are produced by this operator. Thereafter, we discuss the different forms that the complementary *having* clause can take. A special focus is put on the way FGB can be used for mining fuzzy association rules whose head or body are bound to a specific fuzzy value. Implementation aspects are tackled next, and the chapter ends with a discussion about related work.

9.2   An Extended Group By Clause

In SQLf as in SQL, a *group by* clause builds a partition based on the (atomic) values of the attributes specified in this clause (see Section 2.3.3). Then, "*group by A*" leads to a partition where every group is associated with an A-value present in the relation. The idea we advocate here is to extend this mechanism so as to build a partition based on intervals or fuzzy sets of values.

9.2.1   *Use of a crisp partition*

The generic form of such a query is:

> **select label**(A) [, **aggregate**, ...] **from** r [**where** ψ]
> **group by label**(A)
> **using part**(A) = $\{L_1, \ldots, L_n\}$,

where *part*(A) is a partition defined on the domain of A, *label*(A) denotes any label L_i from *part*(A), and ψ is a (fuzzy or crisp) condition.

Example 9.1. Let *Emp* be a relation of schema (*#e, e-name, position, age, w-dep, salary*). Assume that we want to retrieve the average salary for each age class (twenties, thirties, etc.). In SQL, these have to be as many queries as there are age classes. However, it is possible to imagine an expression of the type:

> **select label**(*age*), **avg**(*salary*) **from** *Emp*
> **group by label**(*age*)
> **using part**(*age*) = $\{[20, 29], [30, 39], [40, 49], [50, 59]\}$.

With the data from Table 9.1, the result is:

$$\{\langle[20, 29], 2650\rangle, \langle[30, 39], 3200\rangle, \langle[40, 49], 4500\rangle,$$
$$\langle[50, 59], 6100\rangle, \langle[60, 69], 3700\rangle \}.\diamond$$

In the case where ψ is a fuzzy condition, the only type of aggregate which can appear in the *select* clause is *count*, because of the difficulty of defining other aggregates on fuzzy sets (see Chapter 6). Indeed, the existing approaches dealing with the interpretation of aggregates in the general case (Dubois and Prade, 1990) cannot be used in the framework of SQLf, since they deliver a *fuzzy set* of possible evaluations (only allowing the lower and upper bounds of this fuzzy set of numbers to be computed). In SQLf, a

Table 9.1   Extension of relation *Emp*

#e	e-name	position	age	w-dep	sal(k$)
17	Smith	engineer	51	3	65
76	Martin	engineer	40	5	45
26	Jones	secretary	24	3	19
12	Green	technician	39	3	32
19	Duncan	clerk	28	1	24
8	Brown	manager	54	1	57
31	Harris	technician	29	5	18
9	Davis	janitor	61	1	15
44	Howard	manager	22	3	45
23	Lewis	engineer	62	1	59

single degree of satisfaction attached to a condition such as $agg(A)$ is C — where agg denotes an aggregate and C a fuzzy condition — is needed in order to maintain compositionality.

For a given L_i from $part(A)$, $count(L_i)$ is computed as follows:

$$count(L_i) = \sum_{t \in r \,\wedge\, t.A \in L_i} \mu_\psi(t).$$

A variant of *count*, denoted *count-rel*, can also be introduced to compute the average membership degree inside a group. It is defined as:

$$count\text{-}rel(L_i) = \frac{\sum_{t \in r \wedge t.A \in L_i} \mu_\psi(t)}{|\{t \in r \mid t.A \in L_i\}|}.$$

Example 9.2. Consider the query:

> **select label(*age*), count, count-rel from** *Emp*
> **where** *salary* **is** *medium* **group by label(*age*)**
> **using part(*age*) =** {[20, 29], [30, 39], [40, 49], [50, 59]}.

With the fuzzy term *medium* defined as in Figure 9.1, and the data from Table 9.1, one obtains:

$$\{\langle [20,\ 29],\ 1,\ 0.25 \rangle,\ \langle [30,\ 39],\ 0.7,\ 0.7 \rangle,\ \langle [40,\ 49],\ 1,\ 1 \rangle,$$
$$\langle [50,\ 59],\ 0.8,\ 0.4 \rangle, \langle [60,\ 69],\ 0.6,\ 0.3 \rangle\}.\diamond$$

9.2.2   *Use of a fuzzy partition*

The extension to the fuzzy partition case — which allows vague classes to be taken into account, and permits more robustness by making query results less sensitive to the boundaries of the classes — is rather straightforward.

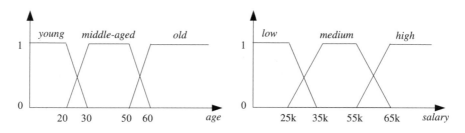

Fig. 9.1   Fuzzy partitions of the domains of (left) attribute age and (right) salary

It is simply necessary to have available fuzzy partitions defined on the attribute domains. However, it is no longer possible to use any type of aggregate in the *select* clause: one is limited to using *count* even when the condition in the *where* clause is Boolean (since the groups themselves are fuzzy). In the following, we assume that Ruspini partitions (Ruspini, 1969) are used, i.e.,

$$\forall x \in X, \quad \sum_{L_i \in P} \mu_{L_i}(x) = 1,$$

where P denotes a partition defined on domain X (see Figure 9.1).

Example 9.3. Consider the partition from Figure 9.1 (left) denoted by *part*(*age*), and the query "find, for each fuzzy age class, the number of employees who earn more than \$30,000". It can be expressed as:

> **select label**(*age*), **count from** *Emp*
> **where** *salary* > 30k **group by label**(*age*)
> **using part**(*age*) = {*young, middle-aged, old*}.

With the data from Table 9.2, the result is: {⟨*young*, 0.8⟩, ⟨*middle-aged*, 3.7⟩, ⟨*old*, 1.5⟩} where each number returned corresponds to a Σ-count.◇

We now have the following definitions:

$$count(L_i) = \sum_{t \in r} \top(\mu_\psi(t), \mu_{L_i}(t.A)), \tag{9.1}$$

$$count\text{-}rel(L_i) = \frac{\sum_{t \in r} \top(\mu_\psi(t), \mu_{L_i}(t.A))}{\sum_{t \in r} \mu_{L_i}(t.A)}. \tag{9.2}$$

The fuzzy *group by* clause makes it possible to compute fuzzy summaries "on demand", in contrast with the approach proposed in Saint-Paul *et al.* (2005) which first builds a summary of the whole database, then uses it to

Table 9.2 Tuples from *Emp* and their degrees

#e	age	μ_{yg}	μ_{ma}	μ_{old}	salary	μ_{low}	μ_{med}	μ_{high}
17	51	0	0.9	0.1	65	0	0	1
76	40	0	1	0	45	0	1	0
26	24	0.6	0.4	0	19	1	0	0
12	39	0	1	0	32	0.3	0.7	0
19	28	0.2	0.8	0	24	1	0	0
8	54	0	0.6	0.4	57	0	0.8	0.2
31	29	0.1	0.9	0	18	1	0	0
9	61	0	0	1	15	1	0	0
44	22	0.8	0.2	0	45	0	1	0
23	62	0	0	1	59	0	0.6	0.4

answer queries. An example of a query aimed at providing a fuzzy summary is given below.

Example 9.4. Consider the query: "what are the ages of the employees whose salary is medium?". This can be expressed as:

> **select label**(*age*), **count from** *Emp*
> **where** *salary* **is** *medium* **group by label**(*age*)
> **using part**(*age*) = {*young, middle-aged, old*}.

With the data from Table 9.2, and using $\top = min$, one obtains:

$$\{\langle young, 0.8\rangle, \langle middle\text{-}aged, 2.5\rangle, \langle old, 1.0\rangle\}. \diamond$$

Example 9.5. Now consider the query: "what proportion of employees from each age class has a salary which is medium?". This can be expressed as:

> **select label**(*age*), **count-rel from** *Emp*
> **where** *salary* **is** *medium* **group by label**(*age*)
> **using part**(*age*) = {*young, middle-aged, old*}.

With the data from Table 9.2, and using $\top = min$, one obtains:

$$\{\langle young, 0.47\rangle, \langle middle\text{-}aged, 0.43\rangle, \langle old, 0.4\rangle\}. \diamond$$

9.3 Having Clause

The different forms of a *having* clause that can be used as a complement to a *group by* clause are described below through the use of a few examples.

9.3.1   *Inclusion constraint*

An example which involves a Boolean condition in the *having* clause is: "find every age class such that at least 30% of the employees from that class have a high salary":

> **select label**(*age*) **from** *Emp E1*
> **group by label**(*age*)
> **having count** $\geq$
>   (**select count** * 0.3 **from** *Emp*
>   **where** *salary* **is** *high* **and** *age* **is** *E1*.**label**(*age*))
> **using part**(*age*) = {*young, middle-aged, old*}.

Another example, which involves a fuzzy *having* clause, is: "find the extent to which all the employees of a given age class have a high salary":

select label(*age*) **from** *Emp E1*
group by label(*age*)
having (**select** #*e* **from** *Emp* **where** *salary* **is** *high*) **contains set**(#*e*)
using part(*age*) = {*young, middle-aged, old*}.

The evaluation of such a query rests on a graded inclusion (see Section 3.4.2). It constitutes the prototype expression for fuzzy association rule mining, and will be detailed in Section 9.4.

9.3.2   *Aggregate$_1$ θ aggregate$_2$*

Even though a limitation exists as to the aggregates which can be computed on a fuzzy set — as already mentioned — it is still possible to evaluate conditions which *compare* two aggregates (Bosc *et al.*, 2003b). The idea is to start with a definition that is valid for crisp sets, and then to extend it to fuzzy sets. In the case where A and B are crisp, it is possible to express the meaning of the statement $agg_1(A) \leq agg_2(B)$ using an implication according to the formula:

$$\forall x, \; [agg_1(A) \geq x] \Rightarrow [agg_2(B) \geq x], \tag{9.3}$$

where x is used to scan the definition domain of agg_1 and agg_2.

     When A and B are both fuzzy sets, the expression $agg_1(A) \geq x$ (resp. $agg_2(B) \geq x$) is more or less satisfied. Its degree of truth $t(agg_1(A) \geq x)$ (resp. $t(agg_2(B) \geq x)$) can be obtained by considering the different α-level cuts of predicate A:

$$t(agg(A) \geq x) = max_{\alpha \in [0,\, 1]} \, min(\alpha, \, \mu_{\geq x}(agg(A_\alpha))).$$

Since "$\geq x$" is a Boolean predicate, its truth value is either 0 or 1, and we have:

$$t(agg(A) \geq x) = max_{\alpha \in [0,\, 1] such\ that\ agg(A_\alpha) \geq x} \, \alpha.$$

If the universal quantifier in Expression (9.3) is interpreted as a generalized conjunction, the satisfaction degree of $agg_1(A) \leq agg_2(B)$ is given by:

$$min_{x \in D} \, t(agg_1(A) \geq x) \Rightarrow_f t(agg_2(B) \geq x), \tag{9.4}$$

where $\Rightarrow_f$ stand for a fuzzy implication (Fodor and Yager, 2000) and D is the definition domain of agg_1 and agg_2. More detail can be found in Bosc *et al.* (2003b).

An example of such a query is: "find the age classes such that the maximum of the technicians' salaries is greater than the minimum of the engineers' salaries". It can be expressed as:

> **select label**(*age*) **from** *Emp E1* **where** *job* = "technician"
> **group by label**(*age*)
> **having max**(*salary*) >
>   (**select min**(*salary*) **from** *Emp*
>   **where** *age* **is** *E1.*label(*age*) **and** *job* = "engineer")
> **using part**(*age*) = {*young, middle-aged, old*}.

In such a query, the *where* clause could also involve a fuzzy condition.

9.3.3 *Aggregate is ψ*

It is also possible to compute the extent to which an aggregate satisfies a fuzzy condition ψ, by means of the approach proposed in Bosc and Liétard (2008) and presented in Section 6.3.2. For instance, when both the aggregate and the predicate ψ are increasing, one may start from the following definition of the statement $agg(A)$ *is* ψ when A is a crisp set and ψ is a Boolean condition:

$$agg(A) \; is \; \psi \Leftrightarrow \exists n \text{ such that } \psi(n) \text{ and } agg(A) \geq n. \tag{9.5}$$

When A is a fuzzy set and ψ is a fuzzy condition, the preceding expression may be generalized into:

$$t(agg(A) \text{ is } \psi = max_{\alpha \in [0,\,1]} \, min(\alpha, \, \mu_\psi(agg(A))). \qquad (9.6)$$

The case where *agg* is not monotonous is more tricky, but can still be dealt with; see Section 6.3.3 and Bosc and Liétard (2008).

An example of a query involving a condition of the form $agg(A)$ *is* ψ inside a *having* clause is: "find the age classes where the average salary of engineers is high". It can be expressed as:

> **select label**(*age*) **from** *Emp* **where** *job* = 'engineer'
> **group by label**(*age*)
> **having avg**(*salary*) **is** *high*
> **using part**(*age*) = {*young, middle-aged, old*}.

Here again, the *where* clause may also involve a fuzzy condition.

9.4   Application to Association Rule Mining

We now explain how the fuzzy *group by* clause can be used for evaluating, in a simple way, fuzzy association rules of the type (*age* is $L_i \rightarrow$ *salary* is L'_j), where L_i and L'_j are two fuzzy labels defined respectively on the domains of *age* and *salary*. As mentioned in Bosc and Pivert (2001), at least two fuzzy extensions of association rules may be considered: those based on (fuzzy or scalar) cardinalities, and those based on fuzzy implications (see also Hüllermeier (2001) for the latter category). In what follows, we do not deal with fuzzy-cardinality-based rules, since they may be somewhat difficult to interpret for an end-user (and also because they cannot be represented and handled easily in a purely relational DBMS).

The approach based on a scalar cardinality (Σ-count) rests on a straightforward extension of the usual definition of confidence. Consider a fuzzy association rule of the type (A is $L_i \rightarrow B$ is L'_j). In this approach, the validity (confidence) of the rule is defined as:

$$\frac{\sum_{t \in r} \top(\mu_{L_i}(t.A), \, \mu_{L'_j}(t.B))}{\sum_{t \in r} \mu_{L_i}(t.A)}.$$

In the fuzzy-implication-based approach, the rule (A is $L_i \rightarrow B$ is L'_j) expresses a constraint on the B-value for each tuple in the relation. The association rule, also denoted by $(A, L_i) \rightarrow (B, L'_j)$, then means: "for every tuple t, the more $t.A$ is L_i, the more $t.B$ is L_j'", i.e.:

$$(A,\ L_i) \rightarrow (B,\ L_j') \Leftrightarrow \forall t \in r, \mu_{L_i}(t.A) \Rightarrow_f \mu_{L_j'}(t.B),$$

where $\Rightarrow_f$ denotes a fuzzy R-implication. In this case, the confidence of the rule is equal to:

$$min_{t \in r}\ \mu_{L_i}(t.A) \Rightarrow_f \mu_{L'j}(t.B).$$

9.4.1 Rules of the type A is $L_i \rightarrow B$ is L'

9.4.1.1 *Computation of the support*

First, we introduce a variant of *count* named *count-g* whose general definition is:

$$count\text{-}g(L_i) = \frac{\sum_{t \in r} \top(\mu_\psi(t),\ \mu_{L_i}(t.A))}{|r|}, \tag{9.7}$$

where ψ denotes the fuzzy condition which appears in the *where* clause of the query. Expression (9.7) computes the proportion of tuples of r which are $\psi \wedge L_i$. Consider the generic SQLf query:

> **select label**(A), **count-g from** r **where** B **is** L'
> **group by label**(A)
> **using part**(A) = $\{L_1, \ldots, L_n\}$.

This allows for computation of the support of every fuzzy association rule of the type "A is $L_i \rightarrow B$ is L'" for a given L'.

9.4.1.2 *Computation of the confidence*

Consider the generic SQLf query:

> **select label**(A) **from** r
> **group by label**(A)
> **having** (**select** K **from** r **where** B **is** L') **contains set**(K)
> **using part**(A) = $\{L_1, \ldots, L_n\}$,

where K denotes the primary key of the relation.

Scalar cardinality.   Using an approach based on scalar cardinality, the confidence of the rule corresponds to the *cardinality-based* degree of inclusion of the fuzzy set:

$$E(L_i) = (\textbf{select } \#e \textbf{ from } r \textbf{ where } A \textbf{ is } L_i)$$

in the fuzzy set:

$$F = (\textbf{select } \#e \textbf{ from } r \textbf{ where } B \textbf{ is } L'),$$

i.e., to the degree μ produced by the evaluation of the *having* clause:

$$\mu = \frac{\sum_{t \in r} \top(\mu_{L'}(t.B), \, \mu_{L_i}(t.A))}{\sum_{t \in r} \mu_{L_i}(t.A)}.$$

R-implication. Using an approach based on a fuzzy R-implication, the confidence of the rule corresponds to the *implication-based* degree of inclusion of $E(L_i)$ in F — see Chapter 3, Expression (3.10) — i.e., to the degree μ produced by the evaluation of the *having* clause when *contains* is replaced by *contains-f*:

$$\mu = min_{t \in r} \, \mu_{L_i}(t.A) \Rightarrow_{\text{f}} \mu_{L'}(t.B).$$

For instance, with Łukasiewicz's implication (*contains-Lu*), we have:

$$\mu = min_{t \in r} \, min(1, \, 1 - \mu_{L_i}(t.A) + \mu_{L'}(t.B)).$$

Example 9.6. Consider the set of rules of the form:

$$age \text{ is } L_i \rightarrow salary \text{ is } medium,$$

where L_i belongs to $p(age)$. These rules can be evaluated by means of the following two queries (the first query computes the supports, the second the associated confidence degrees):

> **select label**(age), **count-g from** *Emp* **where** *salary* **is** *medium*
> **group by label**(age)
> **using part**(age) = {*young, middle-aged, old*},

which, using the data from Table 9.1, the partitions from Figure 9.1, and $\top = min$, returns:

$$\{0.08/\langle young \rangle, \, 0.25/\langle middle\text{-}aged \rangle, \, 0.1/\langle old \rangle\}.$$

The second query:

> **select label**(age) **from** *Emp* **group by label**(age)
> **having** (**select** $\#e$ **from** *Emp* **where** *salary* **is** *medium*)
>   **contains set**($\#e$)
> **using part**(age) = {*young, middle-aged, old*}

returns:

$$\{0.47/\langle young \rangle, \, 0.43/\langle middle\text{-}aged \rangle, \, 0.4/\langle old \rangle\}.$$

If *contains* were replaced by *contains-Lu* in the second query, we would obtain:

$$\{0.4/\langle young\rangle,\ 0.1/\langle middle\text{-}aged\rangle,\ 0/\langle old\rangle\}.\diamond$$

9.4.2 Rules of the type A is $L \to B$ is L'_i

Now consider mining fuzzy association rules of the type "A is $L \to$ B is L'_i" for a given L. Again, two SQLf queries are necessary:

> **select label**(B), **count-g from** r **where** A **is** L
> **group by label**(B)
> **using part**(B) = $\{L'_1, \ldots, L'_n\}$

for computing the support of the rules considered, and:

> **select label**(B) **from** r **group by label**(B)
> **having set**(K) **contains** (**select** K **from** r **where** A **is** L)
> **using part**(B) = $\{L'_1, \ldots, L'_n\}$

for computing their confidence values.

Example 9.7. Consider the set of rules of the form:

$$age \text{ is } young \to salary \text{ is } L'_i,$$

where L'_i belongs to $p(salary)$. These rules can be evaluated by means of the following two queries (the first query computes the supports, the second the associated confidence degrees):

> **select label**(*salary*), **count-g from** *Emp* **where** *age* **is** *young*
> **group by label**(*salary*)
> **using part**(*salary*) = $\{low,\ medium,\ high\}$

and

> **select label**(*salary*) **from** *Emp* **group by label**(*salary*)
> **having set**(#*e*) **contains** (**select** #*e* **from** *Emp* **where** *age* **is** *young*)
> **using part**(*salary*) = $\{low,\ medium,\ high\}$.

With the data from Table 9.1 and the partitions from Figure 9.1, the first query returns:

$$\{0.09/\langle low\rangle,\ 0.08/\langle medium\rangle,\ 0/\langle high\rangle\}.$$

The second query — which corresponds to the scalar cardinality approach since it involves the operator *contains* — returns the result:

$$\{0.53/\langle low \rangle,\ 0.47/\langle medium \rangle,\ 0/\langle high \rangle\}.$$

If *contains* were replaced by *contains-Lu* in the second query, we would have:

$$\{0.2/\langle low \rangle,\ 0.4/\langle medium \rangle,\ 0.2/\langle high \rangle\}.\diamond$$

9.5 Evaluation of a Fuzzy Group By

The complexity of the evaluation of an FGB clause is very similar to that of a regular *group by* clause. Two cases may be distinguished:

- if the attribute appearing in the FGB clause — denote it by A — is indexed, it is possible to directly access the tuples which belong to a given fuzzy class L_i: they are the tuples t such that $t.A \in support(L_i)$. Recall that the support of a fuzzy label is expressed as an interval, and can be straightforwardly determined from the membership function associated with that label. The degree to which tuple t belongs to class L_i is equal to $\mu_{L_i}(t.A)$.
- otherwise, as usual, one may sort the relation on attribute A, and compare the A-value of each tuple with the (overlapping) segments which correspond to the supports of the different fuzzy labels in the partition of $domain(A)$ in order to build the fuzzy groups. Here too, of course, $\mu_{L_i}(t.A)$ must be computed for each tuple t.

As can be seen, the cost of the evaluation of an FGB clause should be more or less equivalent to that of a regular *group by* clause, since the only additional cost is that related to the computation of the membership degrees.

9.6 Related Work

9.6.1 *Extended group by*

Zhang and Huang (2007) propose some SQL constructs to make clustering facilities available from SQL in the context of spatial data. Basically, these constructs act as wrappers of conventional clustering algorithms, but no further integration with database systems is studied. Li *et al.* (2007) extend the *group by* operator to approximately cluster all the tuples in a predefined number of clusters. Their framework makes use of conventional clustering algorithms, e.g., K-means, and employs summaries and bitmap indexes to integrate clustering and ranking into database systems. Silva *et al.* (2009) introduce a similarity *group by* operator in order to group objects with similar values. Our approach differs from Li *et al.* (2007) and Silva *et al.* (2009) in that:

- we focus on fuzzy grouping based on vague concepts, not on similarity-based grouping;
- we do not aim at "discovering" the clusters, since in our approach the groups are explicitly specified in the query (by means of a fuzzy partition), which incidentally gives them a well-identified meaning;
- Li *et al.* (2007) and Silva *et al.* (2009) do not consider a general fuzzy querying framework such as SQLf (where the fuzzy *group by* construct is just one piece of the puzzle) but only extend a particular feature of SQL.

9.6.2 *Fuzzy OLAP*

A few research works, e.g., Delgado *et al.* (2007), Kaya and Alhajj (2008), have been devoted to the introduction of fuzziness into OLAP systems. These approaches have some characteristics in common with that presented here (use of fuzzy partitions, fuzzy association rule mining) but they do not rely on a general purpose database querying language such as SQLf. They instead extend operators such as *roll-up* and *drill-down*, or devise specific rule mining algorithms.

9.6.3 *Fuzzy database summarization techniques*

Developed by Rasmussen and Yager (1997), SummarySQL is a fuzzy query language which can evaluate the truth degree of a summary guessed by the user. A summary expresses knowledge about the database in a statement of the form "Q objects in DB are S" or "Q R objects in DB are S" where DB stands for the database, Q is a linguistic quantifier, and R and S are linguistic terms. The expression is evaluated for each tuple and the associated truth values are later used to obtain a truth value for the summary. The statements considered by the authors are in a sense more general than the fuzzy association rules that we deal with here, since they involve fuzzy quantifiers. However, our approach can easily be extended to capture such statements by relaxing the operator *contains* that appears in the *having* clause, using, e.g., one of the approaches described in Bosc and Pivert (2008). When it comes to mining fuzzy statements, the main difference lies in the fact that Rasmussen and Yager (1997) do not propose any SQL construct to evaluate these statements "in a batch" as we do via the FGB clause: the statements have to be checked one by one and no fuzzy partitioning of the domains is used.

Saint-Paul *et al.* (2005) propose an approach to the production of linguistic summaries structured in a hierarchy, i.e., a summarization tree where the tuples from the database are rewritten using the linguistic variables involved in fuzzy partitions of the attribute domains. The main difference with our approach is that Saint-Paul *et al.* (2005) view summarization as an independent process, which is not performed by means of SQL queries but by a specific algorithm. As mentioned before, the FGB operator enables summaries "on demand", without having to summarize the whole database.

9.6.4 *Mining association rules with SQL*

The use of SQL queries for mining association rules has been advocated by several authors; see, e.g., Meo *et al.* (1998), Clear *et al.* (1999), Thomas and Sarawagi (1998), Yoshizawa *et al.* (2000), Imielinski and Virmani (1999), Rajamani *et al.* (1999), Pereira *et al.* (2003). However, none of these approaches considers an extended *group by* mechanism, and none considers *fuzzy* association rules either. To the best of our knowledge, the only approach which uses a fuzzy extension of SQL for mining fuzzy association rules (or "gradual functional dependencies", as the authors call them) is that of Rasmussen and Yager (1999), which relies on SummarySQL already discussed above.

9.7 Conclusion

In this chapter, we have introduced a fuzzy *group by* (FGB) operator, and have described how it could be integrated into the SQLf language. This operator relies on user-specified fuzzy partitions of attribute domains, and its main goal is to generate meaningful and useful groupings that go far beyond what is captured by the regular *group by* operator. We have shown how this construct makes it possible to generate fuzzy summaries "on demand", as well as to mine fuzzy association rules in a practical way. It is of course important to make sure that queries involving a fuzzy grouping have execution times comparable to those involving a classical *group by*. One can be reasonably optimistic about this issue, given the results presented in Silva *et al.* (2009) about a similarity-based *group by* (SGB), which show that the overhead in this case is no more than 25%. FGB should be even more efficient than SGB since (i) the clusters are predefined, (ii) the use of fuzzy partitions still makes it possible to employ evaluation techniques based on sorts and/or indexes.

Among possible extensions of this work, the following are noteworthy:

- An investigation into the way measures other than support and confidence for assessing fuzzy association rules, see for example Dubois *et al.* (2006), could be taken into account.
- A variant of the approach described here, aimed at expert users, where fuzzy cardinalities would be computed instead of scalar ones. In the context of fuzzy association rule mining, this implies computation of the validity of the rules by means of a technique such as that described in Bosc *et al.* (2001).
- An extension of the format of the rules to be mined, for instance through a relaxation of the universal quantifier based on one of the approaches proposed in Bosc and Pivert (2008) (see also Section 3.4.2.5).

Chapter 10

Empty and Plethoric Answers

10.1 Introduction

When compared to Boolean queries, fuzzy queries reduce the risk of obtaining an empty set of answers, since the use of a finer discrimination scale — $[0, 1]$ instead of $\{0, 1\}$ — increases the chance of an element being considered (somewhat) satisfactory. Nevertheless, the situation may occur where none of the elements of the database satisfies the query even to a low degree. As noted by Motro (1986), there are two possible explanations for the emptiness of a set of answers: either the query has some "semantic flaw" (for example it includes a false presupposition), or the reason lies only in the current state of the database. In the case of a semantic flaw, an explanation may help the user reformulate his/her query. This generally involves having available some additional knowledge about the structure and the content of the database, for instance under the form of integrity constraints. On the other hand, if an empty set of answers is due only to the absence of any satisfactory element from the current database, a solution consists in retrieving data which are *as suitable as possible* with respect to the information requirement expressed by the initial query. In this chapter, we only consider this latter situation, and we present different techniques that can be used for relaxing conjunctive fuzzy queries.

The "plethoric answer problem" (PAP) — which may be seen as the companion to the "empty answer problem" (EAP) — occurs when the amount of returned data is too large to be manageable. In such cases, users have to go through this large set of answers to examine them and keep only the most relevant ones, which is a tedious and time-consuming task. The PAP has been addressed at some length by the information systems community, and two main approaches have been proposed. The first approach aims at summarizing the result either by rewriting the answers using a coarser vocabulary for describing the attribute domains (see, e.g., Ughetto *et al.*, 2008), or by keeping only the most typical ones (see, e.g., Hua *et al.*, 2009). The second approach aims at strengthening the initial query in order to make it more selective (either by adding new conditions or by making some of the initial conditions more drastic). However, not much work can be found in the literature about the PAP in a context of fuzzy queries.

This chapter is organized as follows. Section 10.2 deals with the empty answer problem in a context of conjunctive fuzzy queries, and describes two approaches that may be used to overcome it. The first approach is based on the use of a modifier which softens one or several fuzzy predicates from the query, whereas the second takes advantage of a repository of previously submitted queries, and aims at replacing the failing query with a semantically close one, known to be non-failing. Section 10.3 deals with the plethoric answer problem and also describes two approaches aimed at dealing with it. In the first approach, a strengthening modifier is used to make the fuzzy predicates of the query more selective, whereas the second approach expands a fuzzy query Q with new predicates selected from among those that are semantically correlated with Q.

10.2   Empty Answer Problem

As mentioned above, when the set of answers to a query is empty, rather than returning an empty set, a cooperative system may:

- exploit some domain knowledge in order to explain why no answer was found, thus helping the user reformulate his/her query,
- exploit some domain knowledge so as to automatically construct a modified (relaxed) query.

Between these two extreme possibilities, different ways of interacting with the user may be imagined. In the following, we mainly consider the second strategy. We first describe an approach that uses a weakening mechanism in order to make one or more predicates of the initial fuzzy query more tolerant.

10.2.1   *Query relaxation*

Query relaxation consists of modifying a query in order to find a less restrictive variant. Different methods for relaxing the constraints involved in a query have been defined in the literature (see, for instance, Cuppens and Demolombe, 1988; Guyomard and Siroux, 1989; Motro, 1990; Chu and Chen, 1992; Gaasterland *et al.*, 1992b). Similar work has been carried out in the framework of information retrieval, starting with Salton *et al.* (1983). Most of these approaches rely on a "semantic distance" which makes it possible to determine a modified query that is expected to be as close as possible to the initial one, semantically speaking.

The general mechanism for weakening a query Q may be described in the following way: one must replace Q by its "best" modification Q' in such a way that:

(1) Q' is semantically close to Q in the sense that the elements returned by Q' are still somewhat relevant with respect to the user's need expressed by Q;

(2) the set of answers to Q' is non-empty.

In the Boolean case, two main approaches can be used to relax a conjunctive Boolean query when it fails to produce any answer:

- relaxation by generalization: transforming query conditions into more general ones (Motro, 1986);
- relaxation by removal: it aims at deleting some parts of the query in order to obtain a subquery that is less constraining (Godfrey, 1997).

In the case of conjunctive fuzzy queries, one may either relax some of the atomic conditions, or replace the conjunction by a less drastic operator (such as a mean or a quantifier of the form "almost all"). In the following, we only consider the first strategy, i.e., that based on predicate weakening, which has the advantage of preserving the conjunctive nature of the query.

10.2.2 *Relaxation by predicate weakening*

10.2.2.1 *Principle*

Let Q be a fuzzy query to a given relational database, and let Σ_Q^α (resp. $\Sigma_Q^{0^+}$) be the set of answers to Q whose satisfaction degree is at least equal to α (resp. is non-zero).

In a fuzzy querying framework, the simplest way to relax a query consists of lowering the qualitative threshold present in the query, if any. For instance, a query involving a threshold equal to 0.8 may be relaxed successfully by reducing this threshold to 0.6. In the following, we do not consider this trivial case and we assume that an empty set of answers means that $\Sigma_Q^{0^+}$ is empty.

Relaxing a fuzzy query Q involves weakening the fuzzy constraints contained in Q in order to make Q less selective. Such a modification can be achieved by applying a basic transformation to all or some of the predicates of the query. Consider a transformation T applied to a predicate P ($T^\uparrow(P)$ representing the modified predicate). T is said to be weakening if it satisfies the following properties:

- RC1: $T^\uparrow$ does not decrease the membership degree for any element of the domain, i.e., $\forall u \in domain(A)$, $\mu_{T^\uparrow(P)}(u) \geq \mu_P(u)$, where A denotes the attribute concerned by P;
- RC2: $T^\uparrow$ must extend the support $supp(P)$ of predicate P, i.e.,

$$supp(P) = \{u \,|\, \mu_P(u) > 0\} \subset supp(T^\uparrow(P)) = \{u \,|\, \mu_{T^\uparrow(P)}(u) > 0\};$$

- RC3: $T^\uparrow$ preserves the specificity of predicate P (in order not to alter its semantics too much), i.e.,

$$core(P) = \{u \,|\, \mu_P(u) = 1\} = core(T^\uparrow(P)) = \{u \,|\, \mu_{T^\uparrow(P)}(u) = 1\}.$$

Most of the usual modifiers (see, e.g., Kerre and de Cock, 1999) do not fulfill these three properties. However, in Bouchon-Meunier (1988), a parameterized modifier called ν-*rather* is introduced, whose behavior is described in Figure 10.1, and which is well suited to the problem considered here, since it does comply with the three requirements above. An approach to the relaxation of fuzzy conjunctive queries based on ν-*rather* is described in Andreasen and Pivert (1994, 1995). In the following, we present an alternative approach based on the use of a *tolerance* relation defined on

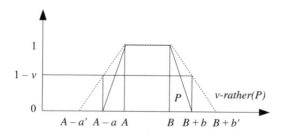

Fig. 10.1 Behavior of ν-*rather*

the attribute domains and the notion of *dilation*. The advantage of this approach over that based on *ν-rather* lies in its more intuitive semantics, as discussed in Bosc *et al.* (2007a).

10.2.2.2 *Dilation mechanism*

Definition 10.1. A proximity relation (or a tolerance relation) is a fuzzy relation E on a domain X, such that $\forall x, y \in X$,

- $\mu_E(x, x) = 1$ (reflexivity),
- $\mu_E(x, y) = \mu_E(y, x)$ (symmetry).

The quantity $\mu_E(x, y)$ can be viewed as a grade of approximate equality of x with y. In a universe X which is a subset of the real line, an absolute proximity relation can be conveniently modeled by a fuzzy relation E of the form:

$$\mu_E(x,\ y) = \mu_Z(x - y),$$

which only depends on the value of the difference $x - y$. The parameter Z, called a tolerance indicator, is a fuzzy interval (i.e., a fuzzy set on the real line) centered in 0, such that:

(1) $\mu_Z(r) = \mu_Z(-r)$. This property ensures the symmetry of the proximity relation E (i.e., $\mu_E(x, y) = \mu_E(y, x)$),
(2) $\mu_Z(0) = 1$, which states that x is approximately equal to itself to a degree 1,
(3) the support $supp(Z) = \{r \,|\, \mu_Z(r) > 0\}$ is bounded and is of the form $[-\Omega, \Omega]$, where Ω is a positive real number,
(4) in terms of the trapezoidal membership function (TMF), Z can be expressed by the quadruple $(-z, z, \delta, \delta)$ with $\Omega = z + \delta$ and $[-z, z]$ the core of Z (i.e., $\{r, \mu_Z(r) = 1\}$).

It is important to emphasize that this kind of proximity relation evaluates the extent to which the amount $x - y$ is close to 0. The closer x is to y, the closer $x - y$ and 0 become. Classical (or crisp) equality is recovered for $Z = 0$, defined as $\mu_0(x - y) = 1$ if $x = y$ and $\mu_0(x - y) = 0$ otherwise. Other interesting properties of the parameterized relation E are given in Dubois *et al.* (2001). In what follows, we shall write $E[Z]$ to denote the proximity relation E parameterized by Z.

Dilation.   Consider a fuzzy set F on the numeric universe U and an absolute proximity $E(Z)$, where Z is a tolerance indicator. Dilating the fuzzy set F by Z will provide a fuzzy set F^Z defined by

$$\mu_{F^Z}(r) = sup_s \, min(\mu_{E[Z]}(s, r), \mu_F(s))$$

$$= sup_s \, min(\mu_Z(r - s), \mu_F(s)), \text{ since } Z = -Z \qquad (10.1)$$

$$= \mu_{F \oplus Z}(r), \text{ observing that } s + (r - s) = r.$$

Hence, $F^Z = F \oplus Z$, where $\oplus$ is the addition operation extended to fuzzy sets (Dubois and Prade, 1988). F^Z gathers the elements of F and the elements outside F which are somewhat close to an element in F.

Lemma 10.1. *Given a fuzzy set F and a proximity relation $E[Z]$, for $F^Z = F \oplus Z$ we have $F \subseteq F^Z$.*

In other words, the fuzzy set F^Z is less restrictive than F, but still semantically close to F. Thus, F^Z can be viewed as a relaxed variant of F. In terms of the TMF, if $F = (A, B, a, b)$ and $Z = (-z, z, \delta, \delta)$ then $F^Z = (A - z, B + z, a + \delta, b + \delta)$; see Figure 10.2. Recall that if $F = (A, B, a, b)$, then $supp(F) = [A - a, B + b]$ and $core(F) = [A, B]$. The scalar a (resp. b) represents the left-hand (resp. right-hand) spread of F.

We emphasize that some practical applications require only one constituent part of a fuzzy set F (either the core or the support) to be affected when applying a dilation operation. We denote by core dilation (resp. support dilation) the dilating transformation that affects only the core (resp. support) of F. The following proposition shows how to obtain such results.

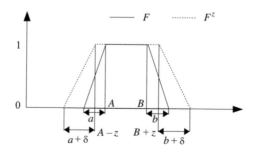

Fig. 10.2   Dilation operation

Proposition 10.1. *Let F be a fuzzy set and $E[Z]$ a proximity relation. We have:*

- *Core dilation is obtained using the family of tolerance indicators of the form $Z = (-z, z, 0, 0)$.*
- *Support dilation is obtained using the family of tolerance indicators of the form $Z = (0, 0, \delta, \delta)$.*

Making use of this proposition, if $F = (A, B, a, b)$ the core dilation (resp. support dilation) leads to $F^Z = (A - z, B + z, a, b)$ (resp. $F^Z = (A, B, a + \delta, b + \delta))$.

10.2.2.3 *Relaxing an atomic criterion*

Let P be a fuzzy predicate and $E[Z]$ an absolute proximity relation parameterized by a tolerance indicator Z of the form $(0, 0, \delta, \delta)$ (i.e., such that only the support of P should be changed). Dilating P allows it to be transformed into an enlarged fuzzy predicate P', defined as follows:

$$P' = T^\uparrow(P) = P^Z = P \oplus Z.$$

Clearly, the modified predicate P' contains the elements of P and the elements outside P which are somewhat close to an element in P. Moreover, we can easily check that the desirable properties RC1–RC3 (Section 10.2.2.1) are satisfied by $T^\uparrow$. Note that a transformation of the same nature was also proposed in the tolerant fuzzy pattern matching setting by Dubois and Prade (1995).

Principle of the approach. Let $Q = P$ be an atomic query. If the set of answers to Q is empty, then Q is transformed into $Q_1 = T^\uparrow(P) = P^Z$. This relaxation mechanism can be repeated n times until the answer to the modified query $Q_n = T^{\uparrow(n)}(P) = P^{n.Z} = P \oplus n.Z$ is not empty. In practice, as pointed out in Bosc *et al.* (2007a), the only difficulty when applying this technique concerns its semantic limits (i.e., the maximum number of relaxation steps such that the final modified query Q_n is not too far, semantically speaking, from the original one). Indeed, there is no intrinsic criterion attached to this transformation which would stop the iterative process when the answer still remains empty (except of course the impossibility of going beyond the limits of the attribute domain concerned).

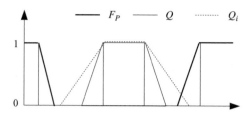

Fig. 10.3   Example of membership functions associated with Q, Q_i, and F_P

Controlling the relaxation. To enable some control over the relaxation process, one solution is to ask the user to specify, along with her/his query, a fuzzy set F_P of more or less non-authorized values in the related domain. See Figure 10.3. The new query to be considered is now written as $Q_i' = Q_i \cap (F_P)^c$, where $(F_P)^c$ denotes the complement of F_P. The satisfaction degree of an element u then becomes $min(\mu_{Q_i}(u), 1 - \mu_{F_P}(u))$. Thus the incremental relaxation process will now stop when the answer to Q_i is not empty ($\Sigma_{Q_i}^{0^+} \neq \emptyset$), or when the core of the complement of the fuzzy set associated with Q_i is included in the core of F_P ($min(\mu_{Q_i}(u), 1 - \mu_{F_P}(u)) = 0$).

Relaxation algorithm. This incremental relaxation technique is encoded by Algorithm 10.1 (where $\Sigma_{Q_i}^{0^+}$ stands for the set of answers to Q_i and Q_i^c for the complement of the fuzzy set associated with Q_i).

Algorithm 10.1. Incremental relaxation of an atomic query.

let Q := P;
let δ be an absolute tolerance value; /* $Z = (0, 0, \delta, \delta)$ */
i := 0; Q_i := Q;
$Q_i' := Q_i \cap (F_P)^c$;
compute $\Sigma_{Q_i'}^{0^+}$;
while ($\Sigma_{Q_i'}^{0^+} = \emptyset$ **and** ($core(Q_i^c) \not\subset core(F_p)$) **do**
begin
    i := i+1;
    $Q_i := T^{\uparrow(i)}(P) := P \oplus i.Z$;
    $Q_i' := Q_i \cap (F_P)^c$;
    compute $\Sigma_{Q_i'}^{0^+}$;
end;
if $\Sigma_{Q_i'}^{0^+} \neq \emptyset$ **then return** $\Sigma_{Q_i'}^{0^+}$ **endif.**

Particular case. It is important to emphasize that, for some kinds of fuzzy predicates to be relaxed, the property of symmetry of the tolerance indicator Z is not required. Consider, for instance, the predicate $P = (0, 25, 0, 10)$ representing the concept *young*. Weakening P boils down to increasing the width of its support $supp(P)$. This has to be done on the right side of the TMF of P. The appropriate family of tolerance indicators will then be of the form $Z = (0, 0, 0, \delta)$, which leads to $T^\uparrow(P) = (0, 25, 0, 10+\delta)$.

10.2.2.4 *Relaxing a conjunctive query*

Among the fuzzy queries involving several predicates, the only problematic class is that of conjunctive queries. Indeed, an empty set of answers returned by a disjunctive query means that every predicate from the query has an empty support with respect to the actual database content. Therefore, it makes sense to relax *all* of the predicates from the query. The situation is the same when the connector, instead of being a disjunction, is an operator which is not zero-absorbing (for instance a mean). In the case of conjunctive queries, however, it is enough to have one predicate whose support is empty for the overall set of answers to be empty.

A conjunctive fuzzy query Q is of the form $P_1 \wedge \cdots \wedge P_k$, where the symbol $\wedge$ stands for the connector *and*, interpreted by the *min* operator, and P_i is a fuzzy predicate.

It is worthy of note that Q can be modified by means of a transformation (in order to perform a relaxation or intensification) in two distinct ways:

- a *global query modification* which consists of uniformly applying a transformation T_j to each predicate P_j. Given a set of transformations $\{T_1, \ldots, T_k\}$ and a conjunctive query $Q = P_1 \wedge \cdots \wedge P_k$, the set of modified queries related to Q resulting from applying $\{T_1, \ldots, T_k\}$ is

$$T_1^{(i)}(P_1) \wedge \cdots \wedge T_k^{(i)}(P_k),$$

where $i > 0$ and $T_j^{(i)}$ means that the transformation T_j is applied i times.
- a *local query modification* which affects only some predicates (or subqueries). Given a set of transformations $\{T_1, \ldots, T_k\}$ and a conjunctive query $Q = P_1 \wedge \cdots \wedge P_k$, the set of modified queries related to Q which result from applying $\{T_1, \ldots, T_k\}$ is

$$T_1^{(i_1)}(P_1) \wedge \cdots \wedge T_k^{(i_k)}(P_k),$$

where $\forall h$, $i_h \geq 0$, $\exists h$, $i_h > 0$, $T_j^{(i_h)}$ means that the transformation T_j is applied i_h times to Pj, and $T_j^0(P_j) = P_j$.

Given a query $Q = P_1 \wedge \cdots \wedge P_k$, if a subquery Q' of Q fails, then obviously the query Q itself fails.

Definition 10.2. Let $Q = P_1 \wedge \cdots \wedge P_k$ be a failing query. Q', a failing subquery of Q, is minimal if and only if no subquery of Q' fails.

In general, a failing query can have one or several minimal failing subqueries (MFSs for short). Identifying MFSs has been considered by several authors (Corella *et al.*, 1984; Gaasterland *et al.*, 1992a; Godfrey, 1997; Kaplan, 1982) as a means of providing cooperative answers to failing Boolean database queries. In particular, an efficient algorithm is proposed in Godfrey (1997) to find an MFS of a query of k conjuncts. This algorithm, which proceeds depth-first and top-down, is polynomial and runs in $O(k)$ time. It has also been shown that finding all MFSs of a query is intractable and is NP-complete. However, finding l MFSs, for any fixed l ($l < k$), can be done in an acceptable time.

Let $Q = P_1 \wedge \cdots \wedge P_k$ be a failing query, $T^\uparrow(Q)$ a relaxation of Q, and $SQ^{[j]}$ a subquery of Q obtained by deleting the predicate P_j from Q. Let also $mfs(Q) = \{M_1, \ldots, M_h\}$ be the set of MFSs of Q and $\{P_{n_1}, \ldots, P_{n_u}\}$ be the predicates that appear in at least one MFS of Q. To characterize the set of MFSs of $T^\uparrow(Q)$ with respect to that of Q, we introduce the following propositions (Bosc *et al.*, 2009c), whose proofs are straightforward.

Proposition 10.2. *If* $T^\uparrow(Q) = SQ^{[j]} \wedge T_j^\uparrow(P_j)$ *with* $j \in \{n_1, \ldots, n_u\}$, *then the MFSs of* $T^\uparrow(Q)$ *must be searched in* $mfs(Q)$ *by substituting* P_j *with* $T_j^\uparrow(P_j)$ *in each element of* $mfs(Q)$.

Proposition 10.3. *If* $T^\uparrow(Q) = SQ^{[j]} \wedge T_j^\uparrow(P_j)$ *with* $j \notin \{n_1, \ldots, n_u\}$, *then* $mfs(Q)$ *is also the set of MFSs of* $T^\uparrow(Q)$.

Example 10.1. Consider a query $Q = P_1 \wedge P_2 \wedge P_3 \wedge P_4$ and assume that $mfs(Q) = \{P_1 \wedge P_3, P_1 \wedge P_4\}$. Then,

- If $T^\uparrow(Q) = T_1^\uparrow(P_1) \wedge SQ^{[1]} = T_1^\uparrow(P_1) \wedge P_2 \wedge P_3 \wedge P_4$, the MFSs of $T^\uparrow(Q)$ are searched in $\{T_1^\uparrow(P_1) \wedge P_3, T_1^\uparrow(P_1) \wedge P_4\}$.
- If $T^\uparrow(Q) = SQ^{[2]} \wedge T_2^\uparrow(P_2) = P_1 \wedge T_2^\uparrow(P_2) \wedge P_3 \wedge P_4$, the MFSs of $T^\uparrow(Q)$ are the MFSs of Q.$\diamond$

As pointed out in Bosc *et al.* (2007a), local query modification of a query $Q = P_1 \wedge \cdots \wedge P_k$ (where all conditions involved in Q are of the same importance for the user) leads to an ordering ($\prec$) between the modified queries obtained from Q. That ordering can be defined on the basis of the

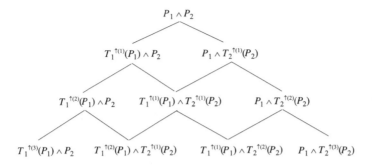

Fig. 10.4   Lattice of relaxed queries (limited to three levels)

number of transformations applied. If Q' and Q'' are two relaxed queries of Q, we say that

$$Q' \prec Q'' \text{ if } \sum_{i=1}^{k} count(T_i^{\uparrow} \text{ in } Q') < \sum_{i=1}^{k} count(T_i^{\uparrow} \text{ in } Q'').$$

The set of modified queries related to Q (i.e., $T_1^{(i_1)}(P_1) \wedge \cdots \wedge T_k^{(i_k)}(P_k)$) can then be organized in a lattice. For instance, the lattice associated with the weakening of the query $P_1 \wedge P_2$ is given in Figure 10.4. In practice, and in order to find a relaxed query related to $Q = P_1 \wedge \cdots \wedge P_k$ that returns a non-empty answer set, one has to deal with the following three main issues when using a local query modification:

- define an intelligent way to exploit the lattice of weakened queries,
- guarantee the property of equal relaxation effect for all fuzzy predicates,
- study the extent to which the user has to intervene in the relaxation process.

The two latter issues have been discussed in Bosc *et al.* (2007a). In the following, we show how the scanning of the lattice can be done in an efficient way by exploiting the MFSs of the original failing query.

Scanning the lattice.   In general, search techniques in a lattice are time-consuming, and result in algorithms whose time complexity is exponential. To make the search over the lattice more efficient, the MFSs of the original failing query may be exploited. The corresponding search technique consists of two steps:

(1) *Enumerating l MFSs of Q.* To do this, one may use the algorithm proposed in Godfrey (1997) which is designed for computing l MFSs

in an acceptable time (when l is not too large). Such an algorithm can easily be adapted in the case of fuzzy queries with no main changes, as pointed out in Bosc *et al.* (2007a). From Propositions 10.2 and 10.3, this algorithm has to be run only once, since the MFSs of any relaxed query $T^\uparrow(Q)$ can be deduced from those of Q.

(2) *An intelligent search technique.* Information about MFSs allows the provision of an intelligent search technique over the lattice by avoiding the need to evaluate some nodes. Indeed, the node in the lattice that preserves at least one MFS of its father node (that is, the node from which it is derived) does not have to be evaluated (since we are certain that it fails). This technique is sketched in Algorithm 10.2.

Algorithm 10.2. MFS-based search for a relaxed query with non-empty answers.

$$\textbf{let } Q = P_1 \wedge P_2 \wedge \cdots \wedge P_k;$$
$$\mathrm{mfs}(Q) = \{P_{l_1} \wedge P_{l_2} \wedge \cdots \wedge P_{l_{m_1}}, \ldots, P_{l_1} \wedge P_{l_2} \wedge \cdots \wedge P_{l_{m_h}}\};$$

```
found := false; i := 1;
while (i ≤ ω.k) and (not found) do
begin
   level(i) := {Qᵢ¹, ..., Qᵢⁿⁱ};
   for each req in level(i) do
   begin
      modif := true;
      for each a_mfs in mfs(father(req)) do
         begin modif := modif ∧ (a_mfs ∉ req) end;
      if modif then
         if evaluate(req) then
            level(i) = ∅;
            found := true
         endif;
      endif;
      if level(i) ≠ ∅ then compute mfs(req) endif;
   end;
   i := i + 1;
end;
if found then return req;
```

In this algorithm:

- $level(i)$ stands for the set of relaxed queries in level i of the lattice,
- $father(Q)$ is the set of nodes from which Q can be derived, i.e., Q is an immediate relaxed variant of any query contained in $father(Q)$. For instance, in Figure 10.4, if $Q = T(P_1) \wedge T(P_2)$, then $father(Q) = \{T(P_1) \wedge P_2, P_1 \wedge T(P_2)\}$,
- $evaluate(Q)$ is a function that evaluates Q against the database. It returns *true* if Q produces some answers, *false* otherwise,
- ω represents the maximal number of relaxation steps for each predicate P_j ($j = 1, k$). Hence, the maximal relaxation of a query $Q = P_1 \wedge \cdots \wedge P_k$ is the modified query given by $T^{\uparrow(max)}(Q) = T_1^{\uparrow(\omega)}(P_1) \wedge \cdots \wedge T_k^{\uparrow(\omega)}(P_k)$. This implies that the lattice is bounded and maximally contains $\omega.k$ levels.

As can be seen, to find the relaxed query with non-empty answers, several candidate queries must be evaluated against the database. One way to substantially reduce the cost of this evaluation is, first, to evaluate the lower bound of relaxed queries, i.e., $T^{\uparrow(max)}(Q)$ and store the resulting items; second, to evaluate each candidate query on the result of $T^{\uparrow(max)}(Q)$.

10.2.3 *Case-based reasoning approach*

10.2.3.1 *Introduction and principle*

The main problem with the type of approach presented in the previous section (i.e., that based on query relaxation) is that it introduces high combinatorics in the case of conjunctive queries — even though the notion of the MFS can be exploited in order to limit these combinatorics, as we just showed — since one has to scan the lattice of possible relaxed queries (which can be huge) and process many of them (which is expensive) before finding a non-failing one.

In this section, we aim to avoid this combinatory explosion by exploring a *case-based reasoning* approach (Bosc *et al.*, 2009a; Pivert *et al.*, 2010). The idea is to take advantage of the queries previously submitted to the system in order to efficiently find a non-failing query as similar as possible to a failing one. We consider conjunctive queries of the form "$Q = P_1 \wedge P_2 \wedge \cdots \wedge P_n$", where each P_i is of the form "A_i **in** E_i", A_i denoting an attribute and E_i a fuzzy set which can be either discrete or continuous. The essential idea is to look for a "good" global substitute to a failing query Q among queries previously submitted to the system (and stored in a repository — also called *query cache* in the following — D^+) whose sets of answers are known to be non-empty. Such an approach implies the availability of a resemblance measure over every attribute domain involved in the database considered, so as to define the notion of *semantic proximity* between queries. With this approach, a non-empty answer is guaranteed in one step, since only one query — known to be non-failing — needs to be processed. Note that this approach is relevant mainly for databases in which deletions and updates are rare or non-existent (a typical example is an archiving system). Otherwise the repository would have to be updated too, which would be a complex and expensive task.

10.2.3.2   *Predicate substitution*

Let $P = (A \textbf{ in } E)$ be a failing predicate with respect to a relation r ($\forall t \in r, t.A \notin E$), where A is an attribute and E is a finite set or an interval, and $P' = (A' \textbf{ in } E')$ a non-failing predicate with respect to r ($\exists t \in r, t.A \in E'$). We denote by *prox* the proximity relation defined over the domain of A.

Boolean case.   We first deal with the case where the failing query only involves Boolean conditions.

Case where E and E' are finite sets.   In order to assess the "quality" of P' as a substitute to P, a measure is needed. It is not, strictly speaking, a proximity measure, since the symmetry property is not desired here. Indeed, one wants to know whether P' is a good substitute to P, but not the reciprocal. Several possible substitutivity measures (denoted by sbs_i later on) are discussed below.

1st idea: Assess the extent to which every element from $(E' - E)$ resembles at least one element from E:

$$sbs_1(P, P') = \inf_{x' \in (E'-E)} \sup_{x \in E} prox(x, x'). \qquad (10.2)$$

The problem with this measure is that the worst element "masks" the others, as illustrated in the next example. In the following, we assume that the resemblance relation on animals depicted in Table 10.1 is available.

Example 10.2. $E = \{\text{hen}, \text{duck}, \text{turkey}\}$, $E'_1 = \{\text{hen}, \text{turkey}, \text{cow}\}$, $E'_2 = \{\text{cow}, \text{rooster}\}$. We have $sbs_1(P, P'_1) = sbs_1(P, P'_2) = 0$, but since there are neither hens nor turkeys in the database — otherwise P would not be a failing predicate — it seems reasonable to claim that E'_2 should be a better

Table 10.1   Proximity relation over attribute *animal*

	rooster	hen	duck	turkey	cow
rooster	1	0.9	0.6	0.7	0
hen	0.9	1	0.6	0.7	0
duck	0.6	0.6	1	0.5	0
turkey	0.7	0.7	0.5	1	0
cow	0	0	0	0	1

substitute than E_1'. However, in the computation of $sbs_1(P, P_2')$, the element cow "masks" the element rooster.◇

2nd idea: Assess the extent to which there is an element from $(E' - E)$ which resembles at least one element from E:

$$sbs_2(P, P') = sup_{x' \in (E'-E)} \, sup_{x \in E} \, prox(x, x'). \qquad (10.3)$$

Here, the difficulty is that the "winning set" may include elements which are very distant from those desired by the user.

Example 10.3. $E = \{hen\}$, $E_1' = \{hen, cow, turkey\}$, $E_2' = \{duck\}$. Here, E_2' should win, since it includes only elements close to the desired ones, contrary to E_1', which includes "cow". However, it is E_1' which wins, since $sbs_2(P, P_1') = 0.7$ while $sbs_2(P, P_2') = 0.6$.◇

3rd idea: Mix the quantitative and the qualitative aspects by measuring the average resemblance degree between an element from $(E' - E)$ and an element from E. For each element x' from $(E' - E)$, the corresponding measure looks for the maximal proximity between x' and an element x from E, computes the sum of these maximal proximities, and divides this sum by the number of elements present in $(E' - E)$:

$$sbs_3(P, P') = \frac{\sum_{x' \in (E'-E)} \, sup_{x \in E} \, prox(x, x')}{|E' - E|}. \qquad (10.4)$$

Example 10.4. $E = \{hen, duck, turkey\}$, $E_1' = \{hen, turkey, cow\}$, $E_2' = \{cow, rooster\}$. We have: $sbs_3(P, P_1') = 0$ and $sbs_3(P, P_2') = 0.45$.◇

Since measure sbs_3 appears the most satisfactory, it will be used in the following.

Case where E and E' are intervals.   We first consider the simple case where proximity is defined in a Boolean manner:

$$res(x, y) = 1 \text{ if } |x - y| \le \delta, 0 \text{ otherwise.} \qquad (10.5)$$

Consider two intervals: $E = [m, M]$ — from P — and $E' = [m', M']$ — from the potential substitute P'. Using the tolerance value δ, interval E is extended into $E'' = [m - \delta, M + \delta] = [m'', M'']$. It is necessary to compute the extent to which E' is close E'', and the expression of the substitutivity measure becomes:

$$sbs_3(P, P') = \frac{|(E' - E) \cap E''|}{|E' - E|}. \tag{10.6}$$

The case where proximity is defined by means of a fuzzy tolerance indicator Z (see Section 10.2.2.1) is slightly more complex. In such a situation, interval E is *dilated* into a fuzzy set E'' according to the calculus described in Section 10.2.2.2 (see also Bosc *et al.*, 2005) and the definition of $sbs_3(P, P')$ becomes:

$$sbs_3(P, P') = \frac{\int_{x \in (E' - E)} \mu_{E''}(x)}{|E' - E|}. \tag{10.7}$$

Case where E is an interval and E' is a set. When P involves an interval E and P' involves a set E', $sbs_3(P, P')$ is written as:

$$sbs_3(P, P') = \frac{\sum_{x' \in E' \wedge x' \notin E} sup_{x \in E} \, prox(x, x')}{|\{x \in E' \mid x \notin E\}|}. \tag{10.8}$$

On the other hand, the dual case (set in P and interval in P') is much more tricky and cannot be captured by Expression (10.7) defining sbs_3 when the attribute domain is continuous. Consequently, we introduce the constraint that a finite set can only be replaced by another finite set.

Fuzzy case. We now move to the case where value constraints are expressed by means of fuzzy predicates. Consider a conjunctive fuzzy query $Q = P_1 \wedge \cdots \wedge P_n$, where any predicate P_i is of the form $(A_i \text{ is } T_i)$ and T_i is a fuzzy term. Here, the fact that Q returns an empty answer set means that there does not exist any element x in the database such that $\top_{i=1,\ldots,n} (\mu_{T_i}(x)) > 0$, where $\top$ denotes a triangular norm generalizing the conjunction. This fact can be expressed by saying that the support of the query relative to the database is empty.

In order to deal with this kind of query, measure sbs_3 needs to be generalized by taking into account the resemblance between the degrees originating from the two fuzzy terms considered. The generalized measure obtained, which can also be seen as a variant of the interchangeability measure proposed in Bosc and Pivert (1997), is defined as:

$$sbs_3(E, E')$$

$$= \frac{\sum_{x' \in sp(E'-E)} w(x') \times sup_{x \in E} min(prox(x, x'), \Psi(\mu_{E'}(x'), \mu_E(x)))}{\sum_{x' \in sp(E'-E)} w(x')},$$

$$(10.9)$$

where $sp(E)$ denotes the support of E, function Ψ assesses the resemblance between two degrees in the unit interval — it can be defined, e.g., as $\Psi(a, b) = 1 - |a - b|$ — and:

$$w(x') = \mu_{(E'-E)}(x') = min(\mu_{E'}(x'), 1 - \mu_E(x')).$$

The weight $w(x')$ captures the fact that it is all the more important to find a good substitute to x' as x' strongly belongs to $E' - E$. It is straightforward to show that, if the sets are crisp, this expression is equivalent to Expression (10.8).

The above definition can be directly extended to the case of continuous fuzzy sets by replacing the sum by an integral.

Example 10.5. Consider the fuzzy sets: $E = \{1/\text{rapeseed}, 0.8/\text{cabbage}, 0.3/\text{wheat}\}$ and $E' = \{0.4/\text{rapeseed}, 0.3/\text{cabbage}, 0.4/\text{corn}, 0.7/\text{broccoli}\}$. Using the most common definition of the difference between fuzzy sets, i.e.,

$$\mu_{(A-B)}(x) = min(\mu_A(x), 1 - \mu_B(x)),$$

one obtains:

$$E' - E = \{0.2/\text{cabbage}, 0.4/\text{corn}, 0.7/\text{broccoli}\}.$$

For "cabbage", the supremum equals:

$$sup(min(0.2, 0.3), min(1, 0.5), min(0.2, 1) = 0.5,$$

for "corn", it equals:

$$sup(min(0.4, 0.4), min(0.1, 0.6), min(0.8, 0.9)) = 0.8,$$

and for "broccoli" we obtain the degree 0.9. Hence, the final substitutivity degree equals:

$$\frac{0.2 \times 0.5 + 0.4 \times 0.8 + 0.7 \times 0.9}{0.2 + 0.4 + 0.7} = 0.81. \diamond$$

10.2.3.3   *Conjunctive query replacement strategy*

Let Q be a failing user query, and consider the set S_Q of predicates $\{A_i \text{ in } E_i\}$ from Q. We assume a repository D^+ of non-failing queries. Each query Q' of D^+ is associated with the set $S_{Q'}$ of its predicates $\{A_i \text{ in } E'_i\}$. The problem is to find the best substitute to Q among all queries of D^+.

Definition 10.3 (substitute to a query). *A substitute to a query Q is a query Q' from D^+ such that:*

i) Q' is addressed to the same relation(s) as Q,

ii) Q' shares at least one attribute from its "where" clause with that from Q,

iii) Q' involves at least one predicate $(A_i \textbf{ in } E'_i)$ which is not subsumed by $(A_i \textbf{ in } E_i)$.

Item ii) of the definition above guarantees semantic proximity between Q and Q' while item iii) is based on the following remark. Even if query Q' involves a predicate which is subsumed by its counterpart in Q, query Q' can be an interesting substitute to Q since the other predicates must also be taken into account. For instance, if query $Q = (A \textbf{ in } \{\text{rabbit}, \text{hen}\} \wedge B \textbf{ in } \{\text{wheat}, \text{cabbage}\})$ returns an empty answer, it is still possible for query $Q' = (A \textbf{ in } \{\text{rabbit}\} \wedge B \textbf{ in } \{\text{wheat}, \text{oats}\})$ to return a non-empty answer, whereas the predicate on A in Q' is subsumed by that in Q. However, for a query Q' to be a possible substitute, it is necessary for Q' to involve at least one predicate which is not subsumed by the corresponding predicate in Q (but note that if this were not the case, the answer to Q' would be empty — since the answer to Q is empty — and Q' would therefore not be in D^+).

The approach that we propose consists of the following three steps:

(1) select the candidate queries from the repository D^+ (and adapt these queries; see the algorithm below),

(2) compute the proximity degrees between the queries retained and the user query Q, through the measure sbs_3,

(3) determine the closest substitute to Q and process it.

Replacement mechanism. It is worth noting that the predicates from Q' which are strictly subsumed by those from Q can be replaced by their counterparts in Q. Indeed, it is not possible for such a predicate from Q (taken individually) to have been the reason for the query failure. Moreover, for every predicate A_i **in** E_i from Q which is not "covered" by Q', i.e., which concerns an attribute on which there is no constraint in Q', one may compute the proximity between P and the entire domain of the attribute considered.

The conjunctive combination of proximities related to the atomic predicates can be performed by means of a triangular norm (for instance the minimum), so as to obtain the overall proximity between two queries. Note that alternative solutions could also be possible; for instance, one might use a mean operator. The substitution algorithm is outlined below.

Let Q' be a query from D^+ which is addressed to the same relation(s) as Q and shares at least one attribute from its *where* clause with that in Q. The five steps of the algorithm are:

(1) replace the *select* clause from Q' by that from Q,
(2) remove from Q' every predicate that concerns an attribute absent from the *where* clause in Q,
(3) replace every predicate from Q' which is strictly subsumed by the corresponding one from Q by the latter,
(4) for the other predicates, compute the proximity between the predicate from Q' and the corresponding one from Q, by means of measure sbs_3, and replace the predicate from Q' by its union with that from Q. In the case of the predicates from Q which are not covered by Q', compute their substitutivity degree relative to the entire domain of the attribute involved,
(5) aggregate the local proximities by means of a triangular norm (the idea being to assess the extent to which every predicate of the substitute query is close to the corresponding predicate from the initial failing query).

In the case of a fuzzy query, the notion of a subsumption can be based on the inclusion between fuzzy sets proposed by Zadeh, i.e., $E \subseteq F \Leftrightarrow \forall x, \mu_E(x) \le \mu_F(x)$.

Detailed example. Let Q be the following failing user query:

select #*id* **from** *Farms*
where *veg* **in** { "corn", "rapeseed" } **and**
        city **in** { "Lannion", "Caouennec", "Prat" } **and** *area* **in** [60, 100];

Assume that the domain of *veg* is: {corn, rapeseed, sunflower, wheat, cabbage, broccoli, potato, rutabaga} and that the associated proximity relation

Table 10.2 Proximity relation over attribute *veg*

	co	ra	su	wh	ca	br	po	ru
co	1	0.4	0.3	0.8	0.1	0.1	0.6	0.4
ra	0.4	1	0.9	0.6	0.2	0.2	0.1	0.1
su	0.3	0.9	1	0.5	0.1	0.1	0.3	0.3
wh	0.8	0.6	0.5	1	0.2	0.1	0.5	0.4
ca	0.1	0.2	0.1	0.2	1	0.9	0.6	0.7
br	0.1	0.2	0.1	0.1	0.9	1	0.4	0.6
po	0.6	0.1	0.3	0.5	0.6	0.4	1	0.8
ru	0.4	0.1	0.3	0.4	0.7	0.6	0.8	1

is given in Table 10.2. Let Q_1' be the following query from D^+:

> **select** #*name* **from** *Farms*
> **where** *veg* **in** { "wheat", "rapeseed", "sunflower" } **and**
> *city* **in** { "Lannion", "Prat" } **and** *area* = 125 **and** *animal* **in**
> { "cow", "pig" };

The query Q_1'' obtained by adapting Q_1' according to the above algorithm is:

> **select** #*id* **from** *Farms*
> **where** *veg* **in** { "corn", "rapeseed", "wheat", "sunflower" }
> **and** *city* **in** { "Lannion", "Caouennec", "Prat" } **and**
> (*area* **in** [60, 100] or area = 125);

The degree computed by sbs_3 for the substitution of {corn, rapeseed} by {wheat, rapeseed, sunflower} equals:

$$\frac{max(0.8, 0.6) + max(0.3, 0.9)}{2} = 0.85.$$

Assume that the proximity over the areas is based on a fuzzy tolerance indicator Z with a triangular membership function of support $[-50, 50]$. The substitution of [60, 100] by 125 is assigned the degree 0.5 (i.e., the proximity degree between 100 and 125; see Expression (10.8)). Finally, the degree computed for Q_1'' using the t-norm minimum is:

$$min(0.85, 0.5) = 0.5.$$

Now consider another query, denoted by Q_2', from D^+:

> **select** #*name* **from** *Farms*
> **where** *city* = "Caouennec" **and** *area* **in** [80, 180] **and**
> *animal* **in** { "sheep", "goat" };

Altering Q'_2 according to the algorithm yields Q''_2:

select #*id* **from** *Farms*
where *city* **in** {"Lannion", "Caouennec", "Prat"} **and** *area* **in** [60, 180];

For the condition on attribute *veg*, we have:

$$sbs_3(veg \in \{\text{corn}, \text{rapeseed}\}, veg \in domain(veg))$$

$$= (0.9 + 0.8 + 0.2 + 0.2 + 0.6 + 0.4)/6 = 0.52.$$

For the condition on attribute *area*, we have (according to Expression 10.7):

$$sbs_3(area \in [60, 100], area \in [80, 180])$$

$$= ((150 - 100)/2)/(180 - 100) = 25/80 = 0.31.$$

Thus, the degree attached to Q''_2 is $min(0.52, 0.31) = 0.31$ and Q''_1 is a better substitute for Q than is Q''_2.

Remark 10.1. In the event of tied results, the cardinality of the result of each candidate query could be taken into account so as to break these ties, provided that these cardinalities are stored in D^+.

10.3 Plethoric Answer Problem

10.3.1 *Introduction*

The plethoric answer problem (PAP) in the context of fuzzy queries can be stated as follows. Denote by $\Sigma_Q^{0^+} = \{\mu_1/x_1, \ldots, \mu_n/x_n\}$ the fuzzy set of tuples whose satisfaction degree with respect to a fuzzy query Q is strictly positive. Assume that Q involves a number k of expected answers. Let:

$$\mu_{max}(Q) = sup_{x_i \in \Sigma_Q^{0^+}} \mu_i$$

and:

$$\Sigma_Q^{\mu_{max}(Q)} = \{x_i \in \Sigma_Q^{0^+} \mid \mu_i = \mu_{max}(Q)\}.$$

If $|\Sigma_Q^{\mu_{max}(Q)}| \gg k$, then we are in the presence of a plethoric answer problem.

This issue often arises because the user query is too general. In other words, the fuzzy requirements in the query are not restrictive enough. To overcome this problem, one can refine the query in order to make it more specific, so as to return a reasonable set of items. The first approach described below, based on predicate modification, assumes that

$\mu_{max}(Q) = 1$ (i.e., there are too many answers which fully satisfy the user's requirement).

10.3.2 Approach based on predicate strengthening

10.3.2.1 Principle

The first way to refine the query consists of intensifying the query's fuzzy constraints in order to reduce the set Σ_Q^1. To achieve this task, a fundamental required property of the intensification mechanism is to significantly shrink the cores of the fuzzy sets associated with the conditions of the query.

As in the case of query relaxation, query intensification can then be performed by applying a basic transformation $T^\downarrow$ on all or some of the query's predicates. This transformation can be applied iteratively if necessary. Three basic properties are required for any transformation $T^\downarrow$ when applied to a predicate P ($T^\downarrow(P)$ representing the intensified predicate), as described in Bosc *et al.* (2008):

- IC1: $T^\downarrow$ does not increase the membership degree for any element of the domain, i.e., $\forall u \in domain(A)$, $\mu_{T^\downarrow(P)}(u) \leq \mu_P(u)$ where A denotes the attribute concerned by P,
- IC2: $T^\downarrow$ must shrink the core $C(P)$ of the fuzzy predicate P, i.e., $core(T^\downarrow(P)) \subset core(P)$,
- IC3: $T^\downarrow$ preserves the left-hand (resp. right-hand) spread of the fuzzy predicate P, i.e., if $P = (A, B, a, b)$, $T^\downarrow(P) = (A', B', a', b')$ with $A < A'$, $B > B'$, $a = a'$ and $b = b'$, and $A' - A < a$ and $B - B' < b$.

The second property allows for reduction of the width of the core, and then effectively decreases the number of answers with degree 1 (i.e., the set Σ_Q^1). The third property guarantees that the data excluded from the core of P remain in its support, i.e., that no data that was initially fully acceptable is then rejected by the intensification.

10.3.2.2 Erosion operation

Let $Z \oplus X = F$ be an equation where X is the unknown variable. Solving this equation was extensively discussed in Dubois and Prade (1983). It was demonstrated that the greatest solution of this equation is given by $\bar{X} = F \ominus (-Z) = F \ominus Z$ (since $Z = -Z$), where $\ominus$ is the extended Minkowski subtraction defined by Dubois and Prade (1983, 1988):

$$\mu_{F \ominus Z}(r) = inf_s(\mu_Z(r - s) \Rightarrow_f (\mu_F(s))$$
$$= inf_s(\mu_{E[Z]}(s, r) \Rightarrow_f \mu_F(s)), \tag{10.10}$$

where $\Rightarrow_f$ is an R-implication generated by the t-norm $\top$, defined by $\Rightarrow_f$ $(u, v) = sup\{\lambda \in [0, 1] \,|\, \top(u, \lambda) \le v\}$, for $u, v \in [0, 1]$. We make use of the same t-norm $\top = min$ as in the dilation operation (see Section 10.2.2.3), which implies that $\Rightarrow_f$ is Gödel's implication.

Let $E[Z]_r = \{s \,|\, \mu_{E[Z]}(s, r) > 0\}$ be the set of elements that are somewhat close to r in the sense of $E[Z]$. The expression above can then be interpreted as the degree of inclusion of $E[Z]_r$ in F. This means that r belongs to $F \ominus Z$ if all the elements s that are close to r are in F. Hence, the inclusion $F \ominus Z \subseteq F$ holds. This operation is very useful for intensifying the meaning of vague terms from natural language. Now, eroding the fuzzy set F by Z results in the fuzzy set F_Z defined by $F_Z = F \ominus Z$.

Lemma 10.2. *Given a fuzzy set F and a proximity relation $E[Z]$, for $F_Z = F \ominus Z$ we have $F_Z \subseteq F$.*

If $F = (A, B, a, b)$ and $Z = (-z, z, \delta, \delta)$, then $F \ominus Z = (A + z, B - z, a - \delta, b - \delta)$ provided that $a \ge \delta$ and $b \ge \delta$. Figure 10.5 illustrates this operation. In the crisp case, $F \ominus Z = [A, B] \ominus [-z, z] = [A + z, B - z]$ (while $F \oplus Z = [A - z, B + z]$).

Again, and in order to satisfy the needs of some practical applications, only one constituent part of a fuzzy set F (either the core or the support) must be affected when applying an erosion operation. We denote by *core erosion* (resp. *support erosion*) the eroding transformation that affects only

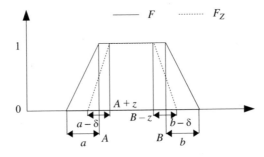

Fig. 10.5   Erosion operation

the core (resp. support) of F. The following proposition allows such results to be obtained.

Proposition 10.4. *Let F be a fuzzy set and $E[Z]$ a proximity relation. We have:*

- *core erosion obtained using the family of tolerance indicators of the form $Z = (-z, z, 0, 0)$,*
- *support erosion obtained using the family of tolerance indicators of the form $Z = (0, 0, \delta, \delta)$.*

By this proposition, if $F = (A, B, a, b)$ the core erosion (resp. support erosion) leads to $F_Z = (A + z, B - z, a, b)$ (resp. $F_Z = (A, B, a - \delta, b - \delta)$).

10.3.2.3   *Erosion of an atomic query*

In the following, we show how the notion of the parameterized absolute proximity relation $E[Z]$ can provide the basis for an intensification transformation $T^{\downarrow}$. We first investigate the case of an atomic query. Let P be a fuzzy predicate and $E[Z]$ be a proximity relation parameterized by a tolerance indicator Z of the form $(-z, z, 0, 0)$. Making use of the erosion operation, the predicate P can be transformed into a restricted fuzzy predicate P' defined as follows:

$$P' = T^{\downarrow}(P) = P_Z = P \ominus Z.$$

Now, if $P = (A, B, a, b)$ then $T^{\downarrow}(P) = (A + z, B - z, a, b)$; see Figure 10.5. Properties IC1–IC3 straightforwardly hold.

Principle of the approach.   Let $Q = P$ be a flexible query containing a single fuzzy predicate P. Assume that Σ_Q^1 is too large. In order to reduce the cardinality of Σ_Q^1, we transform Q into $Q_1 = T^{\downarrow}(P) = P \ominus Z$. This intensification mechanism can be applied iteratively until the database returns a manageable set of answers to the modified query $Q_n = T^{\downarrow(n)}(P) = P \ominus nZ$. An implicit measure of nearness such that Q_k is nearer to Q than Q_l if $k < l$ is then induced by this intensification strategy for atomic queries.

   Let us take a look at the subset of Σ_Q^1 resulting from the intensification process. The items of that subset (which are the answers to the revised query Q_n) can be viewed as the best answers to the original query Q, since they constitute the typical values (i.e., prototypes) of the concept expressed by the fuzzy set associated to Q.

Controlling the intensification. Limiting the amplitude of an intensification process does not appear as crucial as in the case of query relaxation. Indeed, the intensification process only aims at reducing a large set of answers, not at finding alternative ones. It is, however, worth emphasizing that the query refinement process must stop when the upper bound and the lower bound of the core (of the modified query Q_i) are equal to $(A + B)/2$. Indeed, the TMF associated with Q_i is $(A + iz, B - iz, a, b)$. Now, since $A + iz \leq B - iz$ holds, we have $i \leq (B - A)/2z$. This means that the maximal query refinement is obtained when the core is reduced to a singleton.

Note that the risk of obtaining an empty set of answers during the process is excluded when $a > z$ and $b > z$ (since the data that have been eliminated from $\Sigma^1_{(Q_{i-1})}$ still belong to the support of Q_i). Hence, those data are answers to Q_i. Otherwise, it is possible to back up and try another variation (for instance, by adjusting the tolerance parameter Z).

Intensification algorithm. Algorithm 10.3 formalizes this intensification approach.

Algorithm 10.3. Atomic query intensification.

$Q := P$;
let $Z = (-z,\ z,\ 0,\ 0)$ be a tolerance indicator;
$i := 0$; $Q_i := Q$;
compute $\Sigma^1_{Q_i}$;
while ($|\,\Sigma^1_{Q_i}\,|$ is too large **and** $i \leq (B - A)/2z$) **do**
begin
   $i := i + 1$;
   $Q_i := T^{\downarrow(i)}(P) := P \ominus iZ$;
   compute $\Sigma^1_{Q_i}$;
end;
return $\Sigma^1_{Q_i}$;

Particular cases. Note that, for some kinds of atomic queries to be intensified, the property of symmetry of the tolerance indicator Z is not required. Consider, for instance, the query $Q = P$, where $P = (0, 25, 0, 10)$, which represents the concept *young* in a given context. Intensifying P boils down to reducing the width of the core $C(P)$ and thus to come closer to the typical values of P. Here, it is the left part of $C(P)$ which contains the typical values of the concept *young*. The intensification transformation must therefore only affect the right part of $C(P)$ and preserve entirely its left part. The appropriate form of Z that allows this transformation is $(0, z, 0, 0)$, which leads to $T^{\downarrow}(P) = P \ominus Z = (0, 25 - z, 0, 10)$.

Consider now a query Q of the form $Q = \neg P$, where $\neg$ stands for the negation $(\mu_{\neg P}(u) = 1 - \mu_P(u), \forall u)$, and assume that the query results in plethoric answers. To solve this problem, one may apply the intensification mechanism proposed above to Q, i.e., shrink the core of $\neg P$. It is easy to check that this transformation is equivalent to extending the support of P. This means that applying $T^{\downarrow}$ to Q boils down to applying $T^{\uparrow}$ to P. So, we have $T^{\downarrow}(\neg P) = T^{\uparrow}(P)$.

10.3.2.4 *Intensifying a conjunctive query*

Let $Q = P_1 \wedge \cdots \wedge P_k$ be a conjunctive fuzzy query. Assume that the set of answers Σ_Q^1 to Q is too large. Then, obviously, each subquery of Q also results in plethoric answers.

Lemma 10.3. *If $Q = P_1 \wedge \cdots \wedge P_k$ results in plethoric answers, then each predicate P_i of Q also results in plethoric answers.*

This means that, if the plethoric answer problem arises in a conjunctive query Q, it then arises in each proper subquery of Q. In that case, examining the subqueries of Q is useless.

In the following, we consider a global modification strategy which, given a set of intensification transformations $\{T_1^{\downarrow}, \ldots, T_k^{\downarrow}\}$, leads to the set of intensified queries:

$$\{T_1^{\downarrow(i)}(P_1) \wedge \cdots \wedge T_k^{\downarrow(i)}(P_k)\}.$$

The ordering ($\prec$) introduced in Section 10.2.2.4 may also be defined for intensified queries. Letting Q' and Q'' be two intensified queries of Q, we say that

$$Q' \prec Q'' \text{ if and only if } \sum_{i=1}^{k} count(T_i^{\downarrow} \text{ in } Q') < \sum_{i=1}^{k} count(T_i^{\downarrow} \text{ in } Q'').$$

This ordering allows for the introduction of a semantic distance between queries. For that semantic distance to make sense, it is desirable that the set of transformations $\{T_1^{\downarrow}, \ldots, T_k^{\downarrow}\}$ should fulfill the property of *equal intensification effect* (EIE) on all predicates (Bosc et al., 2008). There are several ways to define this property. A possible definition is to consider the ratio of the lengths of the cores associated with the original and the modified fuzzy predicates. This ratio must be of the same magnitude for all the predicates involved in Q, when the transformations $\{T_1^{\downarrow}, \ldots, T_k^{\downarrow}\}$ are applied. Letting $\Delta(P_i, T_i^{\downarrow}(P_i))$ denote this ratio when $T_i^{\downarrow}$ is applied to P_i, we have:

$$\Delta(P_i, T_i^{\downarrow}(P_i)) = L(core(T_i^{\downarrow}(P_i)))/L(core(P_i)),$$

where $L(core(P_i))$ (resp. $L(core(T_i^{\downarrow}(P_i))))$ stands for the length of $core(P_i)$ (resp. $core(T_i^{\downarrow}(P_i)))$. A simple calculus enables the following (with $P_i = (A_i, B_i, a_i, b_i)$ and $Z_i = (-z_i, z_i, 0, 0)$):

$$\Delta(P_i, T_i^{\downarrow}(P_i)) = 1 - 2z_i/(B_i - A_i).$$

Now, given k predicates $P_1, \ldots, P_k$, the EIE property for a set of transformations $\{T_1^{\downarrow}, \ldots, T_k^{\downarrow}\}$ can be expressed as follows:

$$\Delta(P_1, T_1^{\downarrow}(P_1)) = \cdots = \Delta(P_k, T_k^{\downarrow}(P_k)).$$

Thus, to start the intensification process of a conjunctive query $Q = P_1 \wedge \cdots \wedge P_k$, it is necessary to initialize the tolerance value z_i associated with each predicate P_i. Using the EIE property described above, this initialization reduces to setting only one value $z_l (1 \leq l \leq k)$, with the other values being automatically deduced. Algorithm 10.4 sketches this query intensification technique.

Algorithm 10.4. Conjunctive query intensification.

let $Q = P_1 \wedge \cdots \wedge P_k$;   /* with $P_i = (A_i, B_i, a_i, b_i)$ */
/* Initialization step */
choose a predicate P_l $(1 \leq l \leq k)$;
(1): set the tolerance indicator Z_l associated with P_l;
/* $Z_l = (-z_l, z_l, 0, 0)$ */
$j := 1$;
while $(j \leq k)$ **do**
begin
    if $(j \neq l)$ **then**
        compute the indicator Z_j associated with P_j;
        /* using the EIE property */
    endif;
    $j := j + 1$;
end;
/* Intensification process */
$i := 0$;
$Q_i := Q$;

impossible := false;
compute $\Sigma_{Q_i}^1$;
while (**not** impossible) **and** ($|\Sigma_{Q_i}^1|$ is too large) **do**
begin
   $i := i + 1$;
   for $j = 1$ **to** k **do**
   begin
     if $(i \leq (B_j - A_j)/2z_j)$
       then compute $T_j^{\downarrow(i)}(P_j) := P_j \ominus i.Z_j$
       else impossible := **true**
     endif;
     if (**not** impossible) **then**
       $Q_i := T_1^{\downarrow(i)}(P_1) \wedge \cdots \wedge T_k^{\downarrow(i)}(P_k)$;
       compute $\Sigma_{Q_i}^1$;
     endif;
   end;
end;
if (impossible) **then** adjust the tolerance indicator Z_l; **goto** (1) **endif**;
return $\Sigma_{Q_i}^1$;

10.3.3   *Approach based on query expansion*

We now present an alternative strengthening strategy, based on query augmentation and predicate correlation, which is mainly applicable to what may be called *under-specified queries*. An under-specified query Q typically involves a few predicates (between one and three) to describe an expected set of answers that can be more precisely described by properties not specified in Q.

For example, consider a user looking for "second-hand cars which are very recent". The answer set to this query can be reduced through the integration of additional properties like *low mileage, high security* and *high comfort level*, i.e., properties usually possessed by very recent cars.

The query strengthening approach described below aims at identifying correlation links between additional properties and an initial query. These additional correlated properties are suggested to the user as candidates for the strengthening of the initial query. This interactive process is iterated until the result is of an acceptable size for the user and corresponds to what he/she was really looking for.

10.3.3.1 *Fuzzy cardinalities and association rules*

Fuzzy cardinalities. In the context of flexible querying, fuzzy cardinalities appear to be a convenient formalism to represent the number of tuples from a relation that satisfy a fuzzy predicate to various degrees. It is considered that these various membership degrees are defined by a finite scale $1 = \sigma_1 > \sigma_2 > \cdots > \sigma_f > 0$. Such fuzzy cardinalities can be computed incrementally, and maintained for each linguistic label and for the diverse conjunctive combinations of these labels. Fuzzy cardinalities are represented by means of a possibility distribution (Dubois and Prade, 1985a) such as:

$$F_{P_i} = 1/0 + \ldots + 1/(n-1) + 1/n + \lambda_1/(n+1) + \ldots + \lambda_k/(n+k)$$
$$+ 0/(n+k+1) + \ldots,$$

where $1 > \lambda_1 \geq \cdots \geq \lambda_k > \lambda_{k+1} = 0$ for a predicate P_i. Here, without loss of information, we use a more compact representation:

$$F_{P_i} = 1/c_1 + \sigma_2/c_2 + \ldots + \sigma_f/c_f,$$

where $c_j, j = 1, \ldots, f$ is the number of tuples in the relation concerned that are P_i with a degree at least equal to σ_j. For the computation of cardinalities concerning a conjunction of q fuzzy predicates, such as $F_{P_1 \wedge P_2 \wedge \cdots \wedge P_q}$, the calculation takes into account the minimal satisfaction degree obtained by each tuple t for the concerned predicates, $min(\mu_{P_1}(t), \mu_{P_2}(t), \ldots, \mu_{P_q}(t))$.

Association rules and correlation. Given two predicates P_1 and P_2, an association rule denoted by $P_1 \Rightarrow P_2$ aims at quantifying the fact that tuples that are P_1 are also P_2 (P_1 and P_2 can be replaced by any conjunction of predicates). As suggested in Bosc *et al.* (2001), fuzzy cardinalities can be used to quantify the confidence of such an association by means of either a scalar or a fuzzy set detailing the subsequent confidence for each σ-cut. The first representation of the confidence, as a scalar, is used in the following, as it is more convenient to compare fuzzy sets using scalar measures. The confidence of an association rule $P_1 \rightarrow P_2$, denoted by $conf(P_1 \rightarrow P_2)$, is thus computed as follows:

$$conf(P_1 \rightarrow P_2) = \frac{\Gamma_{P_1 \wedge P_2}}{\Gamma_{P_1}}.$$

Here, $\Gamma_{P_1 \wedge P_2}$ and Γ_{P_1} correspond to scalar cardinalities, which are computed as the weighted sum of the elements belonging to the concerned

Table 10.3   Extension of the relation *secondHandCars*

t_i	brand	model	type	years	mileage	optLvl.	secLvl.	horsePw.
t_1	vw	golf	sedan	5	95k	6	8	90
t_2	seat	ibiza	sport	9	150k	3	6	80
t_3	audi	A3	sport	3	22k	8	7	120
t_4	seat	cordoba	sedan	7	220k	4	4	100
t_5	ford	focus	estate	6	80k	7	5	70
t_6	vw	polo	city	13	120k	2	3	50
t_7	vw	golf	estate	4	40k	5	5	80
t_8	ford	ka	city	8	240k	4	3	50
t_9	kia	rio	city	2	10k	2	3	60
t_{10}	seat	leon	sport	2	25k	8	8	115
t_{11}	ford	focus	sedan	4	53k	6	7	90
t_{12}	rover	223	sedan	14	100k	9	8	120

fuzzy cardinalities. With the data from Example 10.6 below, the scalar version of $\Gamma_{recent} = 1/6 + 0.6/7 + 0.2/8$ is $\Gamma_{recent} = 1 \times 6 + 0.6 \times (7-6) + 0.2 \times (8-7) = 6.8$.

Example 10.6. Consider a relation named *secondHandCars* with schema (*brand, model, type, years, mileage, optionLevel, securityLevel, horsePower*) containing advertisements for second hand cars. A sample of its extension is given in Table 10.3. We assume that the finite scale of degrees used for the computation of the fuzzy cardinalities is

$$\sigma_1 = 1 > \sigma_2 = 0.8 > \sigma_3 = 0.6 > \sigma_4 = 0.4 > \sigma_5 = 0.2 > 0.$$

From Table 10.3, we can compute the cardinalities of the predicates *recent* and *low-mileage* (Figure 10.6) and of their conjunction:

- $F_{recent} = 1/6 + 0.8/6 + 0.6/7 + 0.4/7 + 0.2/8$,
- $F_{low\text{-}mileage} = 1/3 + 0.8/4 + 0.6/4 + 0.4/4 + 0.2/5$,
- $F_{low\text{-}mileage \wedge recent} = 1/3 + 0.8/4 + 0.6/4 + 0.4/4 + 0.2/5$.

From this dataset, one can deduce that the rule $P_{recent} \to P_{low\text{-}mileage}$, expressing that recent cars have a low mileage, has a confidence of

$$\frac{1 \times 3 + 0.8 \times (4-3) + 0.2 \times (5-4)}{1 \times 6 + 0.6 \times 1 + 0.2 \times 1} \approx 0.59,$$

and that the rule $P_{low\text{-}mileage} \to P_{recent}$ has a maximal confidence of 1 as all low-mileage cars are also recent in Table 10.3.◇

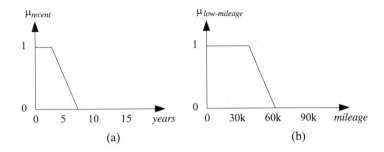

Fig. 10.6   Fuzzy predicates (a) *recent* and (b) *low-mileage*

10.3.3.2   *Shared vocabulary*

As mentioned in Ozawa and Yamada (1995), fuzzy sets can be used to represent what the authors call a "macro expression of the database". Contrary to the approach presented in Ozawa and Yamada (1995), where this knowledge is computed by means of a fuzzy clustering process, it is, in the approach presented here, defined *a priori* by means of a Ruspini partition of each attribute domain. Recall that a Ruspini partition (Ruspini, 1969) is composed of fuzzy sets, where a set, say P_i, can only overlap with its predecessor P_{i-1} or/and its successor P_{i+1} (when they exist), and for each tuple t, $\sum_{i=1}^{n_i} \mu_{P_i}(t) = 1$, where n_i is the number of partition elements of the concerned attribute. These partitions are specified by an expert during the database design step and represent "common sense partitions" of the domains, instead of the result of an automatic process which may be difficult to interpret. Indeed, we assume that the predefined fuzzy sets involved in a partition constitute a shared vocabulary, and that these fuzzy sets are used by the users when formulating their queries. Moreover, it is assumed that the predicates that are added to the initial query also belong to this vocabulary.

   Consider a relation r containing w tuples $\{t_1, t_2, \ldots, t_w\}$ defined on a set Z of q categorical or numerical attributes $\{Z_1, Z_2, \ldots, Z_q\}$. A shared predefined vocabulary on r is defined by means of partitions of the q domains. A partition $\mathscr{P}_i$ associated with the domain of attribute Z_i is composed of m_i fuzzy predicates $\{P_{i,1}^p, P_{i,2}^p, \ldots, P_{i,m_i}^p\}$, such that $\forall z_i \in \mathscr{D}(Z_i), \sum_{j=1}^{m_i} \mu_{P_{ij}^p}(z_i) = 1$. A predefined predicate is denoted by $P_{i,j}^p$, which corresponds to the jth element of the partition defined on attribute Z_i. Each $\mathscr{P}_i$ is associated with a set of linguistic labels $\{L_{i,1}^p, L_{i,2}^p, \ldots, L_{i,m_i}^p\}$, each of them corresponding to an adjective which gives the meaning of the fuzzy predicate.

A query Q to this relation r is composed of fuzzy predicates chosen among the predefined predicates which form the partitions. A predicate involved in a user query is said to be *specified*, is denoted by $P_{k,l}^s$, and corresponds to the lth element of the partition associated with the domain of Z_k.

If Q leads to a plethoric answer set, Q can be strengthened in order to obtain a more restrictive query Q' such that $\Sigma_{Q'}^{\mu_{max}(Q')} \subset \Sigma_Q^{\mu_{max}(Q)}$. Query Q' is obtained through the integration of additional predefined fuzzy predicates chosen from the shared vocabulary on r.

As an example, consider again the relation *secondHandCars* introduced in Section 10.3.3.1. A common-sense partition and labelling of the domain of attribute *years* is illustrated in Figure 10.7.

10.3.3.3 *Strengthening steps*

Correlation-based ranking of the candidates. In the approach we propose, the new conjuncts to be added to the initial query are chosen from among a set of possible predicates pertaining to the attributes of the schema of the database queried. This choice is mainly made according to the conjuncts' correlation with the initial query. A user query Q is composed of $n, n \geq 1$, specified fuzzy predicates, denoted by $P_{k_1,l_1}^{s_1}, P_{k_2,l_2}^{s_2}, \ldots, P_{k_n,l_n}^{s_n}$, which come from the shared vocabulary associated with the database. The first step of the strengthening approach is to identify the predefined predicates that are most correlated with the initial query Q.

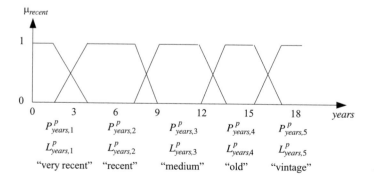

Fig. 10.7   A partition of the domain of attribute *years*

The notion of correlation is used to qualify and quantify the extent to which two fuzzy sets (one associated with a predefined predicate $P_{i,j}^p$, the other associated with the initial query Q) are somewhat "semantically" linked. The degree of this correlation is denoted by $\mu_{cor}(P_{i,j}^p, Q)$. Roughly speaking, a predicate $P_{i,j}^p$ is considered somewhat correlated with a query Q if the group of items characterized by $P_{i,j}^p$ is somewhat similar to Σ_Q. For instance, it may be noticed that a fuzzy predicate "highly powerful engine" is more correlated to a query aimed at retrieving "fast cars" than cars having a "low consumption". Adding predicates that are correlated to the user-specified predicates makes it possible to preserve the scope of the query (i.e., the user's intent) while making it more demanding. It is worth mentioning that the term *correlation* used in this approach means a mutual semantic relationship between two concepts, and does not have the meaning it has in statistics — where it represents similarities between series variations — but rather corresponds to the notion of *set correlation*.

As illustrated in Section 10.3.3.1, fuzzy association rules express such a semantic link that can be quantified by their confidence. Thus, if we consider a query Q and a predefined predicate $P_{i,j}^p$, we compute the confidence of the association rules $Q \rightarrow P_{i,j}^p$ and $P_{i,j}^p \rightarrow Q$ according to the fuzzy cardinalities F_Q, $F_{P_{i,j}^p}$ and $F_{Q \wedge P_{i,j}^p}$. We then quantify the correlation degree between Q and $P_{i,j}^p$, denoted by $\mu_{cor}(P_{i,j}^p, Q)$, as:

$$\mu_{cor}(P_{i,j}^p, Q) = \top(conf(Q \rightarrow P_{i,j}^p), conf(P_{i,j}^p \rightarrow Q)),$$

where $\top$ stands for a t-norm (*minimum* is used in the experimentation described in Section 10.3.3.5). Thus, this correlation degree is both reflexive ($\mu_{cor}(Q, Q) = 1$) and symmetrical ($\mu_{cor}(P_{i,j}^p, Q) = \mu_{cor}(Q, P_{i,j}^p)$).

Using this measure, it is possible to identify the predefined predicates that are most correlated to an under-specified query Q. In practice, we only consider the η most correlated predicates to a query, where η is a technical parameter (set to 5 in the experimentation). This limitation is motivated by the fact that a strengthening process involving more than η iterations, i.e., the addition of more than η predicates, could lead to important modifications to the scope of the initial query. Those η predicates that are most correlated to Q are denoted by $P_Q^{c^1}, P_Q^{c^2}, \ldots, P_Q^{c^\eta}$.

Reduction-based reranking of the candidates. We have shown above how to retrieve the η predicates most correlated with an initial query Q. The second step of this strengthening process aims at reranking those

η predicates according to their reduction capability. As discussed in Section 10.3.1, it is assumed that the user specifies a value for the parameter k which defines his/her expected number of answers. Let $F_{Q \wedge P_Q^{c^g}}$, $g = 1, \ldots, \eta$, be the fuzzy cardinality of the result set when Q is augmented with $P_Q^{c^g}$. $P_Q^{c^g}$ is all the more interesting for strengthening Q as $Q \wedge P_Q^{c^g}$ contains a σ_i-cut ($\sigma_i \in]0, 1]$) with a cardinality c_i close to k and a σ_i close to 1. To quantify how interesting $P_Q^{c^g}$ is, we compute for each σ_i-cut of $F_{Q \wedge P_Q^{c^g}}$ a strengthening degree which represents a compromise between its membership degree σ_i and its associated cardinality c_i. The global strengthening degree assigned to $F_{Q \wedge P_Q^{c^g}}$, denoted by $\mu_{stren}(F_{Q \wedge P_Q^{c^g}})$, is the maximal strengthening degree of its σ_i-cuts:

$$\mu_{stren}(F_{Q \wedge P_Q^{c^g}}) = sup_{1 \leq i \leq f} \top \left(1 - \frac{|c_i - k|}{max(k, |\Sigma_Q^{0^+}| - k)}, \sigma_i \right),$$

where $\top$ stands for a t-norm (*minimum* in our experimentation). This reranking of the predicates that are most correlated with Q can be carried out using the fuzzy cardinalities associated with each conjunction $Q \wedge P_Q^{c^g}, g = 1, \ldots, \eta$.

Example 10.7. To illustrate this reranking strategy, consider a user query Q resulting in a PA problem ($|\Sigma_Q^{\mu_{max}(Q)}| = 123$ and $|\Sigma^{\mu_Q^{0^+}}| = 412$), where k has been set to 50. As an example, consider the following candidates $P_Q^{c^1}, P_Q^{c^2}, P_Q^{c^3}, P_Q^{c^4}, P_Q^{c^5}$ and the respective fuzzy cardinalities:

- $F_{Q \wedge P_Q^{c^1}} = \{1/72 + 0.8/74 + 0.6/91 + 0.4/92 + 0.2/121\}$, $\mu_{stren}(F_{Q \wedge P_Q^{c^1}}) \simeq 0.94$,
- $F_{Q \wedge P_Q^{c^2}} = \{1/89 + 0.8/101 + 0.6/135 + 0.4/165 + 0.2/169\}$, $\mu_{stren}(F_{Q \wedge P_Q^{c^2}}) \simeq 0.9$,
- $F_{Q \wedge P_Q^{c^3}} = \{1/24 + 0.8/32 + 0.6/39 + 0.4/50 + 0.2/101\}$, $\mu_{stren}(F_{Q \wedge P_Q^{c^3}}) \simeq 0.93$,
- $F_{Q \wedge P_Q^{c^4}} = \{1/37 + 0.8/51 + 0.6/80 + 0.4/94 + 0.2/221\}$, $\mu_{stren}(F_{Q \wedge P_Q^{c^4}}) \simeq 0.96$,
- $F_{Q \wedge P_Q^{c^5}} = \{1/54 + 0.8/61 + 0.6/88 + 0.4/129 + 0.2/137\}$, $\mu_{stren}(F_{Q \wedge P_Q^{c^5}}) \simeq 0.99$.

According to the problem definition ($k = 50$) and the fuzzy cardinalities above, the following ranking is suggested to the user: 1) $P_Q^{c^5}$, 2) $P_Q^{c^4}$, 3) $P_Q^{c^1}$, 4) $P_Q^{c^3}$, 5) $P_Q^{c^2}$. Of course, to make this ranking more intelligible to the user, the candidates are proposed alongside their associated linguistic labels (for an example, see the concrete example about used cars given in Section 10.3.3.5).⋄

10.3.3.4 *Strengthening process*

Precomputed knowledge. Because the predicates specified by the user and those that may be added to the initial query are chosen among the predicates that form the domain partitions, one can precompute some useful knowledge that will make the strengthening process faster. Below, we discuss how to compute and maintain precomputed knowledge, stored in two tables.

The first table contains precomputed fuzzy cardinalities. It is of course impossible to precompute the fuzzy cardinalities for all possible conjunctions of predefined predicates, because the number of conjunctions grows exponentially with the size of the shared vocabulary. It is not even useful to store the fuzzy cardinalities of each possible conjunction, as the approach mainly focuses on under-specified queries and produces strengthened queries that contain only correlated predicates. Indeed, queries involving non-correlated predicates are less likely to return a plethoric answer set. Thus, this table only contains the fuzzy cardinalities of conjunctions involving sufficiently correlated predicates. A threshold γ is used to prune some branches of the exploration tree of all possible conjunctions.

This table can be easily maintained as the fuzzy cardinalities can be updated incrementally. Moreover, as we will see, this precomputed knowledge is used to give interesting information — in constant time — about any under-specified query, without computing the query. In particular, it provides the size of the answer set associated with a query and the predicates that can be used to strengthen it. An index computed on the string representation of each conjunction makes this fast access possible.

The second table stores the correlation degrees between each sufficiently correlated conjunction of predefined predicates and each specified atomic predicate. For each conjunction of predicates, the η most correlated predefined predicates are ranked in decreasing order of their correlation degree. This table is checked to generate the candidates that may be used to augment the query.

Both tables have to be updated after each (batch of) modification(s) performed on the data, but these updates involve a simple incremental calculus.

Interactive strengthening process. Recall that a query Q is assumed to be composed of fuzzy predicates chosen among the predefined predicates that form the shared vocabulary. First, the table of fuzzy cardinalities is checked, in order to test whether its fuzzy cardinality is available. If this is the case, it is then established whether the user is faced with a plethoric answer problem according to the value he/she has assigned to k. If so, up to η candidates are retrieved — still in constant time — that are then reranked according to k and presented to the user. Finally, as illustrated in Section 10.3.3.5, the user can decide to process the initial query, to process one of the suggested strengthened queries, or to ask for another strengthening iteration of a strengthened query.

Using the aforementioned tables, this approach guides users in an interactive way from an under-specified query to a more demanding but semantically close query that returns an acceptable number of results.

10.3.3.5 *Experimentation*

We consider a relation *secondHandCars* containing 10,604 advertisements about used cars. This relation has the schema: (*idAd*, *model*, *year*, *mileage*, *optionLevel*, *securityLevel*, *comfortLevel*, *horsePower*, *engineSize*, *price*). The following shared vocabulary, composed of 41 fuzzy predicates, has been predefined to query this relation and to strengthen under-specified queries. The quadruple (a, b, c, d) associated with each linguistic label defines its trapezoidal membership function (where $[a, d]$ represents the support and $[b, c]$ the core).

year: *vintage* $(28, 30, +\infty, +\infty)$, *very_old* $(19, 20, 28, 30)$, *old* $(12, 14, 19, 20)$, *medium* $(6, 7, 12, 14)$, *recent* $(3, 4, 6, 7)$, *very_recent* $(1, 2, 3, 4)$, *last_model* $(0, 0, 1, 3)$

mileage: *very_low* $(0, 0, 20{,}000, 30{,}000)$, *low* $(20{,}000, 30{,}000, 60{,}000, 70{,}000)$, *medium* $(60{,}000, 70{,}000, 130{,}000, 150{,}000)$, *high* $(130{,}000, 150{,}000, 260{,}000, 300{,}000)$, *very_high* $(260{,}000, 300{,}000, +\infty, +\infty)$

optionLevel: *very_low* $(0, 0, 1, 2)$, *low* $(1, 2, 4, 5)$, *medium* $(4, 5, 6, 7)$, *high* $(6, 7, 10, 12)$, *very_high* $(10, 12, +\infty, +\infty)$

securityLevel: *very_low* $(0, 0, 1, 2)$, *low* $(1, 2, 4, 5)$, *medium* $(4, 5, 6, 7)$, *high* $(6, 7, 8, 9)$, *very_high* $(8, 9, +\infty, +\infty)$

comfortLevel: *very_low* $(0, 0, 1, 2)$, *low* $(1, 2, 4, 5)$, *medium* $(4, 5, 6, 7)$, *high* $(6, 7, 8, 9)$, *very_high* $(8, 9, +\infty, +\infty)$

horsePower: *very_low* $(0, 0, 30, 50)$, *low* $(30, 50, 70, 80)$, *high* $(70, 80, 120, 140)$, *very_high* $(120, 140, +\infty, +\infty)$

engineSize: *very_small* (0, 0, 0.8, 1.0), *small* (0.8, 1.0, 1.4, 1.6) , *big* (1.4, 1.6, 2.0, 2.4), *very_big* (2, 2.4, $+\infty$, $+\infty$)

price: *very_low* (0, 0, 2,000, 2,500), *low* (2,000, 2,500, 6,000, 6,500), *medium* (6,000, 6,500, 12,000, 13,000), *high* (12,000, 13,000, 20,000, 22,000), *very_high* (20,000, 22,000, 35,000, 40,000), *extremely_high* (35,000, 40,000, $+\infty$, $+\infty$)

According to these partitions, fuzzy cardinalities of conjunctions involving correlated predicates have been computed in order to populate the table of fuzzy cardinalities and then to identify the $\eta = 5$ predicates that are most correlated to each partition element. On a laptop with a classical configuration (Intel Core 2 Duo 2.53 GHz with 4Go 1067 MHz of DDR3 RAM), it took about 8 s to compute the useful fuzzy cardinalities and to store them in a dedicated table. This process can be made even faster using indexes defined on the relevant relation (i.e., *secondHandCars*). Using a low correlation threshold of 0.05, only 7,436 conjunctions involve predicates that are sufficiently correlated to be considered as possible under-specified queries among the 604,567 possible conjunctions that can be constructed using the shared vocabulary. Among the 7,436 conjunctions stored in the table of fuzzy cardinalities, 41 concern one predicate (one for each partition element), while there are 170 fuzzy cardinalities for conjunctions of two predicates, 382 for three predicates, 695 for four predicates, 1,040 for five predicates, 1,422 for six predicates, 1,808 for seven predicates, and 1,878 for eight predicates.

Example of an under-specified query. To illustrate the strengthening method, consider an example of a query Q composed of fuzzy predicates chosen from the shared vocabulary, involving a quantitative threshold $k = 50$:

$$Q = \textbf{select } 50 \text{ * } \textbf{from } secondHandCars \textbf{ where } year \textbf{ is } old.$$

From a string representation of Q and the table of fuzzy cardinalities, we directly check whether Q corresponds to an under-specified query. If this is the case, its fuzzy cardinality is presented to the user (obviously in a more linguistic and user-friendly way than given here): $F_Q = \{1/179 + 0.8/179 + 0.6/179 + 0.4/323 + 0.2/323\}$.

At the same time, predicates corresponding to properties correlated to the initial query are suggested, if they exist, and are ranked in decreasing order of their reduction capability with respect to k. In this example, the following candidates are suggested, showing the fuzzy cardinality of the corresponding strengthened queries:

(1) *mileage* **is** *medium* ($\mu_{cor}(Q, P^p_{mileage,\,medium}) = 0.11$):

$$F_{Q \wedge P^p_{mileage,\,medium}} = \{1/24 + 0.8/27 + 0.6/28 + 0.4/72 + 0.2/77\}.$$

(2) *mileage* **is** *very high* ($\mu_{cor}(Q, P^p_{mileage,\,very\,high}) = 0.19$):

$$F_{Q \wedge P^p_{mileage,\,very\,high}} = \{1/7 + 0.8/7 + 0.6/8 + 0.4/18 + 0.2/19\}.$$

(3) *mileage* **is** *high* ($\mu_{cor}(Q, P^p_{mileage,\,high}) = 0.37$):

$$F_{Q \wedge P^p_{mileage,\,high}} = \{1/101 + 0.8/106 + 0.6/110 + 0.4/215 + 0.2/223\}.$$

For each candidate query Q', the user can decide either to process Q' (i.e., retrieve the results) or to repeat the strengthening process on Q'. If the latter option is chosen, the table of fuzzy cardinalities is checked in order to retrieve strengthening candidates for Q' (i.e., properties correlated to Q') and their associated fuzzy cardinalities that are ranked according to k. In this example, even if k (50) items can be ranked and returned to the user according to this strengthened query, we suppose that the user selects:

$$Q' = (year \text{ is } old) \text{ and } (mileage \text{ is } medium)$$

for second strengthening step. The following candidates are suggested along with their fuzzy cardinalities:

(1) *optionLevel* **is** *low* ($\mu_{cor}(Q', P^p_{optionLevel,\,low}) = 0.34$):

$$F_{Q' \wedge P^p_{optionLevel,\,low}} = \{1/18 + 0.8/20 + 0.6/21 + 0.4/46 + 0.2/51\}.$$

(2) *optionLevel* **is** *very low* ($\mu_{cor}(Q', P^p_{optionLevel,\,very\,low}) = 0.15$):

$$F_{Q' \wedge P^p_{optionLevel,\,very\,low}} = \{1/6 + 0.8/7 + 0.6/7 + 0.4/22 + 0.2/22\}.$$

Remarks about this experimentation. From this first experimentation on a concrete database, we observe that this query strengthening approach, based on correlation links, gives the users interesting information about data distributions and the possible queries that can be formulated in order to retrieve coherent answer sets. By "coherent answer set", we mean a group of items that share correlated properties and that may correspond to what the user was looking for without knowing initially how to retrieve it.

Moreover, thanks to the precomputed knowledge tables, it is not necessary to process correlated queries (i.e., queries containing correlated predicates) to provide the user with interesting information about the size of their answer sets and the predicates that can be used to strengthen them.

This experimentation shows that the predicates suggested for strengthening the queries are meaningful and coherent according to the initial under-specified queries. Below are some examples of suggested augmented queries Q' starting from under-specified queries Q:

- $Q = (year$ **is** $old)$ **and** $(mileage$ **is** $high)$ **and** $(optionLevel$ **is** $low)$:

  intensified after two iterations into

  $Q'' = (year$ **is** $old)$ **and** $(mileage$ **is** $high)$ **and** $(optionLevel$ **is** $low)$ **and** $(comfortLevel$ **is** $very\_low)$ **and** $(securityLevel$ **is** $low)$,

  with $|\Sigma_Q^{\mu_{max}(Q)}| = 63$ and $|\Sigma_{Q''}^{\mu_{max}(Q')}| = 26$.

- $Q = year$ **is** $recent$:

  intensified after two iterations into

  $Q'' = (year$ **is** $recent)$ **and** $(mileage$ **is** $low)$ **and** $(optionLevel$ **is** $high)$,

  with $|\Sigma_Q^{\mu_{max}(Q)}| = 4060$ and $|\Sigma_{Q''}^{\mu_{max}(Q')}| = 199$.

- $Q = comfortLevel$ **is** $high$:

  intensified after one iteration into

  $Q' = (comfortLevel$ **is** $high)$ **and** $(optionLevel$ **is** $high)$,

  with $|\Sigma_Q^{\mu_{max}(Q)}| = 180$ and $|\Sigma_{Q'}^{\mu_{max}(Q')}| = 45$.

- $Q = year$ **is** $very\_old$:

  intensified after two iterations into

  $Q'' = (year$ **is** $very\_old)$ **and** $(optionLevel$ **is** $low)$ **and** $(comfortLevel$ **is** $very\_low)$,

  with $|\Sigma_Q^{\mu_{max}(Q)}| = 35$ and $|\Sigma_{Q''}^{\mu_{max}(Q')}| = 6$.

Finally, we found that the parameter η was useless in this applied context, because the correlation threshold used during the computation of fuzzy cardinalities already restricts the size of the correlation table to the most correlated conjunction of predicates. However, for some applied contexts involving many more predefined predicates and a low correlation threshold, η can certainly be useful.

10.4   Conclusion

In this chapter, we have presented several approaches aimed at dealing with situations where a conjunctive fuzzy query returns either an empty or a plethoric answer set. This sample of techniques shows that these two problems are not as related as one might think. Indeed, each problem has strong distinctiveness. When a query Q returns no answer, one may either:

- relax Q; but then one has to look for the minimal failing subqueries of Q which cause this absence of answers, so as to target the problematic part(s) of the query (and also in order to provide the user with some explanations), or
- use a case-based reasoning approach and look for a query similar to Q whose answer is known to be non-empty.

On the other hand, when a query Q returns too many answers, one may think of either:

- strengthening Q by making some of its atomic predicates more selective, or
- augmenting Q with additional predicates in order to reduce its scope; but this latter choice requires some rationale for choosing the predicates to be added.

Despite the peculiarities of each problem, it appears that one type of approach, among those outlined above, is able to solve both problems in a somewhat symmetric way: the approach based on a fuzzy tolerance relation, which leads to dilation of the atomic predicates in the empty answer case, and to their erosion in the plethoric answer situation. However, even though the tools used are symmetric (dilation/erosion), the resulting algorithms are quite different, as we have shown in this chapter.

Among the perspectives for future research, it would be interesting to extend the scope beyond selection queries, and consider, e.g., the empty/plethoric answer problems in the context of division queries. In the case where the result is empty, a solution is to make the division *tolerant* (see Section 7.3). However, the plethoric answer situation is more problematic, and the weakening/strengthening of stratified division queries is also an open issue.

Chapter 11

Conclusion

To the best of our knowledge, this book is the first extensive monograph devoted to fuzzy preference queries. The main objectives we pursued were:

- to show that fuzzy set theory constitutes a suitable and highly expressive framework for modeling database preference queries,
- to study the algorithmic aspects of the evaluation of fuzzy queries, in order to demonstrate that this framework offers a good trade-off between expressivity and efficiency,
- to tackle some specific issues somewhat related to fuzzy querying, such as bipolarity (Chapter 8) and cooperative answering (Chapter 10).

Two families of fuzzy queries have been considered:

- Unipolar fuzzy queries, leading to the computation of a single score for each tuple of the result, which makes it possible to rank-order the answers to a query (a complete preorder is obtained). We have shown that the framework considered, namely the SQLf language, makes it possible to express a wide range of preference queries while preserving the main aspects of the SQL standard.
- Bipolar fuzzy queries, made of a pair (contraint, wish), acknowledging the fact that the human mind often makes decisions on the basis of both positive and negative information. Negative preferences correspond to *constraints*, since they specify those values or objects that have to be rejected (i.e., those that do not satisfy the constraints), while positive preferences correspond to *wishes*, as they specify those objects that are more desirable than others. As shown in Chapter 8, the satisfaction of the constraint and of the wish can be used to order the tuples of the result by means of lexicographic order (with priority given to the constraint).

Fuzzy queries have many potential application domains. Indeed, soft querying turns out to be relevant in many contexts, such as information retrieval, in particular on the Web (many commercial systems, e.g., Google or Yahoo, use a technique to rank-order the answers), yellow pages, classified ads, image or multimedia retrieval. One may assume that the richer the semantics of stored information (images or video being a good example), the more difficult it becomes for the user to characterize his/her search criteria in a crisp way, i.e., using Boolean conditions. In this kind of situation, fuzzy queries which involve imprecise descriptions (or goals) and vague terms, may provide a convenient means for expressing information needs. For instance, the flexible route-planning system described in Mokhtari *et al.* (2009) illustrates the relevance and usefulness of fuzzy queries in the context of intelligent transportation systems. It is important to emphasize that, even though relational data have been assumed throughtout this book, many results can be transposed to other contexts, such as information retrieval or multimedia database querying.

Among the topics which have not been dealt with in this book but are closely related to its subject, it is appropriate to mention:

- The handling of "competitive conditional preferences". This corresponds to a new type of database query introduced in Bosc *et al.* (2011), whose format is somewhat outside the scope of an SQL-like language since it involves conditional requirements (which is more in the spirit of a procedural programming language). The idea is to consider preference clauses structured as a tree, of the type "preferably P_1 or ... or P_n; if P_1 then preferably $P_{1,1}$ or ...; if P_2 then preferably $P_{2,1}$ or ...", where the P_i's are not exclusive (hence the notion of competition).
- The modeling of contextual preferences. In Hadjali *et al.* (2010), a fuzzy-rule-based model is proposed for the representation of contextual preferences in a database querying framework. The idea is to augment a query with fuzzy preferences deduced from information regarding the current context of the user. We have not presented this type of approach here since it is not a purely relational one (it implies coupling a DBMS with a rule-based system, which is somewhat beyond the scope of this book).

Considering the benefits of the fuzzy-set-based approach (particularly in terms of expressivity), one may wonder why this approach is not more prominent in the database world when it comes to database preference queries. In our opinion, the two main reasons are related to:

- The strong priority given to efficiency over expressivity by the database community (hence the popularity of Skyline queries, top-k queries, etc). Obviously, there is still some effort required in order to convince mainstream database researchers that fuzzy queries may be efficiently processed, and we hope this book will contribute to that effect.
- The relative difficulty for an end-user to specify fuzzy membership functions and choose appropriate fuzzy operators. However, as discussed in Chapter 5, it is perfectly possible to conceive user-friendly interfaces to make this task as easy as it is in qualitative approaches such as those based on Pareto-order (e.g., *Preference SQL*; Kießling and Köstler, 2002).

To conclude, let us say a few words about a confusion which has not helped make work about fuzzy queries particularly "readable" for the mainstream database community in the past, namely the use of the expression "fuzzy databases". This term actually covers two *orthogonal* issues: fuzzy queries on the one hand, and uncertain data handling on the other hand. Unfortunately, many research papers about "fuzzy databases" mix both issues, and it is often quite difficult to discern what the fundamental issues are; not to mention the fact that very few papers about fuzzy — in the sense of uncertain — databases have a solid theoretical basis. Even though these two issues have a non-empty intersection, we believe it wise to treat them separately in a comprehensive way before investigating that intersection. Both preference queries and uncertain databases are rather old issues (in each case, the first works date back to the eighties), but it is only quite recently that they have become "hot topics" in the database community. Many uncertain database models based on probability theory have been proposed, particularly in the last decade (see, e.g., Benjelloun *et al.*, 2008; Dalvi and Suciu, 2004; Antova *et al.*, 2007 for some recent ones, and Bosc and Pivert, 2010 for an overview and a critical discussion). However, it is quite clear that not all uncertain information is of a probabilistic nature. A typical example is that of a person who witnesses a car accident and who does not remember for sure the model of the car involved. In such a case, it seems reasonable to model the uncertain value by something more qualitative than a probability distribution — which, by the way, would have to be artificially normalized. Several qualitative approaches based on possibility theory (Zadeh, 1978; Dubois and Prade, 1988) — whose strong ties with fuzzy set theory must be emphasized here — have been proposed in the recent years, among which are Bosc *et al.* (2003a), Bosc and Pivert (2005, 2007b,a), and Bosc *et al.* (2009d, 2010c). However, not much work has yet been done on the subject of preference queries to possibilistic databases (we mention Bosc and Pivert, 2004; Bosc *et al.*, 2010b), and many research issues remain to be investigated in that domain. In particular, there is an open question over the extent to which fuzzy queries, such as those studied in this book, could be adapted to a possibilistic database context.

Bibliography

Agrawal, R., Rantzau, R. and Terzi, E. (2006). Context-sensitive ranking, in S. Chaudhuri, V. Hristidis and N. Polyzotis (eds.), *Proceedings of SIGMOD 2006* (ACM, New York, NY), pp. 383–394.

Agrawal, R. and Wimmers, E. (2000). A framework for expressing and combining preferences, in W. Chen, J.F. Naughton and P.A. Bernstein (eds.), *Proceedings of SIGMOD 2000*, (ACM, New York, NY), pp. 297–306.

Andreasen, T. and Pivert, O. (1994). On the weakening of fuzzy relational queries, in Z.W. Raś and M. Zemankova (eds.), *Proceedings of the 8th International Symposium on Methodologies for Intelligent Systems (ISMIS 1994), LNAI 869*, (Springer-Verlag, Berlin), pp. 144–153.

Andreasen, T. and Pivert, O. (1995). Improving answers to failing fuzzy relational queries, in *Proceedings of the 6th International Fuzzy Systems Association World Congress (IFSA 1995)*, pp. 345–348.

Antova, L., Koch, C. and Olteanu, D. (2007). 10^{10^6} worlds and beyond: Efficient representation and processing of incomplete information, in A. Dogac, T. Ozsu and T. Sellis (eds.), *Proceedings of ICDE 2007* (IEEE Computer Society Press, Washington DC), pp. 606–615.

Atanassov, K. (1986). Intuitionistic fuzzy sets, *Fuzzy Sets and Systems* **20**, 1, pp. 87–96.

Bartolini, I., Ciaccia, P. and Patella, M. (2008). Efficient sort-based skyline evaluation, *ACM Transactions Database Systems* **33**, 4, pp. 1–49.

Benjelloun, O., Das Sarma, A., Halevy, A., Theobald, M. and Widom, J. (2008). Databases with uncertainty and lineage, *VLDB Journal* **17**, 2, pp. 243–264.

Bodenhofer, U. and Küng, J. (2004). Fuzzy orderings in flexible query answering systems, *Soft Computing* **8**, 7, pp. 512–522.

Bőrzsőnyi, S., Kossmann, D. and Stocker, K. (2001). The skyline operator, in D. Georgakapolous and A. Buchmann (eds.), *Proceedings of the 17th IEEE International Conference on Data Engineering*, (IEEE Computer Society Press, Washington DC), pp. 421–430.

Bosc, P. (1998). On the primitivity of the division of fuzzy relations, *Journal of Soft Computing* **2**, 2, pp. 35–47.

Bosc, P., Brando, C., Hadjali, A., Jaudoin, H. and Pivert, O. (2009a). Semantic proximity between queries and the empty answer problem, in J.P. Carvalho, D. Dubois, U. Kaymak and J.M. da Costa Sousa (eds.), *Proceedings of the Joint IFSA World Congress (IFSA 2009) and the 6th Conference of the European Society of Fuzzy Systems and Technology (EUSFLAT 2009)*, pp. 259–264.

Bosc, P., Buckles, B., Petry, F. and Pivert, O. (1999a). Fuzzy databases, in J. Bezdek, D. Dubois and H. Prade (eds.), *The Handbooks of Fuzzy Sets Series, vol. 3: Fuzzy Sets in Approximate Reasoning and Information Systems* (Kluwer Academic Publishers, Dordrecht), pp. 403–468.

Bosc, P., Claveau, V., Pivert, O. and Ughetto, L. (2009b). Graded-inclusion-based information retrieval systems, in M. Boughanem, C. Berrut, J. Mothe and C. Soulé-Dupuy (eds.), *Proceedings of the 31st European Conference on Information Retrieval (ECIR 2009)* (Springer, Berlin), pp. 252–263.

Bosc, P., Dubois, D., Pivert, O. and Prade, H. (1997). Flexible queries in relational databases — the example of the division operator, *Theoretical Computer Science* **171**, 1–2, pp. 281–302.

Bosc, P., Dubois, D., Pivert, O. and Prade, H. (2001). On fuzzy association rules based on fuzzy cardinalities, in Z.-Q. Liu and H. Yan (eds.), *Proceedings of the 10th IEEE International Conference on Fuzzy Systems (FUZZ-IEEE 2001)* (IEEE Press, Piscataway, NJ).

Bosc, P., Duval, L. and Pivert, O. (2003a). An initial approach to the evaluation of possibilistic queries addressed to possibilistic databases, *Fuzzy Sets and Systems* **140**, 1, pp. 151–166.

Bosc, P., Galibourg, M. and Hamon, G. (1988). Fuzzy querying with SQL: extensions and implementation aspects, *Fuzzy Sets and Systems* **28**, pp. 333–349.

Bosc, P., Hadjali, A. and Pivert, O. (2005). Towards a tolerance-based technique for cooperative answering of fuzzy queries against regular databases, R. Meersman, Z. Tari, M.-S. Hacid, J. Mylopoulos, B. Pernici, Ö. Babaoglu, H.-A. Jacobsen, J.P. Loyall, M. Kifer and S. Spaccapietra (eds.), and in *Proceedings of OTM*, (Springer, Berlin), pp. 256–273.

Bosc, P., Hadjali, A. and Pivert, O. (2007a). Weakening of fuzzy relational queries: an absolute proximity relation-based approach, *Mathware & Soft Computing* **14**, 1, pp. 35–55.

Bosc, P., Hadjali, A. and Pivert, O. (2008). Empty versus overabundant answers to flexible relational queries, *Fuzzy Sets and Systems* **159**, 12, pp. 1450–1467.

Bosc, P., Hadjali, A. and Pivert, O. (2009c). Incremental controlled relaxation of failing flexible queries, *Journal of Intelligent Information Systems* **33**, 3, pp. 261–283.

Bosc, P., Hadjali, A. and Pivert, O. (2011). On database queries involving competitive conditional preferences, *International Journal of Intelligent Systems* **26**, 3, pp. 206–227.

Bosc, P., Legrand, C. and Pivert, O. (1999b). About fuzzy query processing — the example of the division, in Z.Z. Bien and K.-W. Oh (eds.), *Proceedings of the 8th IEEE International Conference on Fuzzy Systems (FUZZ-IEEE 1999)*, (IEEE Press, Piscataway, NJ), pp. 592–597.

Bosc, P. and Liétard, L. (2005). A general technique to measure gradual properties of fuzzy sets, in *Proceedings of the 11th International Fuzzy Systems Association World Congress (IFSA 2005)*, pp. 485–490.

Bosc, P. and Liétard, L. (2006). Non monotonic aggregates applying to fuzzy sets in flexible querying, in B. Bouchon-Meunier, G. Coletti and R. Yager (eds.), *Modern Information Processing: From Theory to Applications* (Elsevier, Amsterdam), pp. 309–319.

Bosc, P. and Liétard, L. (2008). Aggregates computed over fuzzy sets and their integration into SQLf, *International Journal of Uncertainty, Fuzziness and Knowledge-Based Systems* **16**, 6, pp. 761–792.

Bosc, P., Liétard, L. and Pivert, O. (1995). Quantified statements and database fuzzy querying, in P. Bosc and J. Kacprzyk (eds.), *Fuzziness in Database Management Systems* (Physica Verlag, Heidelberg), pp. 275–308.

Bosc, P. and Pivert, O. (1991). About equivalences in SQLf, a relational language supporting imprecise querying, in *Proceedings of the International Fuzzy Engineering Symposium (IFES 1991)* (IEEE Press, Piscataway, NJ), pp. 309–320.

Bosc, P. and Pivert, O. (1992). Some approaches for relational databases flexible querying, *Journal of Intelligent Information Systems* **1**, 3/4, pp. 323–354.

Bosc, P. and Pivert, O. (1993). On the evaluation of simple fuzzy relational queries: principles and measures, in R. Lowen and M. Roubens (eds.), *Fuzzy Logic — State of the Art* (Kluwer Academic Publishers, Dordrecht), pp. 355–364.

Bosc, P. and Pivert, O. (1995a). On the efficiency of the alpha-cut distribution method to evaluate simple fuzzy relational queries, in B. Bouchon-Meunier, R. Yager and L. Zadeh (eds.), *Advances in Fuzzy Systems — Applications and Theory vol. 4* (World Scientific, Singapore), pp. 251–260.

Bosc, P. and Pivert, O. (1995b). SQLf: a relational database language for fuzzy querying, *IEEE Transactions on Fuzzy Systems* **3**, 1, pp. 1–17.

Bosc, P. and Pivert, O. (1997). On the comparison of imprecise values in fuzzy databases, in R.L. de Mantaras, L. Godo and J. Jacas (eds.), *Proceedings of the 6th IEEE International Conference on Fuzzy Systems (FUZZ-IEEE 1997)* (IEEE Press, Piscataway, NJ), pp. 707–712.

Bosc, P. and Pivert, O. (2000). SQLf query functionality on top of a regular relational database management system, in O. Pons, M. Vila and J. Kacprzyk (eds.), *Knowledge Management in Fuzzy Databases* (Physica-Verlag, Heidelberg), pp. 171–190.

Bosc, P. and Pivert, O. (2001). On some fuzzy extensions of association rules, in M.H. Smith, W.A. Gruver and L.O. Hall (eds.), *Proceedings of the Joint 9th IFSA World Congress and 20th NAFIPS International Conference* (IEEE Press, Piscataway, NJ), pp. 1104–1109.

Bosc, P. and Pivert, O. (2004). From Boolean to fuzzy algebraic queries in a possibilistic database framework, in L.T. Koczy, E. Ruspini, K. Hirota, J. Botzheiin and M. Jetzin (eds.), *Proceedings of the 13th IEEE International Conference on Fuzzy Systems (FUZZ-IEEE 2004)* (IEEE Press, Piscataway, NJ), pp. 547–555.

Bosc, P. and Pivert, O. (2005). About projection–selection–join queries addressed to possibilistic relational databases, *IEEE Transactions on Fuzzy Systems* **13**, 1, pp. 124–139.

Bosc, P. and Pivert, O. (2006). About approximate inclusion and its axiomatization, *Fuzzy Sets and Systems* **157**, pp. 1438–1454.

Bosc, P. and Pivert, O. (2007a). About possibilistic queries and their evaluation, *IEEE Transactions on Fuzzy Systems* **15**, 3, pp. 439–452.

Bosc, P. and Pivert, O. (2007b). About yes/no queries against possibilistic databases, *International Journal of Intelligent Systems* **22**, pp. 691–722.

Bosc, P. and Pivert, O. (2008). On two qualitative approaches to tolerant inclusion operators, *Fuzzy Sets and Systems* **159**, 21, pp. 2786–2805.

Bosc, P. and Pivert, O. (2010). Modeling and querying uncertain relational databases: A survey of approaches based on the possible worlds semantics, *International Journal of Uncertainty, Fuzziness and Knowledge-Based Systems* **18**, 5, pp. 565–603.

Bosc, P. and Pivert, O. (2011). On three fuzzy connectives for flexible data retrieval and their axiomatization, in W.C. Chu, W.E. Wong, M.J. Palakal and C.-C. Hurg (eds.), *Proceedings of the 26th ACM Symposium on Applied Computing (SAC 2011)* (ACM, New York, NY), pp. 1114–1118.

Bosc, P., Pivert, O. and Liétard, L. (2003b). On the comparison of aggregates over fuzzy sets, in B. Bouchon-Meunier, L. Foulloy and R. Yager (eds.), *Intelligent Systems for Information Processing: From Representation to Applications* (Elsevier, Amsterdam), pp. 141–152.

Bosc, P., Pivert, O., Liétard, L. and Mokhtari, A. (2010a). Extending relational algebra to handle bipolarity, in S.Y. Shin, S. Ossowski, M. Schumacher, M.J. Palakal and C.-C. Hung (eds.), *Proceedings of the 25th ACM Symposium on Applied Computing (SAC 2010)* (ACM, New York, NY), pp. 1718–1722.

Bosc, P., Pivert, O. and Prade, H. (2009d). A model based on possibilistic certainty levels for incomplete databases, in L. Godo and A. Pugliese (eds.), *Proceedings of the 3rd International Conference on Scalable Uncertainty Management (SUM 2009)* (Springer, Berlin), pp. 80–94.

Bosc, P., Pivert, O. and Prade, H. (2010b). A possibilistic logic view of preference queries to an uncertain database, in P. Bonissone, B. Bouchon-Meunier, S. Barro, F. Gomide, M. Inuiguchi, J. Keller, R. Kruse and T. Martin (eds.), *Proceedings of the 19th IEEE International Conference on Fuzzy Systems (FUZZ-IEEE 2010)* (IEEE Press, Piscataway, NJ), pp. 379–384.

Bosc, P., Pivert, O. and Prade, H. (2010c). An uncertain database model and a query algebra based on possibilistic certainty, in A. Abraham, H. Prade, T. Martin and A.K. Muda (eds.), *Proceedings of the 2nd International Conference on Soft Computing and Pattern Recognition (SoCPaR 2010)* (IEEE Press, Piscataway, NJ), pp. 63–68.

Bosc, P., Pivert, O. and Rocacher, D. (2007b). About quotient and division of crisp and fuzzy relations, *Journal of Intelligent Information Systems* **29**, 2, pp. 185–210.

Bosc, P., Pivert, O. and Rocacher, D. (2007c). Characterizing the result of the division of fuzzy relations, *Journal of Approximate Reasoning* **45**, pp. 511–530.

Bosc, P., Pivert, O. and Smits, G. (2009e). A flexible querying approach based on outranking and classification, in T. Andreasen, R.R. Yager, H. Bulskov, H. Christiansen and H.L. Larsen (eds.), *Proceedings of the 8th International Conference on Flexible Query Answering Systems (FQAS 2009), LNAI 5822* (Springer, Berlin), pp. 1–12.

Bosc, P., Pivert, O. and Smits, G. (2010d). A database preference query model based on a fuzzy outranking relation, in P. Bonissone, B. Bouchon-Meunier, S. Barro, F. Gomide, M. Inuiguchi, J. Keller, R. Kruse and T. Martin (eds.), *Proceedings of the 19th IEEE International Conference on Fuzzy Systems (FUZZ-IEEE 2010)* (IEEE Press, Piscataway, NJ), pp. 38–43.

Bosc, P., Pivert, O. and Smits, G. (2010e). A model based on outranking for database preference queries, in E. Hüllermeier, R. Kruse and F. Hoffmann (eds.), *Information Processing and Management of Uncertainty in Knowledge-Based Systems (Proceedings of IPMU 2010), Communications in Computer and Information Science*, Vol. 81 (Springer), pp. 95–104.

Bouchon-Meunier, B. (1988). Stability of linguistic modifiers compatible with a fuzzy logic, in B. Bouchon-Meunier, L. Saitta and R.R. Yager (eds.), *Information Processing and Management of Uncertainty in Knowledge-Based Systems (Proceedings of IPMU 1988), LNCS vol. 313* (Springer, Berlin), pp. 63–70.

Bouchon-Meunier, B. and Yao, J. (1992). Linguistic modifiers and imprecise categories, *International Journal of Intelligent Systems* **7**, pp. 25–36.

Boutilier, C., Brafman, R., Domshlak, C., Hoos, H. and Poole, D. (2004). CP-nets: A tool for representing and reasoning with conditional ceteris paribus preference statements, *Journal of Artificial Intelligence Research* **21**, pp. 135–191.

Brafman, R. and Domshlak, C. (2004). Database preference queries revisited TR2004-1934, Tech. Rep., Cornell University, Computing and Information Science.

Bruno, N., Chaudhuri, S. and Gravano, L. (2002). Top-k selection queries over relational databases: mapping strategies and performance evaluation, *ACM Transactions on Database Systems* **27**, pp. 153–187.

Cayrol, M., Farreny, H. and Prade, H. (1980). Possibility and necessity in a pattern-matching process, in *Proceedings of the 9th International Congress on Cybernetics*, pp. 53–65.

Chamberlin, D., Astrahan, M., Eswaran, K., Griffiths, P., Lorie, R., Mehl, J., Reisner, P. and Wade, B. (1976). SEQUEL2: A unified approach to data definition, manipulation and control, *IBM Journal of Research and Development* **20**, 6, pp. 560–575.

Chan, C., Jagadish, H., Tan, K., Tung, A. and Zhang, Z. (2006a). Finding k-dominant skylines in high dimensional space, in S. Chaudhuri, V. Hristidis and Neoklis Polyzotis (eds.), *Proceedings of SIGMOD 2006* (ACM, New York, NY), pp. 503–514.

Chan, C., Jagadish, H., Tan, K., Tung, A. and Zhang, Z. (2006b). On high dimensional skylines, in Y.E. Ioannidis, M.H. Scholl, J.W. Schmidt, F. Matthes, M. Hatzopoulos, K. Böhm, A. Kemper, T. Grust and C. Böhm (eds.), *Proceedings of EDBT 2006, LNCS vol. 3896* (Springer, Berlin), pp. 478–495.

Chaudhuri, S. and Gravano, L. (1999). Evaluating top-k selection queries, in M.P. Atkinson, M.E. Orlowska, P. Valduriez, S.B. Zdonik and M.L. Brodie (eds.), *Proceedings of the 25th VLDB Conference* (Morgan Kaufmann, San Francisco, CA), pp. 399–410.

Chomicki, J. (2003). Preference formulas in relational queries, *ACM Transactions on Database Systems* **28**, pp. 1–40.

Chomicki, J., Godfrey, P., Gryz, J. and Liang, D. (2005). Skyline with presorting: Theory and optimizations, in M.A. Klopotek, S.T. Wierzchon and K. Trojanowski (eds.), *Intelligent Information Systems* (Springer, Berlin), pp. 595–604.

Chu, W. and Chen, Q. (1992). Neighborhood and associative query answering, *Journal of Intelligent Information Systems* **1**, 3/4, pp. 355–382.

Clear, J., Dunn, D., Harvey, B., Heytens, M.L., Lohman, P., Mehta, A., Melton, M., Rohrberg, L., Savasere, A., Wehrmeister, R.M. and Xu, M. (1999). Nonstop SQL/MX primitives for knowledge discovery, in S. Chaudhuri, D. Madigan and U. Fayyad (eds.), *Proceedings of KDD 1999* (ACM, New York, NY), pp. 425–429.

Codd, E. (1970). A relational model of data for large shared data banks, *Communications of the ACM* **13**, pp. 377–387.

Corella, F., Kaplan, S., Wiederhold, G. and Yesil, L. (1984). Cooperative responses to boolean queries, in *Proceedings of ICDE 1984* (IEEE Computer Society Press, Washington DC) pp. 77–85.

Cubero, J., Medina, J., Pons, O. and Vila, M. (1994). The generalized selection: an alternative way for the quotient operations in fuzzy relational databases, in *Proceedings of the 5th Conference on Information Processing and the Management of Uncertainty (IPMU 1994)*, pp. 23–30.

Cuppens, F. and Demolombe, R. (1988). Cooperative answering: a methodology to provide intelligent access to databases, in L. Kerschberg (ed.), *Proceedings of the 2nd International Conference on Expert Database Systems* (Benjamin Cummings, San Francisco, CA) pp. 621–643.

Dalvi, N. and Suciu, D. (2004). Efficient query evaluation on probabilistic databases, in M.A. Nascimento, M.T. Özsu, D. Kossmann, R.J. Miller, J.A. Blakeley and K.B. Schiefer (eds.), *Proceedings of the 30th VLDB Conference* (Morgan Kaufmann, San Francisco, CA) pp. 864–875.

Date, C. (1995). *An introduction to database systems* (Addison Wesley, Reading).

De Tré, G., Zadrożny, S. and Bronselaer, A. (2010). Handling bipolarity in elementary queries to possibilistic databases, *IEEE Transactions on Fuzzy Systems* **18**, 3, pp. 599–612.

Delgado, M., Molina, C., Ariza, L.R., Sánchez, D. and Vila Miranda, M.A. (2007). F-Cube Factory: a fuzzy Olap system for supporting imprecision, *International Journal of Uncertainty, Fuzziness and Knowledge-Based Systems* **15**, Supplement-1, pp. 59–81.

Dubois, D., Fargier, H. and Prade, H. (1997). Beyond *min* aggregation in multicriteria decision: (ordered) weighted *min, discri-min, leximin*, in R. Yager and J. Kacprzyk (eds.), *The Ordered Weighted Averaging*

Operators — Theory and Applications (Kluwer Academic Publishers, Dordrecht), pp. 181–192.

Dubois, D., Hadjali, A. and Prade, H. (2001). Fuzzy qualitative reasoning with words, in P. Wang (ed.), *Computing with Words* (John Wiley & Sons, Hoboken, NJ), pp. 347–366.

Dubois, D., Hüllermeier, E. and Prade, H. (2006). A systematic approach to the assessment of fuzzy association rules, *Data Mining and Knowledge Discovery* **13**, 2, pp. 167–192.

Dubois, D., Ostasiewicz, W. and Prade, H. (2000). Fuzzy sets: history and basic notions, in D. Dubois and H. Prade (eds.), *The Handbooks of Fuzzy Sets Series, Vol. 1: Fundamentals of Fuzzy Sets* (Kluwer Academic Publishers, Dordrecht), pp. 21–124.

Dubois, D. and Prade, H. (1980). *Fuzzy Sets and Systems — Theory and Applications* (Academic Press, New York, NY).

Dubois, D. and Prade, H. (1983). Inverse operations for fuzzy numbers, in E. Sanchez (ed.), *Proceedings of the IFAC Symposium on Fuzzy Information, Knowledge representation and Decision Analysis* (Pergamon Press, Oxford), pp. 391–395.

Dubois, D. and Prade, H. (1984). A theorem on implication functions defined from triangular norms, *Stochastica* **8**, pp. 267–279.

Dubois, D. and Prade, H. (1985a). Fuzzy cardinality and the modeling of imprecise quantification, *Fuzzy Sets and Systems* **16**, 3, pp. 199–230.

Dubois, D. and Prade, H. (1985b). A review of fuzzy set aggregation connectives, *Information Sciences* **36**, pp. 85–121.

Dubois, D. and Prade, H. (1987). Twofold fuzzy sets and rough sets — some issues in knowledge representation, *Fuzzy Sets and Systems* **23**, 1, pp. 3–18.

Dubois, D. and Prade, H. (1988). *Possibility Theory* (Plenum Press, New York, NY).

Dubois, D. and Prade, H. (1990). Measuring properties of fuzzy sets: a general technique and its use in fuzzy query evaluation, *Fuzzy Sets and Systems* **38**, 2, pp. 137–152.

Dubois, D. and Prade, H. (1995). Tolerant fuzzy pattern matching: An introduction, in P. Bosc and J. Kacprzyk (eds.), *Fuzziness in Database Management Systems* (Physica Verlag, Heidelberg), pp. 42–58.

Dubois, D. and Prade, H. (1996). Semantics of quotient operators in fuzzy relational databases, *Fuzzy Sets and Systems* **78**, pp. 89–94.

Dubois, D. and Prade, H. (eds.) (2000). *Fundamentals of Fuzzy Sets, The Handbook of Fuzzy Sets Series* (Kluwer Academic Publishers, Dordrecht).

Dubois, D. and Prade, H. (2002). Bipolarity in flexible querying, in T. Andreasen, A. Motro, H. Christiansen and H.L. Larsen (eds.), *FQAS, Lecture Notes in Computer Science*, Vol. 2522 (Springer), pp. 174–182.

Dubois, D. and Prade, H. (2004). Possibilistic logic: a retrospective and prospective view, *Fuzzy Sets and Systems* **144**, 1, pp. 3–23.

Dubois, D. and Prade, H. (2008a). Handling bipolar queries in fuzzy information processing, in J. Galindo (ed.), *Handbook of Research on Fuzzy Information*

Processing in Databases (Information Science Reference, Hershey, PA), pp. 97–114.

Dubois, D. and Prade, H. (2008b). An introduction to bipolar representations of information and preference, *International Journal of Intelligent Systems* **23**, 8, pp. 866–877.

Dubois, D., Prade, H. and Testemale, C. (1988). Weighted fuzzy pattern matching, *Fuzzy Sets and Systems* **28**, pp. 315–331.

Fodor, J. and Yager, R. (2000). Fuzzy-set theoretic operators and quantifiers, in D. Dubois and H. Prade (eds.), *The Handbooks of Fuzzy Sets Series, vol. 1: Fundamentals of Fuzzy Sets* (Kluwer Academic Publishers, Dordrecht), pp. 125–193.

Friedman, J., Baskett, F. and Shustek, L.J. (1975). An algorithm for finding nearest neighbors, *IEEE Transactions on Computers* **24**, 10, pp. 1000–1006.

Gaasterland, T., Godfrey, P. and Minker, J. (1992a). An overview of cooperative answering, *Journal of Intelligent Information Systems* **1**, 2, pp. 123–157.

Gaasterland, T., Godfrey, P. and Minker, J. (1992b). Relaxation as a platform for cooperative answering, *Journal of Intelligent Information Systems* **1**, pp. 293–321.

Galindo, J., Medina, J.M., Pons, O. and Cubero, J.C. (1998). A server for fuzzy SQL queries, in T. Andreasen, H. Christiansen and H.L. Larsen, *Proceedings of FQAS 1998* (Springer, Berlin), pp. 164–174.

Georgiadis, P., Kapantaidakis, I., Christophides, V., Nguer, E. and Spyratos, N. (2008). Efficient rewriting algorithms for preference queries, in Z.-Q. Liu and H. Yan (eds.), *Proceedings of ICDE 2008* (IEEE Press, Piscataway, NJ), pp. 1101–1110.

Godfrey, P. (1997). Minimization in cooperative response to failing database queries, *International Journal of Cooperative Information Systems* **6**, 2, pp. 95–149.

Goncalves, M. and Tineo, L. (2001a). SQLf flexible querying language extension by means of the norm SQL2, in *Proceedings of the 10th IEEE International Conference on Fuzzy Systems (FUZZ-IEEE 2001)* (IEEE Press, Piscataway, NJ), pp. 473–476.

Goncalves, M. and Tineo, L. (2001b). SQLf3: An extension of SQLf with SQL features, in *Proceedings of the 10th IEEE International Conference on Fuzzy Systems (FUZZ-IEEE 2001)* (IEEE Press, Piscataway, NJ), pp. 477–480.

Grabisch, M., Murofushi, T. and Sugeno, M. (1992). Fuzzy measure of fuzzy events defined by fuzzy integrals, *Fuzzy Sets and Systems* **50**, pp. 293–313.

Guyomard, M. and Siroux, J. (1989). Suggestive and corrective answers: A single mechanism, in M. Taylor, F. Néel and D. Bouwhuis (eds.), *The Structure of Multimodal Dialogue* (North-Holland, Amsterdam), pp. 361–374.

Hadjali, A., Kaci, S. and Prade, H. (2008). Database preference queries — a possibilistic logic approach with symbolic priorities, in S. Hartmann and G. Kern-Isberner (eds.), *Proceedings of the 5th Symposium on the Foundations of Information and Knowledge Systems (FoIKS'08)* (Springer, Berlin), pp. 291–310.

Hadjali, A., Mokhtari, A. and Pivert, O. (2010). A fuzzy-rule-based approach to contextual preference queries, in E. Hüllermeier, R. Kruse and F. Hoffmann (eds.), *Proceedings of the 13th International Conference on Information Processing and Management of Uncertainty in Knowledge-Based Systems (IPMU 2010), LNCS vol. 6178* (Springer, Berlin), pp. 532–541.

Holland, S. and Kießling, W. (2004). Situated preferences and preference repositories for personalized database applications, in P. Atzeni, W.W. Chu, H. Lu, S. Zhou and T.W. Ling (eds.), *Proceedings of ER 2004* (Springer, Berlin), pp. 511–523.

Hua, M., Pei, J., Fu, A. W.-C., Lin, X. and Leung, H.-F. (2009). Top-k typicality queries and efficient query answering methods on large databases, *VLDB J.* **18**, 3, pp. 809–835.

Hüllermeier, E. (2001). Implication-based fuzzy association rules, in L. De Raedt and A. Siebes (eds.), *Proceedings of PKDD 2001* (Springer, Berlin), pp. 241–252.

Ichikawa, T. and Hirakawa, M. (1986). ARES: a relational database with the capability of performing flexible interpretation of queries, *IEEE Transactions on Software Engineering* **12**, pp. 624–634.

Imielinski, T. and Virmani, A. (1999). MSQL: A query language for database mining, *Data Mining and Knowledge Discovery* **3**, 4, pp. 373–408.

Kacprzyk, J. and Zadrożny, S. (1995). FQUERY for ACCESS: fuzzy querying for a Windows-based DBMS, in P. Bosc and J. Kacprzyk (eds.), *Fuzziness in Database Management Systems* (Physica Verlag, Heidelberg), pp. 415–433.

Kacprzyk, J. and Ziółkowski, A. (1986). Database queries with fuzzy linguistic quantifiers, *IEEE Transactions on Systems, Man and Cybernetics* **16**, pp. 474–478.

Kandel, A. and Byatt, W. (1978). Fuzzy sets, fuzzy algebra, and fuzzy statistics, *Proceedings of the IEEE* **66**, 12, pp. 1619–1639.

Kaplan, S. (1982). Cooperative responses from a portable natural language query system, *Artificial Intelligence* **19**, 2, pp. 165–187.

Kaya, M. and Alhajj, R. (2008). Online mining of fuzzy multidimensional weighted association rules, *Applied Intelligence* **29**, 1, pp. 13–34.

Kerre, E. and de Cock, M. (1999). Linguistic modifiers: an overview, in G. Chen, M. Ying and K.-Y. Cai (eds.), *Fuzzy Logic and Soft Computing* (Kluwer Academic Publishers, Dordrecht), pp. 69–85.

Kerre, E. and Liu, Y. (1998). An overview of fuzzy quantifiers — interpretations, *Fuzzy Sets and Systems* **95**, 1, pp. 1–21.

Kießling, W. (2002). Foundations of preferences in database systems, in P.A. Bernstein, Y.E. Ioannidis, R. Ramakrishnan and D. Papadias (eds.), *Proceedings of the 28th VLDB Conference* (Morgan Kaufmann, San Francisco, CA), pp. 311–322.

Kießling, W. and Köstler, G. (2002). Preference SQL — design, implementation, experiences, in P.A. Bernstein, Y.E. Ioannidis, R. Ramakrishnan and D. Papadias (eds.), *Proceedings of the 28th VLDB Conference* (Morgan Kaufmann, San Francisco, CA), pp. 990–1001.

Kim, W. (1982). On optimizing an SQL-like nested query, *ACM Transactions on Database Systems* **7**, 3, pp. 443–469.

Klir, G. and Yuan, B. (1995). *Fuzzy sets and fuzzy logic: theory and applications* (Prentice Hall).

Korth, H. and Silberschatz, A. (1998). *Database system concepts* (McGraw-Hill, New York, NY).

Koutrika, G. and Ioannidis, Y.E. (2004). Personalization of queries in database systems, in B. Salzberg, M. Stonebraker, M. Ozsoyoglu and S. Zdonik (eds.), *Proceedings of ICDE 2004* (IEEE Computer Society Press, Washington DC), pp. 597–608.

Lacroix, M. and Lavency, P. (1987). Preferences: Putting more knowledge into queries, in P.M. Stocker, W. Kent and P. Hammersley (eds.), *Proceedings of the 13th VLDB Conference* (Morgan Kaufmann, San Francisco, CA), pp. 217–225.

Lee, D. and Kim, M. (1993). Accommodating subjective vagueness through a fuzzy extension to the relational data model, *Information Systems* **18**, 6, pp. 363–374.

Leondes, C. (ed.) (1999). *Fuzzy Theory Systems* (Academic Press, New York, NY).

Li, C., Wang, M., Lim, L., Wang, H. and Chang, K.C.-C. (2007). Supporting ranking and clustering as generalized order-by and group-by, in Y. Chan, B.C. Ooi and A. Zhou (eds.), *Proceedings of SIGMOD 2007* (ACM, New York, NY), pp. 127–138.

Liétard, L., Rocacher, D. and Bosc, P. (2009). On the extension of SQL to fuzzy bipolar conditions, in A. Celikylmaz, A. Inoue, V. Kreinovich and A. Ralescu (eds.), *Proceedings of the 28th International Conference of the North American Fuzzy Information Processing Society (NAFIPS 2009)* (IEEE Press, Piscataway, NJ), pp. 1–6.

Lin, X., Yuan, Y., Zhang, Q. and Zhang, Y. (2007). Selecting stars: the k most representative skyline operator, in R. Chirkova, A. Dogac, T. Öszu and T. Sellis (eds.), *Proceedings of ICDE 2007* (IEEE Computer Society Press, Washington DC), pp. 86–95.

Matthé, T. and De Tré, G. (2009). Bipolar query satisfaction using satisfaction and dissatisfaction degrees, in S.Y. Shin and S. Ossowski (eds.), *Proceedings of ACM SAC 2009* (ACM, New York, NY), pp. 1699–1703.

Meo, R., Psaila, G. and Ceri, S. (1998). An extension to SQL for mining association rules, *Data Mining and Knowledge Discovery* **2**, 2, pp. 195–224.

Mokhtari, A., Pivert, O., Hadjali, A. and Bosc, P. (2009). Towards a route planner capable of dealing with complex bipolar preferences, in *Proceedings of the 12th IEEE Conference on Intelligent Transportation Systems (IEEE ITSC 2009)* (IEEE Press, Piscataway, NJ), pp. 556–561.

Motro, A. (1986). SEAVE: A mechanism for verifying user presuppositions in query systems, *ACM Transactions on Office Information Systems* **4**, 4, pp. 312–330.

Motro, A. (1988). VAGUE: a user interface to relational queries that permits vague queries, *ACM Transactions on Office Information Systems* **6**, pp. 187–214.

Motro, A. (1990). FLEX: A tolerant and cooperative user interface to databases, *IEEE Transactions on Knowledge and Data Engineering* **2**, 2, pp. 231–246.

Mouaddib, N. (1993). The nuanced relational division, in *Proceedings of the 2nd IEEE International Conference on Fuzzy Systems (FUZZ-IEEE 1993)* (IEEE Press, Piscataway, NJ), pp. 419–424.

Murofushi, T. and Sugeno, M. (1989). An interpretation of fuzzy measure and the Choquet fuzzy integral as an integral with respect to fuzzy measure, *Fuzzy Sets and Systems* **29**, pp. 201–227.

Ovchinnikov, S. (1981). Representations of synonymy and antonymy by automorphisms in fuzzy set theory, *Stochastica* **5**, pp. 95–107.

Ozawa, J. and Yamada, K. (1995). Discovery of global knowledge in database for cooperative answering, in *Proceedings of the 4th IEEE International Conference on Fuzzy Systems (FUZZ-IEEE 1995)* (IEEE Press, Piscataway, NJ), pp. 849–852.

Pawlak, Z. (1982). Rough sets, *Journal of Computer and Information Sciences* **11**, pp. 341–346.

Pereira, R., Millan, M. and Machuca, F. (2003). New algebraic operators and SQL primitives for mining association rules, in B. Kovalerchuk (eds.), *Neural Networks and Computational Intelligence* (IASTED/ACTA Press, Calgary), pp. 227–232.

Pivert, O., Jaudoin, H., Brando, C. and Hadjali, A. (2010). A method based on query caching and predicate substitution for the treatment of failing database queries, in I. Bichindaritz and S. Montani (eds.), *Proceedings of the 18th International Conference on Case-Based Reasoning (ICCBR 2010), LNAI vol. 6176* (Springer, Berlin), pp. 436–450.

Prade, H. (1990). A two-layer fuzzy pattern matching procedure for the evaluation of conditions involving vague quantifiers, *Journal of Intelligent and Robotic Systems* **3**, pp. 93–101.

Quafafou, M. and Boussouf, M. (1997). Induction of strong figure subsets, in H.J. Komorowski and J.M. Zytkow (eds.), *Proceedings of the 1st International Symposium on Principles of Data Mining and Knowledge Discovery* (Springer, Berlin) pp. 384–392.

Rabitti, F. and Savino, P. (1990). Retrieval of multimedia documents by imprecise query specification, in F. Bancilhon, C. Thanos and D. Tsichritzis (eds.), *Proceedings of EDBT 1990, LNCS vol. 416* (Springer, Heidelberg), pp. 203–218.

Rajamani, K., Cox, A.L., Iyer, B.R. and Chadha, A. (1999). Efficient mining for association rules with relational database systems, in *Proceedings of IDEAS 1999* (IEEE Computer Society Press, Washington, DC), pp. 148–155.

Rasmussen, D. and Yager, R.R. (1997). Summary SQL — a fuzzy tool for data mining, *Intelligent Data Analysis* **1**, 1–4, pp. 49–58.

Rasmussen, D. and Yager, R.R. (1999). Finding fuzzy and gradual functional dependencies with SummarySQL, *Fuzzy Sets and Systems* **106**, 2, pp. 131–142.

Rocacher, D. (2002). On fuzzy bags and their application to flexible querying, *Fuzzy Sets and Systems* **140**, pp. 73–110.

Rocacher, D. and Bosc, P. (2002). About difference operations on fuzzy bags, in B. Bouchon-Meunier, L. Foulloy and R.R. Yager (eds.), *Proceedings of the 9th International Conference on Information Processing and Management of Uncertainty in Knowledge-Based Systems (IPMU 2002)* (ESIA — Université de Savoie, Annecy), pp. 1541–1546.

Roy, B. (1991). The outranking approach and the foundations of ELECTRE methods, *Theory and Decision* **31**, pp. 49–73.

Ruspini, E. (1969). A new approach to clustering, *Information and Control* **15**, 1, pp. 22–32.

Ruspini, E., Bonissone, P. and Pedrycz, W. (eds.) (1998). *Handbook of Fuzzy Computation* (Institute of Physics Bristol).

Saint-Paul, R., Raschia, G. and Mouaddib, N. (2005). General purpose database summarization, in K. Böhm, C.S. Jensen, L.M. Haas, M.L. Kersten, P.A. Larson and B.C. Ooi (eds.), *Proceedings of VLDB 2005* (ACM, New York, NY), pp. 733–744.

Salton, G., Fox, E. and Wu, H. (1983). Extended boolean information retrieval, *Communications of the ACM* **26**, 11, pp. 1022–1036.

Silva, Y.N., Aref, W.G. and Ali, M.H. (2009). Similarity group-by, in J. Li, P.S. Yu, Y. Ioannidis, D. Lee and R. Ng (eds.), *Proceedings of ICDE 2009* (IEEE Computer Society Press, Washington, DC), pp. 904–915.

Stefanidis, K., Pitoura, E. and Vassiliadis, P. (2007). Adding context to preferences, in R. Chikova, A. Dogac, T. Öszu and T. Sellis (eds.), *Proceedings of ICDE 2007* (IEEE Computer Society Press, Washington, DC), pp. 846–855.

Sugeno, M. (1974). *Theory of fuzzy integrals and its applications*, Ph.D. thesis, Tokyo Institute of Technology.

Suppes, P. (1972). *Axiomatic Set Theory* (Dover Publications, New York, NY).

Tahani, V. (1977). A conceptual framework for fuzzy query processing — a step toward very intelligent database systems, *Information Processing and Management* **13**, 5, pp. 289–303.

Takahashi, Y. (1991). A fuzzy query language for relational databases, *IEEE Transactions on Systems, Man and Cybernetics* **21**, 5, pp. 1576–1579.

Thomas, S. and Sarawagi, S. (1998). Mining generalized association rules and sequential patterns using SQL queries, in R. Agrawal, P.E. Stolorz and G. Piatetsky-Shapiro (eds.), *Proceedings of KDD 1998* (AAAI Press, Menlo Park, CA), pp. 344–348.

Torlone, R. and Ciaccia, P. (2002). Finding the best when it's a matter of preference, in P. Ciaccia, F. Rabitti and G. Soda (eds.), *Proceedings of the 10th Italian National Conference on Advanced Data Base Systems (SEBD 2002)*, pp. 347–360.

Trillas, E., Moraga, C., Guadarrama, S., Cubillo, S. and Castineira, E. (2008). Computing with antonyms, in M. Nikravesh, J. Kacprzyk and L. Zadeh (eds.), *Forging New Frontiers: Fuzzy Pioneers I* (Springer, Berlin), pp. 133–153.

Trillas, E. and Riera, T. (1981). Towards a representation of "synonyms" and "antonyms" by fuzzy sets, *Busefal* **5**, pp. 42–68.

Tudorie, C., Bumbaru, S. and Dumitriu, L. (2006). Relative qualification in database flexible queries, in P. Chountas, I. Petrounias and J. Kacprzyk (eds.), *Proceedings of the 3rd International IEEE Conference on Intelligent Systems (IEEE IS 2006)* (IEEE Computer Society Press, Washington, DC) pp. 83–88.

Ughetto, L., Voglozin, W.A. and Mouaddib, N. (2008). Database querying with personalized vocabulary using data summaries, *Fuzzy Sets and Systems* **159**, 15, pp. 2030–2046.

Ullman, J. (1989). *Principles of database and knowledge-based systems* (Computer Science Press, Rockville, MD).

van Bunningen, A., Feng, L. and Apers, P. (2006). A context-aware preference model for database querying in an ambient intelligent environment, in S. Bressan, J. Küng and R. Wagner (eds.), *Proceedings of DEXA 2006* (Springer, Berlin) pp. 33–43.

Wong, M. and Leung, K. (1990). A fuzzy database query language, *Information Systems* **15**, 5, pp. 583–590.

Yager, R. (1980). An approach to inference in approximate reasoning, *International Journal of Man–Machine Studies* **19**, pp. 195–227.

Yager, R. (1984). General multiple-objective decision functions and linguistically quantified statements, *International Journal of Man–Machine Studies* **21**, pp. 389–400.

Yager, R. (1988). On ordered weighted averaging aggregation operators in multi-criteria decision making, *IEEE Transactions on Systems, Man, and Cybernetics* **18**, 1, pp. 183–190.

Yager, R. (1991a). Fuzzy quotient operators for fuzzy relational databases, in T. Terano, M. Sugeno, M. Mukaidono and K. Shigemasu (eds.), *Proceedings of the International Fuzzy Engineering Symposium (IFES 1991)* (Ohmsha Ltd., Tokyo), pp. 289–296.

Yager, R. (1993). A general approach to criteria aggregation using fuzzy measures, *International Journal of Man–Machine Studies* 39, 2, pp. 187–213.

Yoshizawa, T., Pramudiono, I. and Kitsuregawa, M. (2000). SQL based association rule mining using commercial RDBMS (IBM DB2 UBD EEE), in Y. Kambayashi, M.K. Mohania and A.M. Tjoa (eds.), *Proceedings of DaWaK 2000* (Springer, Berlin), pp. 301–306.

Zadeh, L. (1965). Fuzzy sets, *Information and Control* **8**, pp. 338–353.

Zadeh, L. (1975a). Calculus of fuzzy restrictions, in L. Zadeh, K.-S. Fu, K. Tanaka and M. Shimura (eds.), *Fuzzy Sets and their Applications to Cognitive and Decision Processes* (Academic Press, New York, NY), pp. 1–39.

Zadeh, L. (1975b). The concept of a linguistic variable and its application to approximate reasoning — part 1, *Information Sciences* **8**, pp. 199–249.

Zadeh, L. (1975c). The concept of a linguistic variable and its application to approximate reasoning — part 2, *Information Sciences* **8**, pp. 301–357.

Zadeh, L. (1978). Fuzzy sets as a basis for a theory of possibility, *Fuzzy Sets and Systems* **1**, pp. 3–28.

Zadeh, L. (1983). A computational approach to fuzzy quantifiers in natural languages, *Computing and Mathematics with Applications* **9**, pp. 149–183.

Zadrożny, S. and Kacprzyk, J. (1996). FQUERY for Access: towards human consistent querying user interface, in K.M. George, J.H. Carroll, D. Oppenheim and J. Hightower (eds.), *Proceedings of ACM SAC 1996* (ACM, New York, NY), pp. 532–536.

Zadrożny, S. and Kacprzyk, J. (2006). Bipolar queries and queries with preferences, in *Proceedings of DEXA 2006* (IEEE Computer Society Press, Washington, DC), pp. 415–419.

Zhang, C. and Huang, Y. (2007). Cluster by: a new SQL extension for spatial data aggregation, in H. Samet, C. Shahabi and M. Schneider, *Proceedings of ACM GIS 2007* (IEEE Computer Society Press, Washington, DC), pp. 53–56.

Index